SHOCK! HORROR!

Also by S. J. Taylor

STALIN'S APOLOGIST: WALTER DURANTY,
THE NEW YORK TIMES'S MAN IN MOSCOW

SHOCK! HORROR!

THE TABLOIDS IN ACTION

S.J. TAYLOR

BANTAM PRESS

LONDON · NEW YORK · TORONTO · SYDNEY · AUCKLAND

TRANSWORLD PUBLISHERS LTD
61-63 Uxbridge Road, London W5 5SA

TRANSWORLD PUBLISHERS (AUSTRALIA) PTY LTD
15-23 Helles Avenue, Moorebank, NSW 2170

TRANSWORLD PUBLISHERS (NZ) LTD
Cnr Moselle and Waipareira Aves,
Henderson, Auckland

Published 1991 by Bantam Press
a division of Transworld Publishers Ltd
Copyright © S. J. Taylor 1991

A catalogue record for this book is available from the British Library.

ISBN 0593 021061

Typeset in Times by Falcon Typographic Art Ltd.,
Edinburgh & London

Printed in Great Britain
by Mackays of Chatham

This book is dedicated to the memory of
the late Trevor Kempson

Grateful acknowledgement to the following newspapers for their permission to reprint previously published articles:

The *Daily Star*, 'Mr Clarke's Got a Short Memory', by Brian Hitchen, published 14 November 1989; also for permission to reprint, 'Joan Turns Her Back on Loyal Fans', published 18 June 1990.

The *Daily Mirror*, 'A Beastly Affair: It's One in the Eye for Toy Boy Basha!', by Kevin O'Lone, published on 19 March 1990.

Private Eye, 'Lines on the 20th Anniversary of the *Sun* Newspaper', by the illustrious E. J. Thribb, published in the 15 November 1989 issue.

The Philadelphia *Daily News*, 'Gary's Hot Hits', published 31 August 1987, 'There's A Bit Less Odor in the Court', published 23 June 1988, and 'Graham's Near-Fatal Attraction', published 19 March 1988, by Kurt Heine; also 'Double Shooting Erupts in Front of School Kids', by Joanne Sills.

The *Sport*, 'Whoppas of Death', published 11 August 1989; also 'How to Avoid Being a Boar in Bed', by Dominic Kennedy, published 18 August 1989.

The *Sun*, 'A Dead Cert! Punter Bill Tips 4–1 Winner from Beyond the Grave', by Tim Miles, published 16 November 1988, for which the *Sun* made charge of £150.

Throughout this book, the term 'Fleet Street' is retained
to refer to the British national press.

LIST OF ILLUSTRATIONS

ACKNOWLEDGEMENTS

Without the help of George Lynn, former *Sun* reporter and veteran Fleet Street journalist, this book no doubt would have been written, but with infinitely more difficulty. It was George who first mapped out the territory for me, and throughout the research, travel and writing, signposted the way. On at least one occasion, he prevented my falling into a neatly set 'tabloid trap', for which he has my very real gratitude. There is no way I can hope to repay his kindness, patience and well-intentioned and sensible advice.

I also owe a debt of gratitude to Dr Sherrie Good, Community Editor of the *Orange County Register*, who joined me in hot pursuit of a few tabloid types in Los Angeles. She also shared her expertise on the current state of the tort of privacy in the United States. Author Linda Melvern gave me the names of a number of helpful sources when I was just starting out, and Brian Hitchen, editor of the *Daily Star*, showed endless courtesy in extending aid to me. Hitchen also read a draft of the manuscript for which I am grateful. Roger Wood, former Executive Editor of News America, who currently holds the same post at the *Star* in Tarrytown, New York, read part of the manuscript as well; his suggestions were very helpful. Special thanks too to Derek Jameson, whose *tour de force* description of a day in the life of an editor appears in these pages. I must also thank David Sullivan, proprietor of the *Sport*, for giving me unhindered access to his newspapers and staff.

In Philadelphia, Jeffrey Taylor, now reporting for the *Wall Street Journal*, provided me with valuable research materials and also put me on the track of some top tabloid veterans in the city. Mike Nevard, head of Special Projects at the *National Enquirer*, also helped a great deal with sources, as did Vince Eckersley, freelance photographer. When I was criss-crossing Tabloid Valley in southern Florida, Ronnie and Bob Horowitz were particularly helpful. Also the kindness of Tony Miles, Executive Publisher at Globe International, cannot be forgotten. In New York, Brian Moss, deputy features editor of the *Daily News*, and Drew MacKenzie, sub-editor at the *Post*, both went to a great deal of trouble to set me up with informants. Also, Peter Fearon, producer at Fox's *Current Affair*, was unusually supportive through several crises and over a long period of time. I also wish to thank Professor Robert Trager of the University of Colorado and his wife Judy who sent valuable legal materials, and Theresa Walla of the Chicago *Sun-Times* who helped me with important research.

Of especial help was Paul Woolwich, editor of Channel 4's *Hard News*, who not only sent me important materials but changed my thinking in a number of ways.

I also wish to thank Charles Wilson, John Leese, Magnus Linklater, Nigel Dempster, John Sweeney and Fiona Millar for their time.

Of inestimable value were the hours I spent with Lord Rothermere, whose understanding of the way the press works in the UK is outpaced only by his wit in explaining it.

From the beginning, I had the support and encouragement of John Davey, now Director of Blackwell's in the US, who believed in my project. Dr Peter Beal, Deputy Director in the Manuscript Department at Sotheby's, read through the entire typescript, making many helpful suggestions. Diana Battle also read several draft chapters, for which I am grateful. Indeed, her friendship steadied me during the writing of the book. I also want to thank my agent, Caroline Dawnay, who showed great enthusiasm for the project, and my editor, Ursula Mackensie.

Finally, I must thank the participating journalists who gave freely of their time – sometimes hours on end. For obvious reasons, many of them can never be named, but their contributions were indispensable.

Sir Larry Lamb, on the other hand, indicated his willingness to give an interview for £455 plus VAT, but this offer was, alas, declined.

How can you really tear yourself to pieces when there are lawyers who promote law suits to make money, doctors who do unnecessary hysterectomies, big corporations hiding their pollution and environmentally destructive policies. The police are on the take. Maybe my whole view is down, but where drugs is the United States' biggest bloody industry – it exceeds the Fortune 500 listed companies, $90 billion a year now – who the fuck am I to worry about this shit I'm doing? Bottom line: so I chase a few celebrities, so what?

Tony Brenna, 1990
Senior Correspondent
National Enquirer

CONTENTS

A FEW SERIOUS WORDS

In the first significant prosecution carried out under the Licensing Act of 1662, John Twyn, who refused to give the name of the author of an anti-Royalist pamphlet he had published, was sentenced to be hung, drawn and quartered. This entailed being hanged, 'cut down while still alive, his privy parts and entrails taken out and burnt before his eyes, his head cut off, his body divided into four quarters to be disposed of at the pleasure of the King's Majesty.'

The authorities, plagued by anti-establishment types – the progenitors of Grub Street's hacks and Fleet Street's sleazebags – had at last hit upon a way to bring a sense of responsibility to journalists. Hang, draw and quarter them.

Great Britain has a long tradition of self-seeking scribblers and publishers; and an equally long tradition of governmental attempts at silencing them.

In the case of the Licensing Act of 1662, the injection into the populace of new ideas (self-governance and religious freedom) and a new technology (the proliferation of the printing press) had by the seventeenth century caused a virtual blizzard of ephemera to rain down upon the streets of London. It was a period of intense competition, which in turn led to a period of press excess, culminating in governmental suppression.

The same historical process is today taking place in Great Britain, this time with the tabloid press. The permissiveness ushered in during the Swinging Sixties and rendered into newsprint by Rupert Murdoch and Larry Lamb in 1969 initiated the 'soaraway' success of the sensational *Sun*. With the successful injection of a new technology – cold-type – into the newspaper industry in 1986, operating costs were sharply reduced, creating windfall profits. Others imitated the *Sun*'s trend. The result? A new era of press excess . . . and the predictable government clampdown.

In the United States, where the First Amendment to the Constitution prohibits laws being passed suppressing freedom

1

of expression, press freedom is being cancelled due to lack of interest.

In Chicago, the original home of Ben Hecht's 'The Front Page', only two newspapers remain. One of them, the Chicago *Sun-Times*, is in danger of going out of business and may indeed have folded by the time this book reaches the shelves. In Philadelphia, home of the founding fathers and modern-day mafia – known in the jargon as 'a *great* newspaper town' – two newspapers, both owned by one company, survive under a Joint Operating Agreement which allows them to split operating costs while simultaneously 'competing with one another in the marketplace of ideas.'

Says one old-time newsman who works on the Philadelphia *Daily News*, 'I hate to see a newspaper go out of business. When I was a kid, I used to deliver the *Bulletin*, and let's see there was the *Record*, the *Ledger*, the *Inquirer*, of course the *Daily News*. How many's that? Five? That was in the thirties, forties.'

Says a New York *Daily News* editor, 'Ten years ago, there were at least a half a dozen papers in New York. We had the *Journal American*, the *Herald Tribune*, the *World Telegram* and the *Sun*, the *Mirror*, the *News*, the *Post*. The *Daily News* once printed five million on Sundays, four million daily. It's mindboggling.'

What went wrong? A change in demographics. An increasing rate of illiteracy. Rising production costs. *Television*. Then there is the other thing. Says one critic, 'Travel around the country. Pick up the papers of the cities. They're really *bad*. They are badly written. They are *boring*.'

There is a popular idea among press pundits in Great Britain that America got into this fix because it has no national press. But there are plenty of urban centres with a population sufficient to support several competing newspapers. What happened was that all the life and vigour of the popular press somehow leaked into television, carrying with it the mass audience and leaving behind an élitist, establishment press – the mighty Fourth Estate, whose main function has dwindled to setting the news agenda for TV.

The idea of an irreverent press run by rogues, scoundrels, vulgarians and glorified vaudevillians repelled just about everyone. Sensationalism died, and with it, mass readership. In ridding itself of the hacks, America succeeded in ridding itself of a viable press as well. To save the village, they had to destroy it.

The only genuine profit centres left today in the American press are 'the supermarket tabloids' – bizarre hybrids which combine magazine layout and design with investigative newsgathering techniques. To a large extent, they have been manned by Brits, imported either by the late Generoso Pope in Florida or by Rupert Murdoch operating out of New York. In unsynchronized movement, and with the full cooperation of Hollywood's 'hype' machine, the supermarket tabloids succeeded in inventing and exporting the cult of celebrity that encircles the globe today. It is the last outpost of the tabloid mentality in the US, and that means it is held in almost total disrepute by the establishment press; there as here.

The lesson from America is that, without the tabloids and their spirit of irreverence, the press becomes a bastion of conformity dedicated to lofty purposes understood only by the few, an instrument for and by the élite – a danger sign for any society.

The lesson from Britain is that when the tabloids go too far, society seeks to control them, and press freedom for one and all comes under threat.

This book celebrates the tabloid press, its nervy, irreverent and frequently outrageous sensationalizing of the news.

For America, it's an elegy; for Britain, an apology.

It is a record of the last of the good old days.

S. J. Taylor

PART

One

New-Age Tabloids

1

THE EDUCATION
OF SIR LARRY LAMB

Day One was a typical madhouse, organized chaos, presided over by a tall, handsome, slender Yorkshireman named Larry Lamb and a not-so-tall, less-than-handsome, pudgy Australian named Rupert Murdoch.

When they started the interviewing, there hadn't been any telephones; there still weren't enough desks and chairs. Joyce Hopkirk, who edited the Pacesetter Pages, sat atop a desk which she shared bottom to bottom with Nick Lloyd, one of four 'features executives' who were battling it out for top billing. Ten sub-editors were seated at a table tearing through copy while some thirty spares stood uselessly around, in everybody's way, with nothing to do. These were freelancers hired for the night because there had been 'no rehearsals, no dummy runs' and it was anybody's guess how many people it would take to get the first issue of the *Sun* out onto the streets. Nobody had produced any actual words for the paper until now, and now the words were flying all over the place.

That first issue was what those in the business call 'Sunday-for-Monday', the dullest day of the week, and the best Lamb could dredge up for page one was an exclusive about horse-racing: 'Trainer Roy Pettitt', the headline ran, 'has confessed to the Sun that he has been doping his racehorses.' It was blocked out modular style beside a column of boxes running down the right-hand side of the page, each with a white-on-black reversed teaser intended to lure the reader inside. Beneath the horse-racing story appeared a lengthy speculation on the possibility of romance between the twenty-one-year-old Prince of Wales and Lady Leonora, the youthful daughter of the Duke of Westminster. At the top of the page appeared a white-on-red, sanserif masthead, with thick, modernistic letters spelling out 'The SUN'. Stark, energetic and simple, the front-page layout reflected Lamb's description of the paper as 'a young, new, virile campaigning newspaper.' It would bring to the British public 'a new shape, new writers, new ideas.' It would go 'Forward with the People.' It would 'care.'

Inside the forty-six-page paper was a car contest ('Win a Car!'), a free TV offer ('Win a TV!'), a feature on sterilized women ('The Anguish of "No Baby" Wives'), a feature on straying husbands, a pretty girl in a beach jacket, a pretty girl in a bikini, an excerpt from *The Love Machine* by Jacqueline Susann, a horoscope and a two-page spread on the Rolling Stones. Further in, a comic strip pictured a young married Jack saying 'Ulp' and bopping himself on his forehead with the heel of his hand as a sprightly Jill informs him she is pregnant. Another featured a baby named Horatio who says, 'Change my nappy, and I'll follow you anywhere.' In the last, a futuristic couple driving their space car past Luton accidentally run down a woman whose breasts are bared. 'The year', the narration explains, 'is 2170 . . .'

There were, besides all this, a photo of Prince Charles, a photo of Liz Taylor and Richard Burton, a photo of Princess Grace, a photo of a £437,500 diamond and a photo of Mrs Rupert Murdoch. She is smiling and pushing the button that starts the *Sun*'s presses. 'Blast-off day for the Sun!' says the caption. 'A dynamic new newspaper goes into orbit.' Behind the scenes, the presses didn't start.

As the clocks in the building ticked relentlessly on, Larry Lamb – 'taut as piano wire, and filled with a kind of savage energy' – was skidding downwards into despair. 'We were printing in only one centre, London,' Lamb would write later, 'and endeavouring to reach the whole of the British Isles from London railheads by breakfast-time the next day.' With a full-time staff of eighty-five journalists, some of them there only because they believed the paper would fold within days and award them handsome payoffs, Lamb laboured through what he would later call 'the longest day' – 16 November 1969. With an optimism that would run dry by day's end, he had ordered a print-run of 1,650,000.

Lamb's secretary, Marian Davison, was manning the telephones almost singlehandedly. Every few minutes, a public relations man named John Addey would call for Murdoch. Murdoch meanwhile was down at the stone,* in his shirtsleeves, working feverishly

---

* The term derives from hot-metal days when the leaden slugs from the linotype machines were assembled on a large, flat, steel table, formerly a precision-made polished stone surface, before being 'locked up'; that is, their positions finalized and the slugs bolted into a large rectangular frame, called a chase. From this is made the impression for two pages of the newspaper.

alongside his employees. Each time Addey called, Davison would dutifully write out the message, put down the phone, go out to the stone, and pass it along, wait for Murdoch's reply and then relay it back to Addey. 'John Addey said this . . .' she would tell Murdoch. 'John Addey said that . . .' After a few of these messages, Murdoch looked up at Davison and said, 'Fuck John Addey.' Davison walked slowly back to the telephone, thinking it over. 'Oh, well,' she shrugged, 'that's the message Murdoch's given me, and he *is* the chairman . . .'

For designer Vic Giles, a former *Mirror* man lured by Murdoch away from his consultancy business, the first day was also a long one. Since he couldn't be certain how story length would measure up against the space he had allotted in the dummies, Giles 'had allowed for a tremendous number of fillers.' These were the 'Sun Spots', which even today remain an integral part of the *Sun*'s layout. There were dozens of other technical matters to attend to, and before he realized it, he found he had been working upwards of sixteen hours without a break. Sometime after the first edition had arrived, at about nine o'clock in the evening, Giles was summoned to the editor's office. There he found Anna and Rupert Murdoch sitting on the floor, Larry Lamb at his magnificent desk, Bernard Shrimsley on a chair in the corner, each with a glass of wine. Lamb had invited Giles in to tell him what a great job he had done. Murdoch interrupted. 'There's only one thing that worries me, Vic,' he said in his Australian accent, 'and that's the centre spread.' He was referring to a two-page pullout Giles had prepared for display of Susann's *The Love Machine*. 'The white space around the print must be two inches deep. What's that doing?' Murdoch asked. 'Well,' said Giles, 'that's artistic white.' 'And can you tell us what artistic white is?' Murdoch asked. Giles explained it was the white space that opened up the page, making the text seem inviting and easy to read. 'Well, I don't know how artistic it is, but I do know it's cost a lot of trees. We're printing one and a half million copies, and the next time you use that much artistic white, you should think about the number of trees that were cut down to get that effect.' Giles could find no rationale for Murdoch's comment until the rise of the Green Party some twenty years later. 'Along with being first in a lot of other things,' Giles likes to say in retrospect, 'Murdoch was one of the first Greens, if you take what he said at face value.'

Later that evening, a reception had been planned, and hordes of guests, many of them employees, crowded into what had been dubbed 'the Director's Corridor', the makeshift office set up in a corridor where Murdoch shared space with several executives. For those who couldn't make it, a free pork pie and a bottle of beer were delivered to their work site. Lamb was late to the reception. When he finally did get there, he found his way barred by a public relations officer. 'I'm the editor,' Lamb said. 'You're not on the list,' the man countered. Exasperated, Lamb pushed his way past, only to find inside a senior print official vomiting into a wastepaper basket. Another was caught trying to sneak out with a bottle of Johnny Walker Black Label in each of his raincoat pockets.

Anna Murdoch was out in the kitchen where she was helping Marian Davison with the washing up. By the time they finished, it was very late. Davison remembers looking among the stragglers at the reception and seeing Lamb nowhere. She returned upstairs to her office, and looking beyond into the gloom, she could see Lamb, sitting alone, staring into space. 'There he was at his desk,' she says, 'and he was actually depressed.

'The buildup had been going on for weeks,' she says, 'and now he was terribly disappointed with this first paper, the first copy of the *Sun* ever produced. He didn't think it was very good. He was brooding. He wasn't pleased with it at all. He was a poetic sort of man; he really cared. He really took it all to heart and wasn't that good at shrugging things off.' Davison recognized that the lead story wasn't the best one ever written, but she couldn't help feeling that Lamb was overreacting.

'And in retrospect,' she says, 'he must have believed that too, because he had the front page of that first newspaper framed and it hung in his office for years.'

When a captain of industry is toppled, the vacuum created by his absence can become unbearable. There is frequently a great rushing of air inwards and upon occasion an attendant collapse. So it was with Cecil H. King.

The son of Lord Northcliffe's sister and an eminent scholar of Oriental Languages at Trinity College, Dublin, King's unhappy childhood and eventual rise to power would be of little interest, had he not become the chairman of International Publishing Corporation (IPC). Like his famous uncle, who was a pioneer of mass-circulation journalism, King became a publishing magnate. At his height, he employed some 28,000 in his corporate fiefdom. Among the 300 titles he controlled was Hugh Cudlipp's unassailable *Daily Mirror* and the languishing *Daily Herald*, which had been picked up by the Mirror group in 1962.

It is one of the great ironies of newspaper history that the *Herald* would metamorphose into Rupert Murdoch's *Sun*, eventually bringing down the *Mirror* from its toplofty position and changing the face of journalism on two continents.

The *Daily Herald* was born in 1911, a strike newspaper, the bible of the working class. In 1933, its circulation peaked at two million sales a day. But by 1955, circulation had sloped tremendously. King originally bought the paper with the idea of beefing it up and, to this end, commissioned copious market research, all of which would turn out to be wrong. The researchers pointed to a younger, wealthier, more dynamic and more female readership. A move up-market thus ensured, King set about to relaunch the paper under the name of the *Sun*, a newspaper 'born of the age we live in' – the Swinging Sixties.

Vic Giles, who had during his career already designed various titles for the Mirror group and was at the time working on the *Sunday Mirror*, was called in one day to see Cecil King and his deputy chairman Hugh Cudlipp, who asked Giles to help effect the massive face-lift which would change the *Daily Herald* into the new *Sun*. They had also enlisted the clever and precocious Roger Wood, who was to become the youngest editor of a national daily in Fleet Street and later the controversial editor of Rupert Murdoch's New York *Post*. Together, Giles and Wood came up with what they considered a superb design, and at the party at the Café Royal held to celebrate the paper's relaunch, Hugh Cudlipp stood up to praise their magnificent efforts. Unfortunately, he explained to the assembled group, he would be dumping their design because he thought the composing department and printers 'would take umbrage' at its difficulty. Giles believes to this day that, had Cudlipp and King stuck with the original design, the paper wouldn't have fallen into Murdoch's hands.

In September 1964, the scheduled relaunch took place. The new *Sun* was bigger than a tabloid but smaller than a broadsheet – an unenergetic eight-column mutation whose first issue featured five stories shorter than an inch on page one. The paper splashed on the new James Bond film *Goldfinger*, a serious miscalculation in terms of news value, and there were those who believed the paper was never taken seriously after that. But it had other problems as well. Inside, the paper was crawling with pop groups and bouffant hairdos juxtaposed with odd snippets of trade union news and adverts included as a sop to the old readership. Quickly dubbed

11

'King's Cross', the paper's circulation slid dangerously downwards. By 1967, it was losing money at the rate of £175,000 a year.

King likewise was sliding downhill, at a similarly precipitous rate. He had become convinced that Harold Wilson's Labour Government had betrayed its trust to the country. More dangerously, he believed he was the man to right this wrong. On 10 May 1968, he commandeered the front page of the best-selling *Daily Mirror* and plastered his photograph beside a gigantic headline, 'Enough Is Enough'. His message: 'Mr Wilson and his Government have lost all credibility: all authority.' Before its publication, King had shown the infamous article to Cudlipp and to the *Mirror*'s editors. From their reluctance to make substantial changes in the text, King concluded they were in agreement with his sentiments. Meanwhile, behind the scenes, he became more convinced than ever that only a military *coup d'état* could save Britain. With this foremost in his mind, writes Charles Wintour in *The Rise and Fall of Fleet Street*, he requested a meeting with Lord Mountbatten.

> King trotted out his now well-rehearsed scenario of a crisis of confidence which would lead to the disintegration of the government, rioting in the streets, the need for involvement by the armed forces and wound up with the question: would Lord Mountbatten agree to be titular head of a new administration in such a crisis? Sir Solly [now Lord] Zuckerman, then Scientific Adviser to the Cabinet, accompanied Mountbatten to the meeting. According to Cudlipp, Sir Solly rose and said, 'This is rank treachery. All this talk of machine guns at street corners is appalling. I am a public servant and will have nothing to do with it. Nor should you, Dickie.' He then left and Mountbatten, quickly agreeing with him, brought the meeting courteously, but swiftly, to an end.

Soon after this ill-starred meeting, Cudlipp took his now famous decision to oust King as Chairman of the Mirror group. Ironically, the only *coup d'état* King had effected was in the boardroom of IPC; the only casualty recorded in his civil war, his own.

According to some versions of the story, the IPC *Sun* sold to Rupert Murdoch for £60,000; in other versions, the amount is a good deal more; in still others, a good deal less. In all the versions, however, the amount is minuscule, and IPC would have done better to let the newspaper die. Rupert Murdoch had recently purchased the *News of the World*, and it was generally well known within his camp that he would not let his press room, capable of turning out well over 5,000,000 copies a night, sit idle for long. One captain of industry fades from the scene. Another rises in his place.

It has been said that Hugh Cudlipp, upon seeing the first issue of Larry Lamb's *Sun*, gave it six months to live. In view of the fact that the *Sun* would supplant the *Daily Mirror* as the best-selling newspaper in the English language, his words now seem highly ironic. It is similarly ironic that the *Daily Mirror* in large part trained and nurtured the young editor who was destined to cast it into the shade.

Albert Lamb, called Larry by everyone except his mother, was born in 1929 in a small village in Yorkshire. His father, the local colliery blacksmith, died when his son was only ten. His death and the deprivation brought about by the war accounted for the limited education made available to the young boy. Along with what he himself recognized as high intelligence and serious ambition, this fact no doubt contributed to a certain sense of ill-usage, perhaps even bitterness. 'I have worn throughout my life,' Lamb says on the subject, 'a substantial chip on my shoulder, on the grounds that I am not educated, and I should have been.' He wanted to become a journalist, but was instead reduced to taking a job as cashier in Brighouse Town Hall. After a time, he managed to become branch secretary of the union, working his way into an apprenticeship on the union paper. He then moved into shiftwork in London, and got a position sub-editing for the *Daily Mail*, eventually hiring on at the *Daily Mirror* where he worked under Hugh Cudlipp for ten years.

It was clear from the start he was gifted. 'A mess of copy would come in,' says one of his colleagues from the *Mirror*, 'a great pile of paper, and Larry would go through it at breakneck speed, and within, say, ten minutes, on this side he had the stuff that was good and on that side he had the stuff that was rejected. And then he would say, "Well, this is the nub of the story; this is the most important . . ." And he could visualize it as well. I've seen Larry Lamb stand many times and dummy page after page – he was so quick – and say, "This is the whole lot."

'He used to tell me and others how discouraged he was with the *Mirror*. He thought the *Mirror* was going up-market, he thought that a lot of the *Mirror* features in the 1950s and 60s were wrong . . . He said, "*Mirror* readers do not want this type of newspaper. We need to go back to the 'flash' type of newspaper of the thirties and forties."' For the record, Lamb himself would only say, 'I thought I knew where they were getting it wrong.'

13

He did know where they were getting it wrong. On Day Two, 18 November 1969, the *Sun* boasted that all 1,650,000 copies of the first issue had sold out. The paper was a hit, and as Joyce Hopkirk would later say, 'A hit carries you through.

'We were working very hard. We'd go in about ten in the morning and then about seven in the evening there would be a slight slow down, and we'd go into the editor's office to have a drink or to chew over the events of the day, start talking about new ideas and about ten o'clock we'd go home, without having eaten sometimes.

'I think the atmosphere he created made people feel competent; certainly it made me feel confident. The paper did have that energy and that vibrancy that came from people liking each other and being confident and not being afraid to throw ideas into the ring. You know how some people can stifle creativity. They surround their staff with all the trappings, but they make people feel nervous about speaking or communicating. Larry was the very opposite. I mean, he could be very frightening and authoritarian if he thought he was right. But nevertheless, it was a climate where you weren't afraid to throw in an idea.'

Hopkirk's main memory of the early days on the *Sun* was 'this business of doing everything at a gallop. We used to live and eat and drink very hard and we sort of went around in a gang. We were always together – Larry and Bernard Shrimsley and Nick Lloyd and me.' Hopkirk says it was 'like drinking champagne all day long, which we did, we were great drinkers. But we used to work a fourteen-to-sixteen-hour day, that was our life, totally. And I really learned to tell the difference between Krug 62 and carrot water, thanks to Larry Lamb.'

Lamb was the person who taught Marian Davison to make martinis, 'proper martinis, which he liked very dry. And he had to have the lemon twist squeezed. He laughed about stuff like that,' Davison says. Lamb had her order 'the most enormous fridge-freezer, with an icemaker in it, and when this thing arrived in my office, he just said, "Oh, my God, it is rather large. If Rupert comes, can you just walk into it and say good night? He'll think it's another exit."'

Murdoch, according to Lamb, tended not to approve of drinking in the office. 'In my office anyway. We shared many a bottle in his. I defended the practice stoutly on the grounds that the people I invited in were usually those who had already spent eight or ten hours at their desks. They not only deserved a drink, they needed one.

'Furthermore, when they were drinking in my office after the first edition had gone to press, there was only ever one topic of conversation – the paper. Many of our best ideas came at these sessions, when the pressures of the day were receding a little.'

In one story, Murdoch left the office late one afternoon, and after he left, 'the drink started to flow in earnest.' In the middle of the festivities, the office door opened. It was Murdoch, who had missed his plane. Then, so goes the story, Murdoch 'stormed down the corridor,' muttering, 'Let them drink my whisky if they must, but do they have to drink it out of bloody plant pots?'

The *Sun* was located in Bouverie Street, a very ancient printing factory located close to the river. The staff noticed that the pillars holding the floors up had cracks in them, and eventually it was discovered that the whole place was sinking slowly into the ground. They were plagued too by inadequate working space, which entailed most people sharing offices, crawling over one another to get the work done. It was nevertheless, for most of them, the most exciting period in their careers.

Murdoch had a penthouse, with a dining room, and he would invite people up to lunch, executives, heads of department, and other higher-ups at the *Sun*. It was less than lavish. Murdoch gained a reputation for not caring what was on the menu. 'He would eat *anything*,' one staffer says. Lamb, on the other hand, was fussy. He wouldn't touch lamb, said it was 'too fatty'. If there was a strike, Davison often got stuck preparing the lunches in the office. In the beginning, she would trek down to the local Marks & Spencer, buying 'mounds of food' and preparing it herself. Later on, she 'got wise' and ordered the food from the Stafford Hotel. It wasn't unusual, 'after all that food,' for Lamb to send out for fish and chips. He would tell her to send the chauffeur who would then go out in the company Daimler, to pick up the haddock, which was Lamb's favourite, doused in vinegar and wrapped up in yesterday's newspapers.

One of the reasons the *Sun* came together so well, says Mike Nevard, who was Features Editor before going to America to work on Murdoch's *Star*, was that 'we had short lines of communication.' An idea born in the morning could often be found in the first edition. 'If we found out the *Mirror* on Friday was blurbing a series starting on Monday, we would *in hours* create a spoiler series which started on Saturday. Everything,' says Nevard, 'was done by the seat of our pants. At other papers, every idea had to go tree to top, and by the time it got back, the idea was old, or had been changed.'

15

Another of Lamb's ideas, according to Vic Giles, was 'absolutely to pack the *Sun* with news. I had increased the column width, decreased the white space, and we doubled the story counts compared with the *Daily Mirror*, so that Larry Lamb could eventually use the phrase "the paper that's value for money". Even the letters "VFM" became something the readers understood.' One of the sub-editors, a member of the backbench,* remembers Lamb saying he always wanted to see everything important in that day's *Daily Telegraph* somewhere in the *Sun*, even if it was only one 'para'.

Lamb himself was known in the business as a great sub who understood how to condense words without losing meaning. Vic Giles, whose page plans for the *Sun* are still considered classics, believed his designs benefited from a similarly tight use of words. Lamb would hand Giles rough dummies of how to lay out the pages, but very often Giles would do it two ways: Lamb's way, and the way that he himself believed the pages should be projected. 'To Lamb's credit,' says Giles, 'he would take my designs a good half of the time. Most editors,' he adds slyly, 'would have just said, "Look, Vic, I like yours best."'

Lamb was a hands-on editor, always out on the backbench, on the art desk or on the stone. His presence wasn't always welcome. Giles remembers a time when Lamb picked up a perspex ruler and shattered it, saying, 'I *will* have it done my way.' Giles answered, '"I don't think we have any more to say to each other." And the next day, it was as if the incident had never happened.'

Nick Lloyd, later to become the editor of the *Daily Express*, also had something of a surprise during the first week of the *Sun*'s operation. 'We did a feature on homosexuality, a straightforward sort of piece – can't remember the angle, actually – but it was a reputable piece on being gay. It was already on the stone, the page was completed, about four in the afternoon, when it was killed on the basis it would offend the sort of readers the *Sun* was after . . . that they wouldn't like homosexuals. It had actually been set, in a page, and ready to go. The word was that Larry and Rupert didn't think it was right.' But Nick thought they were wrong. 'That was an education for me,' he says now. 'I was a bit mortified by that decision.'

---

* The desk for senior editorial executives located directly behind the table where the chief sub-editor and his assistants work. It is called 'backbench' because of its geographical position and has no relation to the term 'backbench' as it applies to Members of Parliament.

Then, there was the story of the rabid dogs. England's fierce quarantine laws regulating the importation of live animals into the country are credited with achieving the total absence of rabies within its borders. Since it is a disease unknown, the fear of rabies borders on the abnormal in the average Englishman. Lamb took advantage of this phenomenon when he bought a book for serialization called *Rabid*, which he retitled *The Day of the Mad Dogs*. In the book, a couple unknowingly smuggles an infected dog from France to Britain aboard their yacht, the dog infects other dogs and 'soon the country is under siege by ravenous killer dogs.' The *Sun* then made a television commercial for the series, hiring the dogs used in the film *The Omen*. As Lamb tells the story,

> The commercial began sedately, with a middle-aged couple relaxing in the drawing room of their elegant country home with their two dogs. Suddenly the dogs leapt up and savagely attacked the defenceless couple. We showed close-ups of the dogs' foaming mouths (shaving cream) and bloodied victims. Then followed scene after horrific scene of screaming babies waking in the night, fearful parents, hunters out shooting the mad dogs. As a finale, the last scene showed an expiring victim, sweating and moaning in hospital.

The commercial created a storm of protest, to the extent that, by 11.00 p.m. on the day it aired, the Independent Television Companies' Association (ITCA) and Independent Broadcasting Authority (IBA) ordered it off the air. Meanwhile, Giles had done a layout to go with the first part of the series. An artist named Tim Holder had drawn 'the head of a rabid dog with huge fangs, the most rabid dog you have ever seen, with foam running right down the page.' The drawing was so effective, there was a debate in Lamb's office whether or not to run it. In fact, they did, and 'the readership did love it,' says Giles. 'They bought it by the millions.'

There were other gimmicks used to attract readers, with giveaways reminiscent of the backs of cereal boxes. The *Sun* created its own soccer wallchart for kids; a football encyclopaedia; animal cards; a soccer stamp album, with 500 stickers. Along with these came special weekly celebrations, like 'Doggie Week', 'Fishing Week', and the highly touted 'Pussy Week', put forward with much mischief by a knowing staff. Otherwise, there was the 'Tinned Knicker Adventure', which offered knickers in a tin, scented with genuine French perfume. It was said the frequent mention of knickers in the pages of the *Sun* became a bone of contention with Rupert Murdoch, who complained, 'The paper's always full of knickers . . . Can't you find anything else to put in it?'

Regarding sex, the *Sun*'s stance was strictly 'whoopee!'; no apologies. But the Pacesetter Pages also reflected a more serious side: 'We wrote frankly about things like masturbation, menstruation and pre-menstrual tension, cancer of the breast and cervix and other medical problems which were simply not talked about at the time,' says Lamb. Unembarrassed by 'ladies' ' topics, Lamb was light years ahead of his time, not only in the subject matter he permitted onto his pages but also in his treatment of professional women on Fleet Street. Even then, he believed the Street was 'too much dominated by men,' and his view that 'women work harder' was in the late sixties and early seventies pure heresy.

To become editor of the Pacesetter Pages, Joyce Hopkirk, whose career later included editorial positions on the *Sunday Times*, *Cosmopolitan* and *She*, had to present over 200 ideas to Lamb, things like win free nappies for a year or a year's supply of beer or a year off housework. 'That's how I got the job,' she says. Her section of the paper was devoted to the concept that 'there is more to life than washing up, and we thought that our readers were literate, were intelligent. We didn't often do feature materials addressed to executive women, partly because there *were* no female executives, or not very many. Our readers may not have been intellectuals, but I didn't feel we should patronize them or write down to them. The appeal of the *Sun* was that we addressed women in a different way. She may be a housewife, and she may have a baby, but we addressed her in a freer way . . . than she was in reality. And it was done with fun. It was a lark.

'It was the first time a newspaper had tackled so-called magazine subjects. Until then, women's pages were very much in a ghetto of straight fashion. These ideas had appeal to men as well as women because they wanted to read what women wanted to read. But that took a while to emerge, really. It didn't come about on day one.'

Also, at the time, Hopkirk was 'unattached and in the singles market, as it were,' so many of the ideas in the Pacesetter Pages reflected her own interests. 'That's where all the sex came from,' she says. Hopkirk believes she actually was the *Sun* woman, 'rather bossy and crass and sure of myself. You can't be humble if you want to be an editor.'

Another young woman who got her start in Fleet Street at the *Sun* was Sue Snell, who went to work there designing fashion pages in 1972. 'I was treated as an individual,' says Snell. 'My sex was unimportant, whether I did fashion or what I did. It didn't matter. I had a talent, and the *Sun* used it.

'Murdoch would syndicate the stuff we did around the world. It was great fun. If there wasn't a story, we found the story. In summer of 1972, *Stern Magazine* did a thing on the G-string. So I was put on a plane with Brian Aris and sent to St Tropez, where . . . there was not a G-string anywhere. It turned out there was a little island where there's a nudist beach, and a few people had been wearing them there. And so what we did, we went to this little boutique, because the owner said she could crochet things, and we asked her to crochet a G-string. And she crocheted it overnight. Well, we had to have a story. So we created the story and sent the picture: "Variations on a G-string. Why not make one yourself?"'

Eventually, Snell received an offer from the *Evening News* to become fashion editor. When she went to talk it over with Larry Lamb, he said, 'Look, we have a fashion editor here, but you should be a fashion editor. Go. But I will always top by £1,000 anything the *Evening News* offers you.' Says Snell, 'Larry Lamb met you head on. He protected you. For me, it was the best period of my newspaper career. I was treated as a person and encouraged.'

Otherwise, the pages rolled over day after day with the news of the world: the Pinkville massacre in Vietnam, soon to be known as My Lai; starvation in Biafra, blamed by a young columnist named Auberon Waugh upon incompetent politicians; the rise of the 'Hubby Haters', the *Sun*'s catchphrase for Women's Liberationists; the Charles Manson slayings; Woodbridge; Altamont; and every-where hippies, hashish, and a rising tide of 'tit and bum'. It was the age of streaking, and in the spirit of the times, the girls took off their tops to be photographed for the pages of the *Sun*, creating an institution – the Page Three Girl.

In addition, sprinkled in like salt and pepper, were features and photos on Prince Charles, Princess Anne, peg-legged hawks, budgies, and horoscopes. There were also the *déjà vu* stories that regularly headline today's tabloids: Britain's stinking beaches, dog attacks on innocent children, celebrities on the rise, celebrities on the skids. And always in the background, as a continuing refrain, television.

Larry Lamb's contention 'that television was probably the big-gest single area of human interest,' adopted as an operating principle in the early days of the *Sun*, is as cynical an assessment of human values as can be found, even in the world of commerce, and it no doubt accounts in no small part for the newspaper's astounding success. While most publications took the view that television was a dangerous rival, pouring scorn upon the still-young medium, the *Sun* embraced the 'boob tube', making it the centrepiece of its marketing strategy. The formula included 'generic' or 'image' advertising on television, in which the commercials projected the *Sun*'s personality by gathering 'the best and brightest stories and distilling them down to a few words of script along with riveting visuals,' delivered at high speed to create impact. Special features were written to fit the requirements of the ads. And, along with the publication of viewing schedules, TV celebrities became a major staple, the *Sun* 'playing up each and every story about television and television personalities.'

On the last day of publication of the IPC *Sun*, 15 November 1969, circulation stood at 850,000. By December of the same year, just six weeks after Murdoch bought the paper, circulation had climbed to 1,265,000. Within a hundred days of the takeover, it rose to just over one and a half million. 'It was like a rollercoaster ride,' said one staffer. 'It got more and more exciting every day.' Said another, 'You thought it would never end.'

Inside the Murdoch establishment, spirits were high. 'When the *Sun* reached one of its peaks,' says one ex-staffer, 'we went to a party, a black-tie affair, in Rupert's house, which was called Coopersale in a tiny village in Essex by the same name, and in this house, Rupert had a big indoor swimming pool. And some of his top staff members threw Rupert into the pool and then they jumped in themselves. Anna Murdoch thought they would throw her in as well, so she saved them the trouble and jumped in herself. She was in a strapless evening dress, with an embroidered bodice, but she went straight in. She was great, she was really great.'

Such was the euphoria at the top. Down in the ranks, not everybody was so happy about the way things were going. Some of the reporters couldn't adapt to the paper's style. Their stories were slashed, cut to the bone in order to fit the paper's hit-and-run method of covering the news. Sometimes the stories were dropped altogether. 'They were on the wrong paper,' says one ex-staffer, 'and they moaned and they groaned . . .' You could find them in the bars in the evenings after work, complaining about the *Sun* and its methods.

If Lamb got wind of this, he got rid of them – but fast. He told an assistant he didn't want people who were 'even slightly unhappy,' and he would say, 'Go. Don't stay. Go tomorrow. Go today'; or words to that effect. He said he hated firing people, it was like drowning kittens.

One of his staffers, a young Roy Greenslade, who has since worked up the editorial hierarchy to become the editor of the *Daily Mirror*, was by twenty-two already a junior executive on the *Sun*. As Greenslade himself admits, 'I was very young, and I had got too far too quickly, and the pressure made me look around for explanations about things.' Greenslade had, he said, 'a natural left-wing outlook,' and soon he was 'mixing in left-wing circles,' becoming, in his own words, 'very politicized.' The result was that he and a few others 'kicked up a lot of ruckus on the *Sun*, and in the end they brought us in and took the ringleaders and asked us to leave. Larry Lamb did that. Larry was a very fierce man. He wanted to ensure that his newspaper came out, and he didn't want this left-wing caucus organizing trouble. So he persuaded four of us to leave.' Greenslade was happy enough to go, because he wanted to write a book, which he did in short order, before going back to university to finish his degree. Others didn't feel so sanguine about the course of events.

It was said Lamb was the dictatorial type of newspaper editor, highly competent, but ferocious. A lot of people trembled when they were called to his office. 'He wasn't a hail-fellow-well-met sort of man,' said one who knew him well. 'He was the boss.'

One of his colleagues remembers asking an editor whether it was all right to go in to see Lamb and receiving the answer, 'I don't know. It's difficult today. "Simba" has had one circulation manager already this morning, and at the moment he's got his teeth into a deputy editor. So I would advise you to leave it until he's been properly fed.'

Then, there was the problem of what more than one of his colleagues has described as Lamb's pomposity. It was said that his arrogance grew in direct proportion to the circulation, which by the summer of 1978 had reached the four million mark. An unexpected characteristic of the readership, as Lamb was quick to point out, was the large number in the highly regarded 'AB' category, more than *The Times* and the *Guardian* combined.

Essentially, though, the *Sun* remained distinctly down-market, with a high blue-collar readership and a special self-styled vulgarity. Despite this territorial divide, Lamb himself was more and more called upon to meet with important members of state. On occasion, he didn't get it quite right. Davison remembers a time when Lamb was scheduled for lunch with James Prior, who was then Leader of the House of Commons. Lamb told her to go to Fortnum & Mason to buy a jar of peaches in brandy. Prior, it seems, had 'peachy, rosy cheeks,' giving rise to the nickname 'Peaches'. Lamb planned to hold this jar of peaches behind him, presenting it to Prior at the right moment as a kind of practical joke. But when Lamb arrived at the luncheon, he had a change of heart, and when he came back down, he told Davison that Prior hadn't been 'in the mood,' so he hadn't gone through with it.

Another mishap occurred during the period he was 'courting' Margaret Thatcher. Lamb had gone salmon fishing in Scotland, and when he came back he brought back two salmon, one larger than the other. He told Davison to put them in the fridge. One he planned to take home, and one was to go to Margaret Thatcher. 'But I want to keep the bigger one myself,' he told Davison. So she put a sticky label on each of the fish; one with his name, the other with Thatcher's. She then called the chauffeur to make the delivery. Somehow, the story that Lamb kept the big one for himself got into *Private Eye*, much to Lamb's consternation. For Davison, the incident was 'quite terrible'. He had her in and questioned her about how the story got out. She reassured him that she had told no one and didn't know whether the driver or someone else had phoned in the story. After that, Lamb let the matter drop.

About the time he wrote the famous front-page endorsement of the Conservative Party for the 1979 General Election, 'Vote Tory This Time. It's the Only Way To Stop the Rot', Thatcher showed up at the *Sun* offices. Apart from coming to lunch, she would drop in to see Lamb himself, just to have a whisky and take a look at the paper. On these occasions, she made general small talk about Denis's love of rugby, and one time said, 'When Denis is in bed, he must still think he's on the rugby field, because he sometimes kicks me in his sleep.' This cordial relationship, along with the front-page endorsement of the *Sun* for the Tories, is usually cited in relation to the knighthood Lamb was awarded. While Lamb admits that 'Elections are sometimes won or lost on swings of only 1 or 2 per cent of the vote,' he remains characteristically coy on whether it actually got him the knighthood. 'Did it?' he once asked, 'I don't know. I believe it may have been a factor.'

Whatever the case, he took the knighthood seriously, having a small brass plaque placed upon his door at the *Sun* which said 'Sir Larry Lamb'. Said one of his colleagues, 'After he got that knighthood, he became insufferable, absolutely insufferable. He got carried away.' He was said to become less accessible, spending more and more time behind his closed door. Said another, 'He did change after the knighthood. He became pompous. He just did.' And this was from two of his strongest supporters.

Davison, who never called him by his Christian name, herself had a little trouble with the title. She remembers thinking, 'God, I can't bear it. I have to say, "Sir Larry".' But she managed it.

Others managed it as well. Behind his back, though, Lamb was sometimes called 'Lurch'. There is some uncertainty as to the origin of the nickname, whether it was an undeserved joke, stemming from his penchant for drink, or whether it was related to his bad back. Most believe it was the latter, since he often had to walk with a cane, and when he was in pain, which was not unusual, carried one shoulder higher than the other. One other name said to have attached to Sir Larry Lamb, was 'Lord Halibut', pinned on him, according to legend, for returning the fish at a restaurant, perhaps more than once.

He loved Abe Lincoln, and in his autobiography *Sunrise*, made mention of the Gettysburg Address, which Lincoln wrote on the back of a plain brown envelope he found in his pocket as he travelled by train to the scene of the battle. Davison remembers his giving her a copy of the great speech, and she was instructed to keep it handy, where it could be easily reached. Perhaps the speech was the inspiration for the birth of the *Sun*'s masthead, for Lamb writes of taking the job as editor of the paper, then travelling home by train, 'and it was on this trip, on the way back to London, that I created the famous red masthead, since copied in English language newspapers from Fiji to the Costa Brava, with the aid of my young daughter's felt-tipped pen kit, then something of a novelty, on the back of a used envelope.'

Vic Giles, however, somehow gained the impression that Lamb had scribbled the masthead on a table napkin, with Murdoch saying, 'Yes, that's good.' Lamb then gave the masthead to Giles, telling him 'that was the way it should be.' At any rate, Giles figures he could have bettered the design by kerning it. He thinks 'over time, the letters have been driven apart by distortion, as the logo has been extended, leaving too much red space. So,' says Giles, 'it doesn't hang together.'

Besides these discrepancies, there was also the thing with Murdoch. In the scenario presented by Lamb, the day he was hired as editor of the *Sun* was a halcyon moment, Murdoch doing the listening, Lamb doing the talking. 'Certainly,' he writes in his autobiography, 'never again did I find Rupert so willing to listen for so long.' Later on, he would say, with a touch of condescension, that Murdoch's contributions to the paper, 'when he made any, were well meant but not usually helpful. We tended to hope he would forget having made them.' Then too was the little joke they played on Murdoch. Murdoch was a Pisces who said he read the stars. A few of the staff, Lamb among them, conspired to 'massage the forecast', telling him to be 'generous in all things'.

On the other hand, Murdoch's playfulness could sometimes wound Lamb. He writes,

> One of the jokes he was gleefully fond of repeating was that the sun never set on the British Empire because God didn't trust the Brits after dark. It was funny the first time . . .
> I found the Chairman's attitude to my homeland easier to take than his attitude to the paper. In the early days, after his return to the UK, we got the impression that he did not think too highly of the *Sun* or the editorial mix which we had devised. He was often bitterly critical of what we were doing, and it was sometimes difficult, after a painful early morning session with him, to prevent my despondency from showing itself at my own morning conference.

Lamb was not, he believed, 'naturally a pop journalist', and Murdoch's fling with Harold Evans, whom he made editor of *The Times*, went down badly with him. Once, Murdoch called Lamb, telling him, 'I know you are the best of the tabloids. Harry told me.'

> I don't know whether or not we were the best tabloid of the day, but I have no doubt whatever that we were better than *The Times* – and much, much faster.
> Those who had toiled in the Murdoch vineyard through the heat and burden of the day, bitterly resented the patronage which was oozing out of *The Times* headquarters in Gray's Inn Road. We regarded most of the people there as amateurs. And though I wouldn't choose so to describe Harry Evans I was distinctly unamused by the fact that he and the Chairman were discussing the merits of that day's *Sun* before the Chairman had seen fit to discuss them with me.

Later on, Lamb was more specific. There had been, he said, 'a great financial burden of resentment' at the *Sun*, springing from the belief that it was in essence subsidizing the then struggling *Times*. For Lamb, the next natural step in his career would have been

24

the editorship of *The Times*, a post he admits he wouldn't have turned down. 'Unfortunately, I was never a candidate because of the reputation I had acquired at his behest, on his behalf . . . I'm not bitter about it.'

In late 1978, Express Newspapers, who had over the past decade lost more than a third of its readership, came up with a fight-fire-with-fire idea – the *Daily Star*. The decision came from Victor Matthews, later Lord Matthews, whose company Trafalgar House had acquired controlling interest in the Express group. When Matthews asked why the *Sun* was so popular, he was given the answer, 'Because the *Sun* is not a newspaper. It's all tit and bum and racing.' Hence Matthews's vow to start his own similar sheet; one, so goes the story, he wouldn't want to leave around his own home, where children could see it.

The *Daily Star* lived up admirably to Matthews's directive. With a circus layout that fairly burst from the pages, the paper outdid the *Sun* on the *Sun*'s own turf. Where the *Sun* had placed their topless model, the notorious Page Three, the *Star* now featured a 'Daily Starbird'. Shamelessly imitating the *Sun*, even down to the 'Sun Spot', which was renamed the 'Star Spot', the paper used more taping, more italics, more reverses, and more graphics in conjunction with sensational heads and stories to give a sense of excitement and power.

Says Roy Greenslade, 'They then introduced the Bingo game in Merseyside, and it was phenomenally successful. A 17 per cent upsurge in readers, and they realized they had got a great gimmick. Larry Lamb, in his final days, was tired. And nice irony: Larry Lamb was editor of the *Sun* when it sold 850,000 and he took it up way beyond the *Daily Mirror*. He did that because he recognized who the enemy were and he fought them. But by then, he didn't think the *Star* was real competition, he thought it should be dismissed. And he let the *Daily Star* get out of the starting block. He seriously underestimated the fact, that especially in the north – he couldn't get to the north – the paper was providing sport and this silly game, and the *Sun* fell to just over 3,600,000.'

The net result was that as the *Sun*'s circulation dipped, the *Star*'s climbed – to 1.5 million.

Meanwhile, by his own admission, Lamb had acquired 'a reputation for being difficult, for being straightforwardly bloody-minded, which was probably justified, but which wasn't really me.' For his part, Murdoch seemed to lose confidence in Lamb's ability 'to keep the paper on course. Certainly,' writes Lamb, 'he became quite unreasonably critical. When I told him so he reacted, characteristically, by suggesting that I should take six months' leave of absence.' Lamb was given the weekend to consider the offer, but he already knew that Murdoch and Kelvin MacKenzie had been talking.

During the six months, Lamb sometimes rang Marian Davison, and the pair met for drinks at the American Bar at the Savoy. 'It did become clear,' she said, 'he would never come back.'

And what had Sir Larry Lamb learned from taking a newspaper from oblivion to the highest circulation of any daily in the English language? That the only real reward for completing a Herculean task is the pleasure of the task itself? That being boss is better than not being boss? But he probably knew that already.

What Lamb learned was less important than what he taught – that down-market could mean big money, that nobody ever went broke underestimating the taste of the British public, that hard and mean and competent gets the job done.

His acolytes on Fleet Street would pick up where he left off. And men from the *Sun* would gain a certain reputation for tenacity that would reap them big rewards in the United States – *if* they could stand the pace.

2
PAGE THREE PHENOMENA

Their mothers bring them in, their boyfriends bring them in. Sometimes they come in by themselves. That's how it was with Caroline Cossey – tall, lanky, blonde; incredibly exotic. And Yvonne Paul, accustomed to measuring up what will take on the glamour market, knew at a glance Cossey would sell.

Paul runs one of the best-known glamour agencies in London. She was for many years a glamour model herself, climaxing with speaking parts in the movies and regular appearances on *The Benny Hill Show*. With this kind of track record, she is in the perfect position to advise young girls who want to display themselves in front of a camera.

If Paul put you on her books in 1988, your standard rate of pay for ad work would have been £600 a day with your clothes on, £750 with your breasts bared, and £1,000 with no clothes at all. This latter category includes ads for showers, ads for sunbeds, and the undefined 'beauty nude'. Nina Carter did her first nude advertisement when she was seventeen. Says Carter, 'It was a back shot of me curled up in front of a radiator for a central heating advertisement.'

Vivien Neves shot to fame when *The Times* ran her nude photograph in a full-page advertisement for fertilizer. It was the first nude in the newspaper's 186-year history, it created a furore, and it set Neves to thinking: 'I couldn't figure which one it was because I'd done so many pictures kneeling down with nothing on.' Neves had quit school at fifteen, worked briefly at C&A, done receptionist work at a hairdressers. By eighteen she was working at Raymond's Revuebar Strip Club in Soho. 'The girls there didn't care a damn about nakedness, and I bless them for making me feel the same . . .'

Not everyone had it so easy. Susan Shaw's first live assignment without any clothes was at the Earls Court Motor Show in 1971. 'I thought there would be only a handful of pressmen on the stand,' she said. 'But hundreds of other men crowded round like sex-starved animals. They were standing on each other's shoulders, hanging from the railings. I couldn't help thinking: Haven't they ever seen a naked girl before? Surely they must have wives or girlfriends?

'The only way to go through with something like that is to imagine to yourself that you've got something on – a bikini or a dress. You don't look down at yourself and, above all, you don't look at any of the glaring vultures in the face.

'I was shaking all the time, inwardly. I thought, can I go through with it? But it's a job and you can do it.'

For Caroline Cossey, the tall, attractive blonde who showed up at Paul's agency, it was murder. When Paul sent her to see a few photographers, says Paul, 'She really had to psych herself up . . . because she was so insecure. With hindsight I could imagine what it must have been like for her – it's hard enough for any hopeful young girl to be interviewed by a model agency and then be sent to a top photographer. But for Caroline . . . trial by fire.'

Cossey's metamorphosis into the ideal feminine form had been a long and painful one. It included breast implantation, hormonal treatment and castration. Eventually, her appearance would change, her name would change; her entire identity would undergo transformation. But for Barry Cossey, also known as Caroline Cossey, also known as 'Tula', it would all be worth it. For she would become one of Paul's most successful girls, chalking up picture after picture on Page Three, television appearances in Britain and in America; she would dance with the Bluebell Girls, and, as icing on the cake, would become a Bond girl in *For Your Eyes Only*.

The first woman to appear without clothing in the pages of the *Sun* was an unidentified blonde sitting expressionless at the feet of the Rolling Stones. It was a two-page spread in the paper's first issue – 17 November 1969. On Page Three the same day, there was printed the photograph of a young woman dressed in a beach jacket. It was headlined, 'All Systems Go', and the text explained, 'She's just the sort of gorgeous blonde you hope will smile at you on a dull, back-to-work Monday morning.' Ull Lindstrom, who had 'a nice line in brains too,' was studying to be a systems analyst at a computer centre in Stockholm.

In the next few months, dozens of women would grace the *Sun*'s Page Three, including a few who made names for themselves. Kate O'Mara, Samantha Eggar, Joanna Lumley, Britt Ekland, Elke Sommer, Virna Lisi; the list goes on. Then, on the *Sun*'s first birthday, 17 November 1970, the first genuine Page Three Girl appeared – topless, bare-assed, sitting sideways, knees-bent, in long grass; sunlight profiling one bared breast.

The pose was artsy, it was craftsy; the caption astonishingly mindless. 'Birthday Suit! From time to time some self-appointed critic stamps his tiny foot and declares that the *Sun* is obsessed with sex. It is not the *Sun*, but the critics who are obsessed. The *Sun*, like most of its readers, likes pretty girls. And if they are as pretty as today's Birthday Suit girl, 20-year-old Stephanie Rahn, who cares whether they are dressed or not?'

Away in Australia at the time, Rupert Murdoch later declared he was 'just as shocked as anybody else' when the photo appeared. He labelled it 'a daring experiment' that quickly turned into 'a national institution'. Upon reflection, he believed 'It was a statement of youthfulness and freshness.'

The brain-children of Larry Lamb, the newspaper's first editor, 'Page Three Girls' quickly became commonplace in the pages of the *Sun*. For a time, the *Daily Mirror* used them. And when the *Daily Star* was launched, it featured its own 'Starbird'. But somehow the name never stuck. What stuck was Page Three, the page where many readers turned first when they picked up their newspaper.

The convention of the Page Three Girl is a strange one, highly stylized and formulaic, and while the rules are not so rigid as those that govern, say, a Geisha, only a small margin of variation is acceptable. A girl, no younger than sixteen, no older than twenty-five, appears on Page Three, displaying her breasts. Her nipples are erect. She is looking straight into the camera, and she is smiling. Occasionally, she pouts or simpers. No other emotion can be registered. Certainly, an expression of lust or desire would be wholly inappropriate.

In the brief caption that appears alongside the girl's photograph, her 'vital statistics' are given. These are, regardless of height, 36–24–36, given in inches – bust, waist and hips. The measurement of the bust may be enlarged by as much as two inches, the waist by one, although this is not customary. A brief mention will be made of the girl's occupation, or former occupation before she turned to modelling. It will be ordinary. She will not be an astrophysicist or a Ph.D. in microbiology. She will work in a pet store or flower shop. She might have been a check-out girl in a supermarket.

'I am neither ashamed,' says Lamb, 'nor particularly proud to say so, but I suppose I helped to make Page Three a part of the language. In many ways I now wish I hadn't.'

'The *Sun* did not invent the bosom, any more than it invented the permissive society. And thousands of people, including many women, get great pleasure each day from looking at pictures of beautiful girls in a state of undress . . . And if we hadn't emancipated the nipple, I'm sure some other paper would have done it before long.

'However, I do not like to feel that I was in any way responsible for the current fiercely competitive situation in which the girls in some of our national newspapers get younger and younger and more and more top-heavy and less and less like the girls next door.'

What Lamb is referring to, one can speculate, was his own good taste in naked ladies. And, to be truthful, his taste was impeccable. Not for Lamb the fawn-faced, thick-lipped, big-toothed look. His early Page Three girls were free spirits, true flower-children, at harmony with the times. Lithe, statuesque, small-breasted, they often appeared in verdant surroundings, on swings, in the grass, midst woods and ivy.

One of his staffers, George Lynn, remembers once having watched Larry Lamb throw away a batch of Page Three photographs. According to the story, Lamb 'came out of his office and said something like, "Haven't we got any better photos?" The picture editor pulled out a whole batch, and Larry Lamb flicked through them, and threw them away, saying something like, "They're useless. The breasts are too big. Big-breasted girls look like tarts." Then he stalked away. Then the picture editor said, "Christ, he's just thrown away £3,000 worth of pictures."'

For Lamb, there was only one hard and fast rule: the girls who appeared on Page Three had to be 'nice girls'. 'Sleazy pictures,' he said, 'were unlikely to see the light of day – not least because Woman's Editor Joyce Hopkirk and her colleagues in the Pacesetter department had an absolute right of veto.'

But Hopkirk 'wasn't real thrilled' with this responsibility and in the end simply dodged the job 'because life was such a rush. I did talk to the photographers about the girls, but really there was so much else in life. I'm a "words" woman. Larry is a great sort of visualizer. He's got a very strong sense of how to make fairly mundane material look brilliant on a page. That was his great forte. So in the end, it's what your true interests are . . . Perhaps in retrospect, in view of history, I could have done the female nation a great service if I'd paid more attention to that. But I didn't. It didn't interest me. I didn't really approve of it. While I wasn't against pictures of pretty ladies – let's face it,

I make my living by printing them today – I didn't see why they should have, um, you know . . . [laughs] no clothes on.'

Sue Snell, who worked more directly with Page Three, saw it all as 'a bit of a giggle' at the time. 'I come from a farming family, and a friend of my father out in the country had the most wonderful haybarn, and they said we could come. And we went, and the girls took their tops off. They were dressed as red indians. And then we all went and had a farmhouse tea, and we all giggled and laughed about it. It was all fun . . . And I think, now I'm older, "God, was I naïve about that?" Because people sometimes jibe at me and say, "Oh you did Page Three and *that* sort of work." And I react to that terribly much because they don't react as it really was . . .'

Beverley Goodway, Snell remembers, was the photographer who started Page Three. Goodway was a staff photographer, who had 'this nice attitude with models . . . They trusted him. He wasn't a leering old man, he wasn't making money on top of it, and also in those early days, when they took their clothes off, those girls were wonderful. They were in it for business. They knew they didn't have very much time. It meant they made more money. It was fun to do. They never saw the implications, with the feminist movement. I mean, all that came later.

'Those girls in those days, they were really together, I thought. When I was on the *Sun*, I never saw the people that *bought* it. I just saw the people that put it in . . . it was all done for laughs . . . It was only later that I realized how some men might see it.'

Currently a film fashion designer, Snell sometimes works late in Soho and it's only now, after dark, when she sees some of the clients there that 'I suddenly realize how seamy it is.'

The presence of Page Three Girls no doubt contributed to the decision of the local library in Sowerby Bridge, Yorkshire, to ban the *Sun* from its public reading room. Ostensibly dropped because the newspaper didn't fit the library's wooden rods and could therefore be easily stolen, the *Sun*, it slowly emerged, was actually thought 'too sexy for the local inhabitants.' At once recognizing a publicity opportunity, Lamb labelled the town's officials 'the Silly Burghers of Sowerby Bridge', sending his star reporter to cover the story. He then cooked up a contest, first prize: 'Win a Free Weekend in Sowerby Bridge'; second prize: 'Win a Free Week in Sowerby Bridge'. In the glare of publicity, the affair quickly became a *cause célèbre* with 'the Silly Burghers' themselves getting into the act by showing a willingness to go along with the popular sideshow.

More powerful than 'the Silly Burghers of Sowerby Bridge' are W. H. Smith and its competitor, Menzies, the major outlets for newspapers and other reading material in Great Britain. Twenty years after the appearance of the original Page Three Girl, businesses like these still find themselves under heavy pressure to remove photographs of half-dressed women from their shelves. The movement is led in the main by Labour MP Clare Short. Dubbed 'a dragon woman', 'a feminist scourge' and 'the absolute enemy of the working man', Short has nevertheless been dauntless in her anti-Page Three crusade.

In March 1986, she stood up in Parliament and introduced a private member's bill, the Indecent Displays (Newspapers) Bill, which sought to ban Page Three Girls from the newspapers. 'Those pictures,' she said, 'portray women as objects of lust to be sniggered over and grabbed at, and do not portray sex as something that is tender and private.' In the rowdy House of Commons, where members often shout out their objections like youngsters in English public schools, her speech was twice interrupted and once greeted by raucous laughter.

In April 1988, she again introduced her bill, citing the 5,000 letters she had received in its support, twelve of them from women who had suffered rape and who were told by the men raping them that 'they reminded them of a woman on Page Three or that they ought to be on Page Three.' She referred to other letters 'from young women who were sexually abused as children', charging that relatives had used 'those pictures' to justify their abuse. She referred to the power of mass circulation newspapers 'to shape attitudes in our society' and equated her bill to others which restrict materials inciting 'racial hatred'.

Again meeting with rebuff, Short then, in November 1989, led a delegation against the Holborn branch of W. H. Smith, 'in the company of fellow anti-porn campaigners', sweeping up 'a pile of dirty books and magazines' and presenting them to the shop's manager. Said a company spokesman, 'We are all primarily retailers. We do not wish to be seen acting as censors.'

W. H. Smith nevertheless, along with its competitor Menzies, stands in a unique position in Great Britain, one not dissimilar to the United States Post Office, who, before being halted by the US Supreme Court, had the power of life and death over major publications. A magazine as innocuous as *Esquire* was nearly driven out of business when officials within the bureaucracy revoked its second-class mailing privileges on the basis of questionable material.

Otherwise, in America, the great dividing line is the marketplace, and anyone who hopes to sustain mass circulation among the working class will find that scantily dressed women are not a welcome addition. For a time, the New York *Daily News* ran the picture of a bathing beauty on page four. The photographs came over the wires at first from Florida, then from Sydney, Australia, giving rise to the nickname 'the Sydney Beauty'. Essentially, these were cancelled through lack of interest.

As to the supermarket tabloids, they were quick to discover that 'bikini girls, pin-ups, London pictures we got from over there . . . they didn't go over very well. Within six months, we quit using them,' says Christina Kirk, Associate Editor of the *Star*. 'For a long time,' she adds, 'we didn't feel we could use the word "sex" on the cover.'

Early in the history of the *Globe*, when it was still called *Midnight Globe* and originated in Montreal, the editors used to run girls in bikinis. Says John Vader, editor of the *Globe*'s sister publication, the *Sun*, 'We would get letters saying, "If you don't get rid of these nude girls, we'll never look at *Midnight Globe* again." And these girls weren't nude. They weren't half as scantily dressed as they are today.' These were the early days in the *Globe*'s history, when blood, guts and gore set the tone of the publication, and pages were plastered with pictures of corpses that looked like what one might imagine the nuclear melt-down at Three-Mile Island to resemble.

So far as mass circulation on the North American continent is concerned, violence is entertainment, sex is taboo.

In the historical evolution of the Page Three Girl, Samantha Fox is credited with changing the trend from Larry Lamb's small-breasted beauty to the buxom bobby-soxing, sweet-sixteen type. Fox was sixteen when her photograph was first published on Page Three, and since then, says one commentator, Page Three Girls have had 'to appear to be that extremely unusual combination of nursing mother on top and schoolgirl below.' Fox burst the Page Three barriers when her agent, Yvonne Paul, making routine phone calls to various insurance firms about group life and health policies for her models, joked, 'Well, would you just insure someone's boobs?' According to Paul, the *Sun* picked the idea up, running the story on page one under the headline: 'Sam to Insure Her Boobs at Lloyds'. From that moment on, so Paul's story goes, the phones never stopped ringing, Fox's career was assured and eventually, she made her way into the pop music field and on to the green grass of America.

Still the favourite heroine of the tabloids that made her, Fox appears in the headlines regularly and on practically any pretext. One story traces the progress of her career in the United States, after a hand-wringing lead debating whether, at twenty-three, her boobs are drooping or not. In April 1990, under the headline, 'Day I Spat Blood and Thought I'd Die', readers of the *Sun* were regaled with details of Fox's burst ulcer and resultant loss of 38 pounds. The following day, the editorial cartoon showed a microphone with boobs, captioned, 'Sam, Don't You Think It's Time You Stopped Slimming?'

Coming a close second in the race for Number One Page Three Girl is petite but busty Maria Whittaker, whose dark hair provides a natural counterpoint to the blonde Fox. Whittaker's fame makes her worthy of a front-page reversed headline in the *News of the World*: 'Maria's Lost Two Inches Off Her Boobs! See page 24.' On page 24 appears the head, 'Maria Gets 'Em Off! Page 3 Star Sheds 10 lb. and 2 Ins. Off Boobs.' The how-to-do-it article specifies Whittaker's special diet: '8 a.m. BREAKFAST: muesli and skimmed milk, toast with low-fat margarine. 1 p.m. LUNCH: Salad or a tuna sandwich using wholemeal bread. 7 p.m. DINNER: Chicken or fish with lots of vegetables and salad.'

The stories about Page Three Girls don't stop with Fox and Whittaker though. When one Page Three Girl's attractive mother became entangled with a 'toyboy lover', a telephone hotline gave readers the chance to vote whether she ought to have or not. The overwhelming response? 'Get it while you can.'

Meanwhile, another true life drama unfolds when Rachel Garley explains, 'Why I Ditched Lover, 45, by Page 3 Girl, 20'. Garley, the *Sun* says:

> . . . decided to break with Ray Pearson because she was 'suffocating'.
>
> He ORGANIZED every detail of her life – even laying out her make-up and the clothes she wanted to wear.

REFUSED to let her do anything as down-to-earth as shopping.

HATED her even talking to other men – claiming that they were trying to take advantage of her.

Rachel, ironically, found this stultifying . . .

After she split with him, 'I only had to look at a teddy bear that Ray had bought me and I'd burst into floods of tears.

But for the redoubtable Garley, there was a serious moral to her lesson, one from which others might benefit: '*But now I'm learning to live my own life and do things for myself for the first time in years.*'

Perhaps the classic Page Three genre story comes from a *Sun* exclusive which in some ways evokes the perils of the heroine of Samuel Richardson's novel *Clarissa* some two hundred and fifty years earlier. Entitled 'My Tiger Lover Was a Snake', the story is the heart-wrung confession of Page Three Mia Ford, who, when she met Male Model of the Year Danny Mayhew, believed she had 'at last found the man of her dreams.' Ford's story may be told in a few short phrases:

'*a story of trust . . . and betrayal*'
'a smile that could melt ice'
'so genuine, so nice – and so goodlooking'
'*everything a girl could want in one package*'
'got on like a house on fire'
'like schoolkids on a first date'
'the future as if it belonged to the two of us – together'
'*I couldn't believe my luck*'
'a wonderful night of romance'
'melted clean away'
'left on my violet silk bra and panties'
'turned into an animal . . . like a tiger . . . I was his little sex kitten'
'I can't believe this is happening to me'
'reminded me of Tarzan . . . I was his Jane . . .'
'never called me back'
'*smooth operator*'

Back to Tula. 'My £19m Husband Dumped Me for His Momma, Sobs Sex-change Tula'. Her exclusive story is run in the *People* in September 1989.

James Bond bird Tula was dumped by her mega-rich husband the day they flew back from a passionate honeymoon – because his mother found out his bride used to be a BOY.

The statuesque beauty, who became a top model after a sex-change operation in 1974, revealed yesterday how she made love to multi-millionaire Elias Fattal for more than two years before breaking the shocking news that she was once a butcher's boy called Barry Cossey.

But they DIDN'T tell his strict Jewish family . . .

Now Tula is planning to take her husband to court because, after persuading her to give up her modelling career, he has cut off all financial support for her.

'I can't believe this has happened to me,' said Tula. 'Just when life seemed so perfect.'

It is 31 October 1989, and the *Sun* is running a three-quarter page colour spread. It is filled with slender suntanned bodies, glistening under artificial lights. Their poses are arrogant and artificial – even arch. One of the shots is of a bare back, the model wearing only a towel, which plunges provocatively beneath the hips, showing five or six inches of bulging buttocks.

'Feast Your Eyes on Our Tasty Offering of Mouth-Watering Men, Girls!' says the headline. 'Vote for Page 7 Fella of the Year. Phone in your vote and you have picked him.'

By April, we learn that the bulging buttocks have won. 'Fancy a night out on the town with Page 7 Fella of the Year Kevin Petts? Just let your imagination roam free for a few seconds. Then tell us how YOU would like to spend a date with our cuddly Kev – and you could WIN the evening of your dreams with him.

'Former weight-lifting instructor Kevin, 28, is SunWoman's gift to you on our second birthday. The sender of the best idea will have her fantasy come true as Kev takes her on a super spree – courtesy of SunWoman.'

A month before, the *Sport* staged its own 'Hunk of the Year' contest, for amateur contenders: 'Feast your peepers on this, girls. He's the gorgeous guy who out-flexed the opposition to become our Hunk of the Year.

'Slinky Simon Lelley, 24, from Coventry, beat nine other hopefuls for the cherished title by scoring 430 points on the *Sport*'s "Hunkometer".'

Lelley, who wears a black 'wet' bikini, looks unusually handsome and, he is, well, real. Lelley works in a steelworks, and his girlfriend sent in his picture to the contest 'as a joke'. In the background of the photo in which Lelley holds his winner's trophy aloft are hundreds of cheering and laughing women, who, the *Sport* explains, 'are coming to grips with the bulging beefcakes parading their posing pouches.'

In London, a telephone rings in an agent's office. She picks up the phone. 'Oh, hi, Karen,' she says matter of factly. 'No, your breasts were too small. I know you wouldn't want me to lie to you. Well, OK.' The call takes less than twenty seconds.

Across town, another agent calms a worried photographer: 'No, no, no. You'll find that none of *our* male models need any "help" with their posing pouches.'

In classical burlesque, American-style, scantily clad girls – dumb, sweet and stacked – were the inspiration for countless comic skits. They wore high-heel shoes, tassles on their tits, feathers on their bums, and they wiggled. Pull on the tassles, and a bell goes 'ding-dong'. Meanwhile, the comedians are panting like dogs, fanning themselves, pouring water over their heads; anything to 'cool down'.

It was vulgar and tasteless and people loved it. In Britain, Page Three, and now Page Seven, are what most vulgarize the popular press, thus bringing the newspaper business closer to showbiz. The *Sunday Sport*, much deplored by the 'legitimate' press, has, perhaps more than any other publication, lowered the taste threshold in tabloids.

An amateur snap of an overweight lout with sagging muscles, hair sticking out from under his arms, hands stroking a beer gut, graces Page Seven of the *Sport*. His girlfriend loves him.

'Pizza Sue is just topping!' says another headline. 'Super Sue Robinson was a pizza delivery girl until she discovered her own toppings could earn her a much bigger crust in the modelling world.'

Or take 'the World's Hairiest Glamour Model'. 'Human Bath Rug Cindy Bush last night revealed the secret of her modelling success . . . a twice daily shave. The bristling beauty is covered with black body hair because of a rare hormone disorder . . . But now the gorgeous French-woman, who shaves twice a day, has made a clean breast of it. Hairs looking at you, Cindy!'

Or take Vicki Little, whose arms can reach only as far as the nipples around her 'amazing mega-size breasts'. Or Tina Small, the beauty with the 84-inch bust who became a Buddhist nun in Tibet.

Or take 'Gert Bucket', the 69-stone East-Berliner, who 'smashed her way through the Berlin wall' and onto the pages of the *Sunday Sport*.

Go ahead, take her.

Behind the scenes of this merry-go-round is big business. If the first purpose of any institution is to perpetuate itself, the institution of the Page Three Girl has quickly established a financial stronghold, one that is unlikely to go away. What MP Clare Short has labelled 'the Page Three Mentality' is not so much a state of mind as a major industry, one that offers sharp young business men and women an early chance at big stakes.

'Marcelle', whose glamour agency is rated among the top five in London, started in the business only four years ago. Before that, she worked for Estée Lauder. But when she had her two sons, she began looking for something she could do from home. She gave a grooming course – where the clients learned cat-walking, make-up, even drama – and a few of the girls who turned up told her they wanted to become models. Marcelle then sent their pictures around, entered them in competitions and, lo and behold, three of them got jobs.

Today, she manages eighteen girls full-time, and she's had Page Three's in the *Sun*, the *Sunday Mirror*, the *News of the World*, the *Star*, the *Sport*, the *Sunday World in Ireland* and a number of German magazines. She lives in a detached house, furnished with fine antiques, with a Porsche in the driveway. She is thirty years old.

Any girl who wants to become a glamour model begins by sending Marcelle amateur snaps taken by friends or relatives. If these show potential, Marcelle gives her an appointment. The age span for the average glamour model is from sixteen to twenty-five, although a few girls have lasted until thirty. At the initial meeting, Marcelle assesses the girl's potential. 'Right,' she'll say, 'You need to lose weight, gain a few pounds, take exercise, change your hair colour . . .

'We've had girls here who were bleached blondes, and we've said, "Go back to your natural colour." And it's paid off. Then,' she says, 'a photographer does a few test pictures, and he tells me whether he sees potential or not. Normally we can see *some*.'

What Marcelle seeks is 'a bubbling, pretty, fresh look. Personality is most important. The girls must be full of life.' Some of the girls have pleasant personalities, 'very bubbly and very pretty,' but, when faced with the camera, 'boom, they freeze.'

'Different agencies work differently,' says Marcelle. 'I send the girl out to a photographer for test pictures, and then I use a lot of those pictures to build up her portfolio. She might have to buy a few pictures. Model cards, like index cards; that's her cost. Black-and-white index cards will cost the girl between £100 and £150; colour between £200 and £300 for a thousand. But I try to get her a job to cover the cost.

'And then she enters the agency's model book. I charge her to appear in it . . . somewhere in the region of £50 or £60, but West End agents charge up to £275. The girl then gets sent out to casting directors, publicity people, photographers, and ad people. If she doesn't get any engagements after a month or two, I take her off my books.'

Marcelle advises the new model what to wear and what not to wear, and also how to make up her face for photographs. For black-and-white pictures, heavy make-up is advisable. The flashing of the light blows out much of the make-up. Marcelle suggests 'a few charcoal colours, grey, dark black, blue. They can wear any lipstick, so long as it's not too pale. Burgundy is good, or mid-red or dark pink. With colour you use more natural colours. Girls should look a little bit suntanned.'

The girls soon find out that there are 'a lot of rip-offs out there,' says Marcelle. 'There is one guy charging £175 for pictures. And there are agencies that charge a lot of money.'

Also, most beginners don't realize there's a lot of legwork, 'knocking on doors, and so on'. This falls under the general rubric 'professionalism', a term with a very specialized meaning within the glamour industry, where so many of the girls are young, naïve and ill-educated. Says one agent about her most 'professional' model:

> From the minute I told her she was a little overweight, she went on a sensible diet. I also thought her hair was too long and would look better blond, so she had it cut and dyed without a word of complaint. She did everything completely right. If I gave Gillian a booking for seven o'clock in the morning, she would be there at six-thirty. If I told her to take three swimsuits, she would take six. If I told her she needed black boots and she didn't own any, I would never know there was a problem because she would go and buy a pair. If I asked her to have a particular type of dress that was difficult to find, she would just shop around all day until she tracked it down. This attitude was invaluable to Gillian's career. People

started using her because she was so professional, keen and reliable.

But Marcelle has had just the opposite experience. A pretty blonde came in, did a few jobs, but for some reason just 'didn't take'.

'She tried very hard. You get some girls,' says Marcelle, 'you have to stay after them all the time. Do this. Do that. Don't do this. Don't do that. They're late, or they put on weight, or they don't get their roots done. And they get used quite regularly. But the ones whose hearts are in the right place don't seem to get on.'

There is another problem, one that can be more serious. The models are for the first time meeting all kinds of people and seeing completely new lifestyles. They begin to live 'a champagne life', even before they've tasted champagne. 'Some of the girls can't handle it,' says Marcelle. 'They can't take the glare, it goes to their head. They come down with a thump when they realize they aren't Miss World.'

Predictable, too, is the problem with sex. 'The girls sleep with people to get ahead,' says Marcelle, 'on the casting couch, so to speak; more so in this business than most. Some are so *blatant* about it, like photographers and casting agents. And others are flat out propositioned before the photograph in some cases.

'The girls,' Marcelle says, 'gain nothing from this.' Marcelle gives out a standard warning: 'You do not take people at face value. You do not go out for dinner with them. You do not take them seriously until you get it in black-and-white on a sheet of paper telling you you've got the job. Some of the new girls are unaware of that. If they sleep with them, people will help the models for a little while, then another one will come along . . . that's right, they'll get dumped . . . Some of the girls get offended when they're propositioned, some laugh it off. Some get worried: "Oh, God, what'll happen if I see him again?"'

If a girl gets past all these barriers, and she's still pitching, it will take her a year to become established. Pictures can and do improve, some more than others. A moderately successful girl's first year includes an initial six-month period when the girl is going out and promoting herself, and during this time her income can be very low indeed. Then perhaps she can expect monthly engagements to begin trickling in. The second half of the year might include engagements like this: Portugal for a week, three days back home. Then off to, say, Arizona to work for two weeks. Then home for a week and a half. Then off to Mexico for two weeks. For this, the girl would make roughly £2,000. Altogether for the year, she might expect to make £8,000 to £9,000, bearing in mind she will not work everyday in a week, but more likely one day *in* a week. Of that income, Marcelle will collect 22 per cent, agent's fee.

For most of the girls, five years will be the span of their career, and after this, they leave the profession. 'But,' as Marcelle says, 'they often meet very nice people. One girl met a stockbroker, lives with him. The job makes opportunities for them. They've got their boyfriends, but they go out and meet a different class and compare them to the new men, and . . . some boyfriends get the elbow. Some of the boyfriends are supportive and lovely, though. And quite a few keep on.

'If a girl doesn't make it as a Page Three model,' says Marcelle, 'and she still wants to make it as a glamour model, then that's when she might revert to . . . girlie magazines and raunchier modelling.' Marcelle doesn't handle this end of the trade, and refuses to do nudes for men's magazines. She does do 'soft nudes': 'with a very minimum of pubic hair showing, nothing else. It's very tastefully done, not like men's magazines.'

Shelley Lawrence, a photographer's agent, *does* handle the raunchier end of the trade. Young, energetic and worldly wise, she admits quite frankly she likes her work. Lawrence used to be an actress, but loves the selling, the business side of handling photographs. 'The difference is, especially in the theatre, you are always hustling for work. You never have a regular job. Eighty per cent of all the actors in this country are out of work all of the time. This is steady work, regular income, which is what I like. And you're still your own boss.'

Lawrence holds up a release form for a publication in the United States, which in this case is for the magazine *High Society*. She points out two sets of identifications proving that the model is over eighteen. This one has a passport picture and a medical card.

'You have to have a picture of it – the model holding the passport under her chin,' says Lawrence. 'They've had a lot of problems in the States with models being underage and stuff like that so this is the only way they could protect themselves. We never ever shoot anyone unless they are eighteen and unless they bring the identification to prove it.'

These IDs aren't required for topless shots, but for the nudes, and America is the only country that requires the IDs, to date. 'Over here,' says Lawrence, 'you just get the model to sign and write the date of her birth. Anywhere else in Europe or Australia, you don't need anything else at all, not even release forms.

41

'You have to have a very good knowledge of each country, what you can send them, what you can't. The 'strongest' pictures go to the US. A two-girl pose of simulated lesbian acts can sell only in the States or in Scandinavia. And any porn where the girl is touching herself "on Pussy" is sold only in those two areas. Or Amsterdam, where anything goes. Holding the labia apart in the US market is "quite acceptable", but not OK in Britain. It isn't so much the law,' she explains, 'as what the shops will stock.

'What happens is that two companies virtually control distribution – Menzies and W. H. Smith. They dictate what goes in. If they don't like it, they will take it off the shelf.'

The biggest soft porn market is in the United States; in Germany the porn is hard core. And in Los Angeles, where there is a big glamour industry, all major pornography films are made. In England, anything pornographic is taped up and sold only in Soho.

The law in Great Britain prevents the production of any real pornography. Anyone who arranges a two-model pornographic shoot is culpable under the law, although any models who agree to participate are not. Most real pornographers go to Germany where the laws are more lax and there is an open market. The other venue is Amsterdam, and, more expensively, the United States.

'When we sell pictures,' says Lawrence, 'the biggest money we get is first rights – pictures that have never before been published in that country. In the United States, the first rights could be $1600, and the photographs will go into glossy magazines, on high quality paper. With second rights, you will get less money, say $800, and the paper will maybe be matt finish in digest magazines which are smaller. In the United States, there are only first and second rights. In Sweden, Norway and Finland, there are first, second, third and fourth rights.

'The ideal thing is to do a shoot with different clothes and different backgrounds and different lighting, and get two or three sets, split them up, send one set to the States, one to Great Britain and one to Scandinavia for first rights. We try to do two sets in a day, because the purchaser might not like one background. You might say to him, "Well, look, I've got another one using that girl." It gives you a better chance. Potentially, one set of pictures should make you over a period of five years, say £2,000, before expenses – model, rent, everything. You can shoot it in lingerie and if it's not too fashionable, years later you can sell it. Especially in Japan, there's a greater time lag. If the girl is wearing platform heels, and the style goes out, then you lose business.

'Then there are the specialized rights. We can "rent out" the copyright for different things, like calendar rights. We let them use that picture for a year, and we won't sell it to any other calendar *for that year*. But we could sell it for the cover of a magazine. Or for use *in* a magazine.'

When everything is added together – rights, countries, types of shots (calendars, books, magazines, posters) – the potential income is very high indeed. And so is the potential for 'rip-offs'.

Daniel Mayor, a successful glamour photographer who has created images for over 3,000 models, among them many Page Three Girls, says, 'Models get ripped off by photographers, and photographers get ripped off by agents. They sell it and don't tell you they sold it, or sell it for less because they deal with so many photographers. All they want is their quick commission. Or they sell second rights, say, and don't tell you.

Mayor, who has been published in fifteen countries – 'Japan, Sweden, Denmark, South Africa, Germany, the States, everywhere' – explains that a photographer must 'get a reputation that you can go to any market . . . and that you can produce for it, on a long-term basis.

'You send a lot of stuff off, and they say "We don't like the setting, the photography, the girl or whatever." So you find out what is wrong with it. You have to actually please the editor. Every time there is an editorial change, you have to find out what the new editor's ideas are.

'There's no money in Page Three Girls. It's just good publicity. Agents see your work, that's all. The bread and butter in this industry is nude shots.'

Including topless shots, nude shots, simulated pornography and hard core pornography, the glamour industry grosses over £500 million a year in Great Britain alone. Include Europe and America, where the markets are worth revenues in the region of £3 billion and $10 billion respectively, and the industry is bigger than the international music and film industries combined.

For the Page Three Girl, there is a nebulous grey area, an undefined cross-over line, where topless slides into nude, nude into 'open-leg' or 'Pussy' shots, and from there into the world of pornography. Exactly where the model stops is largely self-determined, because photographs that might destroy a Page Three Girl's career in Great Britain can be marketed in Europe or in Japan, where no one is likely to find out.

It is possible for a girl to take on a photographic persona during a session, thus changing her appearance sufficiently that she is not easily recognized. It would take close scrutiny and some sort of tip-off, in most cases, to recognize the girl next door after she has assumed the make-up, the hairstyle, the costume and mood changes that are part and parcel of the business. Add to this the photographer's personal style, plus the changing sets and backgrounds, and it would take a professional's eye to pick out one girl from another.

From time to time in the popular press, a Page Three Girl admits to having done pornographic photographs. These are always portrayed in typical tabloid-ese: 'I was young and naïve'; 'the biggest mistake of my life'; 'the pictures came back to haunt me'. Underneath all this jargon is a cold economic fact: porn – soft or hard – simply pays more money.

It is ten o'clock in the morning, and a photographic session is about to begin. Daniel Mayor, whose father was a landscape artist, has definite ideas about how a model should look under the lights, and he took a course in make-up in order to create the image that has become his trademark. For a time, he studied hypnotherapy, and he uses what he learned there to get a model to perform in front of the camera. Mayor's idea of what makes a beautiful woman is high cheekbones, small nostrils, clean shining hair, and pouty lips, like a baby. 'We were all beautiful babies,' he says.

Mayor will be photographing Tracie, who works in the glamour trade only part-time as a hobby. She explains that she prefers to have a steady weekly salary coming in, and 'if you work full-time, it's harder to have a boyfriend. The male in this country,' she says knowingly, 'is jealous and possessive.'

Tracie has won ten beauty titles, among them, Miss UK (twice), Miss Leeds, Miss Doncaster, Miss Skegness, Miss Lovely Legs, Miss Glamour Legs. There are many different competitions, she explains, for tights, swimwear and so on, and many nightclubs sponsor their own competitions. You enter these contests, not so much for the title, as to advertise your name. If an agency knows you have a title, you can make more money. This can lead to personal appearances at retail outlets, supermarkets, petrol stations and the like.

'It's not very hard really,' says Tracie. 'I mean, you can't put it down to hard work. The hardest part is goin' out and visitin' the agencies . . . takin' trains, tubes. You've got to travel, and you can't be shy.'

Like 80 per cent of Page Three Girls, Tracie is from the north, and her parents were very strict when she started working in the glamour industry. She only lately began going topless. She is twenty-five-years old, and it's a late start. A few years ago, Tracie was a finalist in a beauty contest that Samantha Fox won, and Tracie was asked to do calendar shots abroad. 'I said no because my mum and dad wouldn't like me to do topless. And of course,' Tracie says with regret, 'Samantha carried on.' Tracie believes it was there, at that moment, that she lost out. 'I mean, who wouldn't like to be a *star*?'

Tracie is wearing a fashionable denim overall outfit with long sleeves. It's dark blue, with decorative metal studs across the yoke and padded shoulders. She is wearing black boots that are also decorated with metal studs. Her hair is in hot rollers, and she is wearing no make-up whatsoever. Stripped of all the accoutrements of feminine artistry – flowing hair, make-up, revealing clothing – it is nevertheless a fact that Tracie is a stunningly beautiful girl, with flawless features and a freshness that overwhelms.

Mayor is not overwhelmed. He takes a seat in front of a make-up mirror, and Tracie drops her clothes. She stands naked in front of Mayor without modesty. 'I'm not bothered,' she says, and she obviously isn't. She is tanned all over. She got her suntan, she explains, 'in the back garden.' Says Mayor, 'You can get a very cold look, if your skin's too white. A suntan is better because it looks warm. Everybody wants a warm look. Open your legs.'

Mayor has put baby oil onto his hands, now he strokes her body gently all over with it. 'That way, you don't get too much,' he explains. Tracie has burned herself on her barbecue at home, and he covers it with make-up.

Tracie's body is stunning. She eats healthy foods, she says, and takes weight training. She used to do Karate – 'absolutely fabulous for body tone . . . and it's not as strenuous as aerobics.' Jane Fonda's workout tape? 'That's not so bad.'

As Mayor strokes the oil over her body, Tracie continues to talk. 'Lack of sleep shows in this business,' she says. 'The time of month shows. When I get a bloated tummy from my menstrual period, I take less water.' She shows her pubic hair, which is neatly shaved into a perfect 'V'. She can't have hairs on the leg, she explains. 'There's nothing worse than surrounding hair, especially with high-cut costumes. A lot of girls use wax,' she says.

Says Mayor, 'If that is messy down there, if there are pimples or anything like that, you'll lose a sale.'

Mayor's studio is in his home, and he uses the decorations, like potted plants, rugs, tapestries, from all over the house in order to build the set. If he doesn't like the colour, he paints it overnight. There is a wooden cobra in the corner. 'Yeah,' he says, 'I've used it before.'

A lot of photographers hire their own make-up artists, Mayor explains. But he prefers to do it himself.

By now, Tracie has changed into a shortie navy blue dressing gown, with a monogram on the pocket. She sits before the make-up mirror as Mayor does her face. The dressing table is littered with bottles, cartons, paints and powders. It looks like an artist's palette. 'Right now,' says Mayor, 'I'm putting on a base that's going to last. Because of the hot lights, she's going to sweat . . . and the physical aspect of doing all the posing, all the back bending, and everything else,' he adds. 'The make-up's got to stay on, and she's still got to look good from the beginning of the shoot to the end of the shoot.'

He cakes mounds of translucent fixing powder onto her face. 'She sweats while I'm putting make-up on and any make-up would fall into the open pores, wouldn't it? So I'm putting on as much as possible. I'll put excess on, take it all off later.

'Take the colour of a mass of her body, I've got to match that, blend it in; it's got to correspond. Then I make the face the same colour. As I put the eye make-up on, I always put loose powder under the eyes, so when I brush the powder off, I can take away any loose mascara that's fallen off.'

Mayor is a big man, athletic-looking, with rough and distinct features. He now puts on bifocals to do the close-up work, and for the first time, he looks middle-aged. He is using pencil liner.

'I do everything my own way,' he says. 'I use a highlighter on the eyelids, mix a lot of my own colours.' Tracie is now transformed into a gross creature with long, black lashes, irridescent eyes. Her complexion looks like brightly painted plaster of paris, and her lips are glossy and shining. They are painted a heavy pink – Mayor's trademark.

She unrolls her long blond hair from the rollers, and begins to brush it out. Tracie uses one of the strongest of the mousses to get a thicker look; 'more bounce and height,' she says. Up close, as she teases her hair higher and higher, it seems sticky and webbed. She is using copious amounts of hairspray, so it will hold under the lights. Her nails, she explains, must be painted, not cracked or chipped.

Mayor decides she should wear something light because they have dark colours in the background, so, from among her many flimsy costumes, Tracie chooses a pink camisole affair with cascades of cream-coloured lace. She slips into silk bikini panties and pulls on white stockings with lace at the top; attaches them to a suspender belt. She steps into a pair of silver shoes 'to define her legs', and she is fully dressed.

Since she once owned her own boutique, Tracie knows where to pick up the filmy gewgaws of her profession cheaply. Sometimes, she says, the photographer provides a costume for her.

Says Mayor, 'In England, you have to look "like the girl next door" or "like a right tart". There's no inbetween.'

Tracie is now ready. The fresh pretty girl who sat in hair rollers an hour and a half ago has transformed into an exotic creature. In her shimmering finery, she has taken on the aura of an acrobat or circus performer. 'I feel comfortable behind a camera,' she says. 'People can't touch me.'

Tracie is now ready to go to work. She moves onto the set, under the lights, and the make-up that seemed pasty and gross now seems natural and light. Mayor arranges her on the set. Her right leg is on the stool, her left leg on the floor. She's arching her back. She's leaning back, top down, legs spread. Tracie begins to move, slowly and constantly, as if she were doing a slow-motion dance. She has entered a fantasy world, one she likes. 'If you *enjoy* something,' she says, 'it gives *you* satisfaction, it gives other *people* satisfaction . . .' Tracie is unfastening her clothes, pooching her lips.

'That's a girl,' Mayor says, 'Good. Stay there. Good girl. Good girl. That's a gal. And again. Good. I'm just going to swing over here to get more. Why don't you bring that sideways? Bring some boobs up on that. That's a gal. Good gal. That's it. Hold that. The look I want you to get is a right arrogant look. That's it. Stay there. That's a girl. Good.'

'Show a little boob coming up to the top now. That's it. Throw the head *up*. That's a gal. And again. Good.' Tracy seems to disappear – at least the girl who was here a short time ago. She seems to go inside herself. She is pouting. He tells her what to do. She puts her finger in her mouth, then holds it to her ear. Her mouth is open: 'Keep Pussy out,' he says. Tracie's not embarrassed; she gets an arrogant look on her face. She's very delicate about exposing Pussy. She reaches down, pulls back the labia with her finger, like pulling a small curtain, showing a small rosebud.

You can hear the camera shutter click. Whirring.

'Good gal. All done. Sideways. Leave the boobs out. Bring your legs together. Make one leg further than the other. Leave boobs out. Head up to about there. Hold that. Close your eyes. That's

47

it. Pout the mouth. That's a gal. Well done. And again. Well done. Good gal. Quite good. Go from the back . . .' Tracie turns around, pulls her underwear up, almost like a G-string. 'Open up a bit wider, Tracie. A little bit more. Lift up the top. *Now*. Little bit more forward. That's it. Just about there. Good girl. Hold that. Hold that. And again. Hold that. Good girl.'

3
I CUT OUT HER HEART
AND STOMPED ON IT

In early January 1967, John Ostrom, recently released from an American prison and with no fixed address, committed an act for which he was made to pay dearly: he walked across a buddy's freshly made bed with his boots on, leaving a path of muddy footprints on clean sheets. His pal was incensed, and in a fit of rage, tied Ostrom to a chair, explaining he was going to kill him, but 'not right away – just piece by piece, little by little, so that even in death you will always remember, never forget.' Over the next few hours, Ostrom was slowly butchered; his groin cut open, an arm hacked almost off, his eyes cut out. Three of his teeth were extracted with pliers. At last, and somewhat anticlimactically, his heart was cut out. The murderer then stored Ostrom's dismembered body in a steamer trunk, where it was later photographed, a box of bones, the picture working its way into the pages of the *National Enquirer* through the *ad hoc* network of local reporters and stringers who knew or had heard the sort of thing its founder, Generoso Pope Jr., was looking for.

Something of a whiz kid, Pope had graduated from MIT (Massachusetts Institute of Technology) at the age of nineteen and spent a year working in the government's top secret department of psychological warfare before turning his hand to tabloid journalism. In 1952, he purchased the New York *Enquirer* for a sum somewhere between $70,000 and $75,000.

In these first few years of ownership, Pope discovered for himself a general precept demonstrated by the history of the tabloid press: the lower the common denominator of a newspaper's content, the higher the circulation.

Pope's approach had been far more cynical than the one adopted a few years later by Larry Lamb on Rupert Murdoch's controversial London *Sun*. Lamb's mass readership would grow out of the permissiveness of the Swinging Sixties and his shock value was mainly sexual; Pope based his appeal on the public's prurient interest in violence. By combing the world for bizarre and horrific tales of shark attacks, decapitation, white slavery, chained-up lunatics, and the occasional one-time special, like the story about the deaf farmer who dragged his wife to her death in a hay-turning machine – headlined 'I Couldn't Hear Her Scream' – Pope created what was arguably the most sensational newspaper ever printed in the United States. Its relentless gore carried the New York *Enquirer* from a 17,000 circulation local newspaper into a 1,000,000 circulation national, now dubbed the *National Enquirer* by the ambitious Pope.

Iain Calder, who was destined to become Gene Pope's right-hand man, joined the *Enquirer*'s London bureau in 1964. To him, these early years of the newspaper were 'terrible days, dreadful days, awful days. . . . The standard joke, but there was a lot of truth to it, if they asked you, "Where did you spend '61 to '63?" I think the guy would rather have said Sing Sing.'

Whether by accident or artifice, none of these early newspapers survives; certainly, none is housed in the permanent archives of 'Story Control', the sci-fi name of the current Research Department of today's *National Enquirer*. The records begin in 1967, when the newspaper had passed reluctantly from the profitable 'gore era' into a kind of schizoid phase which incorporated a bit of the old tried-and-true horror with personal beauty tips, celebrity chit-chat and reader-oriented human interest stories.

What changed the tone of the *National Enquirer* was the jump into the supermarkets, thought to be the single most inspired move made by Pope, who is credited with formulating the idea. In order to set up its racks near the check-out, the *Enquirer* was forced to end what tabloid veterans now commonly call the 'I-Cut-Out-Her-Heart-and-Stomped-On-It' period. The basic conservatism of supermarket managers, and their wish not to offend customers, forced Pope to search for a new product to sell. He found it in television.

At a time when 'the boob tube' was being trashed by magazines and newspapers, many of whom would not survive the new competition, the *Enquirer* embraced television, realizing 'that it was becoming one of the major forces in society,' says Iain Calder. 'So we piggybacked on it. And we suddenly found that if you wrote about Lucille Ball, or if you wrote about someone in *The Beverly Hillbillies*, for example, *they* sold better than John Wayne. It was amazing! Our circulation started going up.' So it was that at about the same time Larry Lamb was discovering in London 'that television was probably the biggest single area of human interest'

50

– aside from sex – and interweaving television personalities into the basic formula for the *Sun*, Gene Pope and Iain Calder were independently adopting the same strategy across the seas.

The transition to 'a clean, well-scrubbed family audience' was swift, and in only a few years the emphasis changed to 'human interest, animals and celebrities and medical cures and everything that basically makes life a sunny day,' says one *Enquirer* staffer.

Although Iain Calder was only twenty-five when he joined the staff of the *National Enquirer*, he had already worked for three Scottish papers and freelanced for London's *Daily Mirror*, and it was probably Calder who first inspired in Gene Pope his admiration for British reporters. Schooled in the tough methodology of the Glasgow school of journalists, Calder was the embodiment of their all-stops-out approach to newsgathering. 'In this market,' Calder says, 'you'd do almost anything, I mean, crashing cars, and putting other cars off the road. You would do kinda tricks to beat the competition, things that are now not heard of.' In the normal journalism of today, a reporter goes to the home of a disaster victim and interviews the family. But in the early days in Glasgow, it wasn't enough to get there first. You had to get the family out of the house in order to get an exclusive.

There were 'try-ons', like leaving a sign on the door with a fictitious address where the family could be found. 'And then,' says Calder, 'you would take every picture in the house . . . you'd say, "Does grandma have any pictures? Does aunty have any pictures?" You'd go and get every single picture you could get, so there *was nothing left*. It was like Russia, the devastation as the Germans approached.'

The most aggressive single incident Calder remembers was a trial case, where a killer got off on a 'not proven' verdict, a verdict peculiar to Scottish law which means that the court believes the defendant to be guilty but cannot prove it. In this case, practically every newspaper had paid a member of the family not to talk to anyone else. 'Everybody had someone tied up,' said Calder. 'Someone had his mother, someone had his brother. One newspaper had about twenty-five reporters, about fifteen photographers, another about ten, and everybody was trying to get the killer. As he came down the steps, everybody made a grab. There was a big pushin' and shovin' match.'

Calder was a court reporter, and had just returned to his newspaper's radio car in time to witness what happened next. One paper had hired six thugs, at £5 apiece to get the killer into their car, 'But the guy starts screamin', thinkin' it's friends of the person he killed tryin' to kill him. They bodily threw him into *our* car by mistake. We had a professional driver, and the driver starts takin' off . . . So he's tryin' to put it into gear, the doors are open. One guy is screamin' into the radio, "we got him, we got him!" and they're sayin' "great!" Suddenly the killer fights his way clear, jumps out of the car and he's off, and everybody, dozens and dozens of people runnin' and trailin' after him. We had a paper called the *Daily Citizen*, had no photographers, never thought they could get anything. They're there in their car, they open their door, and the guy jumps in, and they get an exclusive – *that* was Glasgow journalism. It was the most amazing place to get your training, to find out how important it is to get the story.'

Today, there are few lengths Calder won't go to 'to get the story.' A typical stakeout might involve half a dozen or more staffers. If the subject is travelling, Calder might try to get someone sitting next to him on a plane, with a photographer and reporter waiting at the airport where he is planning to land. He would have one reporter waiting to tail the subject in a car, another on a motorcycle, with several people already staked out at his home. Otherwise, Calder would have approached neighbours with offers of cash to use their windows. 'I'd have an infra-red camera in the window overlooking the area or a camera that takes pictures in low light.'

Calder's single-minded determination comes from having worked for Generoso Pope for two and a half decades. Pope, known by most as 'Mr Pope', behind his back as 'GP' or, if you had known him for twenty years, 'Gene', was an enigmatic character who had become a cult figure even during his lifetime. Since his death from a heart attack on 2 October 1988, Pope has been elevated to something approaching canonization. Says one staffer, 'I loved Gene Pope. I didn't know how much until he died . . . You know, everybody remembers where you were when JFK died; it was the same with Gene Pope.'

The New York *Post* took a somewhat different tack when they headlined Pope's obituary, '*National Enquirer* Owner Goes to Meet with Elvis.'

It is a bright Sunday morning sometime in the late 1970s in Lantana, Florida. Before the headquarters of the *National Enquirer*, nestled in a working-class neighbourhood directly behind a baseball field, an American flag ripples gently in the breeze. Surrounding the one-storey brick building is a thick lawn, exactly four inches high, alongside a well-tended garden, lush with vegetation; the pavement up to the front door is lined with poinsettias. A car is driven directly up to the path, and a grey-looking man with a granite face gets out of the backseat. He is about six feet tall, slightly corpulent, a bit on the chunky side. He is wearing a bathrobe. It is Generoso Pope, who has come to the office to water his plants.

Pope believed that, in giving the common people, 'millions and millions of them, relief and escape,' he had himself become something of a blue-collar type. And everything about the way he conducted his life seemed to reinforce his fantasy. He dressed carelessly, wearing shiny suits, his pants held up by a frayed belt that was too long. One staffer couldn't help noticing it swung back and forth in almost constant movement whenever he stood. He was the director on the board of a local hospital, and you always knew the day it met because that was the day Pope showed up in his best jacket – a dusty sportscoat of uncertain age. Once he complained ruefully to an editor that Sears and Roebuck had 'cut out the 100 per cent cotton shorts in the new catalogue.'

He refused to fly, and never took holidays. He tried to stay out of the public eye as much as possible, and like his readers, he lived vicariously through the pages of the magazine. There is a story that a staffer once came back from Hollywood with a graphic description of a well-known starlet 'giving a blow job'. Pope sat through the recital with great interest, full of curiosity, saying at the end, 'Why did she *do* that?'

To most on the staff, however, he remained a distant and menacing figure, a kind of Wizard of Oz who spoke through other people. While he was capable of firing twenty secretaries on Christmas Eve, totally terrifying everybody, he was also known for his acts of extraordinary generosity. Learning that a former writer on the staff had contracted terminal cancer, he 'hired him back on payroll just so the *Enquirer* could pay his last medical bills.'

Pope also contributed generously to local charities – the JFK Medical Center, where eventually he was Board Chairman, the Palm Beach Rehabilitation Center, the Palm Beach Blood Bank, the Florida Easter Seals Society and the town of Lantana. Except for what it could accomplish, money seemed to hold no fascination for him. He was fond of reciting the statement, 'I can't live in more than one house at a time, I can't eat more than one hamburger at a time.'

One veteran of the *National Enquirer*, Brian Hitchen, who is now the editor of London's *Daily Star*, calls Pope 'the brains behind the whole lot. He was never interested in making money, he just *made* a lot of money . . . But he believed in spending it all and ploughing it back in so that he would have at any given time reporters and photographers travelling the globe . . . he indulged in editorial spends that no company I've ever come across could do. He just didn't care. And he would send them on the most flimsy stories on the chance that they might come off.'

Probably the most famous spend occurred when Grace Kelly died. By coincidence, the *Enquirer* had a stringer interviewing a 'Dutch aunt' of Princess Grace in New York, 'and by sheer happenstance, while he was sitting there interviewing her, the phone rings and the palace is calling to say Princess Grace died,' says Paul Levy, then Senior Editor at the *National Enquirer* and now editor of one of the *Enquirer*'s major competitors, the *Globe*.

'So the aunt passes out on the floor, and being a well-trained reporter, he simply stepped over the body – I don't know whether he bent over to see if she was alive – asked who was on the phone and what it was about and was asked by the palace who he was, I don't know which relative of the aunt he claimed, and while she was still lying there, he called me before he called an ambulance for her.'

This gave the *Enquirer* a four-hour start on the story, and staff began phoning all the relatives. 'Half of them were crying, which made us know it was true, and about half we broke the news to.' That afternoon, Levy put together an *Enquirer* team of nine, who flew into Paris by Concorde, moving in about nine others from Europe and Africa 'who had contacts and knew their way around.' They booked rooms in the second-best hotel in Monaco, and as soon as they found out Princess Grace's car had crashed into some farmer's backyard, 'we immediately went and locked him up for the next two weeks . . . We paid him tens of thousands of dollars.' Levy left with all the money that was lying around the office, and a line of cash and credit was set up in Monte Carlo at $20,000 for each reporter.

According to Levy, the only words that Gene Pope had to say to him, as he was 'mounting this huge invasion, his only two words of advice were, "if you miss the plane between Paris and Nice, don't waste time, just charter one," and the second one was "stay the fuck out of the casino with my money." But it was a friendly "fuck".'

David Duffy, who had gone out on the Princess Grace story with Levy and got a good interview from the Archbishop of Monaco, was going on a holiday the next day with his wife. As he came through the door, his wife met him with an envelope from Gene Pope. In it was a cheque for $1,000. 'That's the thing about this guy,' Duffy says. 'He wasn't ashamed of sharing his wealth. He wasn't afraid of spending money on stories, and when you did a good job, he wasn't afraid of letting you know it. He was enigmatic, and he was an extraordinarily strong individual, he was a taskmaster, but he paid for what he got. He was never afraid of paying.'

There was one more thing that Pope had said to Levy before they left that Levy considers typical of the man. Pope had heard an absolutely wild rumour about Prince Rainier's relationship with Princess Grace, and 'could we prove it in two days?'

One other story typifies to Levy 'why Pope was a legend and deservedly so,' and which shows 'the drive, the reputation for being bizarre, his willingness to put his money where his mouth was.' Some years before kidnappings in Iran became commonplace, there were two kidnappings there. The first involved several employees of a corporation owned by Ross Perot, who hired a team of mercenaries and sent them in to free his employees. 'And this stuck in GP's mind,' says Levy. 'And about a year later, an American army sergeant was captured in Iran, and GP called in all the editors and told us to rescue the guy.

'We accept this,' he continues, 'with a straight face, wondering whether we had crossed over into *Alice in Wonderland* . . . There were a few minor questions along the way, like whether this was legal, invading another country. What if we got arrested? Or killed? All of which he brushed aside. "Don't worry about that. I'll take care of that." And one editor immediately opted to become the intelligence and finance chief of this thing, and he would go to Cyprus to set up headquarters. *He* knew a good way of getting out of the office quick. Someone else would set up as paymaster, someone else as intelligence.

'I was in charge of finding the mercenaries to lead this. We were talking about three or four days, not some sensible long-range thing. He wanted the lock-up three or four days later. After about an hour, discussing the ramifications – Should we discuss this with a lawyer? "No, that's not necessary." How do we find this guy? "That's what you're getting paid for." The final question was asked by an editor who shall remain nameless. "Well, what if we get this guy out and he won't talk to the *Enquirer*?" And that editor was fired three weeks later,' Levy says.

So the men all poured out of Pope's office, eyeing one another – 'Here we go again' – and Levy began trying to figure out where he could 'round up some mercenaries'. He called a friend who had been in counter-terrorism for the FBI. 'I said "I got a question to ask you", I tell him the story. And when I last heard from him, he was still on the floor laughing. His one question was, "Are you *out of your mind*?" On a stroke of genius, I called the editor of *Soldier of Fortune Magazine*, which specializes in this, and I tell him the same story, and he almost strangles on the phone, but agrees to try to find somebody. "When are you planning to do this?" he asks. And I said, "Tomorrow". And he cannot believe I'm not high on marijuana or cocaine, calling from some bar. And then we sit there and have this very rational discussion about the difficulties of hiring mercenaries these days and what they would cost, and in the middle of it . . . about one or two in the afternoon, word comes over that the guy has been released. As bizarre as this seems, it was an absolute letdown. And then we sit around, decide whether we call GP and tell him, "Well, we've got it done for you already, we got him out." Which is what we did.'

Levy believes that Pope wasn't power-mad or crazy, but that he knew that 'out of a hundred wild ideas like this, that he was willing to spend money to rescue this guy, or to prove some crazy story about Princess Grace . . . he was willing to spend the money on the ninety-nine losers for that one great story. And he didn't want to know about the money . . . Absolute genius.'

Besides his penchant for dropping bucks, Pope was known for being a workaholic who dominated every aspect of his newspaper. Says Mike Walker, who worked for Pope for nearly twenty years, 'Pope loved people and loved to play, but it was *his* uniforms, *his* ball.' According to this depiction, Pope did all the jobs on the paper. 'He was editor, news editor, picture editor, he was everything,' one ex-staffer says. 'He would take anyone's job over – without knowing what he was talking about.'

'He had a Mafia mentality,' another reporter on the *Enquirer* says. 'Think of Don Corleone, OK? Think about the way the office was organized, the articles editors were capos, the reporters were like soldiers and button men.'

James Sutherland, who is now Associate Editor of London's *Daily Star*, remembers a strange exchange that took place when Pope called him into his office. Pope said:

> 'Right, Jim, I'm going to put you in charge of the photo desk,' and I said, 'Terrific, that means I'll be Photo Editor.' And Pope said, 'No, you can't be Photo Editor because I

am.' So I said, 'What shall I be then?' and he said 'Associate Editor.' And I said, 'What's the difference?' And he said, 'About twenty grand.' And I said, 'Thank you very much.' And that was that.

From his vantage point as virtual dictator, Pope made every decision of importance. An incident that gives insight into his peculiar logic and total control concerns the famed photo taken of Elvis Presley in his coffin. It fell to James Sutherland to train the man who took the Elvis picture, a close relative who would be attending 'the King's' funeral'. Sutherland tried to teach the man to take a photo with a Minox, but, having no luck, finally taped over the controls of the camera, so all he had to do was push a button. The relative then spent all night at Graceland, and afterwards, Sutherland put him on a plane travelling to the Lantana airfield, where Brian Hitchen was waiting.

Says Hitchen, 'I paid the guy $18,000 without knowing what we'd got and put the guy and two other relatives who travelled with him in a locked room with a guard. Then Santo Bucafucci, the manager of the photo lab in Lantana, developed the film. And we got four pictures: one of a chandelier, two of his face and one full-length of the body in repose. And we put the last one on the cover with the headline "Rest in Peace".

'At that time we were selling five million copies a week. But on that issue, we went up to 6.6 million. We put on nearly two million in that week. So after that, I went to Pope and said, "Why don't we reprint the picture for people who didn't get a copy the first time?"

'And Pope said, "Geez, I couldn't do that. That would be commercialism."'

So literally every decision was Pope's decision, no matter how whimsical. The staff sometimes worked under the impression that they didn't produce things for a newspaper but for the Scheduling Room which Pope maintained. In it, he had enough stories and pictures for ten editions of the *National Enquirer*. The story was that once a week Pope would go into the Scheduling Room with his senior editors and choose what was going into that week's issue from whatever was in there. 'A picture could have been in there for two months,' says Sutherland, 'but if he liked it, in it went.'

Says Brian Hitchen, 'They would go to tremendous lengths to research a story. Take quotations, for instance . . . if you get a quote from someone, and it goes on and on at length, frequently there are sentences that are not completed. At the *Enquirer*, you had to tape everything. There are trains of thought that aren't completed, so that any proper journalist would listen to what was said and take out the bits that didn't matter. That way, you'd have what the person was *actually saying*, without all the verbiage.

'When stories were turned in, this would all go down to Pope's Research Department. Now the Research Department was not like it is anywhere else – where they would assemble a whole load of facts for you, so that if you were going out to interview someone, you knew all about them. The reporters went out with whatever they could grab from anywhere, and in writing their story they would use a truncated quote from the yards of nonsense they'd been given, and the research people would sit like battery hens – twenty girls with earphones on – checking the quotes against the tape, and every time a word was exactly as it had been said, they'd put a red tick over it. But if it wasn't what they'd said – "Well, this isn't *exactly* what he said" – then they would throw the entire story back again. So you got perfectly decent reporters who did *not* go round making things up and bending quotes, literally *banging* their heads against a wall.'

There was also a much-complained about numbers system, which, according to one account, rewarded 'sheer drudgery' more than creative and independent work – a countsheet many found 'very difficult to cope with.'

But Paul Levy insists, 'It was a very carefully thought-out system. It was not secret, and it was no different from any other system that rates employees for promotions, raises and quality control . . . Any reporter or editor was welcome to go over and see what his numbers were. The purpose was very frankly both to provide competition – almost *deathly* competition – among the staff and to use that competition to increase the output and quality of staff. If you didn't maintain your standard in relation to your colleagues, you were soon out of there.'

It has been said of Gene Pope that he didn't suffer fools gladly, and, 'if you bullshitted him, he'd fire you on the spot. He was 110 per cent dedicated to the paper . . . if he smelled any lack of dedication around anybody, you were out on a moment's notice,' says Levy. This policy, along with Pope's dictatorial tendencies, led to high tension in the office. Some staffers speculated that he actually liked to have everybody in the office competing against each other, thus cementing his own ascendancy.

They also thought he believed this deathly competition among staff worked as a stimulus, 'and it was, because they would all cut each other's throats as soon as look at one another,' said one staffer. 'Everybody was politics-wise. It honed up those who were successful at it, gave them an absolute killer instinct, so that if you went on a job and the world's press were there, you daren't come back without a story. You would go to all sorts of means to bring in a good story.'

Despite all this pressure, many who worked for Pope liked him. Says Hitchen, 'Pope? I liked Pope tremendously. Just knowing him enriched my life. He was a strange man, he used to whip himself into a frenzy, I mean *terrifying* frenzy . . . he would sit there and his right leg would become uncontrollable, banging up and down like this [demonstrates] and he would try and hold it down like Dr Strangelove, and if he was really angry . . . I remember a time when Walter Cronkite was said to have seen and believed in flying saucers, which Cronkite denied . . . The guy who did the story was Robin Leach, the guy who's now on television in *Lifestyles of the Rich and Famous*. Robin was freelance then, and his articles editor who controlled him was Mike Hoy, who is now the managing editor of *The Times* here, and Pope had a meeting in his rather palatial office and he got so angry, with the leg banging up and down, and all the people in his office on the hard chairs we used to sit on, like a cinema, and Pope actually began to dribble with anger and the dribble ran off his chin and splashed on his desk, and . . . you used to sit there and have to keep a very straight face.'

Pope's admiration for British reporting methods made Lantana the American centre for evacuees from Fleet Street. They came to southern Florida for the adventure, for the sunshine – for the money. Pope essentially believed British journalists were capable of running harder. American journalists tended to be in the business, he thought, 'because they want to right the wrongs of society, and they want to be "investigative and in depth" – not to sell papers.'

'Every country specializes in something,' says a reporter who started out on Fleet Street. 'What the Brits are good at is reporting. Send a British reporter and American reporter out on a plane crash. The American reporter will write "I wept over the funeral pyre of 199 people." And the Brit will write, "Dead, that's what 199 people were last night . . ." They'll cut it right to the bone.'

Also, because the British tabloids depend on circulation rather than advertising as their main source of revenue, Fleet Street journalists think in terms of angles and presentation, and Pope admired this. The idea of 'grabbing the readers at the check-out counter with their 25 cents change' was natural for the Brits. Back home, it was a time of financial hardship and austerity, cutbacks and union woes. So, when Pope made British journalists an offer they couldn't refuse, they accepted, many of them becoming part of what has come to be known as 'the Foreign Legion of Journalism'.

'The *Enquirer* was running a thing – it was wonderful – which amounted to package holidays that were paid. They had this month's tryout . . . they recruited people for it,' says James Sutherland. 'We went and worked for them for a month. They gave you a hotel room, a car and temporary credit cards, and you flew all round America and did stories for them, and pictures for them, and came back home with $1,000 in your pocket. And lots and lots of British journalists took advantage of that and did it, and had no intention of ever going to work there. It was just a nice month, and they gained a lot of experience moving around America.'

For those who did join the staff, it was generally agreed that opportunities for promotion were greater for the British than for the Americans. 'There was a time,' says one American reporter 'when most Americans were averaging only about sixteen or seventeen months on the paper.' This is the period when staffing soared to about 80 per cent British, and consequently, sometime around 1974, Brits became 'quite unpopular in Lantana.' There was the New England Oyster House Bar, and that was where the Brits and Australians holed up. Americans from the *Enquirer* rarely went to this stronghold.

The British suffered, however, from what they perceived as a loss of status. In Fleet Street, there had been 'a certain honour and dignity that came with the job,' says one British reporter. 'You were an NUJ member, a Fleet Street reporter who had made it from the ranks.' In Lantana, the differences were soon obvious.

'If you were pursuing a star, say Muhammad Ali,' says David Duffy, 'and you wanted an interview with him, and you trapped him in a phone box and he burst through the back of the box and escaped from you, in Britain, if you were to tell that to your editor, he would say, "What an awful experience. Go and have a drink or a dinner on me, and I'll see you in the morning." At the *National Enquirer*, you would be in terrible trouble for allowing him to escape. And that's the whole difference in attitude. They don't thank you for coming second, you've got to come first. They've hired you to be the best.'

Veteran reporter Tony Brenna, thought by many to be the best reporter on the *Enquirer* staff, said of his countrymen, 'Some of the British couldn't learn to live with the irrationality of the way Pope edited the paper. They broke out in hives and some of them developed chest pains and ulcers, and I drank too much, and basically it turned them screaming crazy after a while. They weren't allowed to exercise their ego in the Fleet Street fashion. No "Old Boy" network.

'There were a lot of journalistic pirates in Florida, there to have a good time, to travel, to womanize, to do drugs, there was a lot of adventure offered. In return, you had to sell your soul. All very Faustian, put it that way. You had to do whatever they wanted you to do. There was no backing down from the story; you became a journalistic kamikaze pilot. It broke some of them . . . It didn't matter what your own personal opinions were. It all had to be told in lurid quotes and ultra-sensational fashion.

'You would revel in the misery of someone who had been half bitten in two by a shark. You'd want to know exactly how it felt when the teeth clenched . . . and you'd have to know exactly how it felt, to see your son dragged under the water, or your mother burned in a fire, or whatever. There were no limits, and you would be sent back and back and back on a story until you got exactly what they wanted. They'd ask you to write it with five times the depth and detail that any British paper would, and then it would all be condensed down to a page, maybe a page and a half of copy.'

To former staffer Jeff Samuels, 'Pope was a totalitarian lunatic. We came here just to get out of England. He had these skilled and experienced senior reporters – for many it was a demeaning experience – Pope took these guys and broke them down to janitor status. They went down in their own estimation. He would have them at Christmas parties with torches bringing in cars. If you don't like it, then go take a walk. Many of them didn't have green cards, they had been here maybe ten years working illegally. They had children who were all-American kids, wives who loved going down to the Boca Raton Country Club. They had two cars and a boat. Lose the job and you'd lose the country and everything. The whole pressure thing was quite intense there, so that was where they grabbed you by the nuts and gave 'em a good squeeze.

'People needed the job, they needed the paycheques, they needed to be in Florida in the sunshine. You screw up once on the job, and you've lost the whole package. The wife hates you because she can't play tennis anymore. She's gotta go back to some house in Liverpool. The kids hate you because they've got their friends – and all because you haven't placated the Ice Cream Man's outrageous demands on stories.'

'The Ice Cream Man' (*Gelato! Gelato!*) was the nickname assigned Pope behind his back by dissatisfied reporters. Iain Calder was called 'the Ice Pick'. And Paul Levy was named 'the Twinkie Man' because he loved junk food.

Tony Brenna explains that 'at the *Enquirer*, with that type of tabloid journalism, you're moving from ego-creative type of work into power-and-money type of work. You're starting to work for the money more than anything else, giving up a lot of pride and craftsmanship and also . . . in many ways your integrity.'

Lured by the high paycheques – salaries were double those of Fleet Street – the British continued to pour in. Those sent out on assignment would have ten or twelve weeks on the road, then come back to Lantana to as many unopened paycheques.

'That's where you got things like long-haired, loony Brits wandering into the Cadillac concession,' says Samuels. 'The security guys would try to throw them out. They'd say to the salesman there, "Do you have that in green?" And they'd go, "yeah." And they'd go, "I'll have it." And they'd pull out a wad of hundreds and say, "Have that, asshole." And they'd get drunk and lose it. It was rock 'n' roll suicide for a while.'

Samuels believes that was where all the crazy stories came from, 'about people who burst into flames for no apparent reason.' In the United States, the US Supreme Court has ruled that public figures and people in the public eye cannot collect on libel unless they can prove actual malice on the part of the publisher. Samuels says, 'once you sidestep that malice thing, I can prove anything, there's always a way to do it journalistically . . . By asking people, brushing hundred dollar bills in their hands and gettin' them to say "yes", and then gettin' them to sign it, and get them on tape to say it. And then when you sue me, I say, "No, that's what they all said. They lied. They all fooled me, because I was stupid enough to believe them." So given those situations, that was why there was a lot of discontent in the newsroom, and on the road, and you'd be in some godawful place . . . and you'd run into reporters, and they would be drunk and bitchin' and moanin' . . . a lot of discontent, but no way out, nowhere to run away to. This was the Foreign Legion of Journalism and there was no other outpost. There were spies everywhere. Once in a while there would be brawls and fights – it got out of hand – beer-bottle breakings in bars. A couple of guys got really fucked up, and they took credit cards and ran away.'

Samuels recounts a story that shows the less savoury side of Generoso Pope's machine, one that placed him in the centre of the unofficial state of war that grew up between the establishmentarian wing of the *Enquirer* staff and the more rebellious of the Brits.

One morning about eight months after Elvis Presley's death, Jeff Samuels put on his Harley Davidson T-shirt and flew into West Palm Beach. Samuels was carrying contraband goods, which he now intended to sell on the black market for $80,000. It was the original photograph of Elvis in his coffin which had been run on the cover of the *National Enquirer*. Because of Pope's refusal to reprint it, individual copies of the paper, which originally sold for 25 cents, were within a week going for $10; within a month, $100. Samuels had reason to believe a buyer had been located who would reprint the photo on the front of a line of T-shirts.

Samuels rationalized his sale this way. 'It was my original contact in Memphis who had got the pictures of Elvis . . . a cousin of Elvis . . . Had we – me and some others in on the deal – been freelance, the photo would have been our property. But because we were working for them, it was theirs.'

These members of the *National Enquirer* staff set up what they called 'the FINE project' (Freedom and Independence from the *National Enquirer*). They reshot the picture at an angle, so that in any court of law, 'we could argue, we *hoped*, it was a different photo. Then we tried to sell it.

'Everything Elvis is owned by Factors, Inc., out in LA, which means that they take a huge cut on every dollar. If you buy a hound dog comb on Elvis Presley Boulevard, then money comes to them. We took it to Factors first thing. We wanted $100,000. They said, "No, it's tasteless."' Samuels and his partners then made the rounds, with everyone saying roughly the same thing. 'So basically,' says Samuels, 'what we had was a pig in a poke. We couldn't sell it.'

At one point, Samuels says, they would have traded the thing for a case of beer. The whole project had been shelved and forgotten – until he received a call from an old girlfriend who said she had found a buyer. 'So I flew to West Palm, rented this car and drove to this hotel, called and she said, "Yeah he's here." Went to the door, and this woman opened the door . . . There was this dreadful man from Chicago with wraparound sunglasses: "Bob from Chicago." "I've got what you want. Have you got what I want?" So I'm just basically trying to count the money, and I look up and there is this gun to my head. And this cop said, "Don't move." . . . And a staff member came in, saying, "Why'd you do it? Why'd you do it? You were one of our best operators. I don't know why you'd do it."'

As Samuels was looking down at his hands, which had been cuffed, he saw the words, 'Harley Davidson' upside down on his T-shirt. He looked up at the staffer and said, 'Well, I wanted a motorcycle, didn't I, Mate?'

Jeff Samuels, along with his partners, was originally charged by the *National Enquirer* with grand larceny. Within a short time, however, these charges were reduced to petty larceny and finally negotiated out of court. Samuels had 'a very healthy year' as a construction worker before going back into the business. He is now chief writer at Robin Leach's *Lifestyles of the Rich and Famous*. Occupying one of the most prestigious positions in tabloid television, Samuels recognizes that he and his kind have contributed significantly to the continuing decline in the circulation of the supermarket tabloids.

Samuels relishes taking the long view: 'Be it ever so humble,' he says, 'that is my role.'

Despite the internecine strife that occasionally erupted among staff, the *National Enquirer* continued to prosper, so much so that Rupert Murdoch tried to buy the paper outright in the early 1970s. When, predictably, Gene Pope declined his offer, Murdoch put together his own supermarket tabloid.

At the *National Star*, so-called in direct imitation of the paper it planned to supplant (now simply known as the *Star*), morale has always been high, despite an astounding number of changes in the top editorial slot during its short life. It was started in 1973 by a handful of Brits and Australians imported by Murdoch and a hand-picked group of Americans whom Murdoch thought could make the transition to the kind of hybrid tabloid he intended to create. At the head of this invasion of America was none other than Larry Lamb, editor of Murdoch's London *Sun*, soon to become the esteemed Sir Larry Lamb.

Among those Lamb brought with him in November 1973 was Mike Nevard, the Features Editor of the *Sun*. When they went back for Christmas, Nevard said to Lamb, 'I already feel that the *Star* is my baby, and I don't see we'll ever recruit American executives who can run a tabloid like this.' For the next few years, Nevard essentially ran the *Star* during the period of rapid turnover at the editor's desk.

Another *Sun* expatriate on the original *Star* team was Vic Giles, the graphics designer. Giles and Nevard set to work producing a colour brochure for the new *Star*, a kind of 'mock *Star*' printed on high quality paper that was supposed to become the sales vehicle for the publication. But when it was circulated to all the advertising agencies and distributors in New York, supposedly 'to get them wild with anticipation,' says Giles, 'instead we got back a big blast from most of them, saying that what we were planning to produce would never sell in America.' New York hated the style and approach of the stories, and 'the New York *Times* critic of the day said that the cover looked like an advertisement for Dunlop tyres.'

There was an emergency meeting, and before the first issue hit the stands, the cover and much of the inside pages had, in the words of the Brits who were producing it, 'been watered down for the American Public.'

One of the Americans on the original staff who was able to make the transition to the type of paper Murdoch was producing was Christina Kirk. A graduate of the University of Indiana, Kirk was very much a product of American journalism, cutting her teeth early on police reporting in Indiana. In New York, she had worked at the press services until mergers left her out of a job. She then did a stint on the *Herald Tribune*, switching after a short time to the *Daily News*, where she worked in features for ten years. When Murdoch approached her, she decided to give it a try.

'Nothing worked out as we had planned,' says Kirk. 'We had intentions of being a national daily. We were gonna be *USA Today*, I think, but we were fifteen or twenty years ahead of ourselves. So we got into the celebrity tabloid thing. It was planned and it was unplanned. The TV people came and interviewed us. You're going to do axe murders and sex crimes, and I would say, "When did you last look at the *Enquirer*?" Ever since they went into the supermarkets, they dropped that stuff.

'When we first started, we looked like the London *Sun*. We had "leaders", a sports section, consumer news, celebrities and gossip and advice to the lovelorn.'

One of the first shocks to the Murdoch entourage was the strange attitude of the printers toward the proofs they were given. There was steady resistance to everything handed them. Then, an episode occurred that Murdoch hadn't anticipated. Various truckloads of their issues began, says one early staffer, 'disappearing into the crevices.' They simply never got delivered. The rumour making the rounds was that Generoso Pope had connections with 'the mob', and that, in some undefined way, this gave him influence over the truckers. It is said that Murdoch made a quick trip down to Lantana and had lunch with Pope. Whatever transpired there changed the situation. After that, distribution went smoothly.

Other problems evolved, one of the most serious from the mixture of Brits, Aussies and Yanks who wrote the newspaper. Headlines were a constant headache. 'If the word "number" came up,' says Giles, 'we would write it "No." as it is done in England. In the States, it's done with a symbol like a musical sharp. We got all these letters complaining that we had said "no" in the middle of the headline.'

Says Kirk, 'The copy desk had language problems. In England, they go on "walkies", which means, they are taking their dog for a walk. This doesn't mean anything in America. It struck me, in the fast-divorcing languages of Britain and the United States, that the slang of the Brits is sort of 'cutesy-pie'. They have budgies, and tellies and walkies. One of our early criticisms was that the paper didn't sound like it was written in America.

'When we first started, we had more English than Australians, with some Americans. Then it shifted, and there were more Australians. Nowadays, it is still a mix of the three nationalities, and we still have a backbench, like the original *Sun* in London.'

Vic Giles remembers an incident 'typical of Rupert' in those days. 'About five or six weeks after we started,' says Giles, 'the fire alarm sounded. We were then located on the twenty-second floor of 713 Third Avenue, and Rupert came out of his office and said, "Everybody out onto the street, but you can't use the lifts and elevators." So,' says Giles, 'he and I walked down the stairs, the rest of the staff in front of us, and by now, there were bits of smoke about, and we got down to the nineteenth floor. It was about here we discovered that the fire was on the fourteenth floor and as we walked, Rupert and I were talking about the production of the newspaper. "How far have we got?" he asked. "Have you got the dummy with you?" And I said "No," and he said, "Where is it?" and I said, "It's on my desk," and Rupert said, "Go and get the bloody dummy."'

So Giles did as he was told. 'But Rupert waited right there for me, on the nineteenth floor, until I got back.'

Meanwhile, Mike Nevard, who always felt slightly put upon because he was never actually named editor, one day confronted Murdoch directly. Says Nevard, 'I was told I lacked "mature cynicism". What "mature cynicism" has to do with putting out a supermarket tabloid, I don't know.' Nevard eventually ended up editing the competing *Globe* in Boca Raton. Nevard says Murdoch was really 'quite decent' about his leaving; it was an executive on the staff who labelled him 'the traitor'.

The *Star*'s goal has been decidedly up-market and in the past few years it has successfully transformed itself from a newspaper to a magazine – a trend followed by another supermarket tabloid, the *Globe*, and even by the *Enquirer* itself. For purposes of the Simmons readership survey, all three major supermarket tabloids are treated as magazines. But the *Star*, which is produced in Tarrytown, New York, far from Tabloid Valley in southern Florida, has been most successful at carving itself a niche of respectability.

Bigger than its competitors, the *Star* went to colour a few years ago and then began stitching the paper. 'The next stage of our evolution,' says Phil Bunton, Executive Editor at the *Star*, 'will be the glossy cover.' Part of an overall strategy begun when Murdoch still owned the paper, the transformation has a practical goal – getting high quality advertising into the pages of the *Star*. Says Bunton, 'Our readers have colds, use toilet tissue, they wash, but it's been an uphill battle trying to convince Madison Avenue of this.'

'If it's true that the celebrity market is shrinking,' says Bunton, 'as it is, then the only way we'll get growth is through advertising.' It's been a tough sell for their clients. 'Many Madison Avenue executives have never read the *Star* in their lives. Campbell's Soup was a very hard sell. We kept saying, "Our readers drink soup!"'

Meanwhile, at the *Enquirer*, the arrangement of stories and photographs on the page – what's known as the layout – has had less to do with miming magazine pages and more to do with the use of highly sophisticated motivational research. According to the rumours, there is a formula, which has been many times tested, that accounts for the way the *Enquirer* is schemed from page to page. 'If they juxtapose one type of story with another,' says one source, off the record, 'it represents "X" number of papers sold, which is then translated into "X" millions of dollars in revenue. They take it real seriously.'

In 1990, Murdoch sold off the *Star* to MacFadden Enterprises for $400 million, the same corporation that bought the *National Enquirer* after Generoso Pope's death. It was reported that the *Star*'s staff went into a kind of shock when they were told of this merger. After competing for years with the *Enquirer*, sometimes bitterly, the idea of becoming 'a Siamese twin' publication held little charm for many on the staff.

Whether the carefully charted aim of respectability for the *Star* will remain one of the prime objectives of the publication remains to be seen.

Today, the *National Enquirer* that Generoso Pope built has become the generic term for all the supermarket tabloids, which include the *Enquirer*'s sister publication, the *Weekly World News*, the Tarrytown-based *Star*, and the Canadian-owned *Globe*, the *Sun*, and the *National Examiner*.

Iain Calder estimates that one in every ten Americans reads the *National Enquirer* alone; inside the *Star* offices, it is thought their readership is one in twenty. Paul Levy believes that if you combined *all* the tabloids – the top three, plus the *Examiner*, the *Weekly World News* and the *Sun* – and you allowed for the increasing rate of illiteracy in the United States, a staggering one out of seven or eight people read one or another of these products. They represent the only significant tabloid press in America whose profits rely primarily upon circulation rather than advertising.

As for *Enquirer* editor Iain Calder's attitude, he claims victory. 'When Murdoch came over here, he tried to buy us from Pope, and couldn't. So he started the *Star*. When he began in Australia, he ended up bein' Number One. When he went to Britain, he ended up bein' Number One. "So I can come to the United States, and I can do it in the United States," he thinks. This is *the only place* he hasn't been able to do that. The only tabloid. And he's put on his best Australians, his best Britains, and he's still had to be content with bein' Number Two. We're the only ones who stood in the way of the Murdoch steamroller and survived.'

An artist and a
businesswoman

The 12-carat marquise diamond slides out of its setting. *Voilà!* Laurie Brady is holding it in the palm of her hand. It is a handful. She carefully reclips the tearshaped sparkler back into place. The lapis lazuli ring, her favourite, is from Russia. The stone is as big as an egg. She waves away the ruby; nothing special. But at home, she has the biggest black opal in the world.

Brady is wearing a black, pearl-encrusted angora sweater, with patterns overlayed in white leather. Sewn inside the intricate loops and swirls are fancy irridescent dark sequins. Brady is herself a slender, red-headed woman, with eyes like dark pools. When she minces across the room in her four-inch heels, every eye is upon her. No kidding, she looks less than half her age.

'I used to do big promotions with supermarkets, because I was a businesswoman first, and an astrologer second, and I sold my business to concentrate on astrology, and everybody laughed at me. "You'll never make a living." And [laughs] I'm really doing quite well.

'I'm starting a 900-number for the *Star* that goes through A T & T, and it will probably cost $2.00 to call the number. The phone company will get like 50 cents, and we divide the rest. I will have to write 365 charts a year for twelve signs in addition to all my other duties. I write for other publications besides the *Star*, locally, and I see a lot of people and I have workshop and meditation groups and I'm starting a radio show. I'm also starting these two-minute radio spots: it's like "Star" Stars. What happens is I write my predictions, and I have a very clever writer. She makes them kind of bitchy, because I don't have that kind of personality. I predicted Cher would change boyfriends. And she might write, like, "I hope Cher's next tatoo is washable, because, you know . . ." Little zingers like that, she does.'

Brady has been with the *Star* since Rupert Murdoch founded it some eighteen years ago, and from the beginning, she tied celebrities to her column to increase its reader interest. Now Brady herself is the celebrity. She's been on *The Johnny Carson Show* and *Oprah Winfrey, A.M. America* and *60 Minutes*. She's even been interviewed by Barbara Walters. 'And I'm listed as one of the top ten psychics in the world, whatever that means,' she says.

When Brady walks into a restaurant, forks drop. Her waiter registers an instant flash of recognition, and . . . asks for a reading. 'You're going to have a career change around your birthday,' she answers obligingly as he pulls back her chair. She is looking over the menu when a young man in pony tail and black tie approaches her table.

'Excuse me, I'm terribly embarrassed. My girlfriend made me come over here. We want to know if we can get married.' He and Brady chat for a minute or two, establishing the date of birth of the young man and of his girlfriend.

'Well, it's not the most compatible relationship,' she says, the menu still in her hands. 'You can probably work it out. You really need my card because she's having some career problems this year that will reflect on the relationship . . . I'm going to give you my card because before you take a big step like that you should seek advice, and I'm not soliciting business because I'm really quite busy. It's just going to be a little bit challenging this whole year. It doesn't mean you're not going to get married; it just means, you know, if I knew the time of day she was born, I could pinpoint the problem.'

He screams back to his table, 'What time of day were you born?' She yells back, '7.43 a.m.'

Brady outlines his problem in some detail. But the young man is desperate. 'We're *going* to be married in September.'

'I'm not saying it isn't going to happen, I'm just saying it will be put off.' He persists. The waiter is standing by, waiting for Brady to order.

'Look, I'm a professional astrologer. Call me and make an appointment.'

Laurie Brady has been fending for herself ever since her mother tried to pull her out of school and put her to work as a waitress when she was thirteen years old. Instead, Brady ran away from home, spent time in an orphanage, then in a convent. When she was still a teenager, she struck out for Hollywood, where she met Marilyn Monroe and picked up a little money playing bit parts in films. By nineteen, she and six friends had founded a successful nightclub chain that made her a millionaire. 'When you're on the street,' she says knowledgeably, 'you're really on your own.'

From the age of four, Brady has known she was a psychic. But she was under the impression that everybody could predict the future. 'I told my mother once the lady next door wasn't going to make it through the night, and she was only in her thirties and she died. My mother gave me a whack. She thought I was evil. So I learned to keep my mouth shut.'

Despite her early hard times, once she became successful, she and her mother worked out a relationship. 'I bought her a mink coat before I had one,' she chuckles.

Once, when Brady got engaged, she consulted an astrologer and was told she would be married shortly. Instead, she and her fiancé broke up. Brady went back to the astrologer and confronted her. 'I didn't want to upset you,' came the answer. Brady vowed when she became an astrologer that she *would* pass along the bad news, if there was any coming. 'When people come to me, and I have negative things to say, they say, "At least you gave me warning." And I say, "Well, that's what I'm here for," because most people have a tendency to blame the other person when the problem is within themselves. And so once you know what you're doing wrong, then you can take steps to change it and then your whole destiny changes. You change your character and you change your destiny. That's why nothing I say is written in cement.'

Quite often, clients will try to mislead her. 'Women come to me, they say, "I love my husband." I say, "Oh, come *on*. The stars do not lie." And they say, "Well, you're right, I despise him."' Brady emits a rich, low chuckle.

Brady's clients live all over the world. She has regulars for whom she casts a chart, tapes it and mails it to them. If she weren't accurate, she figures, they would have dropped her long ago. Many expect confidentiality, especially the corporations and stock and commodity brokers whom she advises. Earlier in her career, she advised the founder of McDonald's hamburger chain, the National League Oakland A's baseball team – and Betty Ford, wife of former President Gerald Ford.

In addition to the weekly predictions for the *Star*, she does a celebrity special five times a year and a holiday horoscope twice a year. Her weekly column takes about two hours to write. 'I write it as I go along. I take it out of the typewriter and I never proof read it and I never correct it because I'm a perfectionist and if I did that I'd be doing it over and over. I just mail it in or send it by Federal Express. 'Cause all I have to sell is time, and time to me is money.

'Astrology is like music. You can teach everybody to read music, but the difference is between someone who can play – and Van Cliburn. Because you can teach anybody to erect a chart, but reading it, that's where the art comes in. I have to be very good at that.

'Most astrologers are like artists. They would starve if they didn't have an agent. Most really don't know what to do with their gift, they just barely make a living. But I'm lucky. I'm a businesswoman as well.'

4
THE FIRST CASUALTY

It is October 1986, and Harvard University has invited Prince Charles to help celebrate its 350th birthday. Not everyone approves.

Ed Anger, columnist for the *Weekly World News*, a small-circulation black-and-white newspaper and sister publication to the *National Enquirer*, is 'madder than a banker who can't balance his books.' He cannot believe 'those smart-alec hepcats at Harvard' would honour 'nerdy Prince Charles' when they could have invited 'a great American – like Johnny Cash or Lee Iocacca or William 'The Refrigerator' Perry.

'Our forefathers,' he explains, 'were smart, cagey and ambitious guys. They didn't want a bunch of inbred, noodle-brained aristocrats skimming off all the gravy from this new and rich land. And they were sick of being ruled by that loony-tune King George – a man who had an IQ lower than your average dinner salad . . . Who needs blue-blooded bozos?'

Anger, who served in Korea, and to prove it, has a steel-plate where 'half my head was blown away,' was for many years the voice of Red-Neck America – and proud of it. When *Rolling Stone* called him 'the most irresponsibly berserk columnist in America,' Anger was delighted.

The original 'Freeze-dried Baby' publication, *Weekly World News* reaches out to a characteristically American populist readership who, it could be said, move their mouths as they read. So what kind of stories catch their imagination? 'Couple Hides in Bomb Shelter Since 1957!, They Thought WW3 Had Destroyed the Planet'; 'Groom Risks His Life to Marry Bride with AIDS! "We'll Have A Normal Honeymoon", He Vows'; 'Talking Cat! Amazing Kitty Says More Than 100 Words, Say Experts'; 'Fisherman Dies Trying to Land a 15lb. Salmon!'; 'Alien Satellite Spying on Earth'; 'Pharoah's Curse Claims Its 200th Victim.' And so it goes.

For seven and a half years, Ed Anger was the conscience for the *Weekly World News*. It was Anger who said, 'God gave women knees to pray on and scrub floors with.' But surprisingly enough, he welcomed the return of the mini-skirt 'because it signalled the deathknell to the Women's Movement, and their uniform, the pantsuit.'

A typical column: 'Let's Go Slow on Giving Commies Our Fast Food!'

'I'm madder than a fat man with an empty fridge at the move by American businesses to build our fast-food restaurants in crummy Russia,' says Anger. Pepsi Cola, he tells us, is already selling pop there, and now McDonald's is going in. It is, he says, 'the sneakiest trick the commies have ever pulled.

'Let's face it, we are what we eat. And pizza, hamburgers and french fries are the foods that made America great . . . Have you noticed that the Japanese are no longer the little nippers they used to be? That's because they've been wolfing down our type of chow since we whipped 'em in World War Two. Here I am – a middle-aged guy – and I can still kick commie butts.

'Why? Because every day for lunch I gobble down a double-cheeseburger, an order of fries, a chocolate shake and a pack of Twinkies.'

America being the sort of place it is, Anger became a kind of cult figure, who soon had a collection of groupies writing to him and asking him to spend the weekend. One college station in middle-America read the Ed Anger column over the air weekly, with strains of 'God Bless America' as sung by the Mormon Tabernacle Choir, playing softly in the background. And, in the spring, on their way down to Fort Lauderdale, Florida, the unofficial gathering-place of tens of thousands of university students, many would stop in at Lantana to shake the hand of Ed Anger.

They would be directed to a slightly built, slightly balding young Jewish liberal, with burning blue eyes, who turned himself inside-out each week to find somehow, buried deep within his background as a fifth-grade teacher in the black ghettoes of Chicago, the voice of Conservative America. Rafe Klinger – a single parent of two daughters, aged five and six – has one degree in political science from the University of Illinois, a second from Southern Illinois University in Journalism. A great admirer of Benjamin Franklin, Klinger set out to create his own 'Poor Richard'. 'And in my own strange way,' he says, 'I guess I accomplished that. But I don't think I'm like Ben Franklin because I never had as many mistresses as he did.

'We'd get letters,' says Klinger, 'and they would say, "Ed Anger, he's stupid, he shouldn't be allowed to have a voice." And we'd get others that said, "It's a joke, right?" Then we got letters that said,

"Right on, Ed!" And a few wrote in and said, "Ed is too liberal," and those,' says Klinger, '*those*, you wrote down their address, 'cause you never *ever* wanted to go to that town.'

When Klinger speaks of Ed Anger, he speaks as if he is a real person, a separate entity from Klinger himself: 'Ed,' he says, 'was too much different from me. You know, he's different and he's *not* different. He's a facet of my personality and of my beliefs, but he's not really the strongest part of that personality. We all have complementary sides of our personality, a side that's conservative and a side that's liberal, and those sides are always there. So there's a little bit of Ed Anger in me as there apparently is in a lot of people, because that's why he became so popular.

'The key to Ed Anger was to insult as many people as you could.

'I had a hard time when I first wrote him, and I didn't even know what the conservative point of view *was*. I would actually have to get angry. I would have to get into a fit of rage, and then write it. Over the years, I became fascinated with conservative people because I'm a Jewish boy from the big city, and I was raised to be really liberal, and I taught in the ghetto, and I learned to really like black people, and I learned to be comfortable with them and to be part of them culturally in a sense . . . and while I may not be a *raging* liberal, I'm a liberal.

'When I was working as a reporter on the tabloids, I would encounter a lot of conservative people, and I would be thinking, like, these people are putting me on. They are, like, *funny*. Some of the things they said were to me outrageous, that I couldn't imagine somebody actually believing that. I thought they were being sarcastic, I thought they were kidding. Then, later, I realized they weren't kidding. This was the way they actually felt.

'So when I thought of writing a column, I thought, "What better foil? What better than to have someone come from the other end of me, the other end of what I believe in? Maybe I could cast a light on this. Maybe I could make them laugh. Maybe I could be funny," because humour was the major object of this. That's how I got the idea to use a conservative, reactionary voice. The miracle of Ed Anger was that a lot took him at face value, and others saw him as funny.'

Ed Anger so accurately reflected the values of Red-Neck America that, in fact, few ever dared to believe he was a fictional creation, a satirical figure – although many nursed suspicions. Ed seemed truer in the minds of his readers than reality itself, and his aphorisms came to represent the views of a large segment of the followers of the *Weekly World News*.

Ed Anger on Ollie North and Fawn Hall: 'I think Fawn Hall is the perfect role model for American women because she not only stood by her man, she also cleaned up after him.'

Ed Anger on 'SanFran-sissi-co's' Gay Community: 'I guess the gays forgot that the Supreme Court wasn't the only high court to ban sodomy. As I recall, the high court in the sky – presided over by God Almighty – passed a ban on sodomy a long time ago. And when the disgusting cities of Sodom and Gomorrah appealed his decision, the Good Lord turned them into parking lots for camels.'

Ed visits Rome: 'Everywhere you look, you see bricks missing, paint peeling, plaster chipping. Inside and out! You'd think formica and panelling had never been invented . . . That's what this old town really needs. Really, some oak-veneer panelling on the inside, some aluminium siding on the outside, some asphalt shingles on the roof and this place could look great. And how about some astroturfing for the Colosseum?'

Ed visits Paris: 'Why do the Frogs treat us so bad, we saved their butts from the Germans in two world wars. Thank god there was a McDonald's – a decent place to eat.'

Ed visits Venice: 'Why, they could call in the Army Corps of Engineers and have the place drained in no time . . .'

Rafe Klinger sits in a restaurant, beside the Intercoastal in Boynton Beach, Florida. At the mention of Ed Anger's line, 'If you really love your little boy, prove it by giving him a toy gun for Christmas,' Klinger tilts his head to the side, blows outward, shrugs. His white-hot eyes go crazy, like Harpo Marx's. 'It's too mad even to comment on,' he seems to say. Ed can exasperate him, and then he's lost for words.

Klinger was among the infamous forty-seven axed from the *National Enquirer*'s staff after MacFadden Enterprises took over. When Klinger left, Ed went with him. But lately, the circulation of the *Weekly World News* has been wilting, and Klinger believes this may be the reason the Ed Anger column was recently revived. Sadly, without Klinger behind him, Ed has turned into a pitiful old bore, with none of the incisive bigotry of his predecessor. Klinger meanwhile is suing, on the basis Ed Anger is his own persona, invented, developed and nurtured by him. Stay tuned, America.

Phil Bunton, now Executive Editor of the *Star*, then Editor of the

Weekly World News, remembers how 'We came across this small item from the Xin Hua Agency in China, which is the official government news agency, in some American paper – a coupla 'graphs. A Chinaman had been hidden by his parents for some thirty years because he had two heads, and now, thanks to the People's Surgeons, he was going to have one of these heads removed and face the world again. Somehow the idea appealed to Rafe Klinger and he called up the Consulate and they were delighted that an American newspaper actually wanted to do a story on them.

'They said, "We'll line somebody up and you'll have to call them at a certain time, their time," and Rafe and my wife and I all went out to dinner and he had to leave the table to go call. Rafe is a sort of ebullient guy and when he came back again, he couldn't stop talking about it and he blew it up as we sat there about how he had talked to both heads simultaneously.' Bunton sighs. 'The final version wasn't nearly as good as the one that Rafe told over dinner. But that's an example of the sort of story you didn't have to make up on the *Weekly World News*.

'The Chinese government sent us pictures,' he says as an after-thought. 'It always struck me as sort of strange that they would want publicity for this sort of freak show.'

In April 1979, when Generoso Pope decided to shift his production of the *Enquirer* to colour, he didn't want to close down his old black-and-white printing plant in Pompano Beach. Neither did he want anyone from the *Enquirer* to start up a new newspaper, because they might be 'tainted' from the way the *Enquirer* was run. 'Bizarre as it sounds now, the idea was that the *Weekly World News* should be almost like a news magazine, and I gave interviews saying it would be a cross between *Time Magazine* and the *Star*.' Says Bunton, 'It turned out otherwise.'

As for Klinger, who had worked on several establishment newspapers, he had already formed the opinion that 'real' news-papers were 'very hypocritical'. Says Klinger, 'They don't like boatrockers, and being an investigative type, I was always doing that. I got so fed up I was going to leave. Then I heard that the *Enquirer* was starting a new tabloid – the *Weekly World News*. The minute I tried out, I *loved* it. Phil Bunton said to me, "This isn't exactly journalism, your old friends are going to give you trouble." I said, "I know it's not journalism. It's showbiz."'

It was showbiz all right but of a peculiar type – entertainment based on actual facts. The basic plan, according to Bunton, was for the *News* to be made up of 'genuine' stories. 'We used to get in eighty or ninety newspapers from all over the country,' says Bunton, 'and we had people comb through those papers, looking for oddball stories.' For Bunton, the story had to be genuine, true – at least *before* it was subjected to the embellishment of enthusiastic staffers.

'You don't have to make stories up,' he says ruefully. 'They are only too true. Like the woman who broke into the morgue in San Francisco to make love to the corpse of her boyfriend. That story had originally appeared in the San Francisco *Examiner*. They had handled it tastefully, with only four 'graphs. But we were less inhibited. We made a few phone calls to the Medical Examiner's office, and got a few more horrible facts.

'When you are doing that kind of work, you have to laugh. You certainly can't take it seriously. To my mind, though, it's important that it's true. It may seem like a fine distinction, but there are enough stories out there, and the true ones are more imaginative than anything you can make up. Some of my colleagues didn't always worry about the truth . . . The ones about people being impregnated by space aliens, for example.

'But it's not necessary to make it up because there is so much that is really crazy, and it's not well reported by the newspapers in general. We found at *Weekly World News*, if we dug hard enough, we could find them. "Kookie" was a part of America, and it was not being well covered. And it was fun stuff. It was fun escapist reading.

'When I was there, I wouldn't do the kid-made-into-ashtray stories, and I think now they've got a little bit horrible and "Nightmare on Elmstreetish". In my day, I tried to avoid that, although that sounds sanctimonious. But now, they make some of the stories up. No one is going to complain if you make them up.'

The major competitor for the *Weekly World News* is the *Sun*, not to be confused with Rupert Murdoch's *Sun* in London. Part of the holdings of Globe International, owned by Canadian Mike Rosenbloom, the *Sun* sports its own kind of unique humour, labelled 'wacky' inside Globe. *Sun* editor John Vader agrees with Bunton's concept of truth, but takes it a step further.

Says Vader, 'In the tabloids, when a story is true, it is *far more true* than when a daily newspaper carries it. Everybody accepts that what the daily newspaper prints is the gospel truth. If you read it in the paper, it must be so. And many times, a daily newspaper doesn't have time, or is careless about verified facts, and if a reporter is in a hurry, he will slip something in that he doesn't know in fact. When a tabloid does a story, it has a stigma of being "mostly" true or totally untrue. But with most of the tabloids, it becomes almost a *fetish* to get it right. They've got researchers and they've got checkers and they used to have checkers to check the checkers. We do a lot of checking on true stories and also a lot of updating, to make sure nothing has happened between the time we got the story and the time we ran it in the paper.'

Educated at Concordia College in Canada, Vader, who looks like a handsome version of Edward G. Robinson, wanted to be a playwright in his youth. Now, he sits in his *Sun* office, surrounded by issues of his wacky tabloid. A few feet from his head, a headline appears on the cover of one of the issues: 'Lucy and Ricky Are Remarried in Heaven, Favorite Pair Now Together for All Eternity.'

Vader shrugs. 'Who's to say it's not true?

'I think it's like going to a play. You know the play is not really true. It's not an actual event. But while you are there, you want to believe it. It's "a willing suspension of disbelief". And that's what we ask of our readers. So we can't turn around and say to them, "Hey boys, we were really only fooling around." When we entertain in a way that's light,' says Vader, 'we expect you to go with us.

'We won't tell you what's true and what's not true – and don't ask!'

Inside Tabloid Valley – a stretch of land in Florida that runs northwards along the I-95 from Boca Raton, headquarters of Globe International, Inc., to Lantana, home of the late Generoso Pope's empire, now a part of McFadden Enterprises – truth and untruth co-exist in uneasy rivalry. The hi-jinx of the 'wacky' papers have in the public's mind become attached to the self-styled 'quality' papers. Adding to the confusion, the *National Enquirer* still remains the generic name for all the others. Whatever occurs in the supermarket tabloids, it is the *Enquirer* that gets the credit – or the blame.

In 1990, the *Enquirer* employed 109 in editorial, with most reporters making somewhere in the region of $80,000 a year, and most editors making in excess of $100,000, many of them considerably in excess. Why employ so many at such high salaries, so goes the argument, if the only purpose is to make up stories?

The answer is one of deliberate distortion and obfuscation, all carried on in the name of marketing imperatives. This was a direct departure from what came to be known in the early days as the legendary 'Gee Whiz Factor' – said to have been made up by Generoso Pope himself. James Sutherland, who was given the title Associate Editor on the *Enquirer* by Generoso Pope when, in fact, he was the Photo Editor, remembers Iain Calder standing over him, lecturing him on the 'Gee Whiz Factor'.

Essentially the 'Gee Whiz Factor' held that any story or photograph used in the newspaper had to cause a mythical Mrs Smith in Kansas City to sit up, take notice and murmur, 'Gee Whiz!' In his job selecting photographs for the paper, Sutherland remembers visualizing pictures, setting up a lot of assignments for paparazzi and scanning thousands of magazines from around the world, in relentless search of the 'Gee Whiz Factor'.

One theory as to the genesis of the 'Gee Whiz Factor' stems from the tabloids' move into the American supermarket. Globe International's John Vader, remembers what it was like: 'Everything was changing. The suburbs were coming into their own, people were moving out of the cities. The corner newstand was beginning to disappear. The tobacco store that carried newspapers as well as smokers' supplies began to go. The "Mom and Pop" stores started disappearing. The next place where newspapers would be effectively displayed would be in the supermarkets because everybody has to buy food. Today, America buys 85 per cent of its food in supermarkets, and because people are always waiting in food lines, while they are standing there, they can idly go over the covers and pick up something that interests them.

'It was the supermarket managers who quickly became offended at the kinds of stories that the tabloids were doing during the "gore era". When we were first marketed in New York, we were accepted. When we got into the suburbs, parents didn't want their children seeing the paper. Farmers were far more moralistic, more religious. And they just turned their backs on us. The *National Enquirer* had in the meantime changed their format entirely, and lost an awful lot of sales as a result. But eventually, their new format caught on, and it started climbing again. And all the other newspapers followed suit.'

The new format developed during the early 1970s, when all these changes were taking place, constituted the 'Golden Age' of the *National Enquirer*, the period when the 'Gee Whiz Factor' reigned supreme. It was an era of human interest features that wouldn't be matched again by any newspaper in America. There were the tales of blind golfers, maimed children who went on to achieve in maths or in science or in music; of paraplegics who overcame their handicaps. Then there were the animals: gorillas, rhinos, zebras, polar bears. In one issue, a photograph of a lioness named Sheba appeared, with a mouse seated upon her stomach. In another issue, a reader's prize picture showed a small boy having his hair cut. There were stories of hidden treasure, record moustaches, body language, celebrity lookalikes, Moscow's first phone directory . . .

On the medical front, readers were told how to diet sensibly, conquer 'nervous tension', avoid dangerous food additives. They were warned about poorly constructed cribs and dangerous toys and instructed how to burglar-proof their homes. They were told about the effects of television upon their children and the plight of the elderly. It was wide-ranging entertainment with a wholesome bias; and more – a low-keyed attempt at abolishing ignorance. And all for a quarter.

A story on famine in third-world West Africa, written by Harold Lewis, demonstrates the tone of the old *Enquirer*:

> I cradled in my arms a child I sensed was about to die.
>
> Fatima was six years old, and even to the untrained observer, she was obviously too weak to fight off disease. I didn't have to look at her bloated belly to know the hunger in her eyes was desperate and real.
>
> Thousands of such children, potbellied from starvation, await death today in six drought-stricken, underdeveloped nations of West Africa – Upper Volta, Senegal, Mauritania, Mali, Niger and Chad.
>
> Four years of meager rainfall have killed off crops and cattle and brought catastrophic famine to a populace of more than 6 million . . .

The rise of celebrity reporting killed off all this. Slowly but systematically, the human interest stories involving ordinary people and events began to eclipse, celebrity stories taking over the pages. Most were drawn from television, and at first the stories were little more than public relations exercises: 'Mae West at 81', 'Sid Caesar Tells How He Lost 65 Pounds', 'Vincent Price to Remarry', 'Bud Abbott Near Death'. But the interest was there, the readership was there; circulation figures proved it. So there was a redirection of the 'Gee Whiz Factor', now towards celebrity.

The first casualty of celebrity reporting is truth. Inside the tabloids, there was the belief that certain truths were too true for the readership. Says one *National Enquirer* reporter about the death of Elvis Presley, 'Myself and another reporter had the real story, which was that Elvis had overdosed on drugs. But it was easier to go with a made-up story about Elvis going to a psychic the night before his death who told him he was going to die, the "premonition-of-death" thing. They preferred the phoney story to the real story. They thought Elvis was too revered, and they didn't want to tarnish his image right there and then.'

According to another reporter, who was assigned to cover Presley's last moments, the King apparently mistook the ministrations of the Angel of Death for a bowel movement. In this version, his last words on this earth were, 'I'm goin' to take a shit, Honey.' Naturally, the *Enquirer* gave him a more appropriate send-off. 'That kind of change,' the reporter says, 'that's the classic *Enquirer* thing.'

Says an editor from another of the tabloids, 'Readers don't want to believe the truth. The tabloid reader, the public, the movie-watching public, they didn't believe Rock Hudson was gay until he died of AIDS. If the story had come out ten years earlier about his being gay, I don't think people would've believed it. Rock Hudson was the guy who appeared with Doris Day. That's who he was. He was such a big star in his time that you couldn't really suggest anything else.'

Otherwise, the supermarket tabloids are hardly the only news outlets to sell lies for a living. In the apocalyptic story of the death of Princess Grace and the *National Enquirer*'s legendary coverage of the event, only one thing is wrong. Everything. The myth of Grace Kelly's popularity in Monaco is little more than a perpetuated lie that fits the purposes of both the popular and the 'quality' press.

'The first decision that had to be made,' says Paul Levy, after the *Enquirer* team arrived on the scene in Monaco, '*and that decision was made by every journalist covering her death*, was not to report that nobody over there liked her. She was seen as an actress, a business deal, a brokered deal, a marriage arranged by a priest.

'Very few people in the city even had her picture draped in black.

'Princess Grace was practically a hooker in Hollywood, screwed *everybody*. She did not have a good reputation. She was not a sweet virginal young lady. She was in everybody's bed. And, after a number of years in Monaco, she had her own lover, a television and film executive. She was very unhappy and was about to go back to Hollywood. The kids were very unhappy. The excesses in the family . . .' Levy shakes his head, shrugs. 'So we didn't tell how the people of Monaco really felt about Grace. That was our decision.'

It's the same decision made on a regular basis by almost every-one in the business of celebrity reporting.

Says Mike Walker, Gossip Columnist on the *National Enquirer*: 'OK, on my column, the girls, if the crotch on the bathing suit is too low, OK, we send it to retouch and we build the crotch up – OK? Yes, to *that* extent we *conform* to the supermarkets.'

Says Brian Williams, a relative newcomer to the *National Enquirer*, 'We did a celebrity story about a well-known TV star with a real family image. We had this friend of his female lover who was enraged at his behaviour, his degradation of the girl sexually and with drugs. And this friend came to us and wanted us to expose him, and it was pretty damaging material.

'In fact, there were letters, there were dates we were able to confirm in terms of drug treatment, there were arrests which we were able to confirm. There were a number of things that were *pretty* damaging. The celebrity was much older than the girl, and her friend had a motive, that the girl was being degraded.

'But this celebrity has a very good public relations firm. Always, at some point, it is necessary in any story to go to the celebrity themselves or to their firm. In this case it was a poker game from the beginning because most of the materials we would not use. It was not material we would get into. Kinky Sex, for example . . . The *Enquirer* considers itself a family publication.

'Now the way this publicist handles the tabloids is to try to do damage control. And we literally spent three weeks negotiating the story, and the story ended up in the guise of an interview concerning this guy's fiancée's drug use. Now what the publicist was able to do . . . It became an interview with the star himself in which he talked about how he helped his girlfriend recover from her problems. So we were able to narrow the focus of the story, and the damage was minimized.

'Part of what we want to do, especially with people our readers *like* . . . I mean, the assumption is that we want to write all bad things, and that isn't true. I think what we write about are the major crisis points, the rites of passage, and we mark them with the people the community is most familiar with, and that happens to be the celebrity.

'Certain things are simply not publishable, however true they may be. There are certain places where you draw the line:

1. We don't do one-night stands.
2. We don't do any kind of bizarre or non-couple sex.
3. We'll touch on homosexuality.
4. Even a *ménage à trois*, we won't do.

Cleaning up stories, says Williams, 'is something we do out of respect for our reader.'

'Think about auto-erotic asphyxiation. If you cut off the air supply as you're having an orgasm, it increases the sensation, it heightens the orgasm. When we wrote that story, we followed the experts, and we did not define the act, you could not read the article and know what was happening . . . In a way, it was poor journalism; it's also responsible journalism. We took expert advice on how to handle it. Somebody called up really annoyed because we didn't tell them what it was.

'But what happens, if we lose that grounding, that base that, once again, is sort of an anchor for us? If you lose that grounding, then *anything goes*. And what's next? And what's next? And what's next?

'My theory of the *National Enquirer*,' says Williams, 'is that you cannot read it by yourself. You have to tell somebody what you've read. If you read something you can't tell somebody, or you're embarrassed to tell somebody, then we've failed. There's a little bit of acting out; people are shocked, thrilled, touched, but they are never offended or embarrassed. And anyone can come into their house, and see the magazine on the table, and they won't be embarrassed.'

A dozen or so years ago, it became part of the Tabloid Valley legend to speak of the 'Hour of the Jackal' – a cut-throat meeting held every Friday afternoon of top editors who, in hot competition with one another, were pushing to get their own stories into that week's *Enquirer*. It's said that Generoso Pope hired a lot of talent, but was 'slightly frightened of the talent he had hired,' and so engineered a situation wherein they were constantly at one another's throats – instead of his. Says one editor who remembers those by-gone days, 'It was high pressure, highly paid talent. Dammit! Everyone of them wanted their best stories on top of Page One.' In a way, it was this constant competition among staff that led, perhaps unwittingly, to a situation wherein a reporter stretched or even disregarded the truth in order to score points.

Before coming to the *Enquirer* Paul Levy had during his journalistic career, covered the White House, the Supreme Court, the Civil Rights riots; he had won more than twenty awards, including two Pulitzer Prize nominations. He had been named Reporter of the Year in Philadelphia and had taught at the Journalism Schools at Temple University and the University of Wisconsin. Says Levy, 'When I arrived at the *Enquirer*, those files showed more details and facts than I had ever seen. The people down there were not just sittin' there sucking their thumbs.

'The perception from outside was wrong, and I would match the *Enquirer* staff on any major story of general interest, not specialized White House reporting, but a general story. They will be as good. The last persons I hired before I left over there, one came out of Oxford University, the other from the Philadelphia *Enquirer*.

'On a story, you become more aggressive if you're any good. I think tabloid reporters by and large are better than daily newspaper reporters. They know they gotta write and dig and report better. The people who come to tabloids by and far are not the dregs of journalism. They are in fact some of the top people in journalism, who just like the freedom to travel, the fact that they're going to work on interesting stories, not dull stories.'

Iain Calder takes a similar view: 'You're talking about people who know how to get things done. They're not sitting there afraid of losing their jobs. Most of them are very proud of what they're doin'.

'What we're lookin' for is self-motivators, guys who would run through brick walls to get stories. You can't frighten people and you can't bribe people to get stories. They're just people who get excited about things. They want to win, they just *want to win*. They are the kind of guys on the tennis court who'll have a heart attack to get a ball. You can pay them well so they feel good about it, and feel well rewarded, and you can provide an atmosphere in which their performance is optimal, but you can't change them with money and you can't change them with fear. That doesn't mean to say you can't kick ass, if they're gettin' a little lazy . . .'

This aggressiveness has on occasion resulted in kudos for staffers from the establishment press. After the *National Enquirer* published the famous 'Monkey Business' photograph of Donna Rice sitting on Gary Hart's lap in the spring of 1987, Calder says he could 'detect a difference in the attitude from the national press toward the *Enquirer*.' Says Calder, 'Most of the other papers would have given their eye teeth to have gotten one of those pictures.'

Another moment of glory for Calder involved the *Enquirer*'s Seven Dwarfs story. He sent a reporter around the United States asking people if they could name the seven Democratic candidates in the 1988 election. They could not. But, in the vast majority of cases, they were able to name Snow White's seven dwarfs. 'We got compliments for that story from the national press,'

85

says Calder. 'Chicago-based columnist Bob Greene did a whole column on it.'

But others don't share Calder's sanguine view of the *Enquirer*'s increasing credibility. Says Jeff Samuels about the early days: 'Reporters had their skills and talents perverted into a disinformation unit, and they made these quite proud people basically roll over and beg. Because in those days, you didn't fuck around with the facts. At least then. I saw quite ballsy guys do things that were embarrassing, just to keep their jobs. And having said this, I didn't have the balls to quit . . . You would think that Fleet Street is the hardest school of journalism, and it is, but the *Enquirer* is the finishing school. Everything you've learned, you then learn how to subvert it. You learn how everything you hold as inviolable, like facts and accuracy, how to make anything you want true. You specialize in doing bent stories and that's it.'

According to another veteran reporter, one of the major problems was that the editors already had the angle they wanted in their minds, 'and you had to get it'.

Says another, 'They would be having me interviewing two-headed babies and talking to people from the grave, so I used to do it all in a swirl of marijuana smoke.'

So today, what kind of stuff does the keen tabloid talent chase? One story that has made the rounds has an *Enquirer* photographer assigned to go out to the original Temple of Doom to photograph the tangle of poisonous snakes that crawl constantly across it during the night. Two nights on the job: no snakes. So into town he goes, buys a sackful of cobras, rushes back in a taxi – and takes the picture.

Advice to a tabloid photographer from a veteran: 'If you're ever assigned a disaster – train wreck, plane crash – take the time to drop by a toy store and pick up a few teddy bears. If all else fails, you can get a shot of one of these amidst the debris.'

Mike Walker on his staff: 'Most of my people are moles, and in-place people and strange people, cutting-edge people because most of my stuff is very cutting-edge stuff. Not the most earth-shaking stuff in the world: I was the first person in the *entire world* to report that Roseanne Barr and Tom Arnold had tattoos of each other's names on their asses . . . Which at the time was like, "Are you *sure*?" All she had to do was to pull down her pants. "Are you *sure*?" "Sure, I'm fucking sure." And even *I* was a little worried at the time. Events have *since . . . proven . . . me . . . right!*'

*

If there is anything in journalism Tony Brenna hasn't done, it would be hard to imagine what. Before leaving the UK in 1964, Brenna had been with *Advertisers Weekly* and had been managing editor of *World Press News*, which later became *Campaign*. After leaving Fleet Street, he went to the New York *Herald Tribune* and when that folded, he became associate editor for the prestigious journal *Editor & Publisher*, writing about press ethics and the newspaper industry. For three years, he was an advertising copywriter before joining the *Daily Telegraph*'s New York Bureau. They sent him to cover the United Nations, and while he was there, he started working for the BBC, doing about three broadcasts a week for them. It is one of the ironies of tabloid journalism that a reporter of this calibre was enlisted to become one of the *National Enquirer*'s first men to encircle the globe in search of Gene Pope's 'Gee Whiz Factor'.

Brenna believes that when he went to the *National Enquirer*, it was 'the best journalistic experience he ever had . . . in terms of what people really want to read . . . in terms of selling and moving a product.' He quickly became their Number One reporter. 'I could write anything I wanted, once I got the story approved and could go anywhere in the United States without even calling the office. If I was leaving the country,' says Brenna, 'I just had to tell them, and I could go anywhere in the world. Out of fourteen roving reporters, I was the only one who could do that.

'At one point, the *Enquirer* got very much into dog stories and animal stories, and I found out that they ate dogs in the Philippines and treated them very badly, leaving them trussed up in the marketplace with their legs tied behind their backs in the sweltering sunshine. Then they would slit their throats and drink the blood . . . And we wanted to create a big story out of it. We went to the dog markets, got great pictures of dogs trussed up, came back. And we took them to the United Nations and to the Philippines Ambassador at the United Nations and tried to get it raised in the UN. We had a photograph taken of me with the ambassador looking at the pictures, which made a great story.

'Then all the British papers lifted the story after it was published. We got hundreds of thousands of reader letters. I went back to the Philippines and tried to get to Ferdinand and Imelda. All this was whipping up hysteria. In fact, there's nothing wrong with eating dogs any more than there is cows and pigs. We were interested in a major human interest story. And I nearly got killed there.

'They sent me back with a photographer to the dog market in a small village about 300 miles from Manila. They now wanted follow-up pictures. But the dog traders were all aware of it by now, and we were immediately surrounded by howling dog traders with bloody great knives, who were going to cut us to pieces. The Philippine government had been following us because they were worried about what we were doing, and we were saved at the last minute by these government meat inspectors who came rushing in and pulled us out of there before they chopped us up. I mean, they were going to kill us.

'Anyway we closed down all the dog markets in the Philippines, but by now, I had reached the stage where animal rights, or human rights, or good intentions really, which would maybe have been satisfying in the early stages in my career, didn't matter any more. All I was after was stories.

'This is a corrosive process. This goes on week after week after week – catching somebody with someone else's wife, watching them burn animals, going to an earthquake or a gas explosion in Mexico, watching bodies being tossed into mass graves . . . going around only looking for these human interest stories – this sensationalism.

'The earthquake stories all start the same way, "The clock on the village tower stopped at a certain time," there's a kind of formula that you get into. Now you're getting bored with sensationalism, and you don't have any idealism that's discernable left. You're just a sensation-making machine perambulating around the bloody world. Sometimes you gulp and say "Oh my God, what is this all about? Why am I doing this?" But this very process takes over, it corrodes your integrity.

'Because, by now I would've killed you to get that story. You could've been my best friend and I would've cut your throat from here to here. I really would. There were times you'd get drunk and stoned with people to get a story. We were hanging out with some very low-life people. You had to become low-life to get the story. You couldn't get it by being Mr Nice Guy, which was tough, you know?

'Here I am becoming one of the yellowist yellow journalists in the world and I'd spent a good deal of my life writing about pre-trial publicity, journalistic ethics, and propriety and responsibility, you know? It's kind of weird.'

Brenna's eyes are large and blue, and as he has been telling this, his eyes have been growing larger and bluer with frightening intensity.

And you believe him.

PART TWO

The Cult of Celebrity

That popcorn diet in full

Andy Warhol's Interview Magazine *is talking to Madonna
Louise Ciccone in late summer, 1986. And how does the
singer feel about the tabloid
newspapers who feature her
almost daily?*

*Says Madonna, 'I have three
favorite clips: That I have a
shrine to Marilyn in my bedroom, that I believe the spirit
of Elvis is inside my soul and
that I lost fourteen pounds on
a popcorn diet.'*

It is Wendy Henry on the
other end of the line, and
she is desperate. The heavily
publicized launch of the *Sun*'s
new four-page celebrity diet
pullout is scheduled to begin
almost immediately – and the
first celebrity of the series has
just pulled out.

'Well, God, Wendy, I just
don't know,' says Richard
Ellis, the *Sun*'s New York
correspondent. 'Oh . . . I
just saw this new photo of
Madonna, and she looks
like she's lost a lot of
weight. Apparently she's been
doing a lot of exercises.
She's been going around
in frilly lace and bras
and that sort of thing.'

'Great!' says Henry

Ellis rings up Madonna's
publicists, who are unhelpful.
Henry, meantime, is more desperate than ever.

From his reading, Ellis knows
that one of Madonna's favourite foods is popcorn. But he
knows nothing about diets or
losing weight. Henry tells him
not to worry, 'We'll get some
dietician to help us.'

On the morning of 6 August
1986, the *Sun*'s 'Slim Mag' appears on the centre pages of
the newspaper: 'MADONNA
SHEDS 14lb ON DIET OF
POPCORN: *Slim with a Star*'.

In the lower left-hand corner
of the pullout appears Madonna
as she was in July 1985, at the
time of her wedding to Sean
Penn, when she was 'a "well-
rounded" $8^{1}/_{2}$ st'. In the upper
right-hand corner, we see the
'5ft 3in svelte 7st 6 lb' singer
in July 1986, after she lost 14lb
[sic] – in only six weeks.

'At $8^{1}/_{2}$ stone,' the story
tells us, 'the star was getting too big to reveal her
famous belly button in public.'

'Madonna admits, "I didn't have a flat stomach any more. I had become well rounded."'

'The sexy singer, who is by the way vegetarian, often goes into the kitchen to cook up special vegetarian dishes for Sean and herself, using variations of traditional Italian recipes she learned as a youngster, like wholemeal spaghetti with home-made low-calorie tomato sauce and lasagne.'

You too can join Madonna and lose 14lb in only six weeks. Here's how to do it:

'BREAKFAST (200 calories): Half a grapefruit, two wholewheat crispbreads, scraping of marmalade, small glass mixed vegetable juice . . .

'LUNCH (300 calories): Large mixed salad (use raw cauliflower, spinach leaves and grated cabbage as well as the usual salad vegetables) topped with ONE of the following: 2oz cashew nuts or grated walnuts, small tin baked beans, 2oz grated hard cheese. Add lemon juice dressing and one small banana as dessert . . .

'SUPPER (350 calories): 2oz wholemeal lasagne cooked and layered with a mixture of fresh vegetables simmered in a little stock and tomato puree. Top with wholemeal breadcrumbs and yogurt. Green salad . . .'

And don't forget that medium-sized packet of popcorn!

5
FIFTEEN MINUTES

Fame, who needs it?

The tabloids need it, and in the worst way. In England, it's a rare day when some famous individual doesn't make an appearance on the front page of the tabs. Says one editor, 'Put on readers; that's the whole thought. We have to have somebody like Kylie Minogue on the front page, or Jason Donovan, or Michael Jackson. Sales go up something like 1 per cent.'

In America, it's worse. Says Roy Foster, design director at Globe International, 'The British tabloid doesn't rely on that, but the tabloid here relies on the celebrity as its basic commodity. You take the stars out of the *Enquirer*, and what do you got left?'

Says Christina Kirk, associate editor of the *Star*, who handles, among other things, the tabloid's medical reporting, 'In the old days, we used to sell just with a diet, or you could say, "Headaches", or "Arthritis", and you'd sell three or four million copies. You didn't need celebrities. Now we need them.

'You live or die by the cover. You can't guess who will draw. Every year there is a list for what was the best and the worst cover. One particularly bad for us, we put Nancy Reagan on the cover, right after her mastectomy. It didn't sell. That says something about Nancy. And TV people known for the character, not for their own personal story: we put Carroll O'Connor on the cover, and it died. And his was the number one show. The reader is attracted if the star seems to have her own personal story going, her own personal soap opera. Take Liz Taylor, no movie for years, and yet they love to read about her.'

Kirk remembers when Gilda Radner died of ovarian cancer. 'Then when you do a story about what it is and how to detect it and what can be done about it, they are hooked. They want to know, "How did this happen to this girl?"'

In the early 1960s, historian Daniel J. Boorstin isolated for the first time how image had become interwoven into the American dream, creating 'a thicket of unreality which stands between us and the facts of life.' For Boorstin, the same kind of mentality that turns 'a symphony into mood-conditioning' creates a demand for expectations tainted by fantasy and characterized by extravagance. He saw the rise of the image as a form of self-deceit, a kind of 'democracy of pseudo-events' in which 'anyone can become a celebrity, if only he can get into the news and stay there.'

The first 'pseudo-event' was the 'interview', a sort of makeshift news event in which interviewer talked with interviewee about attitudes and opinions, rather than reporting actual events. When it made its first appearance in the mid-nineteenth century, the interview was quickly discredited by *The Nation*, who called it 'the joint product of some humbug of a hack politician and another humbug of a reporter.'

Today, the marketing imperative has made the interview a popular source of information, or in some cases, disinformation, as human models are 'mass-produced, to satisfy the market, and without any hitches.' In this context, a celebrity is nothing more than a person who is primarily known for being well-known; in Boorstin's words, the celebrity is 'the human pseudo-event'.

At the heart of this preoccupation with fame – this cult of celebrity – is Hollywood's creation of instant celebrities through the launch of successful new television series, whose stars quickly become the flavour of the month in the tabloid press. The globalization of the celebrity phenomenon was pioneered in the mid-1970s after the invention of videotape permitted international sale of such shows as *I Love Lucy*, *The Beverly Hillbillies*, *M*A*S*H*, *Kojak* and others. Yesterday, it was Lucille Ball and Buddy Ebsen; today, it's Bill Cosby and Roseanne Barr. The familiar cry of cultural imperialism falls by the wayside in view of the convenience of this simplified visual coding, whereby fame can be easily exported and marketed abroad. It is the staple of the tabloid in which stars share their views on food, marriage, sex, astrology, finance and even God.

Celebrity coverage was originally born out of the film industry when fan magazines sold like hotcakes while simultaneously furthering the careers of early film stars whose visages had tremendous power to attract. These magazines contained little, if any, actual content; their primary purpose was to cash in on a cult phenomenon. But during the 1950s, a scandal magazine named *Confidential* rose to prominence, terrorizing Hollywood with disclosures about the stars' personal lives, special emphasis being laid upon the sexual and the sordid. It was put out of business in 1957 following a libel suit by Maureen O'Hara, whom

Confidential had falsely accused of 'engaging in amorous embraces' with a male friend in a movie theatre. Although the suit ended in a mistrial, the magazine was judged 'guilty of conspiring to publish obscenity' on the basis of the transcripts.

In America today, the supermarket tabloids are a hybrid of the early fan magazines, *Confidential* and low-brow but intensive investigative reporting hijacked from the establishment press. In England, the same sort of 'hype-and-tell' approach bolsters a straight newspaper format filled with news, human interest, oddball occurrences and sport. Says former *Guardian* Editor, Alastair Hetherington, 'the prominence given to television and entertainment personalities, [is] perhaps the nearest thing to a late twentieth-century "opium of the people". In this respect, popular television and the popular press feed off one another.'

As the cult of celebrity took over first the supermarket tabloids, then the British tabloids, finally making startling inroads into the establishment press, a new wave of reporters invaded the West Coast – seat-of-the-pants freelancers who peddled their stories directly to Fleet Street or Tabloid Valley in Florida.

One of them, who deserted the establishment press and jumped on the celebrity bandwagon at the outset of the phenomenon, remembers how it all started. 'The celebrity worshipping syndrome', he says, 'spilled over from the US about fifteen, sixteen maybe eighteen years ago, to Britain, Australia, New Zealand, to Continental Europe later, and finally to the Far East, because they tend to have their own stars. But now all this stuff's been dubbed. Celebrity journalism comes with the worshipping syndrome.

'We're not interested in Lee Remick, we're interested in the fact that Lee Remick had cancer. Or Jill Ireland, we weren't interested in her unless she was dying. It's this kind of exploitive thing which has developed. It's now done in this perniciously personal style. They want to know who's getting fat, and who's freaky. And then who's on drugs and booze and whose life has crashed around them. And everybody now is confessing to have been on drugs and booze and now that's worn out as impact. For Christ's sake, what do we do next? We've done their sexual stuff, we've done their drugs stuff, we've done their adultery, their diseases, we cannibalize them, we eat them up. So you've done it with *Coronation Street*, now let's do it with *Neighbours*, move on to *Dynasty*, and if there aren't any successful TV programmes, we've got nothing to write about.'

The effect of this upon the celebrity can sometimes be devastating. Says Andrew Cowan-Martin, former manager of Kylie

Minogue, who rose from the relative obscurity of an Australian soap opera to the top of the charts, 'Here's a hypothetical case. How would you feel if the tabs had your grandmother on the phone asking her if you were gay? You say, "Get outta here Granny!" But Granny thinks you *are* gay because a national newspaper asks this. Says Granny, "Well I don't know, I've never thought about it. I never thought of her as being gay." Bang! It's a quote. They are talking about it down at the local pub, the whole family falls apart. And it's done as easily as that.

'Normally, a new artist who has become successful – despite the hundreds of briefings and examples they have been shown – when it's presented in bold type about them in front of their face, they freak out. Totally, utterly, uncontrollably upset! Over and over and over you tell them, their friends will turn against them, their family will turn against them, it's not a question of they don't believe you, it's that they haven't experienced it. How can you understand if I tell you when they punch you on the nose, it's going to hurt? I've had it happen to every major artist who has ever made the press. People always turn. Always. Both for the money and for the spite.

'Different stars freak out differently. Some of them cry. If they are intelligent, they analyse it. Some just get bitter and twisted.' To Cowan-Martin, who has witnessed this process many times over, the tabloids are held strictly to account.

But *National Enquirer* editor Iain Calder thinks differently. Says Calder, 'It's not just their relatives or their best friends talking to us. It's their agents and their lawyers. Everybody they know. But see, they're tuned into that. Don't make it sound like they are special people, you know, surrounded by people like this. *They're* like this too. *They* are doing it to *their* best friends. It's not like the stars are an entity within themselves, and everybody around them is a sleazebag. That's not the case. You have as many people among the stars who would do the same thing to one another. It's not like the stars are a group of people beyond reproach. I mean, *some* of them are the people who are doing it.

'See, in Hollywood, it's like politics, it's a dog-eat-dog world. To get to the top there, it takes a certain type of person. They're not all bad, some of them are terrific, but there's the share of the dregs. It's the people who are desperate to become famous, and they'll do *anything*, and they get the "get-rich-quick artists" all around them. These people are famous for trying to get money as fast as they can, and others there behind waiting to climb right over them.

'What happens is, a lot of people who are saying, "I hate the *Enquirer*", are giving us stories. I think you'll find mostly the hostility comes from fear. If you were a star, and you had skeletons in your closet, who would you be afraid of? *People* magazine? No. The *Star*? Not really. The *National Enquirer*? Absolutely.

'The celebs all say, "Well, of course, what the *Enquirer* says, it's not true." Then you find out a few weeks, months later, it's true. Johnny Carson goes and says, "How can the *National Enquirer* say that my marriage is in trouble, they're liars, they're absolute liars." A few months later . . . the marriage breaks up. This was three marriages ago. Tom Cruise. We did his marriage breakup, "Cruise's Marriage Is in Trouble". He gives interviews to *Rolling Stone*, television, "Are you kidding? My marriage is rock solid. Blah, blah, blah, blah." And you know, he then announces his divorce. Of course we're right. He's not going to say, "Gee, the *National Enquirer* was right."'

Says James Sutherland of London's *Daily Star*, an early paparazzo turned editor, 'If someone like Carol Burnett, Eddie Murphy, whoever, has chosen to appear in movies and make millions and millions of dollars – they're all grossly over-paid, making these huge amounts of money out of it – then they become public property. They've sold themselves. They want to drive Cadillacs, Rolls Royces? To have this multimillionaire lifestyle? Well, there's a price to be paid.'

The last decade has seen the most exhaustive invasion of privacy in history, with the most intimate details of celebrities' personal lives flashed around the world. And these personal tidbits are gleaned from anyone close to the celebrity, most usually for cash payment.

Bill Burt, former editor of the *National Examiner*, likes to tell how tabloid reporters approached the Elvis Presley phenomenon. Says Burt, 'It's like when we used to go dancin' at the Hammersmith Palais. You get some girl out on the dance floor and you ask her, "Do you fuck?" and if she says "No", you just leave her cold and go on to the next. Now, one in ten will say "Yes", will say "Sure". So you say, "OK, let's beat it out of here." Saves time. It's the same with Elvis's relatives: One in ten will say "Yes".'

Burt is a Scotsman with an audacious hit-and-run sense of humour, and he is joking. But . . . he's also *not* joking, because he's explaining the way tabloid reporters work. Somebody, somewhere who is close to the star will sell out. That's the certainty.

97

Says Mike Walker, General Editor and Gossip Columnist on the *National Enquirer* since 1974, 'If a man doesn't want money from me, I have to question his motives. I have to ask myself, "Hey, wait a minute. If someone doesn't want to be paid, who *is* this person? You want to tell us *for the concern of mankind? for the good of humanity?*"'

When a new TV starlet comes across the firmament, Walker can work one of two ways, maybe both ways at once: from present to past, or past to present. Where does she live? Who is she married to? What was the last city she lived in? It's simple enough, says Walker, to track someone back, city by city, speaking to people who knew her. 'Wasn't she a bra burner?' he asks. 'Or maybe a lesbian?'

Walker would also go back to the star's hometown. 'I would send a reporter there for four or five days. Her mom's there, her dad's there, her friends, neighbours, and they're all gonna tell me things. Old women are there, and they love to talk. My reporter could talk to her old girlfriends who hate her because she's a success. And I would find every man she's lived with or slept with. This girl has left a paper trail all over . . . *It is so simple.*'

If the methods seem reminiscent of the CIA or MI6, that's because they are the same methods. Time-consuming and costly, this kind of vetting would be practical only for the big-time star and the big-time story.

For the smaller fry, there is a highly systemized operation in which a number of regulars participate. Says one gossip columnist, 'We have a team of reporters in LA. I've got a person I use in London, one in France and the rest of Europe, and they in turn have sources in all the studios – TV and movie studios – and they work the sources week by week, day by day. They go to the parties, to the premières, to the restaurants of Hollywood, and they get to know the gossip and the stories, and then they file them. A lot of the time, the sources are people who work with the stars or are friends. We've got a whole network of freelance correspondents working for us as well.'

Other stories are got simply by manning the phones, and in many cases, sources have never set eyes on the reporters they confide in. 'There is a wonderful anonymity on the telephone,' says *National Enquirer* reporter Brian Williams. 'There is a bias to see things, but I think a lot of times people are more comfortable with you on the telephone. Some people are much happier with whatever their fantasy of you is. I've had people I've dealt with for a year and a half, and I've never seen them. The only time I ever need to see anybody is when they want to see me. The thing about the telephone is, they are always in control. I mean, the *illusion* is of control. For example, with an anonymous tip, someone calls in and they want you to give them some money for it, but they don't want anybody to know and they could get in trouble for it. For them, it's a totally unique experience. For us, it happens all the time.'

For Williams, the soft sell yields more in the long run than the hard sell. 'It's almost a Judo situation,' he says. 'Instead of resisting that, you just sort of be yourself, whatever that is, and hopefully, it's intelligent and charming and honest, and people are so surprised by that. You play against type. All their expectations and preconceptions are invalid, so that there usually is some kind of bonding that takes place. I probably have a dozen sources who say, time and time again, "I can't believe I'm talking to you," or "You're not what I expected from the *National Enquirer*."'

Williams takes on a three-tiered strategy. First, he never argues with anyone. Second, some of his sources are aggressive, some cautious; whatever approach they are taking, he compliments them on that and on what they are doing. 'Also I assure them we protect our sources. If our sources aren't safe, then we can't stay in business.'

David Duffy, who has been with the *Enquirer* for fourteen years, and before that was a veteran of Fleet Street, also uses a softly, softly approach. 'I had a lot of principles hammered into me by wonderful old-time journalists,' says Duffy, 'and one of the rules I've been taught was never to do anything I'd be ashamed of. If I can't get a story by open means, then I wouldn't do it. I won't say I won't employ every means I can, and know which buttons to push and use the psychological tools: An open face, making the person feel confident in you, and having them trust you. To get the person's trust until they say I want to talk to that man again.'

Duffy's career, like many *Enquirer* reporters, is impressive. He has reported for the Manchester *Evening News*, Granada Television, BBC Radio, the *Sunday Mirror*, and he was the Hugh Cudlipp Reporter of the Year in 1975. When he first came to the *Enquirer*, he found being English an advantage. People, he says, believed he would be 'gentlemanly'. Says Duffy, 'It's worked like a charm all over this country.'

Duffy admits it's been especially 'challenging' since he came to work for the *Enquirer* 'because when you say "*National Enquirer*" they run and hide in the hills. But there are a lot of classy people at the *Enquirer*. People expect you to creep, to slither under the door like a snake, and they are amazed and astonished that that doesn't happen.'

If you were to sweep your eyes across the offices of the *National Enquirer* during working hours, you might very well be overwhelmed by how true Duffy's assessment is. Tanned, tall, trim and handsome, both the men and the women look more like graduate students in the Ivy League than tabloid reporters.

This group of reporters, more than any other, face constant fire from the celebrity community, who feel violated and used and who in turn use every method at their disposal, including their fame and popularity to swing public opinion against the journalists.

Says Williams, 'What happens, I think, especially with television, is, they are creating a persona, and they are making a very healthy living off that persona. And I think what we do is we examine that persona, and we trade on that persona and usually, I think, the anger of the celebrity is something like, "Wait a minute. This is *my* persona and *I'm* the only one who's gonna make money offa this persona!"

'I mean, when celebrities sell their wedding pictures for publication in *People*, or in *Life*, or in one of the tabloids, as intimate an experience as you can have, and you sell it to a magazine, then you're strictly into a matter of commerce.'

The fight is not only over who will profit from the persona of the celebrity. Many of the stars have amassed personal fortunes comparable to powerful monarchs or Roman emperors. With money comes power, and like the emperors, celebrities seek to rewrite history favourable to themselves. In effect, powers once reserved for a ruling class have fallen into the hands of individuals who are famous primarily because of their fame. In their intergalactic battle against the tabloids, the star's major weapon is the law.

In the late-1970s, television comedian and film star Carol Burnett sued the *National Enquirer* over an article that said she became drunk in a Washington restaurant and got into an argument with former US Secretary of State Henry Kissinger. Burnett, whose parents had a drinking problem and who herself does not drink, sued. In 1982, in what was thought to be a landmark case, a sympathetic jury awarded her $300,000 in general damages and $1.3 million in punitive damages for defamation of character. However, the amounts were reduced to $50,000 and $750,000 respectively by the trial judge. On appeal, there were further reductions, and Burnett was given the option to seek a new trial or settle. She settled.

Whenever the *Enquirer* settles a case, it is their standard practice to stipulate that the amount of the settlement cannot be disclosed, and for obvious reasons. Burnett herself has no comment to make, and her agent will only say, 'Carol wants to put the case behind her now.' But within the inner sanctum of the *Enquirer*, it is rumoured that Burnett's final settlement was reduced to a relatively insignificant amount – the sum of $75,000 is sometimes whispered one colleague to another.

It was vital to the continuing success of the *Enquirer*'s operation that the tabloid effectively wear the actress down through relentless litigation, or face the same fate as *Confidential* in the late 1950s. In the wake of the Burnett case, the tabloid faced more than $60 million in suits from other famous individuals. Not a single one of them came to court, and when each settlement was reached, as with the Burnett case, the terms of the agreements were not made public.

In Britain, libel action takes on the aspect of a thriving cottage industry, churning out minor defamations day in, day out, to the extent that the cuttings libraries of most national newspapers contain scores of inaccuracies that have paid off small, large or hefty sums to satisfied litigants. Inside the newspaper industry itself, there is a belief that only the libraries of the *Telegraph* and perhaps of the *Independent* are sufficiently updated on out-of-court libel settlements that they are of any use to the researcher. These small libels, most usually filed and settled without public knowledge, are endemic to publishing in a country that boasts the most repressive libel laws in the Western world. A simple author error is usually good for a fiver – thousand, that is. It's a lawyer's heaven, a journalist's hell.

In this setting, the famous enter a sphere of their own wherein the compensations judges encourage and juries grant approach the farcical. Was Jeffrey Archer's pain and suffering from falsely being identified as the client of a prostitute sufficiently grave to entitle him to *half a million pounds*? Have the verbal attacks made upon Koo Stark since her break-up with Prince Andrew been sufficiently painful that she deserves something approaching £1 million? Were the allegations published about Elton John by the *Sun* actually worth the £1 million out-of-court settlement he received?

Compare these to the figures awarded victims of crime from the Compensation Board: a rape is rated at £5,000, loss of an eye, £13,000, loss of hearing from assault, £32,000. When train driver Arthur Barrett disobeyed orders, stopping his train during the King's Cross fire to pick up some 200 trapped passengers from the smokey platform, he was awarded only £8,750 by the High Court for the ensuing psychological trauma and stress he suffered.

There is something in the very nature of fame that makes society place a higher value upon those who have it. It is as if fame creates a different dimension for the famous, and their suffering is worth more than that of ordinary mortals.

Inside the supermarket tabloids, where fame is marketed as a product, there is a recognized 'celebrity curve'; that is, the beginning, the achievement and the ending of fame. When they start out in the business, performers are desperate for a mention in the tabloids. 'In the early days,' says Phil Bunton, executive editor of the *Star*, 'Cher gave many interviews to the *Star* just after her breakup with Sonny Bono. I think she sort of used them to advance her career. But after she became a big movie star, being only a tabloid, now we couldn't get an interview with her in the *Star*, not if we gave her a million dollars. There are quite a few like that. In the early days, they would push themselves into the *Star*. Once established, they don't care anymore. Suzanne Somers, when she was just starting out, would do all sorts of stunts for us. Now she won't. You get Roseanne Barr. Right at the beginning we got an interview. Now she won't talk to any of us.'

In a frank admission of complicity, one publicist estimates that 80 per cent of Hollywood publicists cooperate at some level with the tabloids. Says one, 'I believe that almost every publicist in town deals with the *Enquirer* although most will probably go to their graves without admitting it.' Says another, 'an appearance in the *Enquirer* can tremendously enhance the commerciality of a client.'

But Bunton insists that neither the *Star* nor the other tabloids are in the business of creating celebrity. What he and his colleagues are trying to do is 'figure out who the next star is going to be.

'When Michael Jackson started to make it big, there was an idea that black stars and that rock stars didn't sell magazines; he transcended all that. So we put him all over the magazine. But then, when we put him on the cover for about the seventh month, we didn't sell. We decided he was dead. The trick is to feed the trend, give as much background on them as you can, as kids, who they are going to marry next, and so on. After the slippage starts, it's all over.'

Inside the offices of the *Star*, tremendously sophisticated research has been conducted to get a precise profile of the average reader of the publication. Seventy-five per cent of the buyers are married women in their thirties who take the magazine home, where it is usually read by their husbands and children. 'Our readers have bigger-than-average families,' says Christina Kirk. 'There are two or three kids, and many of the women work. While they do have extended families, television appears, in a sense, to provide their community. We have developed a system which involves focus groups, and in these, we continually hear the same comment from these women: "This is for *me*. This is *my* treat. This is something *I* enjoy."'

A focus group is a statistically selected group of about twelve all-*Star* or all-tabloid readers. There are separate sessions for each group, and a researcher is in the room with them. Those selected for questioning are never told the research is for the *Star*, but generally, by the end of the session, they come to understand this is the case. It takes time to break down the barriers. There is a general reluctance on the part of these people to admit they read the tabloids. Phil Bunton remembers one truck driver. He looked the part, says Bunton, a big man with a full beer belly. And when he was asked what magazines he read, he answered *GQ* and *Vanity Fair*. 'Finally,' says Bunton, 'he got around to admitting that, yes, he did read the *Star*.'

'This is all done behind a mirror,' says Bunton, 'and we watch it and videotape it.' It was through these focus groups that the *Star* discovered the incredible drawing power of Phil Donahue. Although his ratings weren't as high as those of Johnny Carson in those days, what the *Star* staff heard from their focus groups was, 'We drop everything to sit down and watch the Phil Donahue Show.' Says Bunton, 'We found Oprah Winfrey the same way.'

Although market research has helped the *Star* to find the celebrities to fill its pages, focus groups are conducted only about once every two years. Says Bunton, 'In between times, you have to rely on your gut instinct. Whenever we feel the market has changed markedly, we do research to see why sales have suddenly jumped, or are slipping.'

Television personalities usually sell better for the *Star* than film personalities, probably, says Bunton, 'because they come into your home. They seem to become part of your family. When Rusty Hammer committed suicide, there was a great response because people are still watching *The Danny Thomas Show* on reruns. It's almost like a death in the family, and they want to read about it, know about it.

'Generally, though, our readers *do not* read newspapers. They think there is too much bad news in newspapers and on television news. So when they read us, there is a strong element of escapism. In all the focus groups there was an undercurrent of the feeling that "Life is hard", although no one was was willing to say their own life was bad or depressing.'

'When things go wrong for the celebrities, there is often the feeling on the part of the reader, "Thank God that is not happening to me."'

So along with the 'Gee Whiz Factor' isolated by the *National Enquirer*, a secondary reason why people want to read about the stars is the 'Thank God Factor'.

Says John Vader, editor of the wacky American supermarket tabloid the *Sun*, 'One of our problems has been that TV reduced superstars down to just stars. They weren't the same kind of celebrities they used to be. Very few have superstar status. Now, people get very popular in a series, the series gets pulled in the middle of the year, they're gone. They might be a superstar today, but if they lose the role, they lose their status.'

As with books, there seems to be a 'shelf-life' for the famous, one that's growing shorter and shorter as the new technology takes hold. Serious erosion occurred with home video, which gave viewers new freedom to choose what they watch, and when. Cable and satellite transmission has also diminished the effect of network, which once served to channel the viewing public's attention onto Hollywood's chosen performers. Andy Warhol's off-beat statement that pretty soon everybody will be famous for fifteen minutes holds particular significance for an industry splintered by new technology. The knock-down effect on the supermarket tabloids has been a steady lowering of their circulation.

There is yet another problem. Roger Wood, editorial director of the *Star*, says, 'The number of stars who have sufficient chemistry to move the tabloids is smaller and diminishing. It's nothing to do with their popularity on the TV screen, or in the movies. It's to do with themselves personally. Many stars have enormous appeal on screen. Bring them out and they have no chemistry, and no one cares for them. The number of people you can bring off the screen is becoming more limited.

'I remember in the early days of the *Star* when I could run Farrah Fawcett or one or other of the "Angels" on the cover, and I once did for seven weeks running, and every week our sales went up. We can't do that now. There isn't anybody of that stature. Tried and proven people like Oprah Winfrey, for example, she doesn't always work. Sometimes you can put a perfectly reasonable story about Oprah on the cover and it doesn't work. And she's one of the bankers. When you get to the point where the bankers don't work every time, that's a tough poker game.'

From Boca Raton, home of Globe International, drive south on the I-95. Turn right on to Glade Road, and you will find a stylish bar called 'Tycoon'. Here, veterans from Tabloid Valley stop in for drinks after work. On a warm evening in late January 1990, three of 'the Wild Bunch' are airing their gripes: Vince Eckersley, Lee Harrison and Roy Foster.

VINCE: The tabs make the celebs. They create the mystique of these celebrities . . . One star, before she landed a role in *Dallas*, used to call up the *Enquirer*, she used to beg them to run her picture.
LEE: All the bloody soaps on TV were goin' hot in the evenin' and they were bloody good, and now, all we've got is bloody Roseanne Barr and *she* doesn't sell.
ROY: That's right.
LEE: She's such an outspoken—, that there's no mystique.
ROY: You think about it. Who's a great star at this moment?
VINCE: When you're scratchin' about for people like Lisa Bonnett, and people like that . . .
LEE: Where's the Starsky and Hutches of this world? the Erik Estradas of this world? They've all had their day in the sun. Madonna doesn't sell.
ROY: That's only the kids. Their mum isn't going to go out and buy a newspaper about Madonna. She might buy one about Liz Taylor.
LEE: Liz Taylor was somebody up here [gestures].
VINCE: Elvis was another, but Liz was probably the last big star.
LEE: We couldn't use Joan Collins on the cover now, maybe in Britain, not here.
 [All roll their eyes backwards, thinking, as though they are looking for somebody.]
VINCE: Jackie and Liz. Starsky and Hutch. Where are the greats? Don Johnson doesn't work any more, since *Miami Vice* went off the air. Johnson did a couple of LPs, publicity stunts . . . You see, even that, I believe, was out of sheer desperation, because there weren't any greats. Just a bunch of stars who can't last beyond the series they're in. You see Jackie went through the assassination, through the marriage. She's an interesting person.
LEE: Michael J. Fox's claim to fame was his wedding, and he stitched up the *National Enquirer*.

ROY: What's Michael J. Fox got? He appeals to teenagers.

VINCE: We don't have *anybody*!

ROY: The whole thing's gonna fall apart . . . The greatest problem here is the lack of stars. That's where the tabloid market will sag, because that's its basic bread and butter.

LEE: One of the biggest sellers that the *National Examiner* had last year was that 'Elvis Is Still Alive'. There *is* nobody else. They're all still holding out for Elvis.

Hollywood's splintering stardom has little effect on the London tabs because they sit atop the mother load – the soap that can never be cancelled, the stars that can never be dimmed. In an industry where transience is the cardinal rule, it is no exaggeration to say that virtually the entire population of the world charts the course of their lives by the rites of passage of Britain's Royal Family.

It is 7 July 1986, and a new comic strip appears on the pages of Rupert Murdoch's *Sun*, 'Andy and Fergie's Love Story'.

> SIX months ago she was an unknown London working girl. Now she's set to be bride of the year. This is how 26-year-old Sarah Ferguson captured the heart of her Prince.
>
> It all started with her dad, Major Ronnie Ferguson, who had a farm in Hampshire where Sarah and her sister Jane grew up . . .

'I'm so ugly,' a teenaged Fergie complains to a friend. 'No boy will ever want me.' She is gazing into a mirror, critically surveying her features. 'Nonsense,' says her chum. 'Your red hair is sensational.' Over the next seventeen days, we follow Sarah through Queens Secretarial College, her first puppy love, an involvement with a widower twenty-two years her senior, to that first significant visit to Balmoral. We glimpse the first press leak that she and Prince Andrew are in love. Then, on 23 July 1986, she is pictured right after the wedding ceremony, walking back up the aisle on the arm of Prince Andrew as he utters a single word: 'Gotcha!'

Now that's fame.

Even so, as everyone knows, Fergie is small potatoes. The big drawing card is Princess Diana, who, since her marriage to Prince Charles when she was only nineteen, has gained an international celebrity that can be overshadowed only by the Queen herself.

Says Harry Arnold, who for fifteen years was the best known royal correspondent in England, 'She felt like a second wife to me. I could look at her face and know she was in a mood, and

I'd think, "Oh I'd better be careful today." She had a way of giving you a look, and you knew it would be hell. She used to arrive late, and you'd be waiting an hour. She knew you had been waiting and she knew your feet were frozen. And my friend and I would point to our watches, and she would give this sort of flouncing look.

'Or perhaps she'd wake up in a good mood. Then she was great fun to be with, for everyone around her. I don't think there is a man who reported her or, especially, took photographs of her who wasn't a little bit in love with her. And I was a little. She had a way, in my view, of taking scalps. She used to collect men, not in the lecherous way, but in the old-fashioned, romantic way. She would give you a look with lowered eyes, and she'd make you glow. She'd catch your eye and hold it. And she made you feel as if she was making eyes at you.

'You felt for a moment as if you were imagining something. You knew deep down it was a game she played, and a very clever one in a way, not cynical, but by doing this, she won everybody over.

'It would be difficult to be unkind to her. You would think to yourself, if she gave you that look, "What have I done to upset her? What have I written?" Sometimes you'd think, "Oh, the hell with her, I'm gonna write it anyway!" She never had total control, but she used to manipulate us. It's been going on since the Garden of Eden.'

Arnold, along with his sidekick, photographer Arthur Edwards, was selected by Larry Lamb to become the *Sun*'s first permanent 'Royal Team' whose job it would be to 'watch and study the day-to-day movements of the Prince and maintain a continuity which would one day be an important factor.'

Arnold says he and Edwards invented the modern concept of royal correspondents. Before them, 'You had rather aged, serious journalists following King George and the former Prince of Wales, and then the Queen, but nobody did human interest stories about the courtships of the Royal Family and about what they liked to eat, drink, where they liked to go, whether they loved each other, whether they were pregnant and when they were going to get pregnant. When I was made a royal correspondent on the *Sun*, that's what we started. When it is said we are masters of trivia, we are not. Some of our pursuits were trivial, some not.'

When the *Daily Star* decided to give the *Sun* a run for its money, James Whitaker took over as that paper's royal correspondent. Like Arnold, he too became famous as a result of his high profile job, and the rivalry between the pair became the stuff of Fleet Street legend. Perhaps the most infamous was the competition between the two men that ended with the publication of the photographs of Princess Di in a bikini after she had become pregnant for the first time. For Arnold and Whitaker, the barrage of criticism that fell down upon their heads as a result made them virtual pariahs for a time, and they and their imitators were branded 'the ratpack' or, as the satirical magazine *Private Eye* calls them, 'the reptiles'. Neither believes that Princess Di was as angry over the bikini story as the official statement issued from Buckingham Palace indicated. 'She and Charles were in fact asleep when it had been said by the Palace she was furious. She's not as fuddy-duddy as the Palace would have you believe,' says Arnold.

For Whitaker, who dwells on pageantry and whose reporting style is largely ritualistic, royal reporting offered the prospect of a very pleasant style of life. Whitaker is a portly man, whose taste in clothes is impeccable and who is sometimes accused of having taken on a royal aura of his own. He himself admits that after he was sent to cover a polo match where Prince Charles was playing, he was invited into the sponsor's tent, and while partaking of champagne and smoked salmon, thought to himself, 'It's a good way to do reporting.'

Before Arnold left the *Sun* to become the Chief Reporter at the *Daily Mirror*, he shadowed Princess Diana and Prince Charles around the world, getting some of the biggest royal scoops of the last decade. Arnold's methods lean more toward the 'deep-throat' approach of the investigative reporter. Occasionally, he admits, the stories he picked up emanated from disgruntled servants who were expressing hostility. But in most cases, he simply forged a good relationship with a source, and they became friends. In 70 per cent of the cases, he says, no money changed hands.

'My best informant stood on the balcony on Prince Charles's wedding day. And from what I was told, I wrote the story that Charles asked the Queen's permission before he kissed Di. Di said, "Give me a kiss," and he said, "I'm not getting into that caper." Then he turned to the Queen, and asked her, and she said yes. But my man heard it, and I reported it. It caused a lot of furore, but a few days later, the story was confirmed by a deaf-and-dumb reader watching the video. It didn't cost a penny.'

Before the antics of Arnold and Whitaker, journalists covering the Royals were treated very much as part of the royal entourage. Says Joyce Hopkirk, who early in her career was attached to the Palace, 'In those days we weren't ratpackers. We were honoured guests of the palace . . . because we didn't write the same material. We never made things up – any crumbs we got were real crumbs. My most exciting story was that Princess Alexandra wore a hairpiece and that was, "Oh, God, Shock! Horror!" I wondered whether she would talk to me the next morning after it was printed. It now seems so *ridiculous*. Princess Alexandra and I used to, um, compare bunions. But it did make you feel sort of uncomfortable, because you were not a journalist then. You felt you were just one of the courtiers.'

Nowadays, Princess Diana is the closest thing to a 'circulation goddess' the national tabloids have, and no matter how many times her face appears on their covers, she still has the power to boost circulation. In her case, or indeed, with any of the better known members of the Royal Family, any hint of scandal is exaggerated to the breaking point, not only because of their enduring fame but also because of the unwritten rule that Royals do not sue. And except in two cases, this precept has held true.

The first exception, surprisingly enough, originated with the Queen herself over a photograph stolen from the Palace and published in the *Sun* in October 1988. It pictured the Queen, the Queen Mother and Fergie holding newborn Beatrice in a casual photograph the Queen had planned to use for her personal Christmas cards. When she authorized her solicitors to take action against the newspaper for breach of copyright, the *Sun* published an apology and agreed to pay £100,000 to four charities. The second exception to the rule occurred when the son of Princess Margaret, Viscount Linley, sued *Today* over their allegation that he behaved like a lager lout in a local pub. The Viscount won his case, but voluntarily returned the damages he had been awarded.

Aside from these two isolated incidents, it always has been more or less open season on the Royal Family, with little or no danger of serious recriminations in return. The tabloids have always taken snipes at Prince Charles, whose love for the environment, hatred of unsightly architecture, vegetarian diet and genuine concern for English society have made him an unusually good target. Says one royal reporter, 'One of the cruellest headlines was "A-LOON AGAIN".' He remembers how much criticism Edward VIII received for being a playboy. 'He literally neglected his duties. So it wouldn't be out of line for someone to have said, "Why doesn't he go see how people really live by going to some isolated place and living like an ordinary person for a while?" And that's precisely what Charles did. He went out to the Outer Hebrides and lived among ordinary people. And when he did, the headline was "A-LOON AGAIN". He can't win, he really can't win.'

A typical Royal run-around occurred when Prince Edward was reported by one tabloid to have formed a 'touching' friendship with Michael Ball, the star of Andrew Lloyd Webber's *Aspects of Love* in New York. In an unprecedented personal statement to the *Daily Mirror*, Prince Edward angrily denied the implication that he was homosexual, leading to the newspaper's front-page headline, 'I'M NOT GAY'.

A maelstrom of stories followed as the popular press debated the propriety of Edward's public denial. Since its rival the *Mirror* broke the story, the *Sun* took the moral high ground, pointing to the harm done by reports such as the one that appeared in the *Mirror* – a profoundly uncomfortable position for a newspaper whose Royal 'twists' are legend.

But the most outstanding example of bad taste appeared the Sunday after the story broke in the *News of the World*. In proof of the Prince's manly charms, the paper published on its front page a model's account of a near sexual liaison between herself and Edward. The title: 'The Night Prince Eddie was READY: He Tried to Get into My Beddie'.

Fame, who needs it?

6
HOLLYWOOD

5 March 1982. Comedian John Belushi, 33, is found dead in a bungalow of the Chateau Marmont Hotel on Sunset Strip. Cause of death is cited as 'acute cocaine and heroin intoxication'. The final injection of drugs takes place somewhere in the vicinity of 3.30 a.m. Cathy Evelyn Smith, 38, a Canadian, who is with Belushi at the time of his death, is questioned by police and released. Smith returns to her native Toronto.

14 February 1985. Cathy Evelyn Smith, extradited from Canada after lengthy negotiations, is charged in Los Angeles with murder and drug violations in the death of comedian John Belushi. Pleading not guilty, Smith rejects a plea bargain offer and vows to fight charges against her.

8 May 1985. Tony Brenna, Senior West Coast Writer for the *National Enquirer*, faces possible contempt charges when he refuses to testify at a preliminary hearing on the death of comedian John Belushi. Brenna invokes the First Amendment when asked about an interview conducted with Smith in Toronto which formed the basis for a 29 June 1982 article appearing in the *Enquirer*, entitled 'I Killed John Belushi'. According to Deputy District Attorney Michael Montagna, the article was 'the catalyst for reopening the investigation into Belushi's death.'

9 July 1985. The Second US District Court of Appeals rules that *National Enquirer* reporter Tony Brenna should not have been held in contempt when he refused during a preliminary hearing last month to answer questions about an interview with Smith.

10 June 1986. Cathy Evelyn Smith pleads guilty to involuntary manslaughter and three lesser charges in the drug-overdose death of comedian John Belushi.

*

There was the incentive, of course, of the $20,000; that's the amount the *National Enquirer* was offering Cathy Evelyn Smith for her firsthand account of the death of John Belushi. She had been living hand-to-mouth in Toronto after giving police in Los Angeles the slip – even though they had found a hypodermic syringe in her handbag after Belushi's death. What Smith didn't know was that Tony Brenna, one of the two reporters who had tracked her to her hiding place in Canada, had special instructions. 'The office wanted a headline,' says Brenna, 'which was basically "I Killed John Belushi", and they told us there would be no story unless they actually had her saying on tape "I killed John Belushi."'

By all accounts, Smith is an intelligent and canny woman, and Brenna found the only way to deal with her was 'to party with her'. So they partied, doing all the things Smith liked – marijuana, alcohol, a few exotic substances. She had a thing about brandy: 'We did lots of brandy with her, and booze, we had a bar bill of about $4,000 for three of us for two weeks.'

The whole time, they were taping. 'And she wouldn't say it because she knew it could lead to possible legal proceedings. Finally, one evening, after hours and hours of taping, I said to her, "Look, you really are responsible for his death," and she said, "Well, if you want me to say I killed the fucking guy, I will. I killed the fucking guy." And I said, "That's what I want you to say, and it's the truth, isn't it?" and she said it was.

'And we had assured her that she was up in Canada, and the US authorities would not be interested, and we went with the story, *bang*, on Page One, and then the establishment press in the US started to pick it up and quote it, particularly the old *Herald Examiner* in Los Angeles. It became a *cause célèbre*. The police were called in and asked why they'd let this woman go. Lengthy extradition proceedings started, and eventually, we were called in front of the Grand Jury, and suddenly we were on trial too.'

What the court wanted to question were the methods used to obtain the story, and Brenna 'had to dodge very tricky questions from the District Attorney about whether we were all on drugs and drunk. At one stage I was sentenced to thirty days in prison for not revealing aspects of the way the information was obtained.'

Meanwhile, the establishment press, who had vociferously decried Brenna's methods, nevertheless jumped on the bandwagon, running stories of their own on what had happened the night of Belushi's death. Smith was finally sentenced to two and a half years in prison on reduced charges, and Brenna won the J. Edgar

112

Hoover Award for Reporting – 'the only award I've ever won in my entire life.'

Says Brenna, 'Then Bob Woodward came into the story with the full cooperation of the Belushi family and skimmed off all the cream.' In the long run, however, they didn't like what he wrote. There was a film script, which at first everyone wanted, then suddenly nobody wanted, because by now, a Hollywood conspiracy had swung into full operation to suppress the story. According to Brenna, it's part of a systematic attempt 'to suppress everything that is not favourable to celebrities and the money-making machine out here.'

Brenna believes that one of the positive aspects of the *National Enquirer* and the popular press in Britain and abroad, most of whom, at one time or another, Brenna has reported for, is that at their best they examine the underbelly of corruption that informs the lives of Hollywood's celebrities, even if the stories do undergo a form of sanitizing. Otherwise, the whole process would be nothing more than a kind of crazy 'adulation of idols'.

'What celebrities do is not printable. They are the unhappiest people I've ever met. Power corrupts, and most of these people would kill to keep what they've got. Most of them are spoiled, insecure alcoholics or drug addicts. Most of them are also of questionable sexual preference as well. The number of people who are gay or bisexual in Hollywood would be amazing to the average member of the public. They hide all this. There's just as much a gay casting couch in Hollywood now for men as there is for women; maybe there's some justice to that.

'The bottom line is that cheque-book journalism has become a way of life. People in the public eye are very sophisticated now to the fact that they can get large sums of money from books, television, tabloids. So celebrities won't talk to anyone. It is not now possible to do any celebrity stuff that is up front unless you want to kiss the butt of the big PR outfits. All celebrity journalism is now manipulation. It used to be the studios manipulating. Now it's high power publicists. In the show business world, it's packaging human beings into products and manipulating them often far beyond their talents and manipulating the press and everyone around them in order to sell these products.

'Take Frank. He's a bastard. I mean the stuff that hasn't been published about him is much better than anything you could imagine . . . Oh, he's a shit.'

Brenna took particular pleasure in gatecrashing Sinatra's sixty-fourth birthday party. Security was tight, with public relations people swarming all over the premises. Brenna nevertheless made his way in, then walked around holding 'a silver tray and six glasses and bottles of champagne and started serving his guests'. He then ditched the props and took 'a ringside seat for the whole thing'. At the end of the evening, when all the television cameras were on Sinatra, Brenna 'jumped right in front of him holding up the microphone of my tape recorder and said, "Tony Brenna of the *National Enquirer*. A few words?"'

To Brenna's way of thinking, the diplomatic world – Brenna covered the United Nations for both the *Daily Telegraph* and BBC radio – had much in common with the show business industry. For the reporter, the whole goal is to come up with 'the racy political diplomatic story', just as in Hollywood the goal is to find 'the racy, sensational show business story'. There is no question in Brenna's mind that the same degree of hypocrisy exists among the diplomats as the entertainers. 'Everybody was out for themselves, out to exploit, out to gain as much attention and publicity as they could for their particular cause – whether it be political or nationalistic . . . We were subjected all the time to this pre-presentation of news, this pre-packaging of news, the way they wanted it done.' Says Brenna, if you want to get good stories, you have to break out of the establishment mould and 'tell the stories they don't want told.'

Even in the establishment press, stories about sex scandals and spying do better than stories about genuine struggles for independence by oppressed peoples. And even for a newspaper with as secure a reputation as the *Daily Telegraph*, it was necessary to angle the story. 'If you sent a story saying they were renewing the mandate for Cyprus, it would create boredom at the *Telegraph* offices. But if you said, "Cyprus is a ticking time bomb", then you would automatically give them something they could hang a headline on and would use.'

Then, too, there was the interminable boredom of covering Security Council meetings or the General Assembly, 'writing yards of material about rhetoric, none of which ever happened in the real world.'

Some twenty-four years ago, Brenna was among the first to write about Rachel Carson and the dangers of DDT. He broke the story about CFCs in the ionosphere, and with both of these stories, he found it hard going to get his newspaper editor interested at all. Says Brenna, 'I've done everything from drug busts to murder, to medicine, from human interest to political science, from diplomacy to technical trade journalism, and I've been struck by the hypocrisy

I've experienced – in advertising, working to sell people paranoia about their personal appearance, about their own bodies, in order to make them buy products, in order to make the manufacturer rich; in the political and diplomatic world where diplomats are seeking to support only their own causes, their own ideas and to forward their own interests in terms of territorial ambitions – and it all comes down to money.'

His decision to go into celebrity reporting stemmed from a sense of disillusionment with straight reporting. It was just about the time when videotape was making possible the export of American television shows, just at the transition point from international film celebrity to the more short-lived but intensive television celebrity. Along with that came the opportunity for Brenna to move around the world practically on whim.

Among the celebrities Brenna liked personally was the late Richard Burton, and he has a measure of affection for Liz Taylor as well, as do a number of celebrity reporters. When the couple divorced the first time in 1974, England alone sent over thirty reporters, photographers, editors and freelance correspondents some 70,000 miles in fifty-six days to bring back the story of the breakup. When they remarried in 1975, the scoop was Tony Brenna's.

When Brenna got the tip-off, a short time before the world press, he flew immediately to Geneva, worming his way into the confidence of Taylor's lawyers in Switzerland, by being charming, by taking them out to dinner and by promising them good copy. 'I finally found out the couple were taking a flight from Geneva to Tel Aviv, and the press were trying to find out which flight they were on.' Brenna meanwhile called the airline and found out there were only seven vacant seats in first class, 'and I bought all of them'. All the other reporters ended up in economy.

'The plane went from Zurich to Geneva, and Taylor and Burton didn't get on board. I was sweating like hell, didn't know how I would justify buying the seats to the office. In Zurich, I got off and called another reporter and he told me to get back on the plane, they had got a helicopter and were joining the plane almost immediately.'

The pair arrived shortly thereafter, got onto the plane, entered first class and saw Brenna sitting across from them. At the time, Burton was on the wagon, says Brenna, and he knew the only way he could catch his attention was by drinking a lot.

'So,' says Brenna, 'I sit there swigging champagne cocktails. He's watching me, and his tongue is hanging out, and I'm sitting

115

there ordering one champagne cocktail after another, and he's there watching me like a hypnotized rabbit. So when I've had a few drinks and we're about an hour into the flight, I get up and walk across the cabin, I say to them, "Good morning, Mr Burton, Miss Taylor. My name is Tony Brenna, and I'm from the *National Enquirer*, and there's an easy way and a hard way to do this. All I want is a brief interview with you. I want to congratulate you on the fact you're getting back together again . . ." and at this point Liz becomes furious and tells me to go to hell. I refuse to go back to my seat and she sends one of her secretaries up to get the pilot, to ask me to return to my seat.

'At the same time, she goes forward to the cabin, talking to the pilots and what-have-you, and I return to my seat and turn to Burton and say, "Well, you really are a son of a bitch. You're an Englishman as well as I am. I'm just doing my bloody job. I've got the enterprise to get on this bloody plane, I've got seven first-class seats here, I shall be in deep shit if you don't give me at least a few words." He starts to laugh. In the end he moves over to me on the other side of the cabin, and I start pouring champagne cocktails into him, and he's supposed to be on the wagon. She comes back and finds Richard Burton getting pissed with the *National Enquirer*, so she starts screaming at him. She drags him back to his seat. He pops over again to see me, to have another couple of drinks, and we get drunk together, and she's sitting in furious silence across the other side of the cabin with her hairdressers and her secretaries, and the plane touches down in Tel Aviv, and Burton and I are pretty loaded, and she is so angry about what's gone on that she cancels the press conference at Tel Aviv. So I now have a totally exclusive story, which is what the office wanted.'

It was Brenna who arranged Peter Lawford's marriage to Patricia Seaton-Lawford. He ended up being his best man. The way he got to know Lawford was that he had heard all the sensational stories about him, and he just phoned him up.

'He picked up the phone when I called him, and I said, "Peter, is it true you're back on drugs and booze?" and he said, "Who are you?" and I said "Tony Brenna", and he said, "Well, do you know how to spell fuck off?" and I said, "Well, it was F-U-C-K-O-F-F the last time I spelled it," so he said "At least you can spell, which is better than some of your colleagues." I said, "Well, you really are a drunken old reprobate, but let's face it, you do make great copy. Personally, I don't give a shit if you kill yourself or drink yourself into the grave. I'm not fucking interested in you, it's

116

these arseholes who want me to write about you." So he started laughing and said, "Well, you'd better come round."

'So I was supporting him for the last two years of his life by his spilling his guts about all the horrible things that were happening to him. He was going into drug rehab, every time he went in, I paid him £1,000 for his story. Then, I got all sorts of stuff on the Kennedy family through Lawford. And finally my big *coup* with Peter Lawford was I got him married. His girlfriend had been living with him since she was seventeen. I said to her, "Look, he's going to die. You two should get married so that you've got some status when he dies." So I arranged the wedding, got the judge to the hospital. "We'll get you married. We'll have a picture of Peter with an IV in his arm, staggering out of bed," because I thought this was the ultimate exploitation of the Peter Lawford relationship. He didn't mind. He didn't mind anything, he was a prick. Wouldn't in the end do the picture at the bedside but *would* get married.

'I did genuinely like Peter. After his death it was my idea, because Kennedy's family wouldn't bloody pay for his last resting place, so I had him disinterred, and then that was another exclusive story, and then we took his ashes to sea on a yacht, with fucking helicopters above us, I mean, its bizarre. I used Peter Lawford as a product, as a friend when he was dying, after he was dead, and I'm still getting stories out of his widow. And that's how cynical you can get. But, on the other hand, Peter Lawford was just as cynical too. He was using me to get money for drugs and booze, and he had lived in that sort of society all his life, where everybody was using everybody else. It was almost like a symbiotic relationship.'

It is early October 1985, and the world press has gathered in front of the house of Rock Hudson, who has died of AIDS. There are at least twenty TV crews present and thirty photographers. They are not shooting anything because there is nothing to shoot – only an ancient van with peeling paint sitting in the driveway. This is the vehicle that will convey Hudson's body from the house to the funeral home. Time passes slowly; nothing is happening.

At last, attendants inside the house carry Hudson's body bag to the van and put it on the floor, closing the back doors to the van. The van slowly pulls out of the driveway, to the gates where the world press is assembled. Suddenly, a tall, solid man with curly black hair leaps away from the group of newsmen and hurls his body across the front of the van, steadies himself and then shoots through the windshield, over the heads of the driver and his

117

assistant. He gets the only photograph of Hudson's body bag, 'strapped down to a gurney in the back of the van.'

Phil Ramey, the incorrigible paparazzo known throughout the media world for sheer guts and invincible chutzpah, comes under heavy criticism from the press, who have – despite their revulsion – taped Ramey's actions, rushing the footage back to their studios where it appears on innumerable television news shows world-wide that evening.

'I got such shit for that, you wouldn't believe,' says Ramey, 'just because I wanted Rock Hudson in his body bag. The regular news media, their spokesmen were coming up to me, saying, "You embarrassed us all by doing that." But,' says Ramey, 'I got the picture, and I made a lot of money. And I just said, "You're all fucking jealous because you didn't have the balls to do it." There were editorials about me on TV . . . It doesn't bother me at all.

'If they had stopped the van and opened the van up, not one of the crews wouldn't have taken that picture, and I was just doing what I had to do. If I'm not given the opportunity, I just take the opportunity. FUCK 'EM. Yes, I do say Fuck 'em. Some people like me, some don't. A lot of people help me. Listen, I get so tired of these celebrities complaining. If I was making some of the money that these celebrities are making, they could take my picture every day of the week. You know, they spend most of their life trying to get into this business, and then when they get in, they come up with all this bullshit attitude. I don't know where it comes from. The public and the photographs have made the celebrities, and all of a sudden they run and hide and act like immature three-year-olds, along with all their attendant arse-kissing publicists who know nothing about publicity. It's just absurd. They're not all like that but a great many of them are, especially the TV ones.

'It's a self-serving, egocentric business, that's what it is. To be a success in this business you have to have good health and a short memory, or the ability to take non-serious things seriously . . . It's hard to say.'

Ramey became interested in photography as a child when a cousin of his, a Second World War bomber pilot, came back from the war and took up the hobby. He would take the young Ramey around to all of the Lebanese weddings in the community, huge family affairs, and Ramey would hold his equipment while his cousin took the snaps. They used an old-fashioned 35 millimetre camera, using the speed graphics, 'which means you would shoot one picture and take this dark slide out, and put in another.'

Ramey's cousin would take something like twenty photographs, and Ramey would carry the 4 × 5 inch negatives around in a box 'that was maybe three feet long, that held all the negatives and the film.' In another bag, Ramey carried the flashbulbs. Afterwards, the pair of them would go into the darkroom, 'which was a little toilet at the back of my uncle's grocery store, and develop the pictures. In those days you'd have to put a new flash bulb in after every picture. Everything was taken with a flash bulb. Sometimes they wouldn't just go off, but they'd explode, scattering glass everywhere. Gets 'em real worried! We used to think that the guys at the factory would intentionally overload the flashbulbs so they'd fuck up like that. We could never figure a reason why it happened.'

Ramey's education was bilingual. He went to a French and American school, where half of the lessons were in French, half in English. His father spoke French and Arabic, his mother Italian, English and Arabic. Later on, when he was stationed in South-East Asia 'in the employ of her majesty', as he puts it, he picked up a number of Far Eastern languages and today speaks several fluently. Although he was 'technically never in Vietnam', Ramey counts himself 'a full victim of the sixties'. Among the countless jobs he held during the decade was a short stint as a major league baseball licensee, in partnership with another person. At one time, he owned a T-shirt manufacturing company. He'll tell you that on occasion he moved marijuana from coast to coast: 'Is the Statute of Limitations over yet?' He actually started shooting pictures seriously on the West Coast when he used to hang out with the Hells Angels Biker Band. Then, when he was in his late twenties, he went on tour with the Doobey Brothers just about the time they were beginning to make it big.

A dozen years ago, he began shooting celebrities seriously. The scenario for Ramey's early days in the business: thirty or so people, the so-called 'scumerazzi' of Hollywood, standing in front of the same restaurant waiting for a glimpse of somebody famous so they can take their picture; then all of them trying to sell it to the same place. 'And none of them making any fucking money. I didn't make any money,' says Ramey. Then he got smart, began going after the pictures that nobody else would do, the ones everybody wanted. These were the pictures that take time – 'hours and days and weeks of stakeouts'.

'You sit there,' says Ramey, 'and wait for the person to be where you think they'll be; eat when you're hungry. You're in a car, in the bushes, hidden. You don't get pictures by standing

119

outside somebody's house like a moron. Depending what activity there is, you might be there ten, twelve, fourteen hours a day; sometimes you're there all night. Because the real key to getting the picture is the information as to the whereabouts of the people you want to photograph. The real key is information.

'And you get that through contacts, pay-off, schmoozing people, arse-kissing – I've never been much good at that but some people are. A lot of the time people just tell you stuff. You go and talk to the neighbours . . . they just say it, volunteer the information.'

Ramey syndicates his pictures himself, selling them directly to media outlets across the world. His biggest market is Europe. Says Ramey, 'I'm still to this day one of the few, if only, Americans ever hired by English publications. They hire Brits who live here, they don't hire Americans. I get hired because I embarrass the fuck out of all the Brits who work here by getting the pictures that they didn't get. And the newspapers had to come to me.

'Who do I sell to? It's more like, who *don't* I sell to – *Gourmet Magazine*?' In the last year alone, 800 of Ramey's pictures were published. When Ramey started in the business, everybody wanted photographs of the *Dynasty* and *Dallas* stars; for a while everything was Madonna and Warren Beatty, then Marlon Brando and his new baby.

'There's no limit on the amount of money you can get for a picture. It depends what you've got and who wants to buy it. You have to deal with specifics. The Madonna wedding pictures – which I shot from a helicopter, and I got the second best stuff of the Madonna wedding to Sean Penn in Malibu – made low five figures, worldwide sales. The MacEnroe baby pictures, the official set-up with John MacEnroe and Tatum O'Neal and their first baby: those were worth low six figures. Elizabeth Taylor going round the world, worth middle five figures. I chased her all the way to Hong Kong, all around Japan. She hated us.'

Ramey got one of the rare photographs of Warren Beatty and Madonna out on the town which was published in Rupert Murdoch's *Sun* in London, a picture in which it appears that the two stars are waving at Ramey. 'They weren't waving at me . . . They were throwing their hands up in frantic anger. They were pissed off. That picture was shot in the dark, from 150 feet away. They didn't even know I was there until the first flash action hit them. They accused the restaurant owner of calling me, which he didn't. We ended up following them in a helicopter to find out where they went. I had somebody at the house waiting to follow them, but they were so hard to follow down this canyon road that

I was in this helicopter for about three hours. We knew they were going out, and they lost this guy on the canyon road. I followed in the helicopter, figured out where they went, landed on a building about ten blocks away, called the guy on the carphone who was following them on the ground, got him to come and pick me up. Then we waited across the street from this restaurant in the dark. They came out about one in the morning, and we got 'em.'

The major markets for pictures like these are in Europe, France, Spain, West Germany, the Netherlands and Switzerland. London is a world centre. Says Ramey, 'There's no money to be made in South America because the currency is too weak. You might make a $1,000 or $2,000 a year.

'When you're selling, you gotta get the money up front because they just steal it. If they do, there's lots you can do about it. You can go after them. Generally, I find that I have such a bad reputation that people don't try and steal my stuff and if they do I go right after them.

'I had a West German magazine steal something out of a London newspaper and run it. And they have an office here, and I went right after them locally. And they paid up in a couple of days, plus the damages, plus the sales. But you've got to go right after them. You can't let it slide. You get their photo editor's home phone number, and you ring him up at four o'clock every morning for a week. You harass the guy here, and you slap writs on him. You have somebody call up his office three hundred times a day and tie up his phone lines, really fuck with him. Call 'em at three in the morning. If they change their number, get the new number, keep calling them . . . Oh yeah, send messengers by at three in the morning to bang on their door, deliver them warnings. Find out their bank account number and have it attached.'

A photograph can be delivered to practically any market in the world within an hour. Hypothetically, you could shoot a picture at a location in Los Angeles, drive to the lab, take fifteen minutes to process the film, ten to make a print, and seven minutes later, it can be anywhere. The print is put on the drum of a wire photo machine, or in a special transmitter which hooks up to a satellite link. Depending upon the client, you can send it by phone line or satellite.

Photo editors have within the business the reputation for either being unavailable to talk to you, or they put you on hold. 'They don't put me on hold,' says Ramey. 'I would hang up. No one ever puts me on hold any more. Even to this day, if they put me on hold, I wait thirty seconds, no more. I could be in Hong Kong,

I could be in Cambodia, I could be on an island where you don't get another phone connection for six hours, and they know it . . . and I'll put the phone down.

'There isn't a photo editor in the world who wouldn't buy a $5,000 picture for fifty bucks if he could get away with it. They're all fucking whores. Quote me on that.'

Early in his career, Ramey managed to get exclusive access to a big rock and roll band, his first important shoot. He shot about fifty rolls and, since he was a beginner, made contact sheets. Some were acceptable, but most of them had something wrong with them. Ramey couldn't tell what. So he went to an experienced photographer, a friend of his, who took a look at the contacts, then discouraged him from staying in the profession. Ramey says he was so depressed, 'I didn't think I could ever shoot anything again.' So he just withdrew, doing nothing for about two months. Then, by accident, he ran into a girl who was in photography school, and she took a look at the contacts. The problem was a simple one, something elemental, 'and it was so fucking easy to fix, but because I hadn't been educated I wasn't aware. She solved the problem in ten seconds.' He found out later that the professional photographer he went to had been angry he hadn't got the shoot himself. 'And I learned a very important lesson, that when people do that, it's just another technique, like kicking somebody in the head, undermining their confidence, it's another negotiating technique, that's all it is. And never take it seriously, no matter what you think, no matter how much you like the person. There's always that competitive jealous streak that lets them do that to you.'

The competition among the paparazzi is cut-throat. It's common practice for them to change one another's hotel reservations, cancel their plane reservations. 'They'll have your film taken off the plane, use your name, they'll do anything. They're just scumbags.'

The biggest money Ramey ever made out of the London market was 'when Ryan O'Neal beat up his kid and knocked out his front tooth. Ryan O'Neal and his daughter Tatum, had Griffin, the son, under house arrest. And I knew where the kid was, and I waited twelve to fourteen days. Well, Ryan went to the store to get a paper and Tatum went into the shower. She came out of the second floor of the building in a bathrobe, her hair wet, and she's looking around like, desperately. I'm parked across the street on a busy highway. All of a sudden, I see Griffin O'Neal come running out of the house and then trying to thumb down cars to get out of there. I do a U-turn. "Come on, get in." He says, "You gotta get me away from here," and he tells me the whole story. I convinced him to let me photograph him.

'Everybody was trying to get this guy from a block away, and so was I, and so I only had this monster lens, and the shot of him was all out of focus eventually, because he posed, but I convinced him to let me do it, drove him to his girlfriend's house. And I got a set-up, which was unheard of. You know when you have a scandal, when somebody beats up their kid, they don't just let you shoot pictures of them, that's unheard of. And with a big tooth missing, smiling. But I had the story, I had the words, saying, "Look what my father did to me." And I had it, nobody could get it. London was REAL hot for it.

'When I got the picture, I was totally ruthless with it. I agreed to sell it to one paper for £5,000, then called the next person and said, "Well, they'll give me £5,000." "Well, we'll give you £6,000." I said, "I want £10,000." I ended up refusing them, the first paper, even though I'd made an agreement for £5,000. I said, "No, fuck you, I'm not selling it to you now." And the photo editor, four weeks later, he had a heart attack. That picture was big, he was under a lot of stress, and he actually had a heart attack. Ramey gave him a heart attack. He had to leave the business, and they all blamed me. So anyway I ended up selling it to the other paper for £8,000. The pound was trading at about $2.65 and I insisted on being paid straightaway, not in thirty days, so they loved that.

'The only by-line I want is on a cheque. My by-lines are all on cheques; that's where I like 'em.'

The whole time Ramey is talking, he is gesticulating wildly, moving around. He's abrasive and pushy, the born exhibitionist. His swarthy complexion, the dark circles under his eyes, the small gold hoop he wears in his ear, the sense of menace he conveys; all these things combine to give the impression of a modern-day pirate. It's only with the greatest reluctance that he will admit he is a history buff, with a Master's in eighteenth-century literature, who collects stamps as a hobby. Without thinking, he can suddenly turn into a shy teddy bear of a man who listens well and who laughs easily, at little things. He has to watch himself, because if you catch him off-guard, he might seem too generous, too soft, too nice a guy. And as everybody in this business knows, nice guys finish last.

Whizzing along Sunset Boulevard on a sunny afternoon, you are invariably struck by the lush, green gardens surrounding the mansions of Hollywood's wealthiest, impressive edifices set well back from the street and protected by high walls and electronically controlled metal gates. Drive a little further, and you'll hit the fashionable pavement cafés, where the Beautiful People sit comfortably under awnings that protect them from the noon-day heat, chatting, drinking and eating; everyone slender, beautifully groomed and dressed in eerily chic designer clothes. It all looks, well, like a film set, and these are the extras. The stars themselves have disappeared into the shadowy interior of Le Dome, one of the favourite luncheon spots of those who have made it and those who are on the make.

Inside, the slick, green walls take on the effect of jade, and the pink art deco light fixtures cast a soft hue over the patrons, many of whom no doubt welcome the effects of subdued lighting on their fast-fading good looks. In the loos, a special hygienic toilet seat, covered in opaque mobile plastic, spins rapidly around at the touch of a button.

It's an unlikely place, you think, to find two young reporters from London's *Daily Star*, but there they are, chatting, drinking and eating with the best of them. John Mahoney has golden hair, wide blue eyes, and he is prone to blush in an old-fashioned manner, a tendency rendered more fetching by the brittle cynicism of the types who surround him. His partner, Chris Anderson, wears a bristlebrush moustache, wire-rimmed glasses shaped like teardrops. His thick brown hair has gone somewhat awry. The pair are easily the best looking men in the room, and certainly the most genuine. If you are going to trust anyone at all in this town, it will be them.

Both are only twenty-seven, born, incredibly, on the same day, and they seem too ingenuous for the job they've been assigned – foreign correspondents for a London tabloid. And yet, they haven't done too badly for themselves, despite a limited operating budget. They've been here less than a year, and they've already learned the ropes.

Says Mahoney, 'People won't do anything for nothing in this town. And we very rarely pay our sources. About all we do, we take them out for something to eat.'

His partner nods. 'To a large extent,' he says, 'it's a gamble, that you can spend two or three hours at a lunch or in the evening when you'd sooner see your wife – or John's engaged, be with his fiancée – and you can never turn a source down, and of course there may not be any return on the investment. But if you don't do it, you don't get the sources.'

Some sources do expect money, and if the story's good, they'll try to dig it up. Says Anderson, 'One doesn't enquire too closely, but it's fairly certain that they're selling exactly the same material to the *Enquirer* or the other tabloids, and probably have been for many years. And they're very much aware of how the system works, even to the extent they know how much to ask for stories. They'll pitch the price just right. It's a little high for us, but it's not out of the question, and then, they bargain.'

'I've had a couple of people actually draw up their own contracts,' says Mahoney. 'You know, I believe you, but will you sign this? When we first arrived in the US we got caught out and were sold a false story, but the guy who sold it will never get a penny out of London again.

'Over here,' he continues, 'aggression gets you nowhere. You have to be cool and calm and keep your head, especially in potentially awkward situations like that one.' Anderson agrees that 'if you hammer on the door, you wouldn't get the story. We sometimes have to show more initiative and more enterprise.'

Because they are writing for a London tabloid, Anderson and Mahoney are on the lookout for the specialized story, tailored to their market. One topic that's always big in London is the soaps, and Chris Quentin, former hunk-in-residence on ITV's *Coronation Street*, fits the bill. Quentin quit the popular show, went out to Hollywood and married Leeza Gibbons, who hosts America's *Entertainment This Week* at a yearly salary well over the £1 million mark. Anderson and Mahoney found they couldn't get near either of them for an interview. So they hired an American freelance. They briefed him, gave him a list of questions and he set up an interview with Gibbons. Gibbons is especially interested in interior design, and the thrust of the freelancer's story was architecture and home decoration. From the tape the freelancer delivered, Mahoney and Anderson found out that Quentin couldn't get work in Hollywood and the fact was beginning to be a source of friction between the pair. It was a definite scoop. The couple later separated, despite having a newborn baby, Quentin returning to England.

Another early victory was the much publicized Madonna-Sean Penn divorce. Says Mahoney, 'We broke that story in London. One of the first things we did, it involved going to the theatre where Sean Penn was performing just off Sunset, in Westwood. We'd only been in town four weeks, we had limited sources, we were still wining and dining people. We were beginning to think it wasn't going to pay off, and then we got a call from someone we had taken to dinner, saying "Is Madonna a name for you?" Of course she's a name for anyone. Eventually, we got the court records and proved it. It was a good story. We worked late on that one. By the time we'd written the copy and faxed it, it was about midnight.

'Another example of a good source for us, Michael Jackson . . . No one can ever get near Michael Jackson. He talks to nobody. I don't think he CAN talk. We got a Michael Jackson story a few weeks ago, which at first we didn't believe, that his pet chimp Bubbles had been run over and killed in an accident. We could have written it without checking it, like a few of our colleagues have done a few times over here, but instead, we spent a couple of days on it. We got hold of one of Jackson's employees, took him out for a meal, and he told us a load of stuff that was true, and told us about this bizarre funeral gathering in Michael's grand home.'

As far as celebrities go, both Anderson and Mahoney agree you could write a thousand stories that were strictly false, but not actionable and get them by. Says Anderson, 'I could sit down now and write a story about Madonna, totally fictitious, and it wouldn't be actioned, other than probably a rather stern complaint from Madonna that I hadn't spoken to her. I could write on how she was "kind to animals" and even though it's utterly fabricated, it's not punishable by law because you're not accusing her of anything.'

When Mahoney was eighteen, he did fabricate a story, one he still remembers. He was working shifts, on nights, and one of his jobs was to write a picture caption, just six or seven paragraphs about Cliff Richard, who was performing at the Maidenhead Arena. He was told the photographs were coming later. So at about ten o'clock, when he was eager to finish up and get out of there, he wrote a story about how the housewives threw their knickers at Richard on the stage and how the crowd went berserk as he launched into 'Devil Woman', which was a big hit at the time. 'I wrote all this,' Mahoney says, 'and put it in the tray. I came back the next night, and the chief reporter said to me, "Good show on the Cliff Richard story. There's just one thing – Cliff Richard was giving a Gospel reading last night, he was sitting on a stool reading the Bible." And I had housewives throwing their knickers at him.'

It was the most embarrassing kind of falsification, the one where you get caught. But Mahoney notes that in the London press every week, there are dozens of quotes from the stars that are pure fiction. 'These stories about Marlon Brando making comments to the press . . . Superstars don't speak to anyone,' says Mahoney. 'Marlon Brando isn't making comments to anybody.'

'It's very easy to write Michael Jackson has married a sheep, and they're going to have a ewe together, and live in a barn. That's great, but one day he's going to turn round and say he's had enough, and of course, if anybody on this planet has the millions to sue . . . Just one day, he's going to do it.'

Mahoney and Anderson get calls from the London office every Sunday morning, informing them what's in the *News of the World* and the *People* and 'Can you chase it up?' Quite often, they can't confirm the story. There is always the temptation simply to follow it, but they always check it out.

Says Anderson, 'Sometimes you can't check out a story, and it might be true, but you can't write it up. It can be frustrating.'

But that doesn't mean they don't push a story. Says Mahoney, 'We push a story as far as it will go. We don't just accept what we're given. We really do push every story to its limits.'

Anderson nods. 'We'll present it in its boldest, most dramatic way, in colourful language. Occasionally, you have to do or say something unpleasant, something that's necessary on the job . . . We got a tip that Jane Wyman, Ronald Reagan's ex-wife, and the star of *Falcon Crest*, had diabetes, and was going to have to have her leg amputated. I got her home telephone number and rang her. We chatted for a while, and I asked if she was getting involved in any new television shows. Then, after a couple of minutes, she suddenly asked how I had got her home number – they always do that after a couple of minutes – and what I wanted. I told her the truth, asked her if she was going to have her leg amputated. She started shouting. I said that it surely wasn't the worst thing someone could say about her, and surely it was better to get the facts straight by asking her. But she didn't seem to take this view!

'But what if I wrote that story up? The oldest trick in the book is of course, "Jane Wyman today denied rumours—"'

Mahoney: '—or refused to confirm that . . . Actually, what you could write it as, "Ronald Reagan's ex, Jane Wyman, furiously ducked questions last night that she would have her left leg chopped off. The angry ex-wife of the President snapped—"'

Anderson: '"It's my ex-husband who's the hop-a-long, not me!"'

Mahoney: '"Where did you get this story? Who told you this? Who are you?" Let the reader decide—'

Anderson: 'She did, however, confirm that she would not be attending her shooting schedule as originally planned.'

OK, they're young. But they've got the general idea.

Ageing actress
turns back on fans

On Monday, 18 June 1990, Joan Collins's press agents bar both the *Sun* and the *Daily Star* from the London press conference called to promote her first West End play for ten years – Noël Coward's *Private Lives*. Says her spokeswoman, 'We didn't invite the papers because they aren't really interested in theatre.'

The next morning, the *Sun* runs the story just beside their Page Three Girl. Says the headline, 'SNOBBY JOAN COLLINS BANS *SUN* READERS: *Show "too posh" for us*'.

The *Sun* points out that an independent survey shows 2.3 million of their readers go regularly to West End plays. 'We also have more art and classical music fans than any other daily paper.'

Over at the *Star*, the approach is less defensive. An unflattering photograph shows Collins's backside as she huffs past a *Star* photographer. The headline reads, '*Joan turns her back on loyal fans*'.

*AGEING actress Joan Collins turned her back on her fans yesterday. Joan, 58, banned the *Daily Star* and other popular newspapers from a photo call for her West End play *Private Lives* . . .

*Joan was upset by our report yesterday quoting her as saying that British people were lazy. She told the *Toronto Star*: 'Unfortunately, everyone in England thinks the state should do everything for them.' Later, she said she was misquoted.

*So what are Joan's claims to theatrical honours? Well, she starred in *Our Girl Friday, Empire of the Ants, The Stud, The Bitch, Dynasty* . . .

It's an easily forgotten but basic rule: Never cross the bastards.

PART
Three

Sex and Violence

7
LET FUCKING DOGS LIE

It is early on a mild November evening in 1984 when the call comes through to the 19th district on Chicago's West Side. A fifteen-year-old boy has been shot dead while he was standing on a stoop, waiting for a pizza. The reporter on duty drives over to the address. He has been a crime reporter for only a few weeks. He has never seen a body, never even attended a funeral. He arrives before the street is hosed down, and there is brain matter floating in coagulating blood near the gutter. He gets out of his car, walks over to the pool of blood and looks down. He pulls a notebook and pen out of his jacket pocket and starts taking notes, but he finds, to his horror, his hands are shaking so badly he cannot write. 'Getting cold?' a policeman asks, grinning.

In less than a month, the same reporter will be accustomed to pushing his way into a crowded bar past jeering patrons to the scene of a murder. He will realize that many bar murders in Chicago are committed relatively early, in time for coverage on the city's late night television news. He will come to accept that this is the biggest moment in most people's lives, when they can say to a reporter, 'I saw the whole thing.'

A photographer of twenty-five, newly married, is sent to cover the bread riots in Tunisia. 'In a civil war,' he says, 'people go crazy, you never know what's in their minds. A young guy, younger than me, put a gun to my head. He said, "Your life is not worth the price of one loaf of bread." I tried to reason with him. It was incredible, to hear this bloody noise against your head, "click, click."'

In a visit to Idi Amin's Uganda, Tony Brenna, along with a group of other reporters, is led into a courtyard where they watch seventeen people being executed as a demonstration of Amin's power. 'With sledgehammers, they smashed their heads in,' says Brenna. 'We were absolutely in shock, more concerned that we were going to get the same treatment, more frightened. I mean, screw them, are we next? That was basically our reaction.'

Brian Hitchen, now fifty-three, then twenty-six, was working out

131

of Paris when he was assigned to cover the first Indo-Pakistan War, 'which was a very bloody affair . . . You just walked into a village and there were dead all over the place. I'd covered air crashes and therefore I knew what the smell of burning flesh was like. It smells like, you know when you burn a saucepan, an aluminium saucepan, and there's that harsh bit that sticks in the back of your throat? Well it's like that but also like burning pork, and it's that sickly, sweet smell, and also that acrid bit that stays as well. So I knew what rotting bodies smell like, but I'd never seen as many. You'd drive into a village and there in the village pond would be a couple of oxen that were floating dead, and bodies draped all over. The place would be absolutely festooned with vultures, great big things like turkeys walking around, human fat running down their feathers, and bits sticking out . . . a revolting sight . . . and they were so heavy from gorging themselves on the dead that they were sort of waddling, they couldn't have flown.

'So the first time I saw that, I think I threw up, but that was the last time.'

The phrase 'hardened reporters' stems from the many desensitizing experiences newcomers to the field undergo when they choose to go into journalism. The first shock is inevitably the violence. And although violence is alive and well in the UK, America's unparalleled fascination with bloodshed means that most reporters starting-out in metropolitan areas will, at one time or another, be expected to serve time on the police beat. Almost every reporter under forty has a university education, and most of them come from the middle class. A Monday morning in Magistrates Court brings home – perhaps for the first time – the kinds of individuals who will inhabit their world.

During the first few years of reporting, there is much movement from beat to beat as well as from paper to paper, frequently from so-called 'quality newspapers' to daily tabloids and back. This process is called 'paying your dues', and to a large extent, reporters just starting out are expected to work long hours for little or no bucks. So at the same time they are acclimatizing to a new and sometimes horrific vision of reality, they are also experiencing financial hardship.

As if this weren't enough, reporters are also seeing people at their worst, in family, business and social relationships, and watching corrupt city, state and federal officials misspend public funds, cheating the taxpayer and their constituents. Every ideal instilled by school is eroded in a matter of months. Tabloid reporters observe these vices through eyes considerably more jaundiced than their broadsheet brothers and sisters, in part because they see more of them at first hand and in part because of the stark and emotional style of tabloid writing. This is life's seamy side, and in order to survive emotionally, distancing is necessary.

One way to distance yourself is to drink, and alcoholism is endemic to the profession. Says rewrite man Jack Morrison of the Philadelphia *Daily News*, himself a recovering alcoholic, 'I'm not sure why . . . I don't think it's because of the terrible things we deal with. I think it's that the business attracts people who tend to be artistic, dreamers, I don't know, people who may not be in the ordinary flow of society. A lot of emotional cripples in this business, I think. Because we don't really participate in life. We observe it. We stand aside and let other people do the action, and we report it. We don't get out there and try to change the world. We just wait for somebody else to do it, then we report it. We all have opinions about the way things should be, but, except for editorial writers, we don't do anything to change it. Why this makes us drink, I don't have any idea . . .'

In his book *The Bonfire of the Vanities*, Tom Wolfe bears down upon the phenomenon. The mammoth hangovers of British tabloid reporter Peter Fallow so typify the profession that almost every one of New York's British press corps suspects that *he* was the model:

> Fallow opened one eye and saw the telephone lying in a brown Streptolon nest. He was dizzy, and he hadn't even lifted his head. Great curds of eye trash swam in front of his face. The pounding blood was breaking up the mercury yolk into curds, and the curds were coming out of his eye. The telephone exploded again. He closed his eye. The snout of the beast was right behind his eyelid.

Former New York *Post* reporter Peter Fearon, who, like Morrison, is also a recovering alcoholic, most probably *is* the model for the boozing Fallow. Says Fearon, 'The person I was then is not the person I am now. I stopped drinking five years ago. It's fair to say that my connection with Peter Fallow's character has been exaggerated by my friends, although everywhere I go people say it's the same. I'm not sure it's me, but when the *Rolling Stone* version of the book came out, the references to me and my drinking and other attributes were striking . . . It was eerie.'

133

Brian Hitchen, editor of London's *Daily Star*, makes no apologies for the amount he tosses back. 'I defy anyone in a position with this much pressure not to do something excessive,' he says.

Sometimes the drinking just grows out of an outlandish situation. George Lynn, sent along with a group of fellow-reporters on the *Sun* 'to invade France' – an assignment growing out of the ever-fertile imagination of the famous editor of the *Sun*, Kelvin MacKenzie – remembers that most of them were already 'well on their way to being pissed' by the time they crossed the channel, around eleven in the morning. By the time Lynn phoned in the story to the desk, he was 'well past it'. He remembers sitting on a bar stool with the telephone in his hand, dictating the story, when suddenly everything went black. What happened was that Lynn passed out, falling backwards off his barstool. Just as he was tipping over, Nick Ferrari, now a top executive at News International, neatly picked the phone out of Lynn's hand and continued dictating the story, without missing a beat. Lynn fell to the floor, where, unhurt, he gradually came to. When they reached the English side, Lynn's pals deposited him at a hotel in Dover, where he slept like the dead. When he finally woke up, he found attached to his chest his next assignment, with instructions on how to get there.

A second remedy against harsh reality is laughter. But in the context of their daily occupation, reporters come up with pretty strong medicine. After the offshore oil rig Piper Alpha blew up in the North Sea, killing 166 in a powerful explosion which saw flames leaping 700 feet into the air, a joke made the rounds. 'What's got four legs and goes woof? Everyone answers "a dog",' says a reporter on London's *Daily Star*. 'Then *you* say, "No, Piper Alpha."'

Following the Hillsborough disaster, when ninety-five people were killed by asphyxiation from being pinned by crowds against a football stadium fence, reporters were singing choruses of the theme song from the movie *Top Gun*: 'Take My Breath Away'.

A veteran newsman on the New York *Daily News* describes 'a macabre banter in which I am often a willing participant with the police reporters . . . *Question*: What's the difference between the star of the Boston Celtics basketball team, Larry Bird, and Charles Stuart – the Boston furrier who shot his pregnant wife to death, then committed suicide by throwing himself into the Mystic River? *Answer*: Larry Bird jumps before he shoots, Charles Stuart jumps after he shoots.'

There was another case in New York, the editor continues,

'where a mother went berserk and chopped her daughter's fingers off, and the photographer got a picture of the grandfather and another relative looking at the girl's fingers. We didn't print that, but I gave that picture to police headquarters, where there was macabre laughter about it . . .'

In the eighteenth century, Dr Samuel Johnson, the great lexico-grapher, defined a reporter as 'a man without virtue who writes lies . . . for his profit.' Public opinion has changed little since Johnson's assessment. In England, journalists are rated below estate agents in popularity. This is going some distance since, in an unregulated property market, British estate agents are notorious for their unpopularity. On the scale of public contempt, though, the tabloid journalist must surely rate lowest of all. One young reporter for a London daily tabloid confesses that when he goes to parties, he avoids telling people what he does for a living because 'they feel it's their social right to be extremely rude to you.' Others solve the problem by choosing friends inside the profession.

The public's perception that tabloid reporters will 'lie, steal and cheat,' that they will invade house and home, take your mail, go through your garbage, sleep with your wife, pay cash for lies – anything to get the story – is probably true. Much admired in the trade, this relentless pursuit of the news is catalogued in the States under the euphemism 'resourcefulness'. Tell a story of some fantastic hoax pulled by a reporter in order to get the story, and the likely response is a sage nod of admiration and the comment, 'He sounds resourceful.'

There is the story of a young American male reporter who was sleeping with several of the secretaries in the City Hall of a large metropolis. He was nevertheless scooped by the opposition on a budget story. 'He sat there in the bar shaking his head in disbelief,' said one friend. 'He wasn't bragging, understand; he just couldn't believe his girls would let him down.' Even report-ers who conform to the prevailing behaviour codes are often closet wiseguys, describing themselves as 'trouble-makers', 'anti-establishment types' or worse. Unelected, unasked and unembar-rassed, they will strike out at anyone. 'The key to understanding tabloids,' says Rafe Klinger, formerly of the *Weekly World News,* 'is irreverence. *Nobody* is too sacred or too important to go after.' For them, like Henry Ford, history is bunk; all that counts is grinding the story out today. Along with this is a deep strain of anti-intellectualism, a tradition of being streetwise and using com-mon sense. 'Tabloid reporting is like fucking,' says John Mahoney of London's *Daily Star*. 'You can't learn it at school. You either do it or you don't.'

This attitude makes for individuals who are tough, fiesty and thick-skinned. They are the quintessential outsiders. As one experienced correspondent in the 1930s put it, 'Any reporter looking for a bed of roses would do well to go into floriculture.'

What is known as 'paying your dues' in the US is called 'getting into the Street' in the UK – although Fleet Street has been all but deserted by the trade since Rupert Murdoch successfully broke with the unions and moved his operation to Wapping. For many years, there were only two ways in. The first and more traditional way was to come from the provinces. The reporter would make a start on a weekly paper outside London, moving to an evening or morning provincial, and go from there 'into the Street'.

This meant he had served his three years, long enough 'to get his ticket', a reference to membership in the National Union of Journalists. A variation on this theme was for the reporter to come in from a London suburban paper or to freelance or 'take shifts' until he had made the contacts necessary to get a permanent job.

Stuart Winter, who works on the news desk of London's *Daily Star*, was satisfied enough with his job on a local paper just north of London, when he was assigned a story that changed his mind. A multi-rapist was attacking both men and women in the countryside just outside Luton. The neighbourhood, heretofore a safe, middle-class community, began for the first time to lock up their houses, taking the extra precaution of nailing their window panes shut. The case started in the late summer – a period of time known in the business as the 'silly season' when the House of Commons goes out of session, people go on vacations, little is happening and newspapers are desperate for news. Thus, the case got maximum play in the paper.

In on it from beginning to end, about three months in all, Winter found that each time he received a call from police telling him that the rapist had struck again, he would get a shot of adrenalin. When the case ended and things went back to normal, Winter realized he would no longer be satisfied to work where he was. He craved the excitement. He would have to leave his workaday job and 'go into the Street'. Nowadays 'when a reporter calls up and says, "I've got this story," and it's right,' says Winter, 'I get that buzz.'

Richard Ellis, now on the foreign desk of *The Sunday Times*, reported at a paper in Peterborough for three years, at the same

136

time selling local stories to national newspapers. The one that gave him entrée into Fleet Street was a murder case where a woman married to a local celebrity hired some contract killers from Liverpool to do away with her husband. It became known as the 'Kiss-of-Death Murder' because she telephoned her husband, just to make sure he was in the house 'kissed him goodnight down the phone, and then immediately rang the killers to give them the all clear,' says Ellis. It was only 'a small, run-of-the-mill story, but it made the nationals.' After that, Ellis asked for some freelance shifts and ended up doing a couple of weeks at the *Sun*. 'It was terrifying really because as a provincial journalist, you wonder if you have the skills to cope with Fleet Street, where all the best journalists, you think, are, and you wonder whether you can make it in the big league.'

The second way into Fleet Street was through magazines, a route frequently taken by women. One fashion editor in Fleet Street, who worked on the *Sun*, the *Evening News*, the *Daily Mail* and the *Daily Express* before leaving to go into costume design for film, is Sue Snell. She came in through the now-defunct but highly respected *Honey*, an avant-garde fashion glossy that was considerably before its time. Snell always had a good eye; that, plus the impact of the 1960s led her to an interest in fashion. With no formal training, she was thrown feet-first into the highly competitive world of women's magazines. Her first day on the job at *Honey*, she was handed a group of models and a photographer, a copywriter and told to do a twelve-page spread in colour. Snell survived the ordeal, becoming adept at page design and fashion display. The copywriter, who had a first-class honours degree in English from Oxford, became a close friend.

Later, both of them tried for the same job in Fleet Street. Snell succeeded; her friend didn't make it. 'It's because of your bloody legs,' her friend wailed. 'You got the job because you've got good legs!' But Snell is convinced it was 'because of the visual thing. Of course, she was almost too bright . . . They couldn't use that intellectualism. They could have used it in a Bernard Levin column, but that's about all.'

Once on the job, Snell was told by the Features Editor that she should get out into the field. 'You haven't done any reporting, you've only done fashion,' he told Snell. So he gave her the 'Bride of Britain Competition', sending her two days a week for six months to weddings all around the country.

It was on her first trip out that she received her 'initiation'. 'I went to this wedding,' Snell says, 'with a real pro photographer, somewhere in Tewkesbury, and I had to file my story over the phone. And we went back and drank some champagne, and it was very nice, and the next day the phone rang. It was the deputy editor of the paper. He said, "Luv, you know, we're not allowed to have blacks on the front page. That was a black wedding, and you know, we're a racist paper, and we're not allowed to have blacks."

'And I said, "No, it *wasn't* black." I was upset and worried,' says Snell, 'but they were just putting me through it.'

Later, Snell misspelled a word in an article and got a figure wrong in the wages of a girl she was covering. She was briskly fired by the same man who had initiated her. 'You know, Luv, you're very talented, let me call up *Vogue*.'

In the States, the working apprenticeship, whereby a reporter sinks or swim, has been put out of business by the 'J-School'; that is, the Schools of Journalism that are a part of the vast network of state and private universities across America. Each year the J-Schools roll out some 50,000 students to compete for 5,000 or 6,000 jobs in the market-place. In their undergraduate years, the worst thing students have to face is a trigger-happy professor who is trying to flunk out those he believes can't cut the mustard. What do they learn? They learn how to structure a news story, how to write a news lead – who, what, where, when, why, how; the so-called '5 W's and 1 H' – how to lay out a page. And they learn ethics. The Brits disparage this system, putting it down as the '*Columbia-Journalism-Review*-School of Journalism'.

'I reckon the worst thing that ever happened to American journalism was Woodward and Bernstein,' says Lee Harrison, who works for the *Globe* in Boca Raton. 'Everybody wants to be an in-ves-ti-*ga*-tive journalist and get a Pu-*lit*-zer. It's killed tabloid journalism in this country.' But few American journalists with J-School degrees can see much of a relation between their university years and adult life. Says Bill Boyle, deputy City Editor on the New York *Daily News*, who attended the J-School at Boston University, 'My college training is completely removed from what I do for a living.'

And even back in England, things have taken a turn. At one time, every journalist was expected to be proficient in short-hand and typing before he hit the Street. It's different now. Many joining the profession no longer bother with shorthand. One press critic believes the preference for tape recorders over shorthand, Filofaxes over notebooks, is an unfortunate turn of events. These days, media consultant Peter Jackson says, the

138

national newspaper bosses prefer reporters who are just starting out to have put in their time not with provincial newspapers but with news agencies 'because that's where you learn being first is all that matters and the boss can't pay your wages if you don't get exclusives.' Even reporters in their early thirties worry about 'the youngsters' who come in without having served any apprenticeship, their only motivation a sense of aggression. One *News of the World* veteran calls them 'kick-in-the-door merchants' who are tarring everybody with their brush. 'Wapping Kindergarten' other reporters sneer. These rank beginners, so go the complaints, are hired too young, put on short-term contracts and burn out fast. This leads to a worrying rate of staff turnover, one sub-editor on the *Sun* complains. Another worry is that what used to be pure 'hackwork', carried out by bonafide 'hacks and hackettes', is now done by a growing Old Boy network. It is said that there are three Old Etonians, all under thirty, on the *Sun* right now.

The dependence upon freelancers, too, comes under fire. Being a staffer brings a certain measure of independence. But being a freelancer means – literally – no story, no pay.

If 'a blitz' is ordered, which involves ten or even more reporters on the same story, writes Alastair Hetherington, 'the experience of hunting with the Fleet Street "pack" can be painful – or nauseating – to anyone who is sensitive. It takes a hardened character not to be revolted by the readiness of the pack to talk or force its way into the houses of those who may have suffered in a tragedy, to ask merciless questions and then to make jokes among themselves about the replies . . .' An interesting facet of the 'blitz' is that such a group always includes reporters from the 'quality papers' and from broadcast news, many of whom are known for their aggressive techniques. When the time comes to apportion blame, however, it is almost always the lowly tabloid 'hacks' who carry the can.

When former Commons researcher Pamella Bordes fled the national press after her exposure as a call girl by the *News of the World*, she said, 'one [reporter] nearly assaulted me.' Bordes had been involved in a moped accident on the island of Bali and had got 'cut up really badly.' The story made the rounds in Fleet Street that the reporter had actually jerked the bandage from her face, saying, 'Let's see how bad it is, Pamella.' The reporter who did it was not from the lower end of the newspaper trade, as might be expected, but from the middle market. It has become fashionable nevertheless to personify the *Sun* or the *Star* reporter as the aggressive character who will stop at nothing to get what he wants.

Reporters from the 'prestige' papers have tremendous advantages, when it comes to the kind of person they have to spend time with. At the heart of the business is the relationship between reporter and source. The peculiar dependency of one upon the other exists nowhere else. Reporters for the broadsheets most usually cultivate a higher-minded individual for tip-offs than do the tabloid reporters. Tony Brenna explains why.

'You set up a global network of people in powerful places,' says Brenna, 'but they're not the usual people that you're talking about in press offices, arse-kissing people that you have to be around in establishment journalism. We're talking about chauffeurs, cooks, drivers, maître d's, hotel managers, hairdressers in studios, pimps, prostitutes, drug dealers, anybody who can rap on the rich and famous. And you have to feed and nurture this network. You have to drink with these people, hang out with these people, pay them money and make these people your friends. Inevitably, if these are amoral people, you become amoral too. It gets to you. A kind of slightly down, cynical, look-at-the-world-one-way attitude starts to develop, if you take it seriously, which I do. I really can't play with work, to me work is everything. When I do it it's total.'

Besides the reporter's involvement can come another baffling phenomenon, which is found only in the States; that is the existence of a battalion of 'Deep Throats'. Says one city government reporter in Philadelphia, 'I have this guy who calls himself Deep Throat. He likes the intrigue of it. When he gives me documents, he signs himself "Deep Throat". He has this little stamp, and, when he sends me things, he stamps all over the envelope the words, "Private and Confidential" with this little stamp. When he speaks as an official, I use his real name.'

The ultimate moment in a relationship between reporter and source occurs when it is necessary 'to lock up' the source. This simply means to deposit the source in 'a safe house'. Although a source is being paid a huge sum of money, he must be guarded in shifts, so that other reporters can't get at him. All too often, though, the safe house turns out to be the home of the reporter, and the source turns out to be an abrasive jerk. George Lynn, formerly with the *Sun*, tells about a ballet dancer who defected from the Bolshoi Ballet – at least they *thought* she would be a ballet dancer.

'It turns out she was only an interpreter, but we didn't find that out until after we bought her story,' says Lynn. 'When we saw her, we realized she couldn't have been a ballet dancer in a

140

million years. She looked like a three-quarterback rugby player, really a heavy-set girl. She had spent about three months with the government, while the secret service debriefed her. She was going to be released anyway, and we offered to pay her, I forget how much, £10,000 or £20,000, so she could re-establish herself in this country.

'We had never seen this woman, and we were imagining a sylph-like being, and as a matter of fact, she was not at all lovely. But we were *stuck* with her, so we had to do the best we could. So I took this big brawly lass – a member of the KGB herself and that was why she was an interpreter – I took her home to my place. And it was a lovely summer's day. I asked her if she wanted a drink. What did she want, coffee or tea? And she says, "Well, no, haven't you got something else, something stronger?" I says, "Well, I've got some vodka." And she says, "No, vodka's for the peasants. Have you got any whisky?" I says, "Yes." I had several brands of whisky. Obviously, she didn't want coffee. My wife had coffee.

'The Russian girl says, "Well, have you got J&B?" I says, "Yes." She went out and sat on my patio. And she got through a whole bottle – it was about two hours – and the whole bottle went. And my wife, who doesn't drink, sat there in astonishment. I says, "Well, it's all down to expenses."

'One of our reporters, a girl called Anne Beveridge, had a lovely thatched cottage with a lovely stream, and Anne volunteered to let me use her cottage. And I took this Russian girl down to this "olde worlde cottage" in Hampshire. I says, "Well, there's no good giving her the odd gin and tonic . . . She wants whisky." So I was going out and buying bottles of whisky, and of course, Anne had this lovely Waterford crystal set of glass. You see, her cottage was like a film set. Everything was right. It was the right pictures, lights, carpets. It was *superb*. And this bloody woman caused mayhem and chaos in this cottage. Every night she would break one or two of Anne's glasses. She didn't throw them like that [he gestures]. But she was such a *clumsy* bitch.

'One night, I was sitting with this Russian girl, and we really had a heavy session that night, because I was drinking whisky, and at the end of the evening, I discovered that she had broken all of Anne's glasses. To make matters worse, Anne was coming back the next morning. So when she did come, I just opened up the door and said, "Put it on expenses, Darling."'

In the United States, one of the quagmires awaiting the journalist is the adversarial role the press plays to government. In cities where a tabloid competes with a broadsheet, the broadsheet inevitably enjoys status that the tabloid does not. Conversely, the tabloid usually has more clout when it comes to swinging votes, since the smaller paper usually caters more to the densely populated inner-city areas, where the political machine is likely to be in full force, than to the suburbs. Politicians therefore tend to give tabloid reporters a great deal of attention.

As one city reporter on the Philadelphia *Daily News* says, 'They need ink. They need ink big time. There's good ink and bad ink. But the worst is no ink at all. The worst thing we can do to a politician is to ignore him.'

As to the reporters, they find out quick that, in *their* job, they may influence people, but they aren't going to make many friends. The polar position of tabloid reporter to politician means there will be many confrontations and these will often end unpleasantly.

Philadelphia City Councilman Jimmy J. Tayoun speaks to a young *Daily News* reporter who is questioning him in connection with his frequent referrals to a former business associate, Barbara Williams, who now runs the lobbying firm Tayoun used to own.

TAYOUN: I'm so fed up with your paper, trying to zero me in as a yo-yo, it's pathetic, it's a disgrace.
REPORTER: Have you received any remuneration from [Barbara Williams] for any help you may have given her?
TAYOUN: You're a fucking insulting man, and you quote me, OK? And your paper's insulting and you're a dog to even charge me with that. Go find it. Go find evidence and then say 'I've got evidence'. Don't ever ask me that again or I'll smack you in the mouth and throw you out of here. Don't ever do that again. It's not a fair question because I've never taken a dollar from anybody in my life and you know it. That's what galls you and galls your ilk. I've never taken a penny from anybody. Ever. What bullshit. You know, the *Daily News*, I've got this much [gestures] in my files of what I consider to be malicious libel, the toughest libel to prove. If this story goes wrong, I will tell you, I will go borrow $30,000 to find a libel lawyer because I am fed up to here with the paper . . .

The story does not go wrong. Around the *Daily News*' City Hall bureau, the interview goes down as 'The Fucking Dog Story'. Meanwhile, relations between the reporter and Tayoun remain chilly.

'He doesn't trust me,' the reporter says, 'and I don't trust him.'

142

In addition to insult, reporters can face injury. James Sutherland, for years a celebrity paparazzo for the *National Enquirer* before stepping up the ladder to a major editorial position in London, remembers a night when Frank Sinatra got married. 'We wanted pictures of him. He had gone with his wife and mother to a restaurant in Palm Springs. I didn't bribe anybody. I simply went into the restaurant, took four people and paid $200 or $300 for dinner; I had enough money on the expense account to do that.

'I knew where they were going, so I just went, which gave me an advantage over other photographers who would've liked that picture. When they left and started to Sinatra's car, I stepped out of the restaurant with a Leica in my hand and just took a picture. People jumped all over me and the local police were called and all sorts of things. They grabbed at my camera and they tore the flash gun off the top. These gorillas were so bright they thought they had my camera; they must've spent hours trying to get film out of a flash gun. But I still had the camera. Old Blue Eyes stood right behind these gorillas . . . but not coming close enough to get involved.'

Even under the best of conditions, the activity known in England as 'doorstepping', in the US as 'stakeout', requires a certain kind of tenacity. Sutherland once spent a month 'sitting in a car on Fifth Avenue doorstepping Jackie Onassis.

'I used to work with Robin Leach, he's a big celebrity in America now. He and I followed Jackie Onassis all round the world. Anywhere she went we had to go. If she went to the airport, got on a plane, we had to go. When she went for a weekend – she had a house up in New Jersey – we went. Everywhere she went, we went. And I had quite a good relationship with her. She was all right. Every so often she would say "I know you need a picture, but just stay back, don't stick your wide angle lens right up my nose. Go across the street, use a long lens, get a few pictures and then leave me alone." I had that sort of relationship with her for a couple of years.

'Robin and I set ourselves up on Fifth Avenue and she lived at 1040 Fifth Avenue and there was a little door, that was never ever opened. Next to that was 1040 1/2 Fifth Avenue, and we called all the Chinese restaurants, called all sorts of restaurants, gave them that address, 1040 1/2 Fifth Avenue. Then when the Chinaman came along with the lunches, we just jumped out of the car and ate it. We even had a champagne picnic on Fifth Avenue one night. There was a restaurant on 89th Street. The head waiter was a guy called Limpseal. I don't know whether it was his real name or not, but we used to call him up and he'd come round with a silver tray and bottles of champagne for us . . . marvellous!

'Robin and I always had this deal that if she walked out the door – even if we'd just bought a meal – everything went out the window, coffees, everything, and we were off. I think I can still follow a taxi cab through New York City and not lose it . . . and through a lot of red lights, but I never lost her yet, and she wanted to lose you because she had a big, cockerel-green BMW and it used to take a bit of keeping up with. We used to follow her out to New Jersey. She would drive along the I-75, and she'd put all her hazard lights on just to clear the traffic, get in the middle lane and just go in this great big car. But we never lost it. We'd drive Fords, whatever . . . whatever Mr Hertz had.

'A reporter or photographer, they're there to cover every minute. You have to cover every single minute because you couldn't afford to spend, let's say, three weeks following Jackie Onassis to Paris, Athens, whatever, spending all that money, and then say, "I lost it because I went for a cup of tea." You couldn't do that. You had to be there. One has to learn about this business somehow, and the real place to learn about it, I believe, is out there in the streets doing it. How can you send photographers and reporters to cover wars and chase around the streets of New York City, or whatever, if you haven't done it yourself?'

Sutherland often teamed up with Vince Eckersley, also a *National Enquirer* photographer, now a freelancer. 'I had a Pulitzer Prize winner with me,' says Eckersley, 'when I was watching Jackie. I remember, he couldn't handle doorstepping. He couldn't handle sitting in the car for hours. He kept saying, "I'm a Pulitzer Prize winner, I shouldn't be doin' this." He was literally in tears sitting in the car with me. He wanted the *money*, but he couldn't handle it. Couldn't eat his Chinese takeaway in the car.

'When Pope wanted to get rid of him, his immediate superior said to the Boss, "But Mr Pope, he's a Pulitzer Prize winner," and the Boss said, "When did a Pulitzer Prize sell a paper?"'

The best moment in any reporter's career is when he gets a scoop. The worst moment? When he loses it.

In the 1960s Brian Hitchen was working for the *Daily Mirror* when he received a call from one of his contacts – a Russian countess. She said to Hitchen, 'Have you ever heard of a man called Lucky Gordon?' Hitchen hadn't, so she explained that he was coming up at Marylebone Magistrates Court and that Hitchen should go look him up and then call her back. So Hitchen went

144

down and looked at the two or three cuttings in the *Mirror* library. He also found photographs of Gordon, 'who was bald and black and in the nude, and the name of a woman, Christine Keeler, who was also in the shots.'

Hitchen called back the countess, and she said, 'Look, this is a terrific story because the government is involved and MI5 and the War Minister and a Russian Naval attaché and there are two girls – one is Mandy Rice Davies and the other one is Christine Keeler, who are hiding out because they're afraid. And they're broke and they want to sell their story, but I think you can sweet-talk them and get it for nothing.' The two girls were living at the house of a retired brigadier that was just behind the BBC.

'It was Portland Place or Portland Square, something like that,' Hitchen says, 'and it was a cold January night. We bought a barbecued chicken, because they didn't have any money, at the Marble Arch Barbecue, which is now, ironically, the Ann Summers Sex Shop, and a bottle of Johnny Walker Red Label, and we took all this to this flat. Only Christine was there, the other one was out. And she told me the lot, gave me the letters, the "Darling Christine" letters. Told me absolutely everything about Profumo and about the Russian. She said she'd never given him any secrets because she'd never heard anything, and I believed it. I've never heard of anybody going to bed with anyone and saying, "Tell me about the plans for the invasion next week." And Christine was too dumb to remember what you told her anyway. Mandy was the smart one, and Christine just made money out of it. I mean, she got £20 here and there, a fiver and a couple of pounds . . . So Christine gave me all these papers, and she said that she was quite willing to sign a contract with the *Mirror*.'

Hitchen didn't know how much the *Mirror* would pay, but he did know immediately that the story was 'worth a great deal of money'. He reckoned, even in those days, it was 'probably worth £150,000 for the whole lot.' About this time, Mandy Rice Davies came in, and she went into the bedroom, changing into 'a pair of black shoes, black stockings and nothing else – silly girl! and she was rolling a joint in one of those Rizla cigarette machines. The joint was as thick as my little finger, that was a bonfire she was making, and we all sat around this gas stove.' Davies had just come back from the Savoy where she had been with the son of an American film star, who, she said, had given her the pot.

Armed with all this evidence, Hitchen went into the office the following day, 'eager and bright-eyed and bushy-tailed'. He went to the news editor and told him the story. The news editor read over the materials and said that they couldn't print it in the *Daily Mirror*, that it was more appropriate for the *Sunday Mirror*. So the whole thing went out of the editor's hands. But before he sent it, Hitchen took photostats of the letters and the envelopes. The higher-ups of the Mirror Group Newspapers then took over, and the story that came down to Hitchen was that they had been called by Downing Street and confronted with words to the effect that Profumo 'denied categorically these scurrilous allegations,' asking 'Whose word are you going to take? That of a cabinet minister, or that of a whore?'

Hitchen was instructed to return everything to the women, that the *Mirror* wanted 'nothing further to do with it'. 'And I received a cheque from them for £23, because it was a sister paper, and it said, "To Christine Keeler Enquiry", and at that time I was so skint that I cashed the cheque. Now I would have kept the cheque and framed it.' Hitchen kept all of the photostated evidence, sending the originals back, and 'three weeks later, it broke in the *News of the World*, and then over at the *Mirror*, they began scrambling around like blind nanny goats, realizing that they'd really mucked it up. So miraculously, I was able to produce from my drawer the things that they thought we'd destroyed or sent back, but you can't really catch up on a thing like that . . .

'So my biggest scoop was also my biggest miss. It's true.'

The final calamity a newsman faces is the sack, and the most dangerous period is just before or just after a takeover. One of the first acts of MacFadden Holdings Inc. after buying the *National Enquirer* in June 1989 was to lay off forty-seven employees. The corporation simultaneously announced that the *Enquirer*'s annual Christmas tree display, which reportedly cost nearly $1 million, would also be cut. 'Mr Pope was Santa Claus,' the new president of the company said, 'and we just can't afford to be.'

Behind any 'necessary reduction in payroll costs' – present-day corporate lingo for mass firings – lies a rich tradition of sacking in the newspaper business. One of Joseph Pulitzer's editors found out he was finished when he received a cable from Pulitzer saying that he should plan a farewell dinner for himself at Delmonico's. Hearst's New York *Journal* had twenty-seven city editors in thirty-seven months. But the most flamboyant single episode has to be when James Gordon Bennett, Jr., whose father founded the International *Herald-Tribune*, rose from his bed in Paris, went down to the newspaper's offices dressed in red pyjamas and fired everyone sitting on the right-hand side of the room.

146

Some newspaper workers take getting fired in their stride, much in the spirit of Mark Twain, who once said, 'Reports of my death have been greatly exaggerated.' One veteran Fleet Street editor, sacked on a Monday, had by Friday started his own news service. Within weeks, he was making more money than he had in the Street.

When Generoso Pope called in Mike Nevard to face the executioner's block, asking him why the paper had been late going to press the week before, Nevard pre-empted him. '"Because you made it late, Mr Pope, by killing six pages, and I think you made a mistake in hiring me and I made a mistake by coming here," and Pope said "you're right," and that was it.' Nevard became something of a legend in the *Enquirer* offices when he told the dictatorial Pope, 'You know, you run this operation like a vast plumbing system. You have little faucets all over it, and you can open and close the faucets whenever you like.'

Nevard had just talked one of his friends into becoming editor of the *National Enquirer*'s sister publication, the *Weekly World News*. Phil Bunton had travelled for two days through a blizzard to get to his new job. As he was walking in, Nevard was walking out.

Nevard went on to become for many years the editor of one of the *Enquirer*'s major competitors, the *Globe*. When at last he was fired from there in August 1989, he was replaced by Paul Levy, who had just been fired from the *National Enquirer*. Nevard now freelances for the *National Enquirer*. *Plus ça change . . .*

One of the more resilient editors of Fleet Street, Derek Jameson, was editor of the *Daily Star*, the *Daily Express*, the *News of the World*, and managing editor of the *Daily Mirror*. Four years after Rupert Murdoch fired him as editor of the *News of the World*, he re-employed him to run his chatshow on Sky Television. Later, that show was cancelled. Jameson still broadcasts to some twelve million listeners on BBC Radio 2, however.

Earlier in his career, when he was editor of the *Daily Express*, Jameson was ordered to fire Peter Grimsditch, who was editing the *Daily Star*. Of the firing, Grimsditch, who is now the Manchester editor of the *Sport*, says, 'What in the hell does a man have to do to keep his job? I'd given them a newspaper that was selling. By the time they sacked me, the circulation had gone up to 1.2 million. I'd given them a newspaper *from scratch* that was selling 1.2 million copies per day . . .

'So I left them their car, playing Beethoven's Seventh, with the engine running, sunroof open, on Fleet Street, outside the black glass building.'

8
WAR

Blond, blue-eyed, earnest and eager, Bill Hoffmann is about to hit one of life's turnings, but he doesn't know it. Everything about him is middle-class – his education (university degree), his attitude (respectful), his appearance (conservative). He is working for a small newspaper in upstate New York when the call comes through.

Seventeen-year-old Scott Cantrell, 'an associate' of Anita Pallenberg and her common-law husband, Rolling Stone Keith Richards, who 'hung out' at their twelve-room, $250,000 Westchester County home, has blown his brains out in the master bedroom. Pallenberg is in the bedroom with the boy when it happens; Richards is in Paris.

The twenty-four-year-old Hoffmann is present when Pallenberg makes her entrance into the courtroom, fur coat and all, and he is trying to get a private word, 'like, "Excuse me, Miss Pallenberg, I was wondering if you might possibly—"'

He is interrupted by a gang of unruly British tab reporters, dressed in khakies and fatigues, flashes popping, 'and it was "Hey, Anita, baby, how's the kid in bed?" and "Did he poke you in the whiskers?"' And Hoffmann takes one long look at them, and says 'like Whoa.' And he falls in love. And he knows from this point on, his life will never be the same again.

A few years later, Hoffmann is covering a case in Westchester of two attractive young women who were raped by a pair of drug dealers. Afterwards, the men put pillows over their faces and shot them through the head. Both women, one blinded, the other crippled, came to the trial to testify against their attackers, 'almost from the grave', says Hoffmann, 'to nail these guys and put them away for life. It was a great story, but my paper was very shy of it because what they saw was a bloody, disgusting story. I thought, "Well, the New York *Post* will love it," so I called down there and talked to a woman who said, "It sounds interesting. Dictate four 'paras' and if we don't use it, we won't pay you." So I did and hung up.

148

'Ten minutes later, I get this call from a crazed Australian, who is saying, "Mate, Mate, it's a *great* story, it's full of action, you worked it out yourself? Why don't you start working here Sundays?'

Hoffmann was speaking on the telephone to Steve Dunleavy, *the* Steve Dunleavy, Mr Blood and Guts himself – the man who, at sixteen, slashed his own father's tyres while working for a competing paper in Sydney to prevent him getting an exclusive; the man who, during the Son of Sam furore, put on a doctor's smock and sat thirteen and a half hours in the hospital with the parents of Stacy Moskowitz as she lay dying of a gunshot wound to the head; the man who, invited to speak at an establishment conference on media responsibility, showed up with a blonde on either arm. It is *Steve Dunleavy* on the other end of the line.

A few words about Steve Dunleavy.

At age twenty, accompanied by an extremely good-looking and well-to-do blonde of approximately fifty years of age, he makes the acquaintance of an equally young Mike Walker, now the Gossip Editor on the *National Enquirer*, in a nightclub in Tokyo. Walker, also accompanied by a good-looking and well-to-do blonde of advancing years – 'a port in the storm, so to speak,' says Walker – is pleased at last to meet fellow-journalist Dunleavy, whose reporting prowess matches Walker's own. The ladies chat about prowess of a different sort, the competition becomes hot and heavy, and the upshot is – Dunleavy and Walker end up measuring up on the bar of Club 88 in Tokyo.

Unverified rumour: Steve Dunleavy is officially banned from Japan. Reasons: Unspecified.

Some thirty years later, in New York City, a young correspondent from the *Sun*, 'gets calls from the head of the Australian Bureau. "Come by here, bring in a fresh shirt and tie."' Richard Ellis did as he was told, 'and Steve Dunleavy, having been out drinking all night, would be stretched out asleep on the floor, fully dressed, and we would slip off his jacket and shirt and pull the fresh buttoned shirt over his head and put on the tie.' Dunleavy would later awake, have a cup of coffee and bop off to work. Says Ellis, 'It was the most amazing thing seeing him lying there on the floor, his tie immaculately done up.'

Says Bill Hoffmann, 'One woman reporter at the *Post* here first met him in a bar with his pants off.'

Says Brian Hitchen, 'A craggy little guy, now dead, used to live at Steve's whenever Steve went out of town. Steve was single,

149

between marriages. Steve went off on holiday to Australia. So this guy appeared in Costello's, and he had this great long overcoat on. I said, "That's Steve Dunleavy's coat," and he kept walking around in his coat, saying, "Why shouldn't I wear Steve's clothes?"

'This man would take these ladies of the night back to Steve's apartment, and say, "Listen I'm just going out for some cigs," to get out of paying. Then he'd go off for five hours. And one night, he came back after one of these deals, and there was this smouldering couch. This woman had set fire to the thing. And Steve's place was all smokey and scorched. And there was this green telephone, and it was sort of melted, and it began ringing, and he picked it up, and it was Steve phoning from Australia, and Steve said, "Have you burned the place down yet?"

'So when Steve came back, we all assembled at Costello's to see how Steve would react. The guy who had been staying in Steve's apartment said, "I have something to tell you." And he told him about the fire. And Steve said to the bartender, "Give my friend a drink, Freddie." And we all went over and said, "Is that all you're going to do?" And Steve turns to us and says, "What did you expect me to do, kill him?" End of story.'

The all-time classic Steve Dunleavy story:

Dunleavy was in Elaine's and in the mood, and he met a blonde who was similarly inclined. And the two of them went out into the street, and in two feet of snow, they went at it, right there – in the snow. And as they are about it, along comes a snow-plough, hitting Dunleavy in the leg, breaking it in seventeen places.

Punchline: 'And for this, he sued the city.'

Second Punchline: 'And he won the suit.'

Third Punchline: 'The earth may not have moved, but the snow certainly did.'

A Second Version: 'Along comes a snow-plough, hitting Dunleavy in the foot, breaking it in seventeen places.'

Quips Peter Hamill, then rival New York columnist, 'I hope it was his writing foot.'

A mature Steve Dunleavy, fifty-two and reformed, dissipated but still vertical, sits in a studio at Fox Television, where he is the star of the popular tabloid news show *Current Affair*. He protests strongly against the snow-plough story, 'I don't know what story you are talking about. It would appear to be apocryphal.

'For sure I didn't sue the city.'

Rupert Murdoch purchased the New York *Post* on 19 November 1976, from Dorothy Schiff, New York's first woman publisher, no doubt full of plans to revolutionize the American media as he had the British.

Under Schiff, the paper had become a voice for 'honest union-ism, social reform and humane government programmes.' At its inception a strong supporter of Franklin Delano Roosevelt, the *Post* went on in the 1950s to attack Senator Joseph McCarthy, long before it was fashionable to do so, and later sent a black reporter to cover the Civil Rights Movement in the South. Operated under a regimen of strict fiscal accountability, the paper nevertheless attracted high-quality writers like Jimmy Breslin, Orson Welles and Nora Ephron.

Dolly Schiff – intelligent, attractive, statuesque, with that sheen of confidence wealth confers – carried herself with flair. She had been married four times, no apologies; kept a French poodle; smoked with a cigarette holder. 'She was very much Upper East Side,' says Managing Editor Lou Colasuonno, who started at the *Post* twenty-one years ago and has worked under three separate regimes during his career.

'She was a real liberal, really from the Democratic left. When Rupert came, there was a lot of hostility from the staff. It was a writers' paper given over to longer pieces, and all of a sudden we were gobbled up by Rupert Murdoch, the Fleet Street monster who had a reputation for gory headlines, naked Page Three Girls, tiny stories and sensationalism, with the emphasis on style rather than content.

'Everyone expected a three-headed monster with an Australian accent,' says Colasuonno. 'What they got was a business man who was personally a gentleman, a very low-keyed man. He certainly didn't fit the bill as some mad journalist running around and peeking into people's windows. His editors sometimes went a bit far, but not only was it the whole style of journalism, it was a 180-degree turn politically. You went from a left-wing, Jewish, Democratic paper to a very conservative viewpoint. And we did become sensational.'

To Bill Hoffmann, who found the establishment press stultifying, the atmosphere was like 'a breath of fresh air'. He found a staff of aggressive, fearless, dogged reporters, who were more like troops than employees. 'The Australians and the British would say, "Go out there and get us this." They would tell you what they wanted. There was no "Well, let's think about this for a while." They said, "Go out to the scene and get us a story." Or, "We want this headline in the paper; go out and get it." They worked by headline and by concept.

151

'While I was a reporter, I was doing all these things on the *Post* which we cooked up. We would hype things up here and there to get people interested. We basically took one or two facts and created a whole scenario around them. I can't remember exactly, but the Brits would have their version of what happened, and I'd Americanize it, bringing out certain aspects. When you're taking a couple of little facts, and one reporter adds to them, then another, then another, it sort of becomes larger than life, but that's all good fun, I think. Like everyone wants to read about it whether its true, or half true or . . .

'Basically, under Roger Wood, the theory was "Tits, tots, the Mets and pets." The Australians and Brits coming to America was the greatest gift that American newspapers could have gotten. We had been thinking so much about "Will we step on people's feelings?" and becoming so responsible in our reporting methods that it was like, "Hey, who are we serving, ourselves or the reader?"'

American John Cotter, then one of the editors, remembers a rising tide of enthusiasm that buoyed up everyone who was then working on the *Post*. 'You couldn't get people to leave work. After the edition was closed, we'd order up a case of beer, and people were just running all over the place. We had young kids who would do anything for us.

'There used to be a great sexual craziness when the Aussies were here,' says Hoffmann. 'This place exuded sexuality. I think everyone was fucking everyone else. It was like this craziness, this libido in the office.'

Peter Fearon agrees. Everyone was working so hard, he says, they never had the chance to get out of the office, never met any other people. 'So you created situations with people you worked with. It was pre-AIDS, and people were still living as if it were the sixties. Whatever the accusations are, they are probably true.'

But Roger Wood, editor-in-chief of the *Post* for ten years, prefers to remember what he believes the newspaper actually accomplished. Says Wood, 'The *Post* was criticized for almost anything it did. We shook up the newspaper establishment in New York, and none of them liked it. If you look back, the *Daily News* was a sleepy old suburban newspaper. All of its executives went home to Westchester as soon as it was dusk. We forced them to take a much stronger look at the city they were supposed to be serving. The same with *The Times*. I remember *The Times* as barely covering the city at all. No metropolitan section, no interest. You

152

would think that the city was a garden suburb, with no crime, no problems. All that changed.

'I think a lot of the change was catalysed by the very aggressive position the *Post* took as a New York City newspaper, and it was very New York. At the same time the strength of the *Post* was its news coverage, and particularly its city coverage – I mean, we just ran away with the political coverage of the city, and also the Albany coverage. Nobody was beating us. We broke story after story. We probably had the best crime team too. I don't suppose anybody would dispute that. But also, underneath all that, we had a terrific arts section, a terrific leisure section, and a strong, direct, clear, conservative voice on the op-ed page* and in the editorial columns.'

Dunleavy, who was destined to become the best-known metro editor in America, makes claims similar to Wood's, but in somewhat more colourful terms. 'We made the *Daily News* and *The Times* more aggressive, though *The Times* would probably rather open their veins than admit it. They'd end up with their dicks in their hands on story after story. Now they'll put a crime story on Page Two.

'We had a great team of reporters; young, aggressive, eager to learn, best I've ever struck on in my life. God, great reporters.'

But Mike Nevard, a veteran Fleet Street editor brought over from the *Sun* by Larry Lamb, saw it differently. 'What I found was that Steve Dunleavy held the whole thing together. He had to brief the reporters every step of the way. "If you don't get them, have you tried somebody else? Have you spoken to their neighbours? Have you tried to get the neighbours' phone number?" The reporters were basically American. The way I was brought up, if you were given a story, you went out and got it. You did not report back all the problems you had in getting it. It was as if Dunleavy was running a school for real journalists.'

To a large extent, Dunleavy was the linchpin of the *Post*'s operation. Former Fleet Street reporter Peter Fearon remembers 'a fond relationship with Steve. It's very bizarre. The fact was, I would do anything he asked me. If he had said to me, "We need a story. Go and jump off the Brooklyn Bridge," I would have asked, "Which level?" I would have crawled over broken glass, and I guess I loved him in a sort of manly way. He commanded a tremendous amount of loyalty. That's his greatest talent. The

* The page opposite the editorial page.

153

guy is not a writer in reality; try reading some of his stuff. He had major talents, though. He is an amazing leader of people, he commands loyalty, he is a very attractive man to both sexes. Men love him. And women fall to his feet.'

Says Bill Hoffmann, 'Dunleavy was the best editor I've ever had. I miss the guy. I'd have done anything he asked.'

Dunleavy, on the other hand, prefers to credit the team – Editor, Roger Wood; Managing Editor, Ken Chandler, now editor of Murdoch's Boston *Herald*; and, yes, Kelvin MacKenzie, imported by Murdoch from London for 'tryouts' as the *Sun* editor, according to newspaper lore – in creating the atmosphere that caused the amazing climb from a circulation of 480,000 to almost a million.

'I am very similar to Kelvin,' says Dunleavy. 'I'm a little hyperactive actually. Ken Chandler is a lot calmer and more under control, but there was a tremendous spark of energy off all of us. The whole place was like a three-ring circus. Eight editions a day, and we'd pull the thing apart if it suited us, and it would be nothing for us to be there twenty-four hours straight. We should have paid Rupert Murdoch to work there.'

Says John Cotter, now the metropolitan editor on the *Post*, 'A lot of Brits and Australians were here, and we learned a lot. The old *Post* was serious. So bloody serious. Kelvin MacKenzie was great. A lot of people didn't understand what tabloids were: pushing the story as far as it would go and holding it fifteen feet right over the edge, and there were some reporters on staff who were just astonished.

'Kelvin would say, "Mr *So-and-So* is very uncomfortable by what we're doing with the paper," and he would walk with his finger stuck up his behind as he said it.' According to Cotter, it was Kelvin MacKenzie and Roger Wood who worked out the slogan: 'The paper that cares about New York'.

Says Cotter, 'We promoted ourselves. It was embarrassing, but it was funny. And we'd do crazy stories. The public depended upon the *Post*. But at the same time, we did some really terrific stuff, because we could take our shots. We weren't afraid of anybody. Later on, the *Post* was heavily identified with Koch. And with Reagan. And the paper was highly political, in that it was conservative.'

It was a given, once Murdoch had put his imprint on the *Post*, that the political support the paper offered was like no other. Certainly, any politician it chose to back got more than cursory endorsement. During the Murdoch era, then Lieutenant Governor Mario Cuomo said, '*The New York Times* is perhaps the single

154

most credible newspaper in the world. But when they endorse you, you get one column on the editorial page. With Rupert, he turns the whole paper over to you.'

During the election campaign in 1980, says Peter Grimsditch, who was, like so many, imported from Fleet Street, 'We did this crazy American thing of endorsing people. Murdoch had got one of his people to write this incredibly long, boring thing, which *covered* the whole of Page One and then covered the whole of Page Fourteen, endorsing Reagan, which was the obvious step for Murdoch. I had to be in charge of the paper. Actually it was an easy day because you don't have to worry about Page One; you just put all this crap on it. Easy day, I think, so I'll have another cigarette. And, I put the endorsement in and I made it all fit and made it look pretty. Murdoch came down, and it was half past seven in the morning, and he said, "Well, what do you think of it?" I stopped. I said, "If that's what you want to say, it's OK. It's coherent, well argued, well-written, etc. Nothing wrong with it. *Except* for the last two paragraphs." After two and three-quarter pages on why the Democrats were cocking things up, why Reagan was the only man for the job, there were two paragraphs which said, roughly, "If you think all of the above is bullshit, vote Democratic".

'I said, "I don't understand why you are doing this. Just why bother?" He said, "Well, you know why it's there." I said, "Well, I *guess* why it's there is because if you still have any of the Jewish liberal Democratic readers left, it's a sop. But they must be pretty stupid to continue reading the *Post* after two and three-quarter pages on why Reagan should win." He said, "You're right." And he went back upstairs and got it rewritten.'

It wasn't only the editorial pages and the endorsements, says John Cotter, 'there was a lot of twisting and bending on the news side.'

Says Fearon, 'We would call people and lie through our teeth. But my speciality – I was not a street reporter – I had two talents. One, intuition and talent for analysis and understanding. But my best talent was in writing style. I could make a trowel look like a spade, and a spade look like a backhoe, without telling any lies. I could coin a phrase, tell a story. Excitingly, but not accurately, in particular. I was a complete workaholic.'

Fearon showed up at the *Post* of his own volition, but most on the paper regarded him as an *'apparatchik'*. He once wrote an op-ed piece 'under direction'. When the United States invaded Granada, Fearon was told to write a piece putting down the media

155

who were complaining vociferously that the armed forces hadn't taken any reporters along on the campaign. 'So I wrote a piece comparing the situation to the Imperial Japanese Navy inviting the three American networks along when they attacked Pearl Harbor. Everybody thought it was a disgrace, even inside the paper. Ben Bradlee and Helen Thomas were both on a TV news show, and they were incensed at this editorial. I couldn't go on the show . . . because I was too drunk. At one point, some alternative Chicago newspaper critiqued that article and they said, "Peter Fearon" is a pseudonym for Rupert Murdoch himself.'

Peter Fearon says, in essence, 'We would do anything. We felt we were in a life-and-death, mortal combat with the *Daily News*, and as far as we were concerned, anything went.' Some of the outrages pulled on the pages of the *Post* during this era were repulsive but riveting. Like the time when Bill Hoffmann went out to the Bronx, where 'a half-crazed mother threw her two kids out of an eight-storey window on Thanksgiving Day and then threw herself out after. All but one of them died.'

The parents of the woman told the *Post* to stay away from the family, but Hoffmann and a photographer went out anyway and the woman's brothers and sisters let them in. While the photographer took pictures, Hoffmann was doing an interview. And in the middle of this 'a *Daily News* reporter arrived, and I said, "DON'T let him up here. This guy will twist your words. He'll make it seem like your sister was nuts, like she was an unfit mother. You don't want that. You don't want lies about your sister. You want a nice story." So the other brother goes, "This guy from the *Post* is right." And I don't think they spoke to the *News* reporter.'

The single most infamous incident perpetrated by the *Post* was *not* the publication of the letters of serial-slayer David 'Son of Sam' Berkowitz to his teenaged sweetheart, or even giving him a front-page by-line, which caused a furore of criticism. Nor was it the plastering of Berkowitz's adoption papers across Page One, causing adoptive parents everywhere to be concerned about the confidentiality of the transaction.

It was the publication of a photograph captioned 'Sam Sleeps', taken after the killer was behind prison bars. Says Dunleavy, 'It was alleged that we paid a certain amount of money to a person who then allegedly bribed a correction officer to take the pictures. Now I don't know whether those allegations are true, all I know is we had a picture of Sam asleep in prison. I was in Cuba at the time interviewing Fidel Castro, so *my* by-line did not appear on the picture. (Did the Statute of Limitations run out yet?)'

It was reported in the *Nation* that editor Roger Wood was also out of town when subpoenas were issued in connection with the related court case.

Then there was the time Dunleavy managed to beat out the *Daily News* by getting the first interview with Bernie Goetz, the New York 'vigilante' who shot down a group of black youths in the New York subway after, according to his story, they tried to mug him.

Says Dunleavy, 'Goetz was a strange dude. He was celebrated as a Charles Bronson, and it's no question he struck a nerve in the city, but sometimes you have to think that old Bernie was three sandwiches short of a full picnic. A funny thing happened. There's a well-known mafia joint where I and Bob Young, the picture editor on the *Post*, took Goetz. It came about that we were gonna take Bernie down in the subway, but we met him at this mob club, a little bar with machines where we used to drink. Bernie walks in, and all these mob guys, he was a hero to them, they all come up to him and say, "Hey, Bernie, pleased to meetcha." He starts talking guns with them. He's not a drinker, and we got Bernie quite drunk on gin and tonics. And the whole time these guys are talking about guns. So Bernie says, "What an interesting place. They all seem to know a lot about those guns I owned. Was that a hunting club?"

'We tell him, "Don't worry about it, Bernie. Don't worry about a thing." So we took him down, and there he was in the subway. We got him on the same train, and people were watching, and we almost caused a riot, we almost caused a riot in the subway in New York!'

Dunleavy remembers another night when the Iranian hostage crisis was going on. He had a bright idea that he would get the number of the US Embassy inside Iran, and he did. So, sitting at the desk in New York, he dialled direct, and, lo and behold, somebody answered the phone at the other end and could speak some English. So, with Kelvin MacKenzie looking on, he proceeded to do an exclusive interview. Later on, it became something of a fad to give the Embassy a ring, but this was the first time anyone had done it. Says Dunleavy, 'Kelvin was overjoyed. He was jumping for joy, like a ping-pong ball in a wind tunnel.'

Then, when the hostages were finally released from Iran and the *Post* was stuck for a story for the front page, 'Kelvin decided we should have a greeting for the hostages,' says John Cotter. 'So he

157

had Paul Rigby draw a cartoon, "Merry Christmas to the Hostages from the Readers of the *Post*," and there was a place where you could write in a message. Suddenly, two days later, mailbags began to appear in the office, many bags, hundred of pages coming back at us. And somebody discovered that there was money inside of them, a coupla of bucks in each of the letters. They had stuck that in when they mailed them in. To this day,' says Cotter, 'I don't know where those mailbags ever went.

'We did girlfriend stuff, like, "Mail us a picture of your girl-friend" – "The Best-looking Girl in New York" – and we ran that stuff for a while. *Any* stunt.

'There was a subway strike here in 1979 or '80. And Kelvin had decided that the headline was going to be "CHAOS". And it turned out the first day of the subway strike, it seemed like a normal day. And Kelvin just said, "Fuck it. It's CHAOS." And Koch rang here and complained to the managing editor. And Kelvin wouldn't change it. And if I recall,' says Cotter, 'Koch even called Murdoch in Australia, and Kelvin *still* wouldn't change it, and he left here with it "CHAOS", and I think they put a replay on it at the end. But Kelvin was a tough guy. He stood right up to that.' Says Dunleavy, who remembers the incident, 'I can't seem to remember how much actual *chaos* there was. Chaos is a very qualitative thing.'

Regarding the infamous photograph of the corpse of John Lennon on a mortuary block after his assassination, which the *Post* ran on the front page, Dunleavy is unsure 'whether we paid the guy to get in or paid the guy to take it. I think it was a freelance photographer we called "Streetrats" who would literally steal the gold from your teeth. I think we paid an attendant for him to get in for about two minutes. That was another time when the Columbia School of Journalism emitted a great collective moan of disgust. There was nothing gory about the picture. John Lennon dead looks just like John Lennon asleep.'

Says Roger Wood, who took the final decision whether to run the photograph, 'We published that picture for the simple reason that we always seek to publish rather than not to publish. When Grace Kelly was in that terrible car crash, was lying in state in Monaco, that picture was widely used. No one was bothered . . . It's the same when the Royal Family goes. Those pictures are published. No one quarrels with those. I mean, there was John Lennon, perfectly in repose. It wasn't a hideous picture. He was the idol of millions of kids; after that terrible murder, lying peace-fully. Any difference between his picture taken in the mortuary

158

and Grace Kelly lying in state in Monaco is only surroundings. Suppose he'd been taken out and put in St Patrick's Cathedral, and was lying in state there, surrounded by a panoply of prostrata standing guard over his bier, that's "b-i-e-r", the question wouldn't even have been asked.'

In retrospect, patrician Roger Wood – who must in some way or other, as top man at the *Post* for a decade, be related to the character 'Mousey' in Tom Wolfe's *Bonfire of the Vanities* – prefers to be remembered for his editorial vigilance than for some of the more controversial items that appeared on the *Post*'s pages. 'I used to pace through that newsroom every day, and sometimes well into the night, leaning over people, cajoling them, discussing the attack . . . or even worrying, which I think largely one has to give up these days. *The pure sense of grammar*! I used to have a thing about split infinitives. And then I discovered that a lot of the kids on the *Post* did not know what a split infinitive was. So you find yourself first explaining what a split infinitive is, and then explaining why it shouldn't be used. Of course in the end you have to call a day on that one.'

Evaluations of Wood are fascinating, as is Wood himself. To one of his former employees, Wood remains essentially 'a politician who has risen by disassociating himself from failure at just the right moment. Then stepping into the spotlight of success again, at just the right moment. Dunleavy once said he was good at dodging bullets.'

In his formal summing up, Dunleavy characterizes Wood as: 'Mephistopheles . . . Rasputin . . . Woody Allen . . . but mostly Einstein. Never before had anyone better held together a raw rag-tag team of Don Quixotes that had the skill of the Dirty Dozen and the guts of Patton.'

Widely known among friends and enemies as 'the slippery one', Wood himself eschews the word 'slippery', referring instead to his 'invisibility'. It was for many years his proudest boast that his name had never appeared in a newspaper – any newspaper. Another word he uses to describe himself is 'adroit', and he is fond of recounting a couple of anecdotes that give particular insight into the way he operates.

'When I left Oxford,' says Wood, 'I felt the most free-living existence going was journalism. I didn't want to go into the civil service. That's high bureaucracy. And I didn't want to go into corporate life, because that's rather the same. In fact I have a twin, and one summer when we were at Oxford, we worked at London Transport, and we worked in the department which is the forerunner of computers, you know, where they have cards with holes in them. What we did, we ran through age against salary of all the executives, and then when they interviewed us at the end of our summer stint, they asked whether we would like to consider working for London Transport when we'd finished our degrees. And we said, "NO!"

'"Why not?" they asked. We said because it was just like going into the civil service. Everything happens in turn. And they said, "No. That's not true. We promote entirely on merit." So we showed them the graph of their executives, age against salary, and it was an absolute straight line. But journalism isn't like that, so that's why I went into journalism.'

Once in the field, and landed in a position on the old IPC *Sun*, the unsuccessful precursor to Rupert Murdoch's *Sun*, Wood wanted off the staff quickly, but to advantage. One day, at a Christmas lunch, Hugh Cudlipp asked him whether he wouldn't like to go into magazines. To which Wood answered something in the neighbourhood of 'Oh, yes, Sir, please, Sir, immediately.' Then he waited and waited, and when nothing happened, he asked his immediate superior about it. 'All in the ripeness of time, Wood,' came the answer.

So Wood wangled invitations to a great and wonderful party for all the women who worked on the old IPC *Sun*, and 'I said "Now all I ask of you is this: that you stay with me until I tell you it's OK." So when Cudlipp arrived, there I was, surrounded by all these women. I swear to God this is true. My being with all these women catalysed in the back of his mind that he'd thought of the magazine idea, and I appeared to get on very well with women, so the next day the phone rang, and he said, "Come over and see me," and I went to see him and he sent me over to one of the magazine divisions and I ended up on the board, knowing nothing about magazines. Absolutely nothing.'

Says Wood of his relationship with Rupert Murdoch, 'In all the years I was there I don't think he and I have ever disagreed on the stand the newspaper was taking politically, and in point of fact, we'd judged each other so well we very rarely felt any need to discuss it.'

The mere mention of Roger Wood's name to colleagues or competitors brings a smile to their lips, a hesitant intake of breath, as if in surrender to a certain style, a certain irresistible way of viewing the world. Says *Daily News* publisher Jim Hoge, who wears the familiar smile of affection common to Wood's admirers, 'I've known Roger for years and he really is a rogue.

You want him to treat the world as round? He'd be delighted to. You want him to treat the world as flat? He'd be delighted to. "It's all theatre, dear boy."'

So when it all started at the *Post*, the rise in circulation, says one staffer, 'It was the wildest ride you've ever been on. Suddenly it started to rocket. Next thing you know, you're at 550,000; then at 700,000. And so on up the line.'

To some extent, this amazing rise resulted from the introduction of the sweepstakes card game Wingo, another Fleet Street import. It became so popular that it was said doormen of exclusive apartment blocks on the Upper East side and Westside of the city filched the cards when the *Post* was delivered, considering them their due. The *Daily News* was forced to set up a competing game, and the race was on. Bill Hoffmann, new to the paper, made an appointment to interview the mayor, knowing full well the *Post* wanted Koch's endorsement for Wingo but that he had so far refused to give it.

'So I went to talk to the mayor and asked him about everything under the sun – taxes, homicides in the city, fire prevention, etc. Then I said, "Hey, Mayor, we're starting a new game called Wingo" and asked him what he thought. And suddenly, from nowhere, he said, "I love Wingo. It's great fun and gives great cash and everything." So I tape-recorded this, immediately called up the desk and said, "Well, he discussed taxes, homicides in the city, fire prevention, etc . . . And he endorsed Wingo." And they dropped the phone and went "What? What!" They called the managing editor at home and told him the new man Hoffmann got Wingo endorsed by the mayor. So they gave me the rest of the day off and next day it was on Page One.'

Dunleavy tells the story of a couple of *Daily News* reporters who were caught trying to get the *Post*'s Wingo card numbers in Pennsylvania. 'So the *Post* did this string of stories. We made it like one great big spoof. Each day we had a famous felon, giving the *Daily News* advice. These guys' lawyers advised them not to do it, but they did it anyway.

'Another thing. Each day we had a famous person holding a Wingo card. We even got Nureyev. Well, right after Jim Hoge came into town from Chicago, one of our reporters, Paul Tharp, walks up to him in a crowd of well-wishers and hands him a letter of congratulation on becoming publisher of the *Daily News*, and on the back is a Wingo card. Hoge holds it up to read it, and one of our people takes a photograph of him. And the next day, we have a photograph of Hoge with a Wingo card with the caption, "Look who's playing Wingo!"'

Says Hoge, 'They were welcoming me to town, so to speak.'

Such were the madcap antics of the *Post* staff during its heyday. Behind the scenes, however, was a grimly determined Rupert Murdoch, who soon came to realize that New York City was a long way from Fleet Street, and even further from Sydney. In America, papers couldn't survive on circulation alone. Advertising revenue was the key to solvency. Says Peter Grimsditch, who came in mid-war, 'The circulation area of the New York *Post* was vastly extended, so it was sent up to Albany, and as far as New Jersey, and they had plans to send it down to Philadelphia as well. And that's why it was switched to a three-cycle paper, and Rupert's intention was to get it up to a million. And I think that's the sole reason for this very costly exercise – to batter down the barriers that had been put up by the big New York advertisers. The *Daily News* was surviving on its eight pages from Penney's, twelve pages from Macey's, not every day, but often enough, and Rupert was getting absolutely none of this at all.

'He was so intent to get this thing working that he was in the vanway at six o'clock in the morning down in South Street, just after the paper started going up to Albany, and he pointed out that they were sending an old truck up to Albany. "Why are you sending an old truck? You should be sending the new one. The old one, you can use for closer deliveries."'

Says Roger Wood, 'The real reason the *Post* became a twenty-four-hour paper was to retaliate against a preposterous *Daily News* plan to attack the *Post*'s afternoon franchise. The *News* launched an afternoon paper called *Tonight*. So we launched a morning edition of the *Post*; in fact we recycled *Post* editions continuously around the clock bringing out as many as thirteen in a twenty-four-hour period. Exhausting fun. As it turned out, *Tonight* proved to be a frightfully boring upmarket disaster. It put New Yorkers to sleep by the thousands. In desperation the *News* began The Great Afternoon Giveaway Campaign aimed at the commuter and the Wall Street Yuppies. Huge piles of *Tonight*s lined the canyons of Wall Street, despised and rejected. Nobody wanted *Tonight*. Not at any price. Within weeks *Tonight* closed with $20 million down the tubes.'

Acutely conscious that the moral imperatives in America were different from those in England and Australia, Murdoch at times became enraged if nudity was injected into the *Post*. When the Madonna nude shots came out in *Penthouse*, the *Post* ran a topless

162

picture of her, and, says Bill Hoffmann, 'Murdoch hit the roof, came in here and was furious. Said "This is not the London *Sun*, we can't do this." I never saw him angry before.'

When Phil Bunton was working as night managing editor at the *Post*, he experienced much the same thing. Bunton's shift started at ten at night, the presses ran at six or seven in the morning, and Bunton then waited for his replacement at eight before going home. It was Murdoch's habit to show up at the paper at seven, if he were in town, and, says Bunton, 'he'd say, "What the hell have you been doing?" And he'd grab the paper.'

One morning, Murdoch took Bunton down to the cafeteria to look over the paper. At that time, Patty Hearst was about to go to jail for her part in cooperating with the Symbionese Liberation Army. Up until then, the entire thrust of the national press had been that Hearst had been victimized. But the *Post* was running the now-famous photograph of Hearst by a swimming pool, looking carefree and unworried that she was about to go to jail.

'And,' says Bunton, 'printers were all around, and Rupert was in a suit, and everybody was very much aware of his presence. And Rupert was saying, "No, no, no, I've told you again and again I don't want girls on the front page in a bikini!" And then he went through the whole paper, page by page, four times over. People were watching this whole process and trembling. Then, he went back to the front page, and said, "Yeah, I see why you did that," and went back through the whole paper, page by page, and said, "Yeah, it's OK. Yeah, it's a pretty good paper."'

Says Bunton, 'It was probably just the bikini that set him off. He probably didn't even realize at first it was Patty Hearst. At the time, he wanted to raise the level of the *Post* in the City. Also, once Murdoch vented his rage, it was all over, and that was that. Then the paper was OK by him.'

Murdoch was also capable of becoming angry over seemingly insignificant matters. Mike Nevard tells a story where, after working several months at the *Post*, 'doing everything, working from dawn to late at night, never getting out,' he received an invitation to the National Croquet Championships in Central Park. He was to come attired in tuxedo and white sneakers. Nevard thought it sounded like fun, 'So I asked Roger Wood if I could go. "Good idea," he said. So I hired the tux for $33 and went. When Rupert saw the charge on my "exes", he broke off from major financial talks – he was about to buy some company somewhere – hauled Roger in, beefed about Nevard throwing away company money, and knocked the amount off my expenses. Roger told me he'd talked Rupert into relenting, and that I'd get the money, but I never did.'

Such close attention to minute expenses might seem unreasonable, but in fact, the New York *Post* was a tremendous drain on what was developing into the Murdoch communications empire. Not only was Murdoch not making any money from the paper, all told, he lost $150,000,000 on the *Post*, 'before taxes'. Because of its sensational approach, it had been unable to attract advertising, and, as a matter of fact, it was during this era that the famous statement from department store owners made the rounds: 'Your readers are our shoplifters.'

Murdoch cherished the belief, according to Colasuonno, that when the *Post* reached a million circulation, 'they wouldn't be able to ignore us.' Murdoch was probably basing his assessment on the phenomenal climb of the London *Sun*'s circulation under Larry Lamb only seven years before, which had transformed the fledgling newspaper into the highest circulation daily in the English language.

'But,' says Colasuonno, 'they did ignore us. We were printing seventeen hours a day, running a morning and an afternoon paper, and that's a very expensive proposition, two shifts in the print room. He's got guts, he knows the newspaper business, he could walk down here on any given day, and he did earlier on. But Rupert was a lot different when he sold the *Post* than when he bought it. He was huge when he sold it, not nearly so huge when he bought it.' Inevitably, Murdoch found less and less time for the *Post*, which many on the staff liked to believe was his flagship in America. By now, in the gigantic communications network Murdoch was founding, newspapers had begun to take a backseat to television.

He had, in 1985, bought stations in Boston and New York, the latter, WNYW-TV, becoming the foundation for his fledgling fourth network, Fox Broadcasting Company. At the same time, he was legally sidestepping the Federal Communications Commission's rule barring ownership of a television station and a newspaper in the same city, by requesting and receiving temporary waivers from the FCC.

When in January of 1988, Senator Ernest F. 'Fritz' Hollings, on Teddy Kennedy's behalf, slipped a single paragraph into a $600 billion, 1,000-plus page bill, prohibiting the granting of waivers or extensions in cases of this kind, which passed through Congress without debate, in the case of the *Post* at least, they may have inadvertently been doing Murdoch a favour. Murdoch went immediately to court, and eventually the law was declared unconstitutional, because it was obviously aimed at only one individual. He was in time to save the day in Boston, but not in New York.

Meanwhile, with the halt of Wingo in 1986, circulation on the *Post*, which had reached a high of about 960,000, began to deflate and losses were mounting at astronomical rates. Now, with the Hollings-Kennedy law foreclosing any further delays, it looked as though the *Post* would be forced to close its doors.

Says Colasuonno, 'Rupert was up against it. The stench of death was all over this place. Peter Kalikow came in only at the eleventh hour. The paper was two hours from closing down. This was the oldest continually published daily in the US. But New York is an expensive town in which to put out a paper. This is a union town. It's a can of worms.

'I like to think it made Rupert's name in America, and I think that's why he was so reluctant to sell it. He *hated* to sell it, a) because it was the New York *Post* and it comes with all the trimmings, and b) because it was his only losing proposition, and he wasn't used to losing. I think it broke his heart, I really do. I've never seen him down the way he was when he told us. He had always been well-dressed, dapper, composed – a real professional. But now he was really upset, visibly shaken by the turn of events here, and I'd never seen him like that.'

Said Peter Kalikow, who bought the *Post*, 'Murdoch looked like a man who has just seen his daughter married off, then goes up to her empty bedroom for a last look . . .'

Roger Wood's wife, Pat Millar, herself a journalist, thought she had never seen a man look more miserable than Rupert Murdoch. 'His heart was breaking,' she says, 'I know he went to bed that weekend with a cold – and stayed there. So did Roger. At least, they both said it was a cold. But they both knew what it really was. It was a death.'

For Rupert Murdoch the dream of transforming the *Post* into the same success story as the *Sun* had died. As the New York paper's circulation rose and rose, the parallels between the American and the British experience must have been striking. And it *must have seemed*, if he could only hang on, only keep at it, that he would prevail; the tide would turn, the paper would move into solvency, then profit. And it would be one more success story in a string of successes, one more triumph for the world's most famous media magnate.

It just didn't happen that way.

*

In 1984, F. Gilman Spencer, former editor of the Philadelphia *Daily News*, Pulitzer Prize winner, horse-racing enthusiast, high school dropout and all-round roustabout, took over as editor of the New York *Daily News*.

A few words about F. Gilman Spencer.

After serving in the US Navy during the Second World War, Spencer returned home, went straight to the race track and began following his favourite pursuit – chasing women. 'And my mother threw me out of the house. I had been dating a girl whose father was the president of International Latex, and he didn't like me, and he felt I was a total n'er-do-well, and he was right. And the girl wanted me to take a nine-hour vocational aptitude test at the University of Pennsylvania. So I did, and they called me in and said I had two choices: a) I could go into the newspaper business or b) I could commit suicide.'

Spencer had never even read a newspaper, but he nevertheless put in his application at the Philadelphia *Bulletin*, who turned him down flat. So he went across to the Philadelphia *Inquirer* and saw the Director of Personnel there, 'a woman named Doris Yokum, and she said no, and I began to grovel and sob and dragged her to the window and pointed to my car, like little Eva. And she picked up the phone and got a guy on the line, and said "I've got a kid up here and I'd like you to give him a job." Long silence. A second request. Long silence. "Ken, I know where you were last night and who you were with."

'It was 1947, I was twenty-two years old, and I've been in the business ever since. When I came to the *Daily News*, I viewed the tabloids as fairly fun and impudent and irreverent. But I have a belief: "Don't fuck around with the news." If the news was exciting and fun and slightly on the sensational side, and some is automatically like that, then you play it. But you don't blow it up just for the sake of selling newspapers. It's not to be treated as some kind of a gimmick, just because it's a tabloid, just because it has all those heads, just to tell any story you want. There's plenty you can do without jerking it around with this cynical attitude, "Well, we're going to make it up." I'm not a purist nor am I a Puritan. But basically what works for a newspaper is that it is a newspaper, and news is to be believed.'

Meanwhile, Jim Hoge shipped in from Chicago on behalf of the Tribune Company in April 1985 soon after his old newspaper, the *Sun-Times*, had been purchased by Rupert Murdoch.

Both Spencer and Hoge are charismatic characters, each for different reasons. Spencer is colourful, outspoken, tall and handsome

166

in a raffish sort of way. Hoge, on the other hand, is reputedly so beautiful to behold that the New York society press, always on the lookout for *au courant* cult figures, has invented an 'ice-maiden' legend about him which makes especially good copy. Hoge *is* a privileged character *and* a fair-haired boy, who, after an Ivy League education, struck out on his own for the University of Chicago, braved the winds off Lake Michigan, paid his own way through a master's degree, staying at one point in a flophouse, 'and that's exactly what it was, with about sixteen whores, three social security pensioners and me.' He then worked his way up, from reporter to Washington correspondent, then to editor, then to publisher of the Chicago *Sun-Times* – through merit. Surprisingly, Spencer is on the *Social Register**; even more surprisingly, Hoge had his name taken off.

Each man bristles with integrity, Spencer of the old-time, no-nonsense, city editor variety; Hoge of the keeper-of-the-flame leitmotif. These are honest men who believe in a free, responsible and accurate press – American style.

David Banks is a British journalist who did a tour of duty on the *Post*, and then returned to Fleet Street. It was Gil Spencer's idea in 1987 to bring him back over to work on the *Daily News*. At the heart of the decision was the recognition that British know-how and energy informs the massive English tabloid market, and by importing one of the most energetic editors in the business, the *Daily News* could be re-invigorated.

'CHOPPED TO PIECES' is the headline that put Banks on the map so far as New York City was concerned. The story was about a man in Connecticut who put his wife through a woodchopper, and Banks, with typical British gusto, slapped the story onto Page One of the New York *Daily News*.

Says Spencer, 'It was not so much that we were importing crime. It's coming out of New York like trolley cars, and there's so much of it. You can have fifty murders or tries a day and there's blood all over the goddamn place. You've got to ask, "What is news and what isn't?" David Banks is a huge, imposing kind of guy, fun and jolly. But I felt that it wasn't going to work very well. And David meantime got a shot with Rupert and went to Australia to edit one of his papers.

'You can get suckered into replying in kind. We were simply

---

* A book with the names of people the editors believe to be socially prominent, and their schools, the clubs they belong to, etc.

167

operating on two entirely different philosophies of journalism and I thought that would be transferable to our paper, and we talked about it when I was hiring him. But I was beginning to pick up vibrations. People were talking about it, and responding to it. They weren't comfortable. We were getting letters. I felt that the staff, that some of our business people in circulation, were beginning to respond to it. It didn't get to circulation, it was only a six-to-eight-month period.'

The truth is, Hoge does tend to carry on a flirtation with the British tabloid press, but he always stops short of a full-fledged relationship. He cites the colour of London's *Daily Mirror* as the kind of reproduction he aspires to for the *Daily News*. It has been said that he originally wanted to make the *News* into something like Rothermere's *Daily Mail*, a chalk-and-cheese proposition. But most of Hoge's real interest in the British press stems from the Wapping experience. As Rupert Murdoch did in 1986, in an all-out war that lasted some thirteen months, Hoge wants to tame the unions in New York City. He is positively obsessed by it. And many want him to succeed.

'I have a guy,' he says, 'whose job is defined as follows: he is allowed to count the trucks in the truck parking lot. He can't do anything else. He can't touch the trucks, he can't drive the trucks. He just counts them. You go real slow, it takes you half an hour. If you got something else to do, it takes you about five minutes. And he's through for the day. I've got that kind of stuff all the way through this organization.

'I look at the size of the retail market here, and the disposable income, and I chart out what the growth is going to be from now to the year 2005, and I say to myself, my God! If you can get the awesome costs of manufacturing and distribution down, then there is room here for a couple more papers of 200,000–300,000 circulation. Everybody's always said you can't make a go of a paper that size, but there's nothing magical about it.

'On the *Daily News*, we took in $4 billion in advertising and circulation revenue. And we lost for the decade $115 million. We invested $170 million in technology, equipment and better processes, and we still couldn't keep the damn thing profitable. When you look at the union contracts, they require me to have compensation that's more than 50 per cent of my revenues. That's double what it is at any other metro paper in the US, outside of New York. I've got overtime pay that's 13 per cent of my payroll. That's compared to 3 per cent of other major metros. And all of this is built into the workrules that we've got here. I've got trucks

I can only load at 50 per cent capacity because the union's got in these things saying that bundles can only be so big. I've got jobs which are defined like nineteenth-century jobs, by how many moves you can make. The press maintenance group can go in and you can wipe three blankets and you can ratchet three rollers, and that's it. You've done your job. So if you've gotten through your four or five movements in fifteen minutes, you are through for the day, and I pay you for eight hours. If I want you to do anything else, first of all, you have the right to tell me to go fuck myself. If you decide to be a neat guy, and come and do something else, I pay you premium pay.'

Hoge has read all the right books on Wapping – Linda Melvern's *The End of the Street*, Brian MacArthur's *Eddy Shah: Today and the Newspaper Revolution* ('I'm not Eddy Shah,' he'll tell you in passing) he's been to Wapping, he's talked to Murdoch, he's trained his managerial staff and he's ready for, well, Little Wapping, this time played out on the streets of New York City.

Does he mean to win? 'I do, I do!'

Several storeys below him, his white-collar editorial staff stand in knots, whispering and chewing on their fingernails. 'What's the name of this place Jim Hoge keeps talking about?' one of them asks, 'uh, Werping?'

But the war between the New York *Post* and the New York *Daily News*, as anyone in New York will tell you, is only one campaign, though it's been a long and costly one. New York *Newsday*, the 'tabloid in a tutu', as Gil Spencer has christened it, also made its entrance into the New York market nearly four years ago, and to prove it, has lost almost $30,000,000 in the process. It now has a hard-won circulation of something in the neighbourhood of 170,000. With its parent company based on Long Island, New York *Newsday* suffers from bureaucratic problems as well as transport difficulties. The New York *Post*, on the other hand, with its infinitesimal advertising base, is plagued by staggering losses that its new owner, Peter Kalikow, a real-estate magnate listed by Forbes as one of the 400 richest men in America, has so far seen fit to underwrite.

Hoge is in that most uncomfortable position; if he fails, he fails utterly, and the other two newspapers, smacking their lips like vultures over a particularly rich, fat carcass, will pick up the *Daily News*'s circulation with alacrity. If he succeeds, he will in all probability drive the other two papers out of business. Most agree that there is no longer room for more than two newspapers in New York City – the New York *Times*, it goes without saying,

169

and the victor in the long-lasting tabloid war, whoever that might turn out to be.

Says Jimmy Breslin, columnist for New York *Newsday*: 'New York *Newsday* will be that paper. It will be the *Times* and *Newsday*.'

Says Lou Colasuonno, managing editor on the *Post*: 'This paper was founded in 1801 by Alexander Hamilton. I don't think it will ever die.'

Says Jim Hoge, publisher of the *Daily News*: 'I want to be the man who has on his epitaph that he saved the *Daily News*. It doesn't always have to be that newspapers die and close.'

Postscript: The New York *Daily News* went on strike on 25 October 1990. After a long and violent struggle, British newspaper mogul Robert Maxwell took over the newspaper the day it was scheduled to close down – 15 March 1991. Thus ends one more battle in the protracted New York newspaper war.

9
SUBTERRANEAN
CELLAR DWELLERS

In the land of dying newspapers, crime sells.

It is an unseasonably warm day in January 1990 when an elderly woman's handbag is snatched at 92nd Street and Park Avenue, an exclusive neighbourhood in upper Manhattan. As she crosses the street, a van drives up beside her, and one of its passengers grabs her bag. She becomes entangled in the leather straps and is dragged twenty-five feet, her blood painting a wide swathe down the street, before the straps finally snap and her maimed body comes to rest. 'MURDER ON PARK AVENUE' blare the headlines on the front page of the New York *Daily News*.

Says Deputy City Editor Bill Boyle, 'I've been doing crime work a while, and I've been doing it in New York a while, and New York stories are just so off the wall, so crazy – the mayhem is beyond belief at times – that you certainly get jaded. A story doesn't seem to last for weeks anymore. You're lucky to get two days out of it. We got two or three days out of the Park Avenue purse-snatcher story, and that really had all the elements of an important story. The woman was a pillar of society.

'The family handled it a little differently. Essentially they had one woman who served as spokesman for the family, and she said, "Here's what she was like, here's what she belonged to." The husband didn't talk. He didn't want to talk.

'If I was the victim of some tragedy, and three tabloids came after me in New York City, I'm not sure what I'd do. On one level I'd want to just get it out of the way and cooperate, because I know that the press in this city would continue to hound me. On another level I just wouldn't want to be bothered by the papers at all.'

These days in New York City, it's common practice to call a press conference for routine crime stories. It's an attempt by authorities to handle news distribution in an orderly way. Not every reporter is pleased by the silver-platter method of news delivery, though, complaining that 'it takes the thrill out of the hunt'.

'Understand that everybody feeds off everybody,' says Boyle,

171

'and the cops know when it's a big case that they have to have a spokesman on duty all the time. They know when to put extra cops on, they know when a case has to be broken and they know when they can just let something go. The District Attorney's office knows when it has to press aggressively. There's no question the DA's office treated the jogger case a lot more seriously than all the other rapes and assaults. In New York there is a cops-prosecutors-press triangle. If we decide it's big, they have to react to it because the press has decided it's big.'

In New York, three tabloids slug it out for the right to survive. The New York *Daily News*, circulation just over 1,000,000, the New York *Post*, circulation 540,000, and the newcomer from Long Island, New York *Newsday*, running at 170,000. Each hopes the other will falter, since mere survival is becoming more and more expensive every day. In the meantime, in the city where there were 1,900 murders in the last year alone, crime coverage seems to provide the one formula that never fails to sell papers.

Says Boyle, 'The competition here for those types of story is cut-throat, and I think you're going to see them competing more and more. If a reporter comes back without the photo or the quote, they've got to go back. Got to camp out on the doorstep till somebody comes out, got to stake out the house until you get it. That's common. We have street reporters and they don't write the stories. They call them into the rewrite man. The New York *Times* operates differently from the way we do. If you go to the New York *Times*, my impression is that you don't expect to spend eight hours camped outside someone's door for one quote.'

Says Bill Hoffmann, reporter for the New York *Post*, 'What the *Post* has always done is taken what people have thought and made up the headline. They like to get people's internal response to things. Or if no news is going on, they will take a little story and blow it up into a front-page headline. One time, nothing was going on. It was such a bad day that the waves moving was news. The editors said, "Find every little crime that happened today." So our reporters got them and the editors wove them together, and our lead was like "Fear and crime stalk our city", and the head was "MAYHEM ON OUR STREETS".'

Back at the *Daily News*, selectivity is the keynote of the day. Probably more than any other editor on the paper, Bill Boyle deals most directly with the police bureau. He's the one who hears the overnight statistics on killings in the city. 'Inevitably there are three or four. I get a few of those, and I might pick out one and say, "This one might be interesting. Let's pursue it a little bit."' But with 1,900 murders a year to choose from, deciding which ones make the paper isn't always easy. 'Even if you have a name,' says Boyle, 'and you don't always have that, and you start delving into the victim's background, nine times of ten, he's not that interesting. It's just not news.'

There used to be an unspoken rule among killers – call it a gentleman's agreement – that, so far as violent crimes were concerned, police, reporters, women and children were out of bounds. No more. Says one veteran reporter, 'Some of these places we go into here, wow. Forget about it. It used to be a sign of a little respectability to be seen next to a newspaper reporter, someone perceived as connected with officialdom. And also it was fun. Now they don't want to see you . . . they resent you. They resent TV people and that's new. That makes it tougher. Nobody in the press has been killed here yet; a few people have been punched around. It's tough on the nerves.'

Among the reporters working under Boyle are several women, who take their chances right alongside the men. 'We have a woman at police headquarters, and the City Hall Bureau Chief is a woman. These women will go anywhere. They're very tough,' says Boyle.

They need to be. The impression given by New York's Page One stories is of a city under seige. 'VICTIM'S RAGE' screams the head. The letters are superimposed over a large closeup of Viveca Lindfors, who required twenty-seven stitches after her face was slashed by muggers. Her quote: 'You don't want to be kicked out by kids or rats. This is where we live, me and my children and grandchildren, and we're not going to be kicked out by those bastards.' Another morning, and there's a photograph of a police officer holding a machete. 'MIDTOWN MACHETE MAYHEM' says the head: 'Knife-toting man menaces crowd – he's killed after Taser doesn't faze him'.

New York columnist Jimmy Breslin believes the crime problem in New York and elsewhere in America is a legacy of the Vietnam War.

Says Breslin, 'Martin Luther King said that the American bombs falling on Vietnam explode in the United States. That was a great line and it was true. The South Bronx was a victim of the Vietnam War every bit as much as the city of Saigon. The place fell apart.

'The Vietnam War gave us dope. We never had drugs like that. And with it came crime, more crime. Violence gets you violence every time. A violent war in Vietnam; you get more violence at

173

home. You put that into a situation where a large percentage of this city is born without hope, hundreds and hundreds of thousands of young males are about on the streets who haven't finished school, have trouble reading and writing, have never got a job and probably never will have a regular job. They understand at an early age that they're not going anywhere. People using guns all over the place. And then you start major drug shipments into this country, and people gleefully grabbing it, selling it and using it. And you got a major thing. And a problem that so far doesn't seem to have even the beginning of an end.

'The Number One subject in the city of New York is race. It determines everything. It determines transportation, crime, medicine. It's highly lucrative to attack blacks. It's always good business to attack the poor. It's good politics too. You always can get money and votes by attacking the poor. Come on, you cover crime stories, and you wind up making one black look like he represents ten million.

'If you've got time to look at it, you've got to tell it properly. When you say that the schools are unruly, you've got to say, "Well, my God, look what they've got." They've got kids who didn't even have breakfast in those schools; you've got to think of that. If you don't write that these people are in terrible shape because of these monstrous injustices going on, if you don't write that, that's wrong.

'Dickens had a great break. He was writing about poor people who were white.'

The preoccupation with race that dominates the inhabitants of most American metropolitan areas finds its natural culmination in a bizarre case in Boston, which played directly upon the natural expectations and prejudices of a city and, less directly, the entire nation. On the night of 23 October 1989, Carol Stuart, who was seven months pregnant, and her husband Charles were driving home from a natural childbirth class when they were attacked by a black mugger who demanded Carol Stuart's jewellery. Somehow, in the ensuing struggle, the mugger shot dead the young pregnant mother, seriously injuring her husband, before escaping.

A TV crew, who by chance were travelling with emergency workers that night, recorded on videotape the sight of the body of thirty-year-old Stuart, her head blown open, being carried from the family Toyota, where she had been shot, and into the waiting ambulance. The photograph of her body, brain matter discernible, was run on the front page of the Boston *Herald*, a tabloid owned by Rupert Murdoch, then quickly picked up by news publications across America. Stuart's baby, a son, was delivered by Caesarean section. He survived seventeen days. Before his death, Christopher Stuart was carried into his father's hospital room, where, for one last time, Charles Stuart held his dying son.

Meanwhile, Stuart, who had been shot in the abdomen, underwent two operations, one of them a colostomy, spending ten days in intensive care and a total of six weeks in the hospital. From his hospital bed at Boston City Hospital, he composed the farewell letter to his wife that was read out by his best friend at her funeral. 'You have brought joy and kindness to every life you've touched. I will never again know the feeling of your hand in mine.' The funeral was attended by the governor of the state, former democratic presidential candidate Michael Dukakis, and a number of other important state and city officials.

The hunt was on. Young black men all over the city suddenly found themselves subjected to stop-and-search operations by city police. Politicians called for the death penalty. At last, William Bennett, a thirty-nine-year-old black who had done time for, among other crimes, shooting a police officer, bragged to relatives that he was the murderer. In a lineup, Charles Stuart picked out the unemployed Bennett, identifying him as the assailant who had murdered his wife and, indirectly, his then unborn son.

Then, on the morning of 4 January 1990, Charles Stuart checked into a hotel near the Mystic River and went into an all-night supermarket to pick up some junk food, grinning strangely at the night cashier, before returning to his hotel room and changing clothes. He then left the hotel and jumped 300 feet from the Tobin Bridge to his death into the black and icy waters of the river below.

In the aftermath of his suicide, police revealed that Stuart had become, during the course of their investigation, the primary suspect in the murder of his pregnant wife. Evidence was mounting that he had planned to open a restaurant using the money from a life insurance policy he had taken out on his wife only a short time before her death.

The establishment's willingness to accept Stuart's version of events stunned the black community, whose resultant fury was inevitable. Meanwhile, a city had been forced to examine its attitude toward the nature of violent crime.

In the backlash of such a rising tide of emotion, both on the part of blacks and whites, the tabloid journalist is in the first line of fire, mainly because tabloids give more space to crime than do the broadsheets. Most of the tabloids, with few exceptions, are 'city papers', and this means their readership has a high percentage of blacks and other minority groups who expect to be represented fairly on their pages. Ironically, this readership brings the prestige of the tabloids down, while the broadsheet papers float comfortably atop the controversy.

One editor on one of the three New York tabloids was fired from his job because, it was alleged by staffers present at the time, he used a racial slur while seated at a bar after work one evening. Says the accused, 'It wasn't true, but I was just sacked, not given a chance to answer it. The management more or less conceded that they had made a mistake. There had been suits against one of the tabloids on the basis that minorities weren't being promoted, and essentially, the management didn't want any trouble. So I was basically blacklisted in New York for eighteen months. And I was bitter. I felt betrayed by the paper, and I felt that they had thrown me out for no reason at all – out of fear. And I felt I was slandered. They paid me money, but I'm still bitter.'

Such is the fear among white tabloid reporters in New York that they have unwittingly altered their manner of speaking, carefully omitting any words that could, under any circumstances whatsoever, be construed as racist. 'The reason why a lot of papers folded in the inner city,' one editor says, 'was a flight of "the population" out of the city into the suburbs.' There is a reluctance here for the editor to say 'white flight', the term sociologists were using freely ten years ago. 'Now,' the editor continues, 'we have a crop of people who can't read, or won't read, or don't want to read!' He doesn't identify who that group might be.

Another journalist mentions the high number of unidentified young black men who die nightly at 'known drug locations'. Without thinking, he identifies these as so commonplace they are no longer newsworthy; he pauses, then takes his comments off the record, because 'they could possibly be misunderstood'.

Still another privately concedes that most deaths in metropolitan areas are suffered by law-abiding citizens who live in the ghetto beside hardened criminals. As a general rule, he says, whites need not live in fear because most crimes are 'black-on-black'.

A notorious exception occurred in Central Park in April 1989 when a woman jogger was 'wilded' by a group of Harlem youths. Community passions were unleashed during the trial a year later. Eight rape suspects, aged fourteen to seventeen, were accused of beating, slashing and raping the victim, using a pipe and a brick to bludgeon her head when she tried to fight them off. Left for dead in a ravine, she gradually worked her way out of a coma and back to a life approaching normality. The youths, whose cold-blooded videotaped confessions made light of the attack, showed no remorse for their actions. Sources from within the detention centre where they were being held told reporters that the youths laughed and sang as they compared notes of what they had said on tape.

Parents of the youngsters, however, as well as many in the black community, say the event was blown out of proportion by a competitive press. Said the mother of one, 'She's back jogging, she's back working. My boy spent a year in jail. For what?'

Other blacks are reportedly enraged by the case simply for the reason that dozens of beatings and rapes take place every day in the black community with only passing notice. The very term 'wilding', which held such wide currency in national and international news coverage, was simply a misunderstanding by white reporters of black dialect, some believe. The youths gave their reasons for what they were doing as 'Wild *Thing*', the name of a popular rock song; it was transformed into an act of communal mayhem by the unconscious prejudices of white reporters, according to the theory.

Bill Boyle directed the reporters who covered the story for the New York *Daily News*. Reporters from the paper went to the homes of each of the youths. Says Boyle, 'We knew the name of the victim and we had her picture, but all the papers agreed not to use it or print it. The kids are all identified. They were largely good kids, whose parents were lower middle class. I think six of them lived in a place called Schoenberg Plaza which is a high rise – a middle-class subsidized housing project. Their parents were prison guards and sanitation men – working people. That's part of the interest in the story. You wouldn't think it would have been this kind of kid that would have done it. New York City is really getting crazier and crazier. I feel things have got worse in New York since I've been here.

'I think what I felt when it happened was that this is awful, horrible, what's happening to the city. I think the problem is deep. We've had eight years of an administration that's cut funds to the city for education, drug programmes and everything else. I think that's the start of the problem. You've got young kids being raised without any values, and you've got a drug problem that's out of control.

'You've got waves of new immigrants coming into the city, and the problems are just so overwhelming, that I just don't know if

177

they can be solved. I think politics is the only solution we have, but I don't think it can be handled by the people who run this city. We have a new school superintendent who seems to mean business. That may help. A new police chief. I don't know if he'll be effective.

'It's everybody's problem, because this is probably the greatest city in the world, it's at the centre of everything. I go through Grand Central every day, and it's like Baghdad. Unbelievable. It's worse in Penn Station. The UN is just a block away, and they're being killed and mugged too, people from all over the world.'

The publisher of the New York *Daily News*, an optimist and an idealist, believes the proper forum for solving the problem is the tabloid press. His view of what a tabloid is capable of achieving is distinctive. He sees the tabloid press, and the role of the New York *Daily News* in particular, as part of the solution to the city's problems. Says Jim Hoge, 'I think it's terribly important to try. What is the future of America, and particularly these big cities? It is to be the most diverse democracy anybody ever laid their eyes on. New York City by the year 2000 will be a city without a majority population. There's going to be about 30 to 33 per cent Hispanic, there'll be 24 per cent black, 12 to 15 per cent Asian and the rest will be white. There will be no single majority group. The emerging middle class in New York is going to be blacker and browner and more Asian than anything that's ever been seen in this country, and Los Angeles is going to be not far behind it.

'Somebody, if they care about newspapers and the role they play, has to say "We want to appeal to those audiences. We want to find the ways both to get them to talk to each other, fight with each other and bond with each other. The *Daily News* has historically in my opinion been a newspaper of emerging middle classes. I think it got its view of itself not when it said we are the paper of Irish and Italian Catholics, no. We are the paper of the Irish and Italian Catholics *when* they were the core of the emerging middle class of New York. But the paper is set up, it's reason for being there, is to link in with whatever the groups are which are emerging into the mainstream of American life. Now it's different. We still have a big core of the second and third generation of these white ethnic groups. It's part of our readership. But I think we have to be building now black readership, Hispanic readership, Asian readership.

'And every day you are making these people, just by cutting your product, address issues they would just as soon ignore, and that's what makes me comfortable. And you become the centre

Tony Brenna, reporter, *National Enquirer*: 'Bottom line: so I chase a few celebrities, so what?' (Interviewing Glenn Ford.)

Brian Hitchen, editor, *Daily Star*: 'Information is only a commodity, like bread...We sell it, so why shouldn't they?'

Larry Lamb, first editor of the *Sun*: 'I have worn throughout my life a substantial chip on my shoulder, on the grounds that I am not educated, and I should have been.'

Marjorie Proops, advice columnist, *Daily Mirror*: 'Human beings are subject to the same disasters they always were. The past wasn't that rosy.'

Joyce Hopkirk, first Pacesetter editor of the *Sun*: 'I was unattached and in the singles market, as it were...that's where all the sex came from.'

Roy Greenslade, ex-editor, *Daily Mirror*: 'I know all the tricks.'

George Lynn, retired reporter, the *Sun*: 'I actually switched on one of the blow torches to see if it was working. And it did work. It was very hot indeed.'

Kelvin MacKenzie, editor, the *Sun*: 'How about "F" for "Fuck off"?'

The late Generoso Pope, founder, *National Enquirer*: 'I can only live in one house at a time, I can only eat one hamburger at a time.'

Paul Levy, editor, the *Globe*: 'So the aunt passes out on the floor, and being a well-trained reporter, he simply stepped over the body, and he called me before he called an ambulance for her.'

Iain Calder, editor and president, *National Enquirer*: 'You'd go and get every single picture you could get, so there *was nothing left*. It was like Russia, the devastation as the Germans approached.'

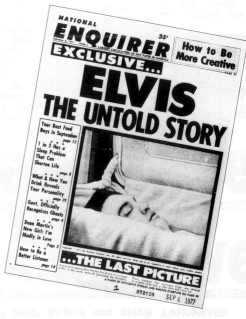

The famed collectors' item. When Generoso Pope died, the New York *Post* headlined his obituary, 'Enquirer Editor Goes to Meet with Elvis'.

TOMORROW: SARAH TAKES A BUS

Fame.

THE STAR SAVES BLACKIE

Don MacKays's editor told him to buy the donkey. MacKay: 'What if it's dead?' Editor: 'Buy the corpse.'

Tina Dalgleish, former investigative reporter, *News of the World:* 'One in ten people is potentially corrupt.'

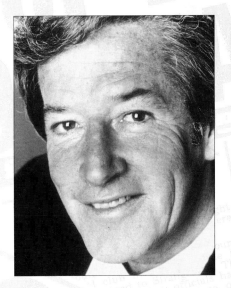

Steve Dunleavy, former metro editor, New York *Post*: 'Fuck 'em if they can't take a joke.'

Jimmy Breslin, columnist, New York *Newsday*: 'And that's the business – ARSE POWER. SIT. Don't walk around and talk about this story, don't swagger, don't tell me how much you had to drink, or how great you are or how tough it was. Just sit there and write. In silence, please.'

Lou Colasuonno, managing editor, New York *Post:* 'Everyone expected a three-headed monster with an Australian accent. What we got was a businessman who was personally a gentleman.'

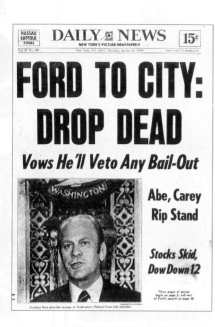

The most famous American tabloid headline.

Jim Hoge, publisher, New York *Daily News*: 'It doesn't have to be that newspapers die and close.'

Kurt Heine, crime reporter, Philadelphia *Daily News*: 'There are some people who are just completely evil, nothing redeeming in them at all.'

Drew Robertson, editor, *Sunday Sport*: 'Ask a comedian if his material is funny. Ask him.'

Trevor Kempson, chief investigative reporter, *News of the World*: 'Scotch, sex, cigarettes and sunshine.'

David Sullivan, proprietor, *Sunday Sport*: 'If I was sellin' the most papers in the country, that would be the most respectability that I would want.' (With Miss Face and Figure, 1990.)

of the community's dialogue and the issues that it has to thrash out. You're one of the steam valves. Just talking to people who are like yourself or went to the same school as you, just never seemed to me what journalism was all about. I think it's more important to get down there where I think it's more combative, where there's more difference of opinion, where there's more difference within the audience and where sometimes people get more emotionally committed because they've got more at stake. You take the issues of public schools, of taxing levels, of affordable housing. The people I live with through my newspaper, goddamn it, these are big things for them!

'I think a paper, the way the *Daily News* will be in about five years from now, can truly serve a very broad and diverse middle class, and be profoundly respected for it. I think it will happen.'

Meanwhile, several floors below Jim Hoge's office, Bill Boyle covers actual crime. 'You're dealing with people. You're dealing with people at their most basic, their most horrible; also at their most poignant, and it's a way to present people in those lights. It's not always that you're dealing with people at their lowest. Many times there's heroes, there's tragedy. Sometimes there's good news. The jogger recovered, remember.'

At night, he takes the train out of Grand Central Station and returns to his home in the suburbs. His wife is a schoolteacher, his son is in the little league and loves baseball.

'We had a six-inch story the other day about some guy who went to his estranged wife's house, and she was with her boyfriend, and so he stabbed her, the boyfriend and her two kids. Then he went to his apartment, stabbed himself and set the apartment on fire. Is that supposed to affect me personally? That's just a six-inch story.'

But somehow, despite his denial, one gets the impression it does affect Boyle. His wife, he'll tell you, is 'an upbeat person, much more so than I am.' What she keeps reminding her husband is that it's only a job. And if he tends to be silent a bit too often, or appears morose, he'll say the reason for it is easy to understand.

'Black Irish'.

In Philadelphia last year, there were 500 murders, 'not the highest rate in the country,' rewrite man Jack Morrison points out, perhaps defensively. 'Here you get an erroneous feeling of danger. Of the 500 murders, only one or two are of ordinary people who go into the city to shop or something like that. That only happens once or twice a year. It's mostly friends and relatives killing each other,

179

domestic knifings, muggings, that sort of thing – or drug dealers. They're not all worth high play in the paper.'

Morrison is quick to point out that the Philadelphia *Daily News* is 'full of information about the entire world.' He picks up 'the budget', the paper's listing of all the stories that moved overnight. There are two stories on the dangers of lead poisoning, a story on the closing of the Trauma Unit at Temple University Hospital, one on an injunction placed on the state anti-abortion bill, another on the Mummers who each year stage a parade in the city on New Year's Day, one on the Regional Burn Unit and at last a story on a sex discrimination case. The rest are in one way or another connected with crime.

Out of twenty-three stories listed on the budget, thirteen of them deal with crime in the city.

The reason for this, says *Daily News* crime reporter Kurt Heine, is the nature of the coverage. At night you get the 'fresh mayhem'. Then in the daytime, 'you get a new shipment of fresh mayhem, along with the opportunity to rehash old mayhem . . . in court hearings and such.'

By comparison with New York, Philadelphia is a cosy city, with its unintimidating 500 murders. Yet it was in Philly that the most bizarre single episode ever to occur in the history of American crime fighting took place. On 13 May 1985, police were given the go-ahead to drop a bomb on a predominantly black, middle-class neighbourhood.

Says an editor who was on duty when it happened, 'The paper knew that the police were going to move in, so people on staff were alerted to stay, and they did stay, but no one would ever expect the mayor to bomb the neighbourhood. I had been working overnight, so I was told to go to a hotel room and get some sleep, and as I was lying there, I was watching TV. And I remember watching the helicopter, and then something coming out of it, and then all of a sudden the fire started, and then I remember seeing the fire for real outside my hotel window, which was a high rise, and then I got up and I just went back to work. So, you'll have to go a ways to top that.'

Says rewrite man Morrison, 'You reach a point, if you've been in this business for three or four decades, that you've written every story that can be written. Then something like that comes along. Nothing like that has ever happened in history . . . you know, a guy drops a bomb on a row house in his own city, burns up eleven people, six of them kids.'

The problem started in 1983 when a militant cult moved into

a West Philadelphia row house. Members of the cult, who called itself MOVE, wore ragged, dirty clothing and kept their unwashed hair in long, matted ringlets of the Rastafarian style, called dreadlocks. The cooking of food was prohibited by the cult; even meat was consumed raw, and soon the children who were part of the group began eating out of neighbours' dustbins as an alternative to the raw food they were being offered at home. Part of MOVE's doctrine had to do with the cultivation of animals, and soon a stable of stray dogs and cats appeared in the back yard. Along with them were insects and rats, who, under the principles the cult lived by, were afforded the same protection as other animals.

MOVE members refused to pay gas or water bills and threatened to kill a city worker who came to turn off the water. At one point, men from the cult chopped down park trees, dragging the trunks back to their house, where they constructed a fortified bunker. In it, they installed a loudspeaker and began broadcasting angry and profane speeches against neighbours who by now had lodged a number of formal complaints against them with the city.

In the aftermath of the episode, police finally moved in, and cult members opened fire on them. After the exchange of thousands of rounds of ammunition, the decision was taken by the Police Commissioner, with the Mayor's approval, to use an 'entry device', i.e., to bomb the house. The fire that resulted from the bombing destroyed the entire neighbourhood, including sixty-one houses and the belongings of 263 people.

Such is the spirit of Philadelphia, where, it will be remembered, the Founding Fathers wrote the Declaration of Independence, that a joke began to make the rounds. It goes:

Question: 'What's the only place in the world where the mayor bombed his own city?'

Answer: 'Philadelphia.'

Punchline: '*And* he was re-elected to office.'

Moral: '*And* most voters were relieved . . . because the other candidate, he was trouble.'

Within the corridors of the Philadelphia *Daily News*, where Kurt Heine reports, other reporters regard him with awe; his ability to turn a phrase is legendary.

Heine is one of a lonely breed. In a country where investigative reporting alone confers status, Heine loves words, specifically tabloidese. One of the last Americans who can write it, he is probably the American who writes it best.

Heine became addicted when he was reporting in Trenton, New Jersey. A novice night police reporter up against two old pros, Heine felt distinctly vulnerable. Each night he sat listening to a police scanner, and then, desperate, he would race out to wherever anything was happening to see if he could scrounge a story. His competitors were complacent enough to think they could weight the story simply by listening.

One night Heine heard a report of a stabbing at a local rollerskating rink. With only a half hour to deadline, Heine raced out to the location to find hundreds of teenagers in the street, 'not causing any trouble,' says Heine, 'but ready to.' As he got out of his car, he saw a youth being taken away in an ambulance. A police officer, who remembered Heine from his nocturnal presence at every crime committed in the city, gave Heine the exclusive. Heine raced back and wrote the story.

On the paper at the time was a new editor, employed by the owner to jazz up the coverage. A tabloid hack 'who had been writing larger headlines by the day,' says Heine. The editor became red in the face from the excitement of Heine's story, slapping a gigantic headline across the front page of what had until then been a staid community news sheet – 'TEEN SLAIN IN ROLLER BRAWL'. Says Heine, 'The next day, people were calling in by the dozens and saying "Cancel my subscription." But after that the paper jumped on any kind of a crime story, using that kind of tabloid display, and the editor stayed on.'

This is when Kurt Heine turned into a tabloid man. The values of the tabloid had been 'imparted to me', he says, and from that point on, he never looked back.

Some of Heine's best stories were written when Gary Michael Heidnik – a white man who kidnapped six black women and chained them in his basement, raping them daily and eventually murdering two of them – went on trial in Philadelphia. Heidnik, a diagnosed schizophrenic with a penchant for making big money on the stock exchange, repeatedly beat the women, torturing them in unspeakable ways, and fed them on the remains of one of the murdered women, which he mixed with dogfood. The self-appointed head and only member of a church he founded himself, Heidnik dreamed of fathering a race of children who, he imagined, would be reared in his basement. Writes Heine,

He had but one master and one mission.
For Gary Michael Heidnik, nothing else mattered.

182

He would rule a warped subterranean world of enslaved women and sire the basement babies that God wanted.

He would do it, he told a psychiatrist, to fulfill 'a pact with God' . . . The newborns would be breast-fed, then weaned onto the human flesh of one of the women he had killed, sawed apart, and stored in his freezer. . .

During the three-week trial, Heine wrote dozens of stories on the demented Heidnik: probably the most unique, the Gary Heidnik weather report. The trial took place in June 1988, and that month it was unseasonably hot in Philadelphia. Temperatures were daily reaching 85 degrees in the courtroom, and along with high humidity and the horrific revelations taking place in court, things were becoming less and less bearable. Heine and his editor were talking about this one day and decided they should do some kind of story on the subject. The result is a tabloid classic.

How hot is it?

So hot that accused torture-murderer Gary Heidnik took his first shower in seven weeks, by his lawyer's estimate.

But not hot enough for Heidnik to launder the fetid Hawaiian shirt and baggy pants he has worn to court appearances for more than a year.

Heidnik showed up for his murder trial yesterday with his shoulder-length hair and shaggy beard washed and combed, a day after Common Pleas Judge Lynn M. Abraham issued an order directing that Heidnik be allowed to shower at the city Detention Center on Tuesday night . . .

Defense lawyer A. Charles Peruto Jr., who was relieved that Heidnik's aroma had dropped a few notches yesterday, explained the span between his client's showers: 'It was due to the fact that it was inconvenient for him to take a shower and that his personal habits are right up there with Charles Manson's.'

Heidnik owned three cars, a fur-lined Dodge van, a Cadillac and a Rolls Royce. During the trial, someone mentioned in passing that the Rolls had a Chevy engine. Heine was intrigued and asked police for permission to go and look at the car. Eventually, a couple of months after Heidnik was arrested, Heine was allowed into the pound, and, he says, 'Here is this Rolls Royce. The windows are all down, the interior is all rotting from the rain coming in, and

183

the police don't care. So I'm in this car, and I'm trying to open this hood to find out what kind of an engine it has, and I can't find the hood release. It's a Rolls Royce. I've never tried to release the hood of a Rolls before. So I have this portable telephone, and I call this Rolls Royce dealer, and he said, "Well, you reach right under the dashboard, and it looks just like part of the dashboard, and you pull this little place just next to the steering wheel." So I try this, and I don't have any luck. So I call him back, and finally we decide since this is a right-hand drive car, the release is on the other side. . . . So I open the hood, and sure enough, there is this beat-up, second-hand Chevy engine in this Rolls Royce. So while I'm in there, I notice his collection of tapes, and I acquired these.

'When I spoke to Heidnik's lawyer about the Rolls Royce with the Chevy engine, the lawyer went right along. So I got my lead:

> Gary Michael Heidnik, accused sex-slave killer, may have ruined his Rolls Royce by replacing its original transmission and hand-crafted engine with junkyard Chevrolet parts.
>
> 'Not only does he have a dual personality, but he has a car to match,' said Heidnik's lawyer, A. Charles Peruto Jr., who claims Heidnik is insane. 'It fits completely.'

'Then,' says Heine, 'I started listening to the songs, and they turned out to be really quite prophetic, like "Shackles on My Feet".'

> He eases behind the wheel of his Rolls Royce and sets off, trolling North Philadelphia's streets for young women he might lure back to his home for sex and, perhaps, a stay in his basement breeding chamber.
>
> Accused torture-murderer Gary Michael Heidnik presses a cassette tape into his cheap stereo and turns the volume knob as far as it goes . . .
>
> Even before one of the muffler-clamped sex slaves escaped the basement dungeon in March and told police of her captivity, Heidnik's neighbors had remarked about the ear-splitting music that blared from the horror house 24 hours a day.
>
> The radio volume knobs were turned up almost all the way in both of Heidnik's cars when police hauled them away.
>
> Some of the women who survived the captivity testified in court that Heidnik wanted to sire a family with them in his basement. They said he had installed loudspeakers near

184

the subterranean man-sized pit where they were periodically shackled when he thought they had misbehaved.

Heidnik would boost the loudspeaker volume to deafening levels when he left the house, so the captives' screams for help couldn't be heard by neighbors, the women said.

In another of Heine's stories, he seriously discusses 'Heidnik's corpse problem.' 'His solution?' Heine writes, 'A food processor from Sears.'

Says Heine, 'I have a voice in my mind when I write. It's not the voice of a writer, though. It's the voice of a reader . . . The voice of the Philadelphia *Daily News* [laughter]. And it says to put things in the bluntest possible way, so if the subject is an extreme of human behaviour, the writing really shows that. I know that part about the "corpse problem" sounds humourous in a sick sort of way, and I'm not sure why, but I think that might be a lot of what the perceived humour is, somebody saying it so blunt. I'm not a humourous person, I'm not a funny person.'

If anything, in fact, Heine is a serious man. During the course of the trial, which Heine attended every day, he found he couldn't help becoming 'sad and morose because there were these women, who came pretty much one after another, and all of them were pretty pathetic people to start with.

'Black women are fairly low on the social scale in poorer areas, especially in the neighbourhood this guy was prowling. And he would pick the most defenceless black women to prey upon – prostitutes, women who were mildly or completely retarded – and would subject them to unimaginable torture. And the way some of them would talk about it was the thing that upset me; just in a completely affectless way, in a monotone, "Yes, just another thing that happened to me. Yesterday my foot got run over by a car, and today I got chained up in a guy's basement."

'I found the horror so intense that I couldn't leave it at work. It affected my sleep. I talked a lot to my wife about it. It helps just to say "This is how horrible this person is." To a large extent, talking to my wife works. Drinking doesn't work.' Heine's wife is an abuse counsellor at a women's shelter in Philadelphia, and they have two children, one six, another two and a half. Heine and his wife share the household responsibilities and the parenting of the children.

Says Heine, 'I'm a bit of a housewife. I'm usually in a bad mood when I'm doing vacuuming and cleaning chores. I hate to do them so much, but after they're done, they're a real accomplishment. The other household things like cooking and playing with the children, I'm always in a good mood. Maybe the vacuuming is how I got Heidnik out of my system.'

To Heine, Heidnik was 'partly evil, partly demented. There are others who are just plain bad, nothing redeeming in them at all.

'Something a lot of people don't realize is the capacity for evil. Unless you see a person who has it, and I have, it's foreign to your mind. I guess there are a lot of people like that running around, but they don't show it to the average middle-class person that often. And when it shows itself, it's just so overwhelming.

'I've actually found myself hating someone I've never even talked to. Not Heidnik, but another guy who comes to mind. He was some kind of a sexual pervert. He raped a number of women and then he did some bizarre stuff; like he broke into a woman's apartment when she wasn't at home, and he took her underwear and shaped it into the shape of a person in her bed. Then he found some pictures of her and he stabbed knives in the picture in the middle of this underpants arrangement. He had tried to rape a woman in a very expensive suburb, and for some reason, he ran out of her house, and a few minutes before that, he had broken into another woman's house, and she had called the police. And a policeman had been called out of his station – he was usually a desk man – to see if he could catch this guy, and he saw the guy. And the guy somehow wrestled the cop down to the ground, and he somehow got hold of his own gun and shot him with it at point-blank range, completely cold, and then ran off.

'There are some people. . . . The death penalty is applied far too often by the courts, but there are some people who are just completely evil, and . . .' Heine gestures hopelessly in favour of the death penalty.

Killing about the same time as Heidnik was a twenty-eight-year-old man named Harrison 'Marty' Graham, but as Heine puts it, Graham attracted less attention, 'probably because he is so foreign to the mind. He was just from another world, the darkest recesses of the ghetto. Heidnik had some nice cars and some stocks, he had an interest in things that regular people have an interest in . . . and he's white . . . I guess that has some small amount to do with it.'

The apartment where Graham killed seven women was known as 'a shooting gallery', that is, a place where drug addicts go to get high. Extremely popular at this location was a $2 mixture of Ritalin, a stimulant, and Talwin, a pain killer, that gives 'a cheap, quick high' after it is cooked and injected into the vein. It is known on the street as 'Rs & Ts'.

186

Graham was said by one court-appointed psychologist to be suffering from a mental illness called alloplastic psychosis. Although the individual's thought patterns may appear to be normal, his acts 'are sick', especially those connected with sex. One of the symptoms may be the practice of necrophilia, an act committed by Graham on one or more of the six female corpses found stored in a locked bedroom in his dishevelled apartment, where open buckets and bottles substituted for washroom facilities. A seventh corpse, thrown out on the roof, was found rotting beneath a mattress where Graham had hidden it several months before his crimes were discovered. Heine was assigned the court case, and his stories chronicle the degradation of the ghetto in America and of the addicts who inhabit it.

> He choked her during sex until she couldn't breathe.
> He waved a machete at her until she bowed to his deviant whims.
> He hacked off the seat of her pants and had his way with her while she slumbered in a drug stupor.
> She believed him when he said he had murdered his old girlfriend.
> And the stench of death made her sick.
> Yet Paula Renee Pinder, who said she endured that and more during the two years she was accused serial slayer Harrison 'Marty' Graham's live-in lover, kept coming back – even after Graham dumped her for other women . . .
> Why did she repeatedly return?
> In an apathetic voice with her cheek propped on her fist, she said she returned for a variety of reasons, from drugs, money and shelter to Graham's 'kind, attentive side,' for which 'there was still sort of an attraction.'

During the murder of one of his victims, a friend of Graham's watched him choke a girlfriend to death, but did nothing to help her. After the killing, Anthony 'Tony Carlos' Ogelsby was shown Graham's collection of 'rotting bodies stacked in the stinking bedroom of his North Philadelphia apartment. He said he walked away, vomited, and rushed out to inject himself with three bags of cocaine. "The smell," Ogelsby said in an even, detached voice, "I couldn't stand the smell . . ." When Assistant District Attorney Roger King asked why he didn't try to help Brooks, Ogelsby replied: "I was going there to get high. I didn't go there to protect nobody."'

Graham was a child of the ghetto, early in his life farmed out to a foster mother. Throughout the trial, she remained loyal to Graham, characterizing him as 'a good boy who is retarded and illiterate. She said she tried to teach him to read and write, but settled for "training" him that "he must eat, keep himself clean, and pay his rent."' When he came to her, he was a tiny child 'with a mysterious scar across his forehead and pus-filled boils covering his body.

He didn't talk, wasn't toilet-trained, and cried almost constantly.

His mother was in jail, where she spent two years for child neglect, and Graham, his older brother and younger sister were placed by the city in a foster home. Graham can't remember how he got the scar.

His mother, questioned by the prosecutor about her relationship with her son, had few answers:

*Why was she jailed two years for neglecting Graham and two of her other children in 1961?

*Why did Graham wind up in a foster home for five years?

*Why did Graham's father run away?

'I tried to tell him it wasn't my fault,' said Jeter, 43, who gave birth to her first child when she was 12 and had Graham, her second baby, when she was 14. 'But he keeps asking about it.'

As Jeter recounted the story of her son's broken life, Graham sat upright in his chair, awake and alert for the first time in almost two weeks of court.

He was 7 when his mother regained his custody. By then, Jeter said, he would beat his head into walls whenever he sat down.

In his closing argument, Assistant Attorney Roger King said that Graham was a symbol of 'what is wrong with this city.' It was a glimpse into 'a ghetto world where the majority can't read, the police ignore drug shooting galleries, dope addicts live amid their own excrement in boarded-up houses, and apathy's grip is so strong that seven women vanished, their corpses putrefying for months before anyone noticed.'

Says Heine, 'During the trial the father of one of the dead

188

women came most every day, and Marty Graham's mother came most of the time with her boyfriend, and there were a couple of other guys who were just homeless guys who got interested in the trial somehow. And every day, after they got out of the homeless shelter, they would head over to City Hall and sit in on the Marty Graham trial. It was a big courtroom, seats over 100 people. And some of them just went to sleep in the back. There were maybe eight or ten in all.'

Harrison 'Marty' Graham was given a life sentence for the murder of the first woman. Judge Robert A. Latrone, who considered Graham's sentence for five days, then sentenced Graham to life for each of the next six killings. Because of an anomaly in the Pennsylvania legal system, however, a previous murder conviction can be considered 'aggravating', and for this, you can go to the electric chair. In Graham's case, with the single previous murder conviction, if he appeals his life sentence for any of the others, he can then be put to death by the state. Lawyers in the case said they knew of no other sentence like it in Pennsylvania history.

Says Heine, 'It's a beautiful sentence really. He's got life, and he'll never even ask for parole. He'll never, never, never get out.'

In the meantime, buried deep in his high-security prison cell and forgotten by everyone except the reporter who wrote his story, Graham lives on – a symbol of the degradation of the ghetto that produced him. He is what happens in America's no-go zones, where crack cocaine, heroin and unsavoury drug cocktails are king – the shadow-world of the American dream.

10
PERSONAL SERVICES

She is a delicate woman, with sunny blond hair that curls softly into a pageboy. Her high cheekbones, classically straight nose and frosty smile betoken the aristocrat, as do her clothes and jewellery. For the publicity photograph accompanying her latest book, she has chosen a three-strand pearl choker with diamond clasp, matching earrings, a strapless ballgown, and long white kid gloves. Sydney Biddle Barrows, 'descended from an English Puritan who emigrated on the famous ship to America in 1620,' is otherwise known as 'The Mayflower Madam' who once ran 'the world's classiest call-girl service.' But this was only after she was busted by cops in New York City and after Peter Fearon went to work on her.

At the time of the story, Fearon was an illegal immigrant, a veteran newsman and self-styled 'trouble-maker'. He had come to New York with 'five grand in my pocket and the names of two contacts.' Just as the money was giving out, somebody suggested he look up a man named Steve Dunleavy, who was then Metro Editor on the New York *Post*. Dunleavy put Fearon on the desk as a rewrite man, and before long, he had worked into a permanent position, to some extent by default, since, after six weeks on the job, union rules required that he become a member of staff.

One of Fearon's jobs on the paper was to go in on a Sunday when there wasn't any staff and 'kickstart the week'. The Friday afternoon before one of these Sundays, there had been a police raid on an escort agency, and several young women were arrested. The story, Fearon remembered, had appeared in the last edition of Friday's paper. It seemed unusual because there are so many escort agencies in New York, 'nobody much bothers with them.' But very little else was going on, so he sent Leo Sachs to investigate. Sachs had received a tip-off that one of the women, Sheila Devin, was high profile but he wasn't sure in what way. On Monday, Fearon alerted Dunleavy that he thought the story might be worth going after.

What they came up with was the name Biddle Barrows – which seemed to ring a bell. So they looked it up on the *Social Register* and found the unusual combination of last names with a dagger beside it. They then cross-checked it with some records of the original crossing of the Mayflower, and sure enough, there was the name. All they had to do now was to confirm Barrows was the same woman who had been arrested the Friday before. After some digging, they came up with business records and handwriting samples confirming that Sydney Biddle Barrows was in fact Sheila Devin. They decided to go with the story.

Fearon has a clear memory of sitting down to put it together, 'trying to write very carefully, making it look like we knew more than we did.' He remembers tapping in a slugline that seemed snappy – 'The Mayflower Madam' – so he wrote it into the body of the story.

The name was 'the key to the whole thing,' he says. 'Without the tag, it was just another story about a madam who ran an agency. Everybody made money who used that name: the Mayflower Madam herself, the guy who ghost-wrote her book, the guy who wrote the article for the *New York Magazine*.' Everybody, that is, except Fearon.

Meanwhile, behind the scenes, the *Post* was piling up sleaze on the girl. But in order to make the story sell, they had to keep 'making up glamour stories'. The escort service became the 'world's classiest call-girl service'. It was run by 'the Mayflower Madam', and Sydney Biddle Barrows became something akin to a demure débutante who had arranged personal services for important lawyers, clergymen, Arab princes, film stars and politicians, none of whom she ever named. Fearon believes it's because they never existed, except in the lore of tabloid journalism.

In the end, Fearon was so successful in elevating the story that television took it up, creating a climate suitable for consumption by the masses. Today Barrows continues to prosper as an authority on sexuality, Peter Fearon has himself moved into television and the American public has the kind of heroine it traditionally takes to its heart – the fallen woman with heart of gold, a kind of latter-day Hester Prynne.

What really sells newspapers in the United States is mayhem and violence, with sex in large part diluted by the imperative of the moral majority. Thus, every metropolitan daily keeps on staff a large and highly trained force of reporters whose speciality is crime. In England, sex is what sells. And staffers specialize in using the unorthodox methods that produce the ever-popular sex exposé.

Standard operating practice is to go undercover to produce the scandals that are the bread and butter of the tabloid press. One of the more common scams is to entrap a prostitute by pretending to be a businessman, asking her to your room and then, after she asks for the money, revealing you are a reporter.

A standard Fleet Street story on hotel hookers goes like this. A reporter is on an out-of-town assignment with a photographer and is looking for a quickie story. They come up with the idea of ringing an escort service, asking for an escort for the evening. The plan is for the photographer to get into the wardrobe, and when he hears the reporter say a code phrase, like 'Darling, you've got lovely knickers,' he jumps out and snaps the girl. Ideally, this takes place at the very moment the reporter is saying, 'I'm a reporter from the *Sun*.'

So the agency sends a girl to the hotel and the desk clerk calls them and they say, 'Yes, send her up to Room 204.' The photographer jumps into the wardrobe. The girl comes in, the reporter offers her money for sex, the girl says 'yes' and begins taking her clothes off. At which point, the reporter says in a loud voice, 'Darling, you've got lovely knickers.' And nothing happens. So the reporter repeats the code phrase, 'Darling, you've got lovely knickers.' Again, nothing happens. One last time, the reporter shouts out, *'Darling, you've got lovely knickers!'* The girl throws on her clothes and flees, certain that the reporter is a sexual pervert. The reporter opens the wardrobe door to find the photographer fast asleep.

At this juncture, the author of the tale takes a swig from his pint, leans forward, and asserts emphatically one of the catchphrases of Fleet Street: *'True story.'*

Another similar tale has a different twist. A reporter for the *News of the World* has been working undercover in Paris for six months to expose 'The Ten Top Vice Madames in Europe.' He has rented a suite in Paris's exclusive George V Hotel, and as many as eight girls a day are coming through, many of them models for top flight modelling firms, 'models during the day, highrolling at night.' This is about fifteen years ago, and even 'in those days, they are charging as much as £250 a throw.' On principle, the reporter never succumbs to the charms of the women he writes about. But one of them attracts him. Stunningly beautiful, she is the wife of a member of the French aristocracy, complete with a castle and grounds – a businesswoman who owns a chain of boutiques across Europe. On the side, as she travels around, ostensibly buying wares for her boutiques, she is working as a high-class hooker. Eventually, the reporter publishes a front-page story on the woman.

A few months later, he goes to France and looks her up. She comes to the phone and says, 'How could you do this to me?' and he just answers, 'It was the story. But I really do like you so much, and the story is all over now.' She agrees to meet him, they talk, she forgives him. And they have an affair.

'*True story.*'

These Fleet Street tales pale into insignificance, though, beside those of Lindi St Clair, a.k.a. *Madam* Lindi St Clair, the Lady of Laxton Manor. St Clair is a prostitute who, according to *The Sunday Times*, 'earns her bread and butter beating the living daylights out of perfectly compliant clients.' She once ran for political office as the Corrective Party candidate, with a 51-point platform – 'one for every inch of her bust' – featuring such slogans as 'Free sex on the National Health Service' and 'Free condoms with milk'. St Clair, who runs a fourteen-hour-a-day business, sometimes appears in scarlet lace pantaloons and corset. On Valentine's Day 1990, she scandalized Parliament by sending special messages to various MPs, seventy-two of whom she claims to have bedded. She signed the cards 'the Queen of Tarts'.

It has been known to happen, from time to time, that this well known lady of the night picks up her telephone, dials the number of the *News of the World* and asks to speak with Trevor Kempson, the chief investigative reporter there. It was Kempson who, on 9 January 1977, exposed St Clair as 'an evil woman who trades in torture' in a story headlined 'What Goes on Behind the Bars at Number 58b'. St Clair is a friendly sort who never forgets a favour. 'I have a lot to thank you for, Trevor,' she says in her plummy voice. And, in actual fact, she does.

In those days St Clair was running a torture chamber near Earl's Court when Kempson heard of her existence. He also heard she had a two-way mirror where you could watch what she did with her clients, and he thought he could base a story on the fact that important men were putting themselves into a situation that had a potential for blackmail.

Upon reaching her house, Kempson discovered a brass plaque with the aphorism, 'Abandon hope all ye who enter here.' St Clair, who was clothed from head to foot in leather, invited him in, explaining that she took only specialized clients who had been personally recommended to her. But Kempson bluffed his way in by saying he had heard about her on a plane and wanted to

193

try out her services for himself. At last she agreed, and he was given an apointment for two days later, she being 'fully booked at the moment.'

When Kempson returned at the appointed hour, he was escorted into a torture chamber that invited comparison with a painting by Hieronymus Bosch. He saw 'a clothes horse . . . with a rubber waterski suit, medieval costumes, transparent rubber dresses, a university mortar board and gown, schools' gym slip and beribboned straw hat.' There were also 'whips, canes and rubber replicas of male and female genitals . . . on display.' St Clair's equipment, Kempson says, came from Hamburg which is one of the world centres for the trade. Of all the services on offer, Kempson picked out rubberwear, at a cost of about £200, because, he says, 'I thought it was safest.' He found out otherwise.

'"You're into bondage, aren't you?" she asked. I protested loudly,' Kempson says, 'but, the more you protest, the more you like it, they think, and she put this dog collar around my neck, buckled one of the straps up top, one at bottom, then tied my wrists behind my back, put a rubber mask over my head, tied my ankles up and threw me on the couch.'

He was instructed to wait there for twenty minutes, and indeed, no alternative presented itself to Kempson, who said, 'I was wetting myself with fear, almost. And I thought, "I don't even know where the bloody mirror is."'

When she came back, she said, '"You loved that, didn't you?" And I said, "No I didn't, I just like being in rubberwear." She said, "No, you don't, you loved that. You love being beaten, don't you?" My legs were still tied, but she let those off, and she put a rubber cloak on me, with a hole here [motions to his genitals] and sort of led me off to the rack, and I was then six foot tall and I was afterwards six foot two. As she strung me up, the handcuffs were cutting into my skin.'

After an interminable time hanging about, Kempson was rejoined by St Clair, who said '"Now for another £200, I'll show you where the mirror is." She took me into a room, and she pulled back a picture, and I looked through and realized it was the room where *I'd* been, and I thought, "Bloody hell, who's been looking through at *me*?"'

More than a dozen years later, Kempson, who is now fifty-eight years old and one of the single most respected figures in tabloid journalism, ruminates about the experience. He sits back in his chair, takes a puff of his cigarette, a swallow of Scotch. He looks you in the eye quizzically, shrugs his shoulders. 'This is what people do. I'm sorry, Darling.'

The Queen of Tarts has travelled quite a distance since that first article appeared in the *News of the World*. When the paper came to her door to inform her that the exposé would appear in the next issue, the twenty-two-year-old St Clair yelled down from the top of the staircase, 'You can **** off, I'll sue . . . Tell them what I do in my own house is my own business. Tell them I'll sue if they publish anything about me.' Later, on the telephone, she relented a little: 'At least,' she said, 'my clients can come and release their fantasies somewhere.'

After a time, St Clair became quite chummy with the press, and Keith Deves made it a habit of dropping in on her now and then just to keep up on events. Deves was for many years the *Sun*'s self-styled 'Dirty Affairs' correspondent. 'If the vicar ran off with a choir girl,' Deves says, 'somebody else was assigned the story. If the vicar ran off with a choir *boy*, I did the story.' Deves is also remembered for his massage-parlour exposés. In a single afternoon, he had so much baby oil massaged into his skin that at one establishment he slid off the table.

At the time he became close friends with St Claire, she was battling with the Inland Revenue to have the implements in her torture chamber declared tax deductible. One day around lunch-time, Deves called, and according to the story, she said, 'Oh, hallo, I can't talk to you here. Let's go round to the pub.' So they went down to the local, and he asked her what was happening. They got to chatting and before they knew it, two hours had passed.

And suddenly St Clair jumps up and says, 'Cor, I forgot about Mr Jones. *I left him on the rack*, and he's only paid for twenty-five minutes!'

They rush back to the torture chamber, and there is this middle-aged, balding man on this rack, covered in perspiration, and wriggling frantically. St Clair goes up to him and he says, 'Where were you, Lindi?' To which St Clair replies, 'Don't worry. I've just been talking to my friend here. He's a reporter from the *Sun*.'

St Clair has taken her place in the lore of the tabloid press as the sweetheart of 'personal services', a phrase which she originated and which, for several years, was the name under which her business was incorporated. And if you were to call the editor of a well-known newspaper in London to ask for her phone number, he might very well ask, 'Home or Dungeon? I'll tell you what, I'll give you both.'

195

St Clair's success, along with the exploits of the legendary Cynthia Payne, has led to tabloid spin-offs of similar tales, many a good deal seedier than their prototypes. George Lynn, reporting for the *Sun*, was assigned a personal services story, and since he was unused to this kind of reporting, he admits to feeling slightly uneasy about the whole thing.

What had happened was that a prostitute specializing in sado-masochism, who was also the lesbian partner of a woman named Margi Dunbar, had been found dead in a bar. Dunbar, also a prostitute, was a suspect in the case. Like the dead woman, she had a torture chamber on the Cromwell Road which she had set up in competition with her former lover. As soon as he received the assignment, Lynn set out, accompanied by a photographer, down to her flat. Dunbar had been declared an unfit mother, and before she would give Lynn the story, she insisted he go with her to the Social Services to help her get her son back.

Says Lynn, 'She was wearing a mini-skirt up to here [he draws a line high across his thigh with his finger] and a dress down to here [he draws a line low across his chest], and *I* was trying to persuade this Social Welfare Officer that this was a suitable person to have custody of her young son. Which . . . I must say, I wasn't very convincing. You can't be very convincing when she's sitting beside you and she's got her skirt up to here and her blouse down to there. And I had no chance of helping her get custody. It was all sort of a game, sort of a con really to get her to tell me what happened between her and her lesbian partner.'

And that, Lynn says, is what happened. Even though he failed to get the boy returned, Dunbar took him over to her torture chamber, and on the way there, with the photographer driving while Lynn took notes, she told him her life's story.

Once in the basement flat, they found electric hot air paint strippers, plastic macs, torture racks, whips, stocks, *and* a few blow torches. 'These were certainly real blow torches. I actually switched one on to see if it was working. And it did work. It was very hot indeed. And while I was talking to her, we took all the photographs we could.'

The one which appeared in the *Sun*, alongside Lynn's story, shows a thick-waisted trollop in panties and black bra, with one strap falling provocatively off her shoulder. Behind her, on the wall, written in uneven and menacing letters, are slogans like, 'YouR NOtHING But SCUm!!', 'LicK MY BootS DOG!!',

'BEG foRgiVENESS WoRTHLESS SLAVE!' and 'YouR LifE iS NotHING fouR DEATH iS NOTHING'.

The photographer, Margi Dunbar, and George Lynn, who had picked up some white wine at a local supermarket, sat down, and Lynn got the rest of her story while they all had a drink. 'About one or half past one,' Lynn says, 'I said to the photographer, "Now, you look after Margi, and I'll go and phone the story over. I don't want to do it from here."

'I went over to a hotel across from the flat, and I went into the downstairs and for some reason all the hotel phones were out of order, and I said to the girl, "Is there a phone in the hotel that's working?" and she said, "Well, there's one on the first floor landing." So I went up this very quiet corridor, and I was on the telephone, describing the torture chamber – lesbian lovers and plastic macs and paint strippers and blow torches – and out of a room came these two youngish Americans, and I suddenly realized that this young couple who were obviously honeymooners were waiting for the phone and they were standing, horror-stricken, behind me listening to every word I was saying.

'And I put my hand over the phone and turned around and said, "I'm very sorry. There's nothing to be upset about. This is not what England is like. This is just the way I earn my living. And, uh, I'm sure you're going to enjoy this fabulous country of ours."'

Another woman who is fully familiar with the range of personal services on offer is Tina Dalgleish. Dalgleish made her way into the newspapers via an escort agency, but not as a call girl – although if you ask her today how she earned her living for seventeen years, she will answer with three words: 'sex, vice and corruption.'

Dalgleish was a secretary at the *News of the World* when she received the telephone call that changed her life. Her boss Trevor Kempson was on the other end of the line, asking whether she would help him out with a story line. What he wanted was for her to go along to an escort agency and sign on. So Dalgleish, a stunning redhead with a remarkable figure, put on a mini-skirt, a fur coat, and a big floppy hat, and went to an agency just off Tottenham Court Road. In her shaking hands, she carried a gigantic handbag that held a large reel-to-reel tape recorder, state-of-the-art in the 1970s.

Once inside the agency, she was greeted by 'a horrible little man' who gave her the forms to fill out for the job. As she slowly filled in the appropriate spaces, Dalgleish read each of the questions aloud for the benefit of the tape recorder. Even as she was completing

197

the form, two Americans came in and chose her for the evening. Somewhat nonplussed, Dalgleish said she couldn't start until the following week and dashed out. Then she walked across London, to save the taxi money Kempson had given her. She was supposed to meet him in Shepherd Market, and as she walked across the small square in her outlandish costume, a man in a bowler hat stopped her and asked how much she charged. 'I was in at the deep end,' Dalgleish says.

Kempson probably knows more about sexual deviation than anyone in the business. He had dealt with 'animalism, bestiality, sado-masochism, prostitution, lesbianism, male homosexuality, torture . . . in Mexico, in Rio, in Amsterdam, in Sweden, everywhere . . . I know about them because of the job. England? I mean the English are the most extraordinary race . . . heavily into sado-masochism. Tremendously heavily into it. The infliction of pain is absolutely appalling. And defecation and urinology, there's a hell of a lot of that in this country.'

Over the next two decades, Kempson would introduce Dalgleish to the underworld of vice and corruption, and the two would pose so often as man and wife that they would react to each other with the same naturalness as if they were actually married.

After hearing about Dalgleish's reactions that first day, Kempson spotted her as 'a winner without doubt. She was so cool. I mean . . . we went to one orgy down at Eastbourne. The hotel was closed down for the winter . . . and there were about forty people there and they were all guys in Scimitars and Mercedes and Jaguar cars, some of them from the House of Commons, which I won't mention, and honestly it was just like a daisy chain of sucking off and arse-fucking and every bloody thing going. We spent three days in that hotel and nobody ever sussed out we weren't a couple. We had a kind of telepathy between us, you see. I knew virtually what Tina was thinking and she knew what I was thinking and if one got particularly bad with Tina, I'd say, "Just take it easy with her, she'll come across. I know she likes you." And we just played it that way, and three days went by, and nobody sussed us out at all. We've done it time and time again and never got suspected. Never once.'

Dalgleish says 'I used to make things up as I went along. I loved to do that, and Trevor would pick up on things.'

The longest she and Kempson went undercover as a married couple was nine months. During this time, Dalgleish was living with her boyfriend. 'He didn't mind. He accepted it. It was nothing to do with him, that's how I saw it. My job was my job. He was an artist. I didn't tell him how to do drawings, because he was the artist.

'When you do wife swapping,' Dalgleish continues, 'or pretend to be a prostitute, you never sleep with them. You make excuses. But you can never say, before you go into these sorts of things, my excuse is going to be "X". You've got to watch the situation as it materializes and judge from that. An example, if it's Trevor, is, you can have a row. Other excuses are that it's the wrong time of the month. It literally happened a few hours earlier or you wouldn't have come along. In some instances that doesn't wash, but you can turn around and say you don't like it. I've done that. Or I've said I can't stand the sight of blood, it makes me vomit, you can actually say that. Other times, you can say you're too drunk. But you never actually *get* drunk.

'If someone tried to cuddle or kiss me, I would just say, "Don't smudge my lipstick." You have to be careful, they could have herpes, or whatever. *They* think you're only playing hard to get. Or we say, "This is an initial meeting. Nothing happens first time, we'll wait to see if we get to like each other."

'You have to pretend it's not you really. You have to go on the personality of the person you're pretending to be.'

In the seventeen years that Kempson and Dalgleish worked together, neither ever slipped up on a name. 'Trevor never ever called me Tina,' she says, 'and I never called him Trevor.'

One of their specialities was the spouse-swapping story. 'You might ask yourself,' says Kempson, 'why expose wife and husband swapping? It's a private activity, so why expose them? I'm in total agreement.' But Kempson did the first spouse-swapping exposure in England when he was on the *People*, and some half a dozen or more similar exposés in the years following, and he says, 'all of them have always been contacted through contact magazines. Some were millionaires, some doctors, and some local politicians. If they are willing to put themselves on show in public by advertising,' Kempson figures, 'they deserve to be exposed.'

The process takes time, something like nine months, and during that period, Kempson and Dalgleish would send a couple of dozen letters out to contacts found in the magazines, along with photographs. One of the rules of the game is that you never commit yourself in writing and you deliberately keep the content of the letter vague. And you have to be patient. The letters have to filter through the agencies to a box number. In the meanwhile, you have to procure an accommodation address for replies. An accommodation address can be acquired from the *Evening Standard*, and it costs about £5 a week to have mail delivered there. About once a week, you drop by and collect any letters held for you. Then, you begin phoning people who are dotted all over the country and arranging to see them.

Whenever Kempson and Dalgleish visited a couple in their homes – on the initial meeting – they carried along a bottle of vodka and a bottle of Scotch, which they always left behind. Most of the homes they visited were immaculate, a detail that seemed to Dalgleish to be at odds with her expectations. And only about 10 per cent of the people were actually attractive, 'the rest were mediocre . . . they're the ones that sort of look out from behind their net curtains,' she says. 'Very, very few were the sort that you would say were outgoing or gregarious. The average age was about thirty, although the ages could vary from twenty to sixty.'

Kempson and Dalgleish were always careful the first time out, because many of the people involved in this sort of thing are acquainted with one another and, as Dalgleish put it, 'you have to go in cold, not knowing if you've already met some of their friends. Nine times out of ten you get all the stuff you want about the individual couples in your first meeting.'

Exactly why *do* people want to swap spouses, at best picking up a quick thrill, at worst risking exposure? According to Dalgleish, everyone has different ideas about why they do it. Many of the men said that they needed it, that one woman couldn't satisfy their desires. But the wives were often a different matter. If you talked to them separately, she says, 'nine times out of ten the wife didn't want to do it; they were just doing it to keep their marriage together. They preferred taking the devil they knew to the devil they didn't.' In one case Dalgleish remembers, the husband didn't take part in the sex, but watched his wife. His wife did it, she said, only to please her husband.

Dalgleish remembers one particularly poignant case, in which the wife was Danish 'and really attractive'. The husband was blond and muscular, 'the Aryan type'. The woman worked on computers and to get her picture Dalgleish took her for tea at the Ritz. 'We got a beautiful picture of her,' she says, 'and when we told her who we were, she said, "I only do it because it pleases my husband. I don't like doing it at all."' Both Kempson and Dalgleish really liked her and thought she had 'class, real class'. Dalgleish figures in the long run they did the woman a favour because it stopped her husband cold.

The counterpoint to this pair was a couple in Birkenhead. 'He was about forty-five,' Dalgleish says, 'she was about twenty-two. He had a gut and she was fat.' What they liked was for the wife to dress up in sexy underwear and get paraplegics in their wheelchairs at the bottom of a set of stairs. Then she would stand at the top, taunting them to climb up.

When the *News of the World* was about to expose someone, the procedure was to call them on the telephone a few days before or, if they couldn't be reached, to send a telegram asking them to ring a number, one which turned out to be Dalgleish's office. This was to give advance warning. In some cases, people would simply disappear before the story appeared. But in one of the cases, when the man phoned Dalgleish and discovered that a story about his sexual excesses would appear the following Sunday, he committed suicide.

He was a school teacher with two sons, and he simply told his wife he was going to a vintage car rally for the weekend. Instead, he went into the countryside, and 'topped himself', as Dalgleish put it. She was summoned to appear before the inquest, and there, Dalgleish herself was besieged by a hostile press. 'A couple of national newspapers both had a go. To my mind, they were bad . . . they were giving their opinions on something they were not part of. He was not only a liar, but a coward, a coward who could not take on the responsibility of what he'd done and face his wife. The distress he caused his wife and children by killing himself was far greater than by being exposed about some nookie.'

The Queen's Counsellor in the case forced Dalgleish to read the dead man's suicide note in the courtroom. Then he asked her, '"Does that not upset you?" and I said, "No, not really. I can see how it would upset his wife, but it doesn't upset me." I felt sorry for his wife and children more than I ever did for him. She seemed a very nice lady.'

But reactions to the crisis of exposure differ. When one couple was told of their impending doom, the man of the house replied, 'Be sure to send along a copy of the photos, Mate.'

Dalgleish remembers once suggesting that they expose some of the men with money, the company-director-with-Rolls-Royce-who-wants-to-meet-willing-lady type, to find out if they were genuine. She went to meet six of them. 'And,' she says, 'do you know? All of them were the most genuine men I ever met. Fabulously wealthy, but very lonely. There was one twenty-seven-year-old financier in the City; we checked the registration of his Rolls and it was his, not just a chauffeur borrowing it. The man turned out to be married and said his wife didn't enjoy going out and having dinner but preferred to have dinner parties at home. There was no longer any sex between them. He just wanted someone to take out for lunch, and "maybe have nookie with once a month, something like that." He took me to a fabulous restaurant where all his friends and colleagues were. I felt so sorry for him, I didn't have the heart to ring him up and tell him who I was. I just let it die. And one man even introduced me to his eleven-year-old son. His mummy had gone to Canada to visit relatives and never came back . . . I didn't write about it because it would have been too painful for everybody involved.'

By the time she had been in the business for several years, though, Dalgleish had become almost immune to any sort of surprise. She remembers taking an inexperienced member of staff to his first orgy. It was a high-class affair, organized by a Harley Street gynaecologist, being held behind Sloane Square. 'There was a notice on the stairs that said nobody could go above that certain mark with their clothes on, and an in-house video so you could watch people copulating on the floor. And there were daisy chains, ten to twelve people all joined together in a bundle. And this new guy had never seen anything like it. To me, it was all water off a duck's back, I'd seen it all before. And there was the spread. There was salmon, beautifully decorated, from Harrods. And I had a look round, and all these people were copulating, and I looked at one bloke, and he said, "Tina! What are you doing here?" "Working." "You've not!" He was one of my contacts. And I said, "Shut up. You've never seen me before. All right?" He almost died when I walked in and saw him at it! I loved it!'

'In all the time I worked with her,' says Kempson. 'I only once saw Tina freak.

'It was about the last story we ever did together. We went up to a torture chamber in the mountains above Malaga. You had to drive up a goat track to get to it.'

Neither Kempson nor Dalgleish spoke Spanish, and Kempson's French was limited, so they found themselves asking a goatherd, halfway up the mountain, 'the way to this luxury villa. I was laughing my socks off,' says Dalgleish. 'He was moving his hands all around, and Trevor was following his hands. We got there in the end. It was an initial meeting, because these people had a club, and you paid to go for weekends, for these horrible weekends . . . masochistic and sadistic weekends . . . or for a week or a fortnight, in couples or by the half dozen. It was a package holiday, flight and accommodation included, an all-in deal.'

The house had been selected precisely because it was inaccessible and secluded and because much of what happened took place outside. It 'advertised' through a contact magazine.

The host was a rough-looking man with a dark beard, and his partner was a pear-shaped woman with straight hair that hung limply down the sides of her face. She had a dour personality, but he was outgoing. The couple had pooled their resources to buy the place and were at the time installing a swimming pool. In the four or five hours they were there, Kempson and Dalgleish were shown around the grounds, which included kennels for humans, where people were chained up with collars on as if they were dogs. Then the woman showed Dalgleish her photo album, with 'pictures of stocks built for boobs and boob-crushers.' There were 200 photographs of women who were being beaten or installed in these devices, sometimes with dozens of needles stuck into their nipples. There were pictures like this of the hostess with blood dripping down. 'It freaked me,' Dalgleish said. 'I just flipped.'

Kempson says, 'They were the most appalling sadists I've ever come across. They were hanging women, wives, girlfriends, with spikes through their nipples and spikes through their clitorises up in the ceilings, and they were whipping them . . . and there was blood all over . . . and Jesus, you almost threw up. And I said, "I like it, but my wife doesn't." And the man of course immediately went for Tina and started telling her what he'd love to do to her and everything else.'

When Kempson and Dalgleish finally left, they went to the end of the road, took a wrong turning and found the road was blocked off. 'Tina just went berserk. She was so freaked out, she was picking up huge boulders and chucking them around. If I'd gone through the gap she was trying to prepare, we'd have just nose-dived into a bloody great gully. I had to slap her around the face and pull her back by the hair into the car. We drove to a lovely hotel back at Puerto Banus, and by that time she'd come to.'

To this day, Dalgleish doesn't remember the incident. She has a vague memory of trying to clear the road, but nothing else. 'I guess,' she says, 'I was trying to move mountains.'

Dalgleish is now retired from the business and, as a secretary in her office describes her, is 'only a housewife now.' She lives with a former photographer for the *People* and their two children. She tends to be inward-looking and doesn't go out of her way to have people into her home or to go out to theirs. 'It's true,' she says, 'I distance myself.

'One in ten people is potentially corrupt. If you look across a room, you can just about tell which ones. I think people who think about it in their heads are just as guilty as those who have the affairs. It affects their relationships just as much, like hiding girlie magazines under the bed.

'The deception,' she says, 'is there.'

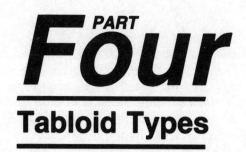

PART
Four

Tabloid Types

11
TREVOR AND TINA

'It was the end of the war, and we had sweets coupons,' says Trevor Kempson, fifty-eight, Chief Investigative Reporter on the *News of the World*. 'You couldn't buy sweets without coupons. I went down the drive from Merchant Taylors' to the newsagent, with my cap and scarf on, and the lady said, "You know, I'm not allowed to sell you boys the *People*, the *News of the World* and the *Empire News*." And I said, "But I want them and I'll give you all my coupons and I won't take any sweets," and she said "That's bribery . . . but all right, as long as you don't tell your housemaster."'

Kempson took his stack of newspapers back to the school, sneaked them into the toilet and read through the lot. It was the days when Duncan Webb, the first big name in investigative reporting, was doing his well-known exposé of a Maltese vice gang – five brothers in the West End who had made millions of pounds out of prostitution. In Kempson's mind, no one had ever seemed as evil as these gangsters and nothing so exciting as the prospect of exposing men like them.

'I hate, I loathe, I despise injustice. I really do, I hate it. I hate that about other people, people who hurt other people, I despise them for it. *Why* do they do it? I *hate* hurting people. I will only ever make a hurtful or offensive remark to somebody if I see them hurting somebody else and that person is incapable of standing up for themselves.' Thus it was that Kempson made his decision to become a reporter, 'to expose people who were bad and to defend people who couldn't defend themselves.'

When Kempson told his father, an accountant who lived a respectable and conservative lifestyle, he was, predictably, horrified; he had hoped his son would become a lawyer or perhaps an accountant like himself. When Kempson told his headmaster, he said, "You'll spend the rest of your life, Kempson, going around jumble sales, womens' institute marmalade competitions and standing at funeral gates taking down the names of the mourners." And that's exactly what I did do.'

Kempson's first reporting job was on a small paper in Devon, and his assignments there were just what his headmaster had predicted. But while he was there, two sheep died in Exmoor. Kempson heard from a local vet that they'd died of anthrax, 'and I wrote it up in about three paragraphs and sent it to the *Daily Express*, and they used it word for word.' For all intents and purposes, Kempson was hooked. From this point on, he could never be lured back to the respectable life.

Then he moved to the Dorset *Daily Echo* at Weymouth, an evening paper, for thirteen months, then on to a Berkshire freelance agency. In his territory were Windsor, Ascot, Broadmoor, Harwell, Henley-on-Thames and Cheam School, where Prince Charles was a boarder. It didn't take Kempson long to discover that it was more exciting freelancing than working for a local. He spent the next seven years working for *Paris Match*, *Life* and almost every one of the national papers on Fleet Street.

Kempson bought his first Jaguar when he was twenty-three – he paid cash for it – and he's had a new one every year of his life since then. He also bought a house, and during these years, he married and had four sons. Again, within a short time, his income allowed him to secure the education of his boys. By the time he was thirty-two, he was earning something in the region of £17,500 a year, 'which was a lot of money in those days,' Kempson says. When he went for an interview at the *People* for a full-time position, the editor said, 'Well, you make £7,500 more than I do. I can only pay you £37 and 10 shillings a week, the salary of the second highest paid reporter here.' And Kempson said, '"I'll take it." The editor said "You must be mad," and I said "Well, perhaps I am but that's the job I want." And I was happy.'

Since then, Kempson has travelled to fifty-seven countries, to Brazil alone twenty-four times. He has gone undercover dozens of times, sometimes for as long as nine months. It was Kempson who masterminded the exposure of the Undersecretary of Defence, Lord Lambton, telling of his involvement with two prostitutes; Kempson again on the BBC payola scheme, in which popular radio disc jockeys were accused of accepting bribes of money and sex in exchange for plugging records on 'Family Favourites'; *and* Kempson has been responsible for putting behind bars some of London's most notorious gangsters, among them the well-known Bernie Silver. He has been beaten up, his life threatened, and when all that failed, he has been offered fulsome bribes. According to *Gentleman's Quarterly*, Kempson has 'the dubious honour' of being the most highly respected reporter among the tabloids.

Self-admittedly, Kempson has 'a short-fuse', and that kind of comment is the sort that raises his ire. Nothing makes him angrier than for someone to put down the *News of the World*, where he has reported for over two decades.

'I've got a very, very vicious tongue, and I think very, very quick . . . and I've been in verbal punch-ups, and occasionally physical ones, defending what I believe, that the *News of the World* does a really good job, I really do believe that. On one occasion, I was at a cocktail party and I was so sick of everyone going on about it. It was the vice-consul in Singapore who was attacking the *News of the World*, and I just said, "Now you don't admit that you buy it and you don't admit that you read it but I bet you are one of these people who comes down in his dressing gown in your suburban home on Sunday morning, sneaks the copy from between *The Sunday Times* and the *Sunday Telegraph* and goes back, sits up in bed, reads it, gets a fucking great hard-on and then tries to make love to his wife. And of course all his friends turned round and laughed like hell.'

If Kempson is one of the most respected reporters in tabloids, he is also one of the most picturesque, with a homespun code of ethics that affects every decision in his life. Described by his colleagues as 'a lovely man', he is affable, chatty and comfortable, just the sort of guy you'd want to tell your life story to.

As for Kempson, he'll always tell you whatever you want to know about himself, because it fits in with his philosophy – that you can't have it both ways. You can't expose what you know about other people, day in and day out, without telling other people what they want to know about you, no matter how embarrassing those disclosures might be.

Says Kempson, 'I've got a motto in life: Scotch, sex, cigarettes and sunshine.'

As for the Scotch, Kempson knocks back a bottle every day of his life, without showing any external effects. As he sits drinking slowly from a tumbler-sized glass, one right after the other, he'll tell you about the sex.

Kempson cannot, he will explain, have an affair with a person unless he has 'rapport with her. I'm a romantic. I've been infatuated many times, in love many times, and I've loved a few times, but never all three, except for one person. She's a very wonderful but jealous woman. I'm not jealous at all. I learned with Mavis

Gromwell, who came from Pudsey in Yorkshire. She was a few years older than me, but I fell in love with her from a distance when I was a teenager. And although I never saw her again, she wrote me a four-page letter and taught me it was the most self-destructive thing ever to be jealous in life.

'I have been punched up all around the kitchen by an irate husband, because of his wife, I was having an affair with. I was in the wrong, and when I walked into my local at the time, about two days afterwards, grazes down my face, people said "Oh, what are you doing here, Trevor? How can you come out and have a drink? I mean, you've been having a punch-up with So-and-So because you've been having an affair with his wife." I said, "And I deserved the punch-up. In fact, I deserved a bloody sight more than I did get." I subsequently met at parties that guy, who's about six foot four inches tall, and we had a chat, he introduced me to his new wife, and that's it. If I do something, I expect to take the consequences . . . I'll tell you one thing I can't stand – hypocrites. I despise hypocrites.'

And speaking of sex, Kempson would like to know, 'Who in the hell do men think they are that they can do it in five minutes and then turn over and go to sleep? Ideally, 50 per cent of the pleasure should go to the lady and 50 per cent to the man. If it can't be like that, 49 per cent to the man and 51 to the lady.'

As to the cigarettes, Kempson smokes, in the course of each day, between thirty and forty; between forty and sixty if he is under pressure. 'Most I ever got up to was 100.' His concession to his health is a filter. 'It was Ronnie Biggs, the mail train robber, he put me onto the filter about fifteen years ago. I'd chased a murderer down to Rio, and I saw Biggs there, and he asked me, "Why don't you smoke with a filter?" and I said, "Well, only poofters and the head of the secret police down there smoke with a filter." And he said, no, I should start, so I did. It's my only concession.'

Like all city dwellers who lead complicated lives, Kempson nurtures a fantasy – that when he retires from the newspaper business, he will move to Pangbourne, Berkshire and settle down in a riverside flat and get the best Mercedes that money can buy.

As to his reporting acumen, which is legend in Fleet Street, he chalks it down, in large part, to determination to win, plus good luck. 'Anybody who tells you he did it without luck will be lying.'

In April 1968, a small paragraph appeared in a French newspaper, saying that some 131 members of Brazil's Indian Protection Service

(IPS) had been arraigned on charges of murder, rape, pillage and stealing the mineral rights of the Indians they had been set up to protect. The then editor of the *News of the World*, Stafford Somerfield, sent for Kempson and informed him he was going to Rio de Janeiro to do the story. 'I said to Stafford, "You're joking." He said, "No, get your visa and go." The next lunchtime, he asked if I'd got my visa, and I said, "Go on, Stafford!" I thought he was joking, because I was always saying I wanted to go to Rio, and he said, "Well, if you don't go I'm sending somebody else." So I hightailed it down to Rio and booked into the Leme Palace Hotel, and it was my first time in South America, and I didn't know where to start.'

Within the week, however, he had come back with the story, a horrific tale of mass murder that was tantamount to genocide against a backward people. It was a story which would receive a great deal of attention in the establishment press. What had occurred in the hinterland of Brazil, deep within the rain forest, was that low-paid employees of the government, stranded for months or even years at a stretch in solitude and primitive conditions, discovered within themselves, like Conrad's hero Mr Kurtz, 'a heart of darkness'.

In some cases, pioneer invaders, mainly German, intent upon mining the natural minerals and precious gems in the jungles, bribed members of the IPS to overlook what was in effect a private war they were waging against the primitive tribes who made their home there. These 'pioneers' cleared vast areas of land for farms, often using the Indians as slaves. Those who tried to run away were tortured to death in unspeakable ways, publicly, as an example to the others. There were cases where villages were gunned down with machine guns when they resisted the settlement of their area by white invaders. In one documented case, the natives were injected with the smallpox serum by a white man posing as a medical doctor. When they died, their clothes were given to other tribes to spread the disease. In another, Indians were given sugar laced with cyanide. Most horrific were the stories of IPS members themselves, who abused the natives sexually, and as the atrocities continued unchecked, these abuses grew in number, taking in at last children, both male and female, in evergrowing numbers. Many of them were sold into prostitution for direct payment to members of the IPS.

The IPS, set up by the Government originally to prepare the primitive natives in the interior for civilization, had, in effect, become the very people who were fomenting the atrocities against them.

For Kempson, the difficulty of getting the story was compounded by the fact that not only had he never been to Rio, he didn't speak the language and he hadn't the first idea of how to proceed. When he arrived, he found most of the world press were there as well – 'guys from *Paris Match*, *Stern*, *Life*, *Saturday Evening Post* . . .' The next morning, they all went together down to the Ministry of Defence, where they were categorically denied access to any details.

'So,' says Kempson, 'they all said they'd hire light planes and get mosquito nets, interpreters and go into the interior.' Kempson called through to his assistant editor and gave him a report on what was happening, requesting funds to go along, but was refused. 'You are expected to do this on your initiative,' he told Kempson. 'I said to him, "Well, I can't fly up there and hire planes and get mosquito nets and learn Portuguese *on my own initiative*." To which my assistant editor just said, "Don't call me again."'

Kempson thus found himself stranded in Rio, knowing he was going to get fired, 'So I thought I might as well enjoy it while I was down there. But how do you enjoy yourself when you know you're missing the story?' He remembers taking a bottle of Jack Daniels down to the Copacabana beach, feeling very depressed, and there he met a German businessman. He told him the problem. The businessman immediately asked, 'Have you offered anyone *money*?' When Kempson said no, he explained that this was the way things were done in Rio.

So Kempson went back the next day to the Defence Ministry and asked the beautiful secretary of an official there out to dinner that night. 'The next morning,' says Kempson, 'she rang and asked me to come down to the office. When I got there, the official came out and said, "I am going for lunch now, I will be back in precisely one hour. Goodbye." And the secretary said, "Come with me." We went into his office and all the files were on his desk – all in Portuguese, mind you – of who was arraigned, in which prison, and a detailed account of what had gone on, how the German pioneers were trying to get the mineral rights of the Indians and had colluded with the military. And the atrocities.

'So she photostated it all for me, and I had two more days there in which I visited three of the military officials, very, very high ranking, who were in prison. I saw a lot of their wives, got the story, flew back to England, had everything in Portuguese. I was then living in Reading, which is very near the BBC monitoring station, where they had all the linguists. I went to a Portuguese translator, and I paid him £100 of my own money to do the whole lot. I wrote a five-part series on it. And all those who went out with their mosquito netting and planes got nothing, and I got everything, including interviews with the three guys who were arraigned on charges of murder. That was determination plus luck, *a lot of luck*, and my editor called me in and congratulated me and told me to up my expenses, which I did.'

One of the things that still irks Kempson, over twenty years later, is that *The Sunday Times* ran an article in its magazine less than a year after his article appeared, which appeared to use information that had already been published under his name. 'In those days *The Sunday Times* was owned by Lord Thompson – I mean the heavy establishment papers used to treat us like dirt – and yet there was my information in his magazine.' It is just one of the many cases, he believes, of the broadsheets feeding off the tabloids while at the same time criticizing their content and style.

Among his other attributes, Kempson is a first-degree witch. He is still able, even though it was many years ago, to recite the chant he was taught when he went undercover for six months and infiltrated a coven. 'If you ever betray the secrets of witchcraft,' it goes, 'better that you fall forward on this dagger and die now.' At the moment Kempson took the vow, 'one of the princesses, as they call them, had a dagger in my navel and the other one had one in my back. Everybody was naked, including me, and one of the girls was mucking about on the altar doing obscene things.' Kempson was in a basement flat in Notting Hill Gate, posing as a wealthy chicken farmer from Devon by the name of Trevellyan Westmacott.

The *News of the World* had been approached by one of the witches who wanted to sell them the story. But he was unable to give them the proof they needed in order to make the story stand up. So the assignment fell to Kempson to convince the coven he wanted to become a witch. 'It's not easy to do. They treat you with a tremendous amount of suspicion, and they check you out.' From a legal standpoint everything Kempson wrote had to be absolutely accurate. This meant that the ceremonies he took part in and every word he wrote had to be on tape. 'So how do you do that when you're naked?' he asks.

'Well, I spent about three days going around bars and thinking, and I went to the British Museum and got out all the books on witchcraft and read them. *Terribly* boring stuff. What I did was . . .

213

I had a beautiful leather case made up that supposedly contained vials of very expensive preparations for injecting into chickens. And whenever I would turn up at one of these meetings, I would pretend that I had just got back from Wolverhampton, or to the Isle of Man where witchcraft is very heavy, and I had this briefcase with me. And they accepted it. As soon as the handle went down there was a minute hair plunger, which activated a tape recorder that lasted for about three or four hours, with a specially high powered microphone which would pick up at about thirty to forty feet, and it just recorded absolutely everything.

'So this lasted about five to six months before it got into the papers. When it came to the point that we were going to run the story – we always have to have a showdown – some of these people were extremely erudite. One was a Catholic priest. Others were middle and upper-middle class. When they knew that we were going to expose them, three or four of them went to their lawyers, and they came into the office and said that they were going to take out injunctions to restrain us from publishing. The lawyers sat there with their clients and said that they would sue us for libel. One of the men said, 'You can't have any proof, it's your word against ours.'

'And I went to the filing cabinet – I had written the story by this time – and first I got out the typescripts and galley proofs, and a tremendous amount of quotations. They just sat there and lied and said, "No, it never happened." And the lawyer said, "You couldn't possibly quote anybody verbatim," and I went to another cabinet and got out the carefully catalogued tapes and played their own voices back to them. And they just collapsed. All of the lawyers said they couldn't represent their clients any more. And we published, and we didn't get a single suit.

'We ran a five-part series and put on about 175,000 circulation in the first week alone.'

When Kempson finds himself in highly charged sexual situations for his paper, the question arises whether, in fact, he gets any pleasure out of them, and the answer is no. To his way of thinking, the situation is not unlike that of a surgeon who operates on a good-looking woman. 'Ask him, did he get a turn-on, and he'll say no. He's just doing a job. And so am I.'

There is a photograph of Tina Dalgleish, taken when she was twelve, that sticks in her mind. By then, her father had deserted the family and her mother was struggling to bring up four children on her own. For the picture, Dalgleish's coarse red hair had been cut at home and parted crookedly down the middle. She was wearing National Health glasses, and one of her front teeth was missing. This was the image she carried of herself through the years. She had no idea she was attractive until she grew up and moved to London, where she set out to earn her own living.

She landed a secretarial position on the *Daily Mail*, and without her bosses knowing it, she began doing rewrites for a few of the reporters there. Sometimes she helped them 'fiddle their expenses'. Then 'the Night of the Long Envelopes' took place, when a large number of editorial staff were given their walking papers. Disillusioned, Dalgleish resigned and signed on as a temp at the *News of the World*. There, she had the good fortune to go to work for Kempson. 'We had a natural reaction to each other and we got on very well.

'People in and out of the office used to think we were having an affair, but we never did. If we had, we'd have never been able to work with each other so long. We could never have been so honest with one another. It would have just complicated life. We're friends, that's not too hard to understand. I'm actually in Trevor's will, I get the Jaguar.'

Like Kempson, Dalgleish had something special that other reporters didn't have. For one thing, she could go out alone on potentially dangerous assignments and come back whole.

Dalgleish was doing a story on heroin dealers and had an inside source named Sally who said she would show her a drug-processing operation. One evening, after the two of them had had an expensive meal on the *News of the World*, Sally took Dalgleish along to World's End to a clothing store that sold 'way-out clothes and stayed open until late at night.' In back of this shop, says Dalgleish, was a man 'cutting up cocaine and heroin and God knows what else.' As they had planned, Sally introduced Dalgleish as someone who used drugs regularly, a heroin addict. What happened next, Dalgleish hadn't bargained for. It was also something they hadn't thought of on the paper when they had gone over how she would handle the assignment. The man cutting the drugs insisted Dalgleish take a hit. She sized up the situation and figured he wasn't going to let her leave in one piece unless she did, so she held out her arm for the needle.

There was no pleasure in the drug for Dalgleish. She became violently ill, and rushed to the toilet where she vomited. Sally meantime made the excuse that she had been drinking, had in fact a drinks problem, and that plus the drugs must have made her sick. When Dalgleish staggered back, the two of them left. But on her way out, she became sick again and went behind a Bedford van and vomited once more. She had managed to get a sample of the drugs and had to take it up immediately to the office where it would be locked up, 'so it could be taken to a public analyst who would then determine the purity. And it was 70 per cent pure Persian,' says Dalgleish, 'a very strong dosage. I could have died.' Dalgleish believes if she hadn't eaten, she probably would have.

She ended up sitting in the front hall of the *News of the World* on Bouverie Street with her informant Sally. She was having trouble focusing, because one of the side-effects of heroin is tunnel vision. At this moment, Murdoch's Number One at the time, Bruce Matthews, who is now retired, walked past and said, 'Hi, Tina, you look dreadful. What are you doing here?' Dalgleish said, 'Read about it in the paper.' The story went onto Page One as part of the overall investigation the *News of the World* was conducting. Her part got the page lead.

Says Dalgleish, 'The guy went to prison for six months, and Scotland Yard came down and arrested me for using, dealing and possession. They were unable to proceed, though, because there was such an outcry from the rest of Fleet Street, who said they should be out after the real villains, not the people who expose them.'

But after the incident, Dalgleish notes, the laws were changed – for the worse. Reporters could no longer do what Dalgleish had done without culpability under the Code of Conduct.

A less dangerous assignment for Dalgleish was to pose as a Playboy Bunny, where, it was thought, some of the girls working there were 'on the game'. It was Dalgleish's job to find out if that were true. When she applied at the club, Dalgleish was taken on immediately, and after two weeks of training, was measured for her costume. 'It was really tight because I have flat ribs, and they put wire bones in, and I was gasping for breath. You had to stuff the costume with toilet paper, and wear tan tights underneath, black tights on the top, to give a shimmer.' Dalgleish was given a name, 'Scarlet', because of her red hair, and put to work. The hours were from eight in the evening until four in the morning, with a half-hour break. Some of the girls had to work parties upstairs. One of the bunnies would come around and say, 'you and you and you and you,' and these girls would disappear. So then, says Dalgleish, she would have to work twelve tables instead of six. One of the floor managers was fired on the spot for talking to Dalgleish. He was a German, and he was sitting at the bar, ready to start work one evening, when he began 'telling me the full dirt, just pouring his heart out to me.' And one of the other managers walked over and sacked him for consorting with the staff. 'They were very harsh,' says Dalgleish.

The girls who were willing to sell sexual favours, which was strictly prohibited by the club, used sugar packets to make their contacts. 'They were usually the ones who were illiterate, and cocky,' says Dalgleish, 'and they would write their numbers on the sugar packets and pass them on to customers.' When she made this discovery, about eight weeks after she began, Dalgleish left the Club.

One of the girls there told Dalgleish she wanted a black costume, but had been assigned some other colour. When Dalgleish left, she said she could have the one that had been made up for her. 'And do you know?' Dalgleish says, 'She sat down and cried and said it was what she'd always wanted – a black bunny outfit. It was really weird.'

Several years later, Dalgleish's older brother went to a rugby match, and afterwards, he decided to go for a pint. In the pub, there was a copy of a newspaper on the bar, and he looked down and said, 'I know that face.' At that time the *Sun* was splashing a story on prostitution at another London club, and the picture editor couldn't resist pulling Dalgleish's picture from the *News of the World* file, even though it was six years old and she was no longer even working for the paper. 'And all these guys were saying to my brother, "That's your sister? I thought you said she was a reporter." Trevor called me up about it, and he was laughing like a drain.'

Dozens of times in her career, Dalgleish posed as a night club hostess or a spouse-swapper or an easy make, and aside from the time she had to take the hit of heroin, she never found a situation she couldn't handle. One of the other women reporters who tried a similar assignment ended up being sexually abused. Says Dalgleish, 'I would have just bopped the guy on the head. I don't know why she didn't do it.'

One of the biggest stories Dalgleish and Kempson ever did was on 'The Maltese Mafia', a group of vice-kings who, for eighteen years, ran a huge prostitution ring in the Mayfair area of London. Says Dalgleish, 'They used to really beat the girls up, threaten to break their limbs, black their eyes.

'We had an informant, and he was the only one who knew what

217

one of the gang, Frank Melito, looked like, but our source couldn't be pictured in the photograph we took of Melito. Our guy knew where this chap lived, in the Water Gardens, a massive tower block of luxury flats in Marble Arch.

'The way we did it, one of us had to find out what Melito looked like, so we could identify him for the photograph. So I decided I would do a washing powder survey and go by his flat.'

Dalgleish made up her own enquiry sheet, photostated it, got a clipboard and went through a number of flats in the Water Gardens, filling in the blanks on the form so the whole thing would look genuine. She then knocked on Frank Melito's door.

'There were all these locks and chains on the door,' she says, 'and when they opened it, there were all these heavies. I said I was from the agency and asked for the resident of the flat. They told me to mind my own business, and started to shut the door. But then from nowhere this little man appears, and I ask if he's the resident and he says, "Yes", and I say "I'm doing a soap powder survey" and he says, "Come in, come in, come in." He had a Yorkshire terrier and a Chihuahua, ratbag dogs, and I thought, "I'm up here on the seventeenth floor. All the bolts are fastened on the door, and it's a long way down." Of course, I had my tape recorder going.

'He only invited me in because I was attractive, that's all. We already knew he controlled many prostitutes, and his regular girl-friend was a hooker as well. But he still said, "Why don't you come out with me this evening?" I said, "I'm very sorry, but I've got to go back to my flat to cook for the girls." He tried to get me to stay for the afternoon, but I said I had to do thirty more interviews and couldn't get paid until I did my quota.

'So he said he'd get them done for me, and I said, "Well, who are you then?" Now, he had given me a whisky and water, in a big glass. And I knew he wouldn't let me go until I finished that drink. You know that sort of thing, you can sense it. So I finished the drink in no time at all, and I was thinking of somewhere to get the photographs. So I said I'd meet him at Flanagan's in Baker Street, at lunchtime. But he never turned up. When I called him back, he said he could only meet me in the evening, but that was too dicey, since the photographer would need to use a flash.'

What Dalgleish finally did was to wait outside the Water Gardens for three days with the photographer so she could finger Melito for him. For Dalgleish, her role in the Maltese Mafia case was a small one: 'I just came in at the end for the photographs.' But for Kempson, it was all-consuming.

218

A thread of continuity runs through Kempson's exposure of the Maltese Mafia.

He is a small boy of twelve, hiding in a toilet, reading about Duncan Webb's exposure of the Messina Brothers – the five Maltese brothers who controlled all the vice in London. Some go to jail, others are deported. Multi-millionaire John Gaul takes over. When Kempson, now a man, is reporting for the *People*, he helps expose John Gaul, who in turn sells out to Bernie Silver and another gang. And these are the men who run the last major vice empire in London; these are the new Maltese Mafia.

The then deputy editor of the *News of the World*, Bernard Shrimsley, dropped in on Kempson one day, asking if he had any ideas about what stories they might do next. Kempson did have an idea – a vice ring centered in Mayfair that is headed by Bernard 'Bernie' Silver. Other names pop up: Anthony Mangion, Emmanuel Bartolo, Frank Melito, Victor Micallef, Joseph Mifsud, Romeo Saliba; others. Shrimsley gave him the OK, and Kempson went to work on the case for three months, 'and I got so well into it that it got known to Scotland Yard. One of the most senior Crime Squad officers there then came to my editor and said that he'd got a thirty-two-strong team of officers set up personally and single-mindedly to destroy this empire. He was a very honest guy, this particular officer, but he said I was interfering in what he was doing.'

The editor called Kempson off the case, as he had been virtually ordered to do by Scotland Yard. But Kempson stayed in touch with a couple of officers on this specially hand-picked team. 'And every now and again, I used to meet them and ask them how it was going, and they said, 'It's not going any fucking-where, Trevor. Every time we try and do anything, Silver and his gang seem to know about it beforehand, and nothing happens.' If the squad staged a raid on one of the houses of prostitution, they would find it had been locked up for the night; if they went for ten of their places, *they* would be locked up for the night.

Armed with this information, Kempson went back to his editor, asking for another two months on the case. He got a month. The key to the case was ownership, and the vice lords had made every single effort to conceal their ownership of the properties where the prostitutes were operating – in Curzon Street, in Soho, all around the London Hilton. Unless Kempson could prove that these men owned the properties, he couldn't prove that they were linked to the web of prostitution that encircled Mayfair. In the meantime, all the properties on the land registry were listed under cousins, third-cousins, 'grandmas,' says Kempson, 'aunties. If you prove somebody's relative owns a property, it doesn't mean a thing.'

What they forgot, says Kempson, was the water and electricity bills, which he and Dalgleish traced back to the properties. So he had that. Then, on the week before publication, Kempson got sixteen reporters and three photographers, 'and I took thousands and thousands of pounds up to the office to give out to each reporter, and we photographed all the notes and took the serial numbers. Then we gave each reporter a pile of money and sent them round to the different houses, beautiful houses, to see the prostitutes and make their excuses – they were too drunk, or whatever, and leave – but pay them the money anyway. They all went in roughly at the same time. Now, every night, collectors from Bernie Silver went around and collected the money. They would then go back to his flat, and along with the other three main ringleaders, they would all count out the money. And then the first thing the next morning, the collectors went to the bank and deposited the money.'

But this time, some of the collectors brought the money back to Kempson's office, where they checked out the serial numbers. The money had gone full circle, through the girls, back to Bernie Silver's flat, where they had hidden tape recorders of the gang counting out the money – literally saying, 'We had a good take tonight' – and then back to Kempson to be photographed. 'And that's how we did it.'

During the weeks preceding the final exposure, Kempson was working something like 110 hours a week, 'and getting virtually no sleep at all,' when he received a call from someone saying he should meet him one morning at St James's Park. There had been so many calls like these, of people who were trying to give him information, that he didn't bother to tell anyone. He just showed up on the spot where he had been told to wait, a park bench, and sat down as instructed.

In a short while, two men approached him, saying, 'Mr Trevor, we have something for you.' They handed him a briefcase which Kempson thought might contain documents, but instead, when he opened it up, it was a massive pile of £10,000 in used notes, 'which was a lot of money in those days. And I looked at them both and I just said, "Look, I've never taken a ha'penny in my life and I'm not going to start now. Thank you very much for the offer. If you've got some information, I'll take it but I don't want any money."'

So the *News of the World* published, and then passed along all their evidence to Scotland Yard, Kempson appearing at the Old Bailey to give evidence on behalf of the police. Between them, the major gang leaders got a total of thirty-five years: Silver was jailed for six years; Mangion for five; Bartola for five; Melito for four, and so on down the line.

A few years pass, and one day Kempson receives a call. A man with a foreign accent says, 'This is me, Mr Trevor. Come out to Simpson's with me for lunch.' Kempson has no idea who the person is. He has never heard his name, he has never heard his voice. The man says, 'You remember that time in the park? I was the person who sent the money, and when the two came back, I said, "If he won't take that, he can't be bribed." You cost me millions of pounds.'

Kempson accepts the invitation, and they go out to lunch. They become friends, and from time to time, whenever he feels like it, Kempson's friend gives him a call, saying, 'This is me, Mr Trevor. Come out to Simpson's for lunch.'

'And,' says Kempson, 'that probably is the greatest accolade I've ever had, though it comes from a criminal. Although I cost him so much money and so much aggravation, he still admits to the fact that I did it honestly, which I did.' As to Bernie Silver, he has, on two or three occasions, had someone ring around Christmas time, passing along the message that 'Bernie Silver sends his regards'. And Kempson always sends back the same message: 'When are we going to meet for drinks?' Once, Kempson got back an answer of sorts. 'Bernie still thinks you owe him money for getting such a good story.'

Then, again, it sometimes happens that Kempson will be standing in a hotel, or a bar, and suddenly, a person he doesn't recognize will come up to him and say, 'Hello, Trevor. You remember me. You exposed me two years ago, or three, or whatever.' They shake hands. And then they are off.

In the seventeen years that Kempson and Dalgleish worked side by side, sometimes as a team, sometimes separately, they came to know one another through and through. 'Tina could drink as well as I can, and keep absolutely stone cold sober,' says Kempson.

'You have to have some fun, you can't go on every day, day in, day out. There was one occasion we'd been all up and down the country, and we booked into this hotel in Cardiff and it was our last night on the road and we were going back to a big party

221

at my house the next day – I was married at the time – and we booked in and we were so euphoric, because we'd been on the road all that time and dealing with all these seedy people and we had this one last couple to go to. So we drove about forty miles and spent three hours with them and we drove back through the fog and the ice and we get to the hotel. And the night porter comes out: "We need the keys to our room," we said. "And can we have two coffees, two drinking chocolates" – this was just for the two of us; we were booked in as Mr and Mrs Bloggs, you see – "and about four of those miniature brandies and about eight whiskies." It was really late, and the guy asked where the rest of the people were. So Tina took the key up to the room and I waited, and took up the drinks, but forgot the room number.'

Kempson thus ends up on the first floor of the hotel, knocking on what he thinks is the door to their room. A woman he doesn't know comes to the door, is furious, threatens to call the police. Kempson moves on to the next floor. The same thing happens again. 'As a matter of fact,' he says, 'we were on the fourth floor, so I got slagged off three more times.

'In the morning – I'm terrible in the morning, I'm OK once I've got out of bed, but *otherwise*; and in the morning Tina is absolutely brilliant on two hours of sleep and, *pow*, she's up and jiving around the room with the radio playing, yeah, swishing away with her face, and her boobs sort of bobbing – and I said "Tina, for God's sake, turn off that row!" Anyway, in the end I couldn't stand it anymore and I got her by her long red hair, and I shoved her into this wardrobe and locked the door and said you stay there while I shave. "Let me out," she said. And I'm shaving, still half asleep, and I say "Christ, better get the porter up to take down these cases." And I pick up the phone and say, "Can you come up to our room?" So this little guy comes trotting in with this trolley, and I go back to shaving, and Tina is on the floor inside the wardrobe, thinking "He's got to let me out sometime, the silly old bugger." Just about then, Tina gets upset and shouts "For Christ's sake, Trevor, you've had enough fun. Let me out, for God's sake now." So I unlock the wardrobe. Course she's taken off her bra and panties, hasn't she? And she comes out stark naked, and the little guy . . .'

Kempson discovered, about four years ago, that he has cancer of the spine, a kind of bone cancer, that's now in remission. 'They did a bone marrow harvest,' he explains, 'took it out of my spine, my chest, and they froze it. Now they've got enough, if it gets bad again, they can put it back in.

'It's certainly changed my life. I've mellowed. The grass is certainly greener, so much greener, even if it's piddling with rain. Every time I open the curtains in my bedroom, I think, it's another day.'

Dalgleish left journalism nearly ten years ago. 'I loved it all, though, my time on Fleet Street. I was there at the very best time, before they went to Wapping. Before I left, they closed down my old investigative team and sent me out to do interviews with celebrities on *Coronation Street* and *Neighbours*. People like Jason Donovan. I'm not interested in actors and actresses and things like that. It's not me. I couldn't hack doing that.'

She left her job, moved to the countryside and became a housewife. She now has two children, and she's gone back to university to study French.

One day, Kempson called her, 'Said he had something to tell me. I had a feeling it was something awful, that there was trouble. I arrived before him for lunch and when I saw him, he'd aged ten years. He was in a lot of pain, you could tell.'

Kempson told her about the bone marrow harvest, that things looked optimistic. 'You're not having my Jaguar yet, Tina,' he said.

'Sod the Jaguar,' she said. 'It's the Mercedes I'm after.'

Postscript: Trevor Kempson died from pneumonia on 4 December 1990, a short time before this book went to press.

Dear Marje

Says Proops, 'Quite a lot of letters come from gays, homosexuals, because it's well known that I have lots of sympathy and am not the least bit condemnatory. They can write to me frankly and know that I'm on their side. And I get a lot of letters from men with sexual problems, like impotence. The way that women worry about the size of their breasts – Are they too small, too flat, too jutting? – men worry about the size and shape of their penises. They sometimes send measurements or lifesize drawings. It's a symbol of their masculinity. It doesn't bother me personally. It troubles me only insofar as it troubles the man who wrote the letter.

'I just write back and point out to a majority of these men that the female vagina is very accommodating and can take any shape or size from the thin ones to the great big banana-shaped ones. All they have to do is find a woman who loves them and will help them. And sometimes I send them a leaflet that gives fuller details than I can give them in a letter.

'Also the women write very frankly. In the beginning, women didn't write about their orgasms, but now they write about them all the time, complaining if they don't get as many as they want.'

For Proops, who has heard it all, the problems are the same as when she was just starting out. 'Human beings are subject to the same disasters that they always were. The past wasn't that rosy. But then, women couldn't write about their orgasms. They just had to bear their lot in silence. It's good that they now feel they can write. When people write a long letter, they invariably say, "I feel much better that I've got it off my chest, now that I've told you." Even if your only function is to be a shoulder to lean on, it's better than no shoulder at all.'

Proops was a columnist on the *Mirror* when she took a trip to America. In New York, she met Ann Landers, the widely syndicated personal advice columnist whose name is literally a household word across the country. What Landers

224

was doing seemed important to Proops, and she returned to England with the idea she might try the same thing.

'So I went to see a psychiatrist practising in London.' He talked with her for a time and then decided she had the right qualities – a sense of sympathy and a sensitive nature. So he agreed to train her for the job. This involved seeing her during her lunch hour three or four times a week, giving her books to read, sending her to lectures and on courses, including marriage guidance counselling. 'Then there came a day,' she says, 'when he said, "You're ready to start."'

Contrary to popular belief, letters that appear in the *Mirror* are never faked, nor do any of the other agony aunts Proops knows fake their letters. They are edited, though. Some are twenty or thirty pages long; the record for Proops was seventy-two pages. So they usually need to be shortened for publication. Proops has a full-time staff of five people to help, but any answer that appears in the *Mirror* was written personally by Proops – in longhand. 'I like to see the words growing, and I don't think machines can take the place of that feeling.'

The people who write to Proops, she believes, are readers who are intimidated by authority and either don't know how or are too timid to seek help elsewhere. The upper classes are accustomed to seeing doctors and solicitors. Says Proops, 'They've gone to school and have been brought up to have a lot of self-assurance.' But the people who write to Proops are in many cases the under-privileged, the ill-educated, those who have nowhere else to turn.

She encourages them to get medical help or legal advice, or to see a counsellor, if they need it. 'I can say to a frightened reader, "A doctor has seen many a vagina. He won't be worried by yours."'

This kind of straight talk earned Proops a great deal of criticism when she first started. She is said to be the first journalist in the country to print the word 'masturbate'. Whenever this charge is levelled at her, she always says, 'Yes, I masturbated all over the *Daily Mirror*.'

But there is a difficult part to the job, a part that isn't funny. The things people write to her are frequently upsetting. What worries her the most are the letters about child abuse. She has recently written a letter to a grandmother who wrote in fear about her son-in-law whom she believes is abusing his wife and their children as well as the baby. She has described all the signs to Proops in her letter. 'And there is very little I can do to help her . . . So I carry it with me. It's the only thing I can do.'

She tries to shut the work off at night, 'but it's not always possible to do that. If I had known all those years ago when I first went to see that psychiatrist how difficult it would be, I am quite sure that I would not have gone to him, that I would not have undertaken this job. But then, in living, you never know what's going to happen to you, where things will lead, how they will develop.'

12
NEWS JUNKIES

In the wintertime in northern England, the sun sets early. By four o'clock, darkness has enfolded the stark countryside surrounding St Helens, and the miners who live there begin to think about the comforts of a pint and a bit of talk. Amidst the sound of rising male voices, a young man named Richard sits in a miners' social club with a group of outsiders, London mates, who have come up to join the pickets at nearby Bold Colliery where the strikers call themselves 'the most militant in Lancashire.' Richard is quiet-spoken, somewhat intense; an earnest man. He wears a scraggy beard, and he is dressed in cheap lace-up boots, dark corduroy trousers tucked untidily inside his boot tops, a non-descript T-shirt. He hasn't bothered to take off his light blue nylon-filled jacket nor the woollen scarf that's knotted tightly round his neck. The date is January 1985, and the National Union of Mine Workers, led by Arthur Scargill, is eleven months into a strike marked, among other things, by violence and bloodshed, vandalism and thuggery.

A man known to Richard walks into the club and over to the table where he sits, along with five or six other members of the Socialist Workers' Party. He tells them they're all to go to another club, so it's everyone up and out and into the minibus parked outside. Richard climbs into a seat in the back as the others pile in behind him. But once the doors of the van shut, the driver doesn't start the engine; he just sits there waiting for something to begin.

The head of the delegation now turns and addresses Richard. 'We've had this phone call,' he says 'saying you are a reporter for the *Sun*.' That's it. That's all he says.

Richard's head is spinning. He is terrified. He has thought about this minute for the past five weeks, ever since he infiltrated the Socialist Workers' Party in London, the possibility of its happening. And if it did, he had decided, he would confess on the spot. Now he changes his mind. Three or four seconds pass before he denies the charge.

'Which was a mistake,' says Richard Ellis. 'Silence was the giveaway. I should have said "no" straightaway, or should have confessed. I don't know why I decided to deny it. I thought there would be no mercy. Those seconds I waited, it was almost a fatal hesitation. Then I said, "No, that's ridiculous."

'There followed about twenty minutes of intense questioning in this car park, going back over this story about who I was and what jobs I'd had. I'm in the minibus, remember. I'd made up a brief story that I had worked as a farm labourer in Sussex. They checked my hands. And they were soft.

'"It doesn't feel to me you've been a farm labourer," one of them said. Luckily, I'd said I worked as a mushroom picker. "And if anybody has ever picked mushrooms," I told them, "you know it doesn't give you callouses on your hands." One guy who had picked mushrooms agreed with that, and that helped. Fortunately, it was dark, and they couldn't see me shaking.'

One of the miners spoke up, said he wanted to take Ellis out to a pit, where they should give him the beating he deserved. Some of the Socialist Workers believed Ellis and didn't want that to happen to one of their supporters. They decided to take a vote.

'In the end,' says Ellis, 'I just said, "Well, do what you want, I've come in to help you, and if you want to beat me up, then beat me up." And they voted and I won four to three to be let go. But they said I had to go back to London where they would have me checked out. Then they offered to give me train fare, and I said, "No, I don't want your money. Just drop me off by the motorway, and I'll hitch back." It was supposed to be an act of defiance.'

They drove Ellis out to a motorway roundabout and let him out. 'Terrified and shaking like a leaf,' he started running down the motorway, 'always thinking the minibus would come back around.' A few miles down the road, he found a phone box and called Roy Greenslade, at that time an editor on the *Sun*, who sent a taxi out to pick him up.

Ellis was then twenty-four years old: 'I was a kid trying to play a man's game.'

Several weeks before, Ellis had shown up at his girlfriend's house armed with a bottle of champagne and flowers, chocolates; the whole bit. Martine Dennis remembers thinking, 'What a sweet man! And I started quaffing the champagne. I was young and naïve,' she says, 'and unprepared for what these gifts might mean.' Ellis then explained to her that the editor of the *Sun*,

228

Kelvin MacKenzie, had come to him and asked him to go on special assignment.

It was almost the truth. The *Sun* believed that the Far Left was partially funding the long-lived miners' strike and that they were behind much of the violence on the picket lines. These charges had been repeatedly denied by Arthur Scargill and the NUM. The *Sun* had already sent several reporters to get the story, but none had succeeded. When they asked Ellis, he agreed to have a go, but only under his own conditions, and these were that he do the thing undercover.

It meant that he and Dennis would have to abandon their holiday in the Gambia, which they had booked only a few days before. He now delivered this news. It happened that Dennis worked in local radio at LBC, and neither she nor Richard had had any time off that summer. This was to be their first holiday together, the one where they mapped out their future. Dennis was furious.

'But more about the job he was doing than losing the holiday. And I said, "Come on, for such a shabby story, you're giving up a holiday?" And then it came down to, "Exactly what are your political beliefs, Mr Ellis?"

'We'd been going out together for only a short while, and it's always a difficult sort of problem – me with my liberal politics – and then running into a guy who works for the *Sun*. We were going to dinner parties, and I would preface my introduction with apologies. "Look-they're-not-all-as-bad-as-they-seem sort of thing." And I'd look at him and think, "I hope I know what I'm saying." We had some very stormy sessions, in terms of racist, sexist jargon that was spewing out of that paper, and fundamentally Richard and I were all right. But I wanted to test him through and through, especially with the miners' strike. It was a very trying period.'

Dennis understood in some distant, undefined way that the job could be dangerous. The words 'undercover work' represented something like that in her mind, but she hadn't 'really bargained for the physical intimidation he found on the front line. Cerebrally, I dealt with it. But not fist to fist, I hadn't gotten that far.'

The holiday was duly cancelled, and Dennis ended up seeing Ellis only on rare occasions. When she did, she was shocked by his appearance.

'He had to grow a beard and it was red! He looked an absolute mess. Very thin, living the life of an unemployed labourer on £23 a week. He would phone when he got the chance. He would usually know what my work pattern was – I was doing shiftwork – so maybe I'd see him for a morning, always he'd be dressed in these awful clothes and that disgusting beard. We'd have a ceremonial conversation and that was it.

'When he finally finished the assignment and described what had happened, *then* I became more frightened than I had ever been. I hadn't anticipated . . . He was very, very lucky. It was quite upsetting to hear his account and to read the account in the newspapers. And then I got these phone calls from my friends. "Did Richard really do that? Did he really mean all he said?" My friends, some of them have the leftie tendency. The trouble with my friends, they would rather be blind than see the truth. The messenger bringing the bad news often gets shot. After a while, I started to distance myself from it.'

Meanwhile, Ellis was disillusioned by the way MacKenzie chose to use the story. Ellis had written about police violence against the miners, which he had witnessed, and also he was quite struck by 'the intense division that the miners' strike caused within the community, that brother was against brother, sister against sister, villages split down the middle, and that division would take years to heal, if it ever did.' In Ellis's story, these two aspects were reduced to two paragraphs. To his way of thinking, they were an integral part of the objective presentation of what he had witnessed.

For Ellis, who now reports for *The Sunday Times*, the experience represents a major difference between tabloid and broadsheet reporting. 'If I had done that story for *The Sunday Times*, they might have rightly led on the miners' hit squads, who attacked colleagues going back to work, but they would have included the rest of it. And in fact the SWP [Socialist Workers' Party] *was* supporting and financing and encouraging the violence that was there during that strike. It's an example of how tabloids do good work, but because of what else they do, they negate their impact.'

For Ellis and his girlfriend, the experience helped consolidate the relationship, and in September 1985, they were married in New York City, where Ellis was reporting for the *Sun* and Dennis was foreign correspondent for the BBC at the United Nations. When they returned to England, Ellis joined the Foreign Desk of *The Sunday Times*, and Dennis became a news reader for Sky Television. They now have a two-year-old son, Joshua, for whom they split domestic responsibilities, Ellis taking him on holiday on his own whenever his wife can't get away.

For Dennis, the vital thing was that they finally get to the hub of what they believed, since she is both black and Hispanic. In her liberal community of mixed races, she had to be absolutely certain that she and Ellis would belong, as a couple. 'My friends,' she says, 'are still my friends; and they adore Richard.'

Don MacKay is standing at the bar of the Golf Club, a private club just off Fleet Street, and he is inspecting the bartender's measure of gin in the glass sitting before him. 'What's all this they've been saying about me being wild? I'm not wild at all. I'm a sensitive guy. Ask Nicola. She's the best thing that ever happened to me. Maybe they're right. Pre-Nicola I was wild. Been seeing her three or four years.

'Put it this way. I've slept on Brian Hitchen's couch in his office more often than he has. General silly things: I've stood at the bottom of Fleet Street so I could shout, "I'll take on all comers!"

'When I first came to Fleet Street, because of my own nervousness . . . There's two ways you can arrive in Fleet Street . . . You can arrive very quietly and just quietly earn your spurs and be accepted. Or you can come and shout "I'm here". Guess which one I chose?

'Apart from the fact that people looked and thought, "Who's this little funny person from the provinces? Who does he think he is?" But they found out. I made some very good friends then. I made some very good enemies as well. There was a lot of hard drinking, a lot of hard working, a lot of driving up and down motorways, jumping on and off planes, it was good fun. It also cost me my marriage and my two daughters . . . but it was good fun. Invariably I'd get home on a Saturday morning. Well, where else does a daily newspaper man go when the "Sundays" have moved into his office?'

When MacKay was working for the *Star* – it was sometimes an eighteen-hour day, not that MacKay minded that – Brian Hitchen sent him to Germany to do a story about a missing child. It was a British sergeant's child from the Rhine army who had vanished from a NAAFI. Predictably, the mother was hysterical, but in this case, even more so than usual, because in Germany, there was a large baby-buying ring in operation. MacKay told his wife he would be gone for three days, maybe four. He flew out on a Tuesday and finished the better part of the piece on that afternoon. The next morning, in the middle of an interview with the sergeant's commanding officer about the ways in which the army was acting to retrieve the missing child, MacKay received a call telling him 'to catch the first plane back, somebody's blown up the Household Cavalry, the Blues and Royals, IRA bombing.'

231

MacKay was on the next plane, and from Thursday onwards he was reporting on the Hyde Park bombing. That next morning, the Lifeguards, determined to carry on with the traditional ceremonial ride-out, went out carrying the tattered banner of the Blues and Royals. MacKay wrote a long colour piece on that. 'What I didn't count for was this television report that night, when I was actually doing this riding-out piece. I was shown on the TV coverage when I was meant to be in Germany.' Eventually, MacKay made it back to his house, which was in Northamptonshire, on Saturday. As he pulled into the driveway, his eldest daughter, who was then four or five, was playing in the front garden. When she saw her father, she cried out, 'Daddy, what are you doing here?'

'And I thought,' says MacKay, 'that's me, in trouble straight away. So she ran into the house and I walked in behind and my wife was upstairs and the little one ran to the bottom of the stairs and she turned round and gave me one last, lingering look from the top of the head to the tips of the toes, and back again, shook this little blond head of hers, sighed, and shouted up the stairs, "He's home. And he's been drinking again."'

'Marriage is the biggest casualty of tabloid journalism, *I* think,' says George Lynn, a thirty-years plus veteran of Fleet Street. 'And the fact remains that I'm probably only one of two or three people on the *Sun* who hasn't been through a divorce. The divorce rate on the *Sun*, and indeed, upon every paper is *very* high. When my sons were growing up, I barely saw them. My wife did all the decorating around the house. She brought up the children. Of course, nowadays, wives won't do that. To be honest with you, I've neglected my family many times. When I should have been home, helping my wife, I was out writing stories. I mean, the story becomes the most important thing in your life.

'What happened, I was born in Camberwell, in the slums, in south London, in a tenement building. My father was a London costermonger. He was a cripple. When he was a baby, his mother dropped him. My grandmother dropped him, and his spine was smashed, and the first fourteen years of his life, he lay in effect in what was an open coffin, and he had a hump, he had a humped back . . . So he couldn't get a full-time job. He used to sell fruit from the stalls in the street. Early in the morning, about three o'clock, four o'clock, he would go to Covent Garden. He would pull a heavy barrow, this iron-rimmed barrow, from Peckham to Covent Garden. He filled the barrow up with lemons. And he used to pull it all the way back . . . loaded up, with crates of lemons, all the way back to Choumert Road, in Peckham. And he used to sell lemons, and my mother used to help him. Oh, oh . . . that was that. I'll tell you what . . . I didn't know what it meant.

'Fortunately, I passed an examination and got through grammar school.'

But by the time Lynn was fourteen, he was already working as a copyboy at United Press. He had planned to stay in school, 'but then the war started in 1939, well, there's not much point in staying in school when there's a war on.' When he was seventeen, he joined the Royal Air Force and became a radio navigator. Among the forces taking part in the raids over Germany after D-Day, Lynn says it was the only time he was religious in his life. When he was discharged from the service in 1947, he applied to go to university but was rejected on a technicality. 'I was not in formal education when I entered the service; that means you were debarred to getting a grant to go to university. So I became a reporter instead.'

When Gladys Lynn first met her husband, she was in the Women's Auxiliary Air Force. She had gone into the service in 1944, and she met Lynn when they were both on home leave. She and two of her friends had agreed to go to a dance at New Cross Palais with a group of young people, and when she got on the tram, 'there was George with them and we were introduced and we were sitting on the tram and he was next to me and that was it from there.'

There was on her part an immediate recognition that Lynn was ambitious, 'and when we got married, I was sort of with him on that. I was ambitious for him. The way things were going, I realized I was going to be married to journalism. The hours he worked, the places he went. Well, I realized that was his job, he loved doing it. If we were to stay together, obviously I had to support him on that.'

Gladys Lynn made curtains, hung wall paper, painted; 'kept the place looking nice.' When the children were young, they were in bed by half past six. She would then go to work on the jobs she hadn't been able to finish during the daytime. 'But I was quite happy. I read a lot. I still do. I had lots of hobbies – embroidery, knitting. I didn't sit at home doing nothing. There was always something I could find to do. If I hadn't been happy, I wouldn't be with George now.

'He could go to his job contented, knowing the boys were well cared for, the house was happy. I think that's why he could get along so well with his stories. I knew that he loved his home, the boys, me, and I knew as soon as he finished the job, he couldn't get home quick enough to see us.'

Before Lynn went to work for the *Sun*, when he was freelancing on Fleet Street, he did a story for the *News of the World* on a group called 'The Marmalade', and one of the band members was married to a well-known Swedish actress, Leena Skoog. One evening, Lynn came home and told his wife he was going to have a shower and change; he had to go out. He told her he was going to dinner with 'The Marmalade'. But that afternoon, Skoog had called Gladys Lynn and invited her to the dinner as well, 'And George never mentioned it,' she says. 'I was sore about that. I suppose I'm still a little angry, after all these years. I never mentioned it at the time though.'

Says George Lynn, 'I guess I'm just a male chauvinist pig.'

Says Gladys Lynn, 'Well, I think journalists just are.'

Nick Lloyd edits the *Daily Express*; his wife, Eve Pollard, the *Sunday Mirror*, and their relationship is, without doubt, unique. They are the only husband-and-wife team on the face of the planet to edit major city newspapers. And in the same city.

Says Lloyd, 'We met in a pub, when I was on the *Sun*, and she was on the *Sunday Mirror* and we were both married to other people and we had a passionate grand affair. Our careers have grown with our relationship, so it's not as abnormal as it might have been. But it's pretty abnormal because we only ever have one day a week *if* we are off together, so our lives are governed by newspapers and work, but by *different* newspapers and . . . we are both sensitive about criticism from one another, in the way husbands and wives are sensitive about being taught to drive together. I can take criticism from outsiders or colleagues and she can too . . . It hurts more from somebody you are in bed with. We are fiercely competitive with one another, underneath it, and I think Eve thinks she could do my job better than I can. She watched me edit two newspapers and be a deputy editor, and she thought, "Well, if he can do it, I can do it." And so she sort of ploughed in. It's a roller coaster relationship.'

Eve Pollard's divorce from her first husband is a friendly one. 'I've just had two very nice, very intelligent husbands,' she says. 'If Nick and I go away, my daughter and my son go together to my first husband's house. Friendly divorce, it's the only way.'

Pollard is overwhelming. She is big-bosomed, big-boned, good-looking and brassy. She is also bossy. In fact, she is not unlike the women immortalized in the Katherine Hepburn–Spencer Tracy comedies of the 1940s – and there is that touch of Tracy in Nick Lloyd.

In the editorial chair, Pollard takes charge completely – although she's capable of infinite patience at unexpected moments. Pollard's mother worked in her father's firm, and she believes that was the deciding factor in her own ability to go in and get the job done. Says Pollard, 'I believe that women are as capable, as clever, in different ways sometimes, as men. But I believe the way to influence men is to go about your work and be as successful as you can. And that works more powerfully than feminism. The more women are seen working efficiently, the less men will see us as having two heads. Women are loyal. They remain sober; during the day, anyway. And they're learning to compartmentalize their lives like men can. It's pure adrenalin being a journalist, and very difficult to pull yourself off.'

When Pollard started in the field, she had no specific goal to become an editor: 'It was unheard of,' she says, 'for a woman to edit a paper on Fleet Street.' But then she was hired from the *Observer* to become Women's Editor at the *Sunday Mirror*. 'I was twenty-two and pregnant. Not barefoot,' she says. They had always had women's editors who wrote about situations like hers, but no one had ever actually done it. Pollard stayed in the job for nine years, 'during which time, I got divorced, got remarried and had another baby.'

Lloyd often fixes snack meals for himself when he gets in from work, sometime between nine and ten-thirty. By then, his son Oliver, who is nine, is already in bed. If Pollard gets in before him, she'll throw something together for the two of them.

'Eve obviously cooks on Sundays, sometimes big lunches, and she'll cook dinner,' he says. Otherwise, he can cope with domestic chores 'pretty well'. A lot of the time, the two editors are asked to attend social functions, along with luminaries in the media, theatre and business world. Both seem to thrive on this lifestyle.

Says Lloyd, 'One way we've found to solve a problem: Chuck a lot of money at it. That helps. We have a nanny, and a daily, and they are organized by Eve and she sorts and arranges the shopping, but the nanny does it. The laundry is organized by the daily. And basically I do my bit with the kids, but Eve does keep all the balls in the air, I think. The thing is, if the adrenalin pumps and you're having fun, then it should work. But you can't want to be a suburban mother-figure and do it.'

Pollard's daughter by her first marriage has been accepted by Cambridge, where she will study archaeology and art history. On

Saturdays, Pollard's busiest day on the *Sunday Mirror*, Lloyd spends time with their son. They go to parties, to the cinema or to soccer matches. They work on Oliver's homework together, play golf, or football, a game that's lost its charm for Lloyd 'as I get older'.

'Once, we had a fantastic Saturday. We thought we might go and watch Arsenal play Derby. Maxwell owns Derby. So I asked Eve, "Can you see if you can get tickets to the game?" Within two minutes, Maxwell called, and said, "I understand you want to come to the game. Why don't you come with me in my helicopter?" Maxwell was really very sweet. He found out Oliver wasn't very enthusiastic about science, gave him a science lesson about the Antarctic, gave us a big lunch in his penthouse, and we talked about life. Then we got in the helicopter and we went to the game. What a day out for a nine-year-old!'

At the end of each day, Lloyd and Pollard talk over what's happened in the news, discussing the politics of the newspaper game, and according to Lloyd, they've found they're not much use to one another in terms of advice. 'We disagree as much as we agree. So there is a kind of debate, and not much common ground. That's what enlivens life. We don't have a unified front on anything, on people or owners or anything. People think we'll be a unit, but we're not a unit. We're two separate human beings. We fight. But that's good; as long as you can cope and you don't sulk, it's fun.

'You make accommodations without admitting it. You adjust, but you don't actually say you're adjusting, even while you're still arguing. We're like nuclear deterrents. In the end, nobody's going to be the one to use the bomb.'

One of the best-known names in tabloid journalism is Marjorie Proops, who is known for her plain-speaking, straightforward advice column in the *Daily Mirror*. What most of her readers *don't* know is that, in addition to writing the well-known column, Proops is also an assistant editor on the paper and a director of the company. She is a shrewd and able businesswoman with a heart of gold – the ultimate ideal of the modern-day career woman.

Proops will tell you 'it's a man's world' and if she has been successful, it's only because men have allowed it. The man who most helped her in her career was her husband of fifty years, her beloved 'Proopsy', who died only recently. 'It wasn't always easy and it wasn't always good, but I miss him terribly now, and I'm very lonely without him.'

The company director of a construction firm, Proopsy accepted immediately and without complaint the proposition that his wife would go on working after their marriage. Said Proopsy, 'Fine, I'll help you.' And he did. He did the shopping, helped around the house, 'long before women considered themselves equal,' says Proops. 'He was years ahead of his time.' Every morning, the couple left the house together, Proopsy with his briefcase under his arm, Proops with her carryall.

'By now,' says Proops, 'we had a son. And when he was five, he woke up covered in spots. And I said to Proopsy, "I think he's got measles, and I'm going to ring the doctor." And he kissed me on the cheek, and said, "Don't worry." And the wonderful assumption was that I would be the one to stay at home. I was furious. But then I realized: This is basic, it's basic to men. Whatever their apparent beliefs, in the end you have your role as wife and mother. *And* I was earning more than he was. When we met in the evening, I told him how angry I was, and we made up. He said he had done it without thinking.'

When Proops's husband died, she considered writing a piece on it in her column. But she decided against it. 'I didn't want to burden my readers,' she says. But whenever she receives a letter about a bereavement, she writes back personally, saying, 'I know what it's like and I know what it is and I'm with you. And old Marje is human and fallible and has the same feelings. And you're not alone.'

'As everybody knows, we went through a very bad patch, the so-called "Gabbert era", which was dreadful,' says Brian Hitchen, editor of the *Daily Star*. 'But I do believe that we now have dumped the baggage of history and that people really don't remember or care about that episode any more. But it was a most difficult time.'

It was Hitchen's fate to follow Mike Gabbert's act. Hitchen had been Deputy Editor of the *Sunday Express* for fifteen months when he went on holiday to Marbella, 'feeling a bit brain-dead', because he and Robin Esser had just put 160,000 circulation on the *Sunday Express*. Gabbert edited the *Daily Star* for eight weeks in autumn of 1987, and he had become famous throughout England for introducing the infamous 'nipple regime' to its pages. There were sixteen-year-old girls topless throughout the newspaper, 'and the readers of course voted with their feet,' says Hitchen, 'and marched away.'

After three days in Marbella – 'where it rained like mad every day' – Hitchen received a call from the Managing Director of Express Newspapers, Andrew Cameron, asking him what he would take to be editor of the *Star*. Hitchen's wife was standing next to the phone and could hear the conversation, 'and she was waving and saying, "No, No, No, No; *Don't!*" because she knew how much trouble we'd have making it decent.

'So I said, "A great deal of money."

'So he said, "Money isn't a problem," which seemed to me a step in the right direction, and she's still waving and shaking her head vigorously. Then she writes on one of those notepad things, "*NO!*"

'So I said "and a great many stock options and a top-of-the-line Jaguar."

'So he said, "No problem." And "What else could I have?" and he said "Anything you like, no problem."

'So I said, "OK." And I asked about Gabbert and Andrew said, "Well, now you've told me this, I'll fire him tomorrow morning."

'So I said, "I'll be on the plane tomorrow morning too."'

Hitchen sighs. Nothing is as certain, he believes, as the inevitability of getting sacked if you are an editor. 'Somewhere the kitchen clock-timer is turned, you don't know how far its been turned, and one day it goes off, and that's it, your time is up: "Come in Number Thirteen. We got a twenty-three-year-old whiz kid who'll screw it all up, but we're going to give him the job." Or you suddenly have a massive heart attack, or whatever, and die. That's the way it works.'

'Soon as you start in the morning,' says Derek Jameson, who edited the *Daily Express*, the *Daily Star*, the *News of the World*, each in its turn, and held top editorial positions on the *Daily Mirror*, 'your head starts buzzing with unanswered questions about your rivals.

'Eleven o'clock: first conference. Then, you are invariably summoned to see the proprietor or one of his right-hand administrators, who will no doubt have some scathing comments to make on that morning's product; where you went wrong, things you noticed long before they did. And of course, many of the most glaring errors they haven't even noticed because they lack the professional experience and ability. You know a lot more than they do, you see, but that never stops them.

238

'Then you return to your desk and there's no doubt five or six people waiting to see you. Somebody has been offered a better job by a rival paper and can't make up his mind to take it or not. Which means he will stay if you pay him more money. If you pay him more money, that means several other people of equal status will want more money. Why should you pay him more than people who do the same job? The sports editor is there because he wants to send somebody to Australia to cover a rugby tour. Do we really want to spend several thousand pounds for five rugby reports from unpronounceable names in Australia? He's then got the job of selling me the idea of this rugby tour in Australia.

'While we're dealing with that the political cartoonist is hovering nearby with five or six drafts in his hand of thoughts on the day's main cartoon. You don't really like him or his work, you think the cartoonist in the other paper's much better, but you have to go through the motions of treating him as the greatest cartoonist in history; otherwise, he will get the vapours and be looking for another job. Remember that top cartoonists are in short supply, and you sometimes have to go all the way to Australia to find one – a good draughtsman with some pithy comments – he can end up earning more than the editor. So you take a very dim view of this fool hovering about here with his bits of paper who earns more than you do. And there's always the danger that he'll go off and join one of your rivals, so you have to keep him happy.

'The leader writer: You look at him and think he's so over-educated, he writes his leaders in Latin and then translates them back into English to make sure that people like myself can't understand what-the-hell he's trying to say. You have to decipher his words and language to make them readily understandable to millions of people. Not that anyone reads the leader column. Its most avid admirer is the proprietor who fancies himself as something of a political expert, is probably looking for a peerage, always wants to keep on the right side of the government, and so he feels he ought to read the editorial columns and be an expert on them, so you've got to get the leader column right for the sake of the proprietor. You know only one reader in seventeen will actually plough through all that verbiage.

'So when you've sorted that lot out, your secretary reminds you that you've forgotten your wife's birthday. It's now around twelve-thirty and you ought to be in your car because you've got to have lunch at the Commons with a tycoon who's got great plans for the redevelopment of London, and you know he's a villain who can't be trusted, but he's too powerful and important to offend.

For starters, his company spends half a million pounds a year on advertising in your paper. How late can you leave it before you go to lunch with him? There are four or five other people who want a word, but you should be on your way to lunch, so you have to do a quick mental adjustment who you're going to talk to before you rush to the front door and jump into your office car.

'And when you finally arrive for lunch fifteen minutes late and cursing the London traffic, you then have that awful business of having a couple of large ones before you sit down to eat. That usually means large gins and tonics. I can't drink. Drink has a bad effect on me. I've never been able to drink, so by the time I've had two large gin and tonics, the best part of a bottle of wine, and a liqueur afterwards – because the tycoon creates the impression that if you don't share his table, his booze and food, then you're somehow passing judgement on him – you have a long boring lunch, too much to eat, too much to drink, and you get back to your office at three-twenty. For years you've been preaching to your staff that they should get their lunch over within an hour, and here you are, you left before one and its now three-twenty. You've then got to catch up on what's gone on in your absence. It could be that four or five major stories have broken.

'You're not at your best. One of the reasons that you are the editor is that you are able to stand up to the rigours of this existence, so that you're still *compos mentis*, but you're probably a bit woozy, a bit befuddled; you'd dearly like to go and lie down for an hour. So you shut the door and tell the secretary you're not in to anyone, and start tackling the morning mail which you should've looked at at ten o'clock. There are three threats of libel action there; there's a very dear and old friend who's been mortally offended by something in the gardening notes. There are always at least fifty problems in the in-tray to be dealt with at some time or another. And they're still queuing up in the outer office to have a word with the editor.

'Just as you sit down to this lot, the secretary reminds you that you have an interview at four-fifteen with a job applicant, who works on another paper and who you are desperate to poach. So you've got to be at your most smarmy, ingratiating, over-flattering. You've got to do everything possible to persuade this journalist that they're the greatest journalist of all time and their talents are wasted where they are working, but you can't pay more than . . . You've hopefully discovered from your contacts what they're earning, not what they *say* they're earning. (They will always add several thousand to what they're actually earning.) It can be a

240

lengthy and tricky business. You usually start off by talking about the days when you worked together twenty years ago as young reporters because the odds are that you know them anyway. Fleet Street is a very small, incestuous community. You tend to know all the others. This takes a lot longer than it should and by the time you've finished, it's time for the afternoon conference.

'You decide what the most likely story is for the front page, what else is going on in the paper. After the conference you'll be talking about the paper, future projects, ideas, movement of staff, and so on until around six-thirty. By that time, there's only one thing to do and that's to get out of the office and into the office pub, and have a few drinks, go back to the office and have a look at the front page. By seven to seven-thirty everything's ready to print. Now begins the long wait until the first copies of the paper come out around ten o'clock. Of course, I'm talking about the old hot metal days – it's all done much more quickly now with photo-composition and new technology – but this is how it was in my day.

'So every night of the week, you would have a wait of a couple of hours for the paper to come out. Frequently, they're spent in the office pub where you're fair game for everybody in Fleet Street to come and bend your ear, whisper gossip about some rival newspaper editor after your job, give you a character reading, tell you why your front-line headline this morning was the worst of the lot, a disgrace to your paper, and how they would have done it differently. This is very wearing, because you're drinking all the time. You've had that huge lunch and you had too much to drink at lunchtime. You're now drinking again in the pub, or else you open the booze cupboard in your office and spend an hour or two there with executives, cronies, visitors, whatever, so a great amount of drink is taken. Then the paper comes up. By ten-thirty you've got all the rival papers as well.

'There is a secret system by which the newspapers exchange early copies, so you can see what the opposition is doing. If one of them is missing, you fear the worst because it usually means they've got some fantastic exclusive story which will be a five-minute wonder and you'd desperately like to have on your front page.

'You then have the great frantic chase to catch up with the rivals. You list stories that they've got and try to stand them up independently. Your newsdesk will be seeking confirmation of other stories. If you can't get that confirmation, you pinch the story anyway, and change the wording here and there, and pray that it's true, that it's not legally dangerous. This is where the editor is putting his entire career on the line because, if you get that wrong it could be a very costly mistake. Look at the Jeffrey Archer case.

'Having done your worst to stir up the entire organization and get everyone on their toes, you stagger out of the office about twelve or twelve-thirty. Elated, if you've got the best story; depressed, if someone else has. You've had far too much to drink, worked under far too great pressure, but you've done the very best you can to keep your paper on top, and juggled all these balls without any of them falling down and hitting you on the head. You fall into bed at one o'clock in the morning. There's every chance the phone will ring at two o'clock and the proprietor will be there saying, "What's this bloody crap on the front page? If I've told you once, I've told you a thousand times we don't want pop stories on the front page." You then have to justify yourself and what you've done to the proprietor, who takes it all very darkly, is not at all moved by your protestations and arranges to see you at ten-thirty the following morning in his office to explain further. You're then supposed to go to sleep for a few hours until you start the whole cycle all over again.'

God is a hack

In the tiny Spanish village of Villanueve de la Vera, high up in the Sierra Mountains, Don MacKay and Stan Meagher sit out of doors drinking San Miguel and waiting for their dinner. 'Suddenly,' says MacKay, 'there's this screeching sound and a cloud of dust, and this car emerges, and out pop . . . the competition.' MacKay, who is reporting for the *Star*, is the picture of serenity.

Only four days before, Mac-Kay was sitting on the news desk at the *Star* when he gets a call from his editor: 'What are we doing about this bloody donkey?'

'Bloody nothing.'

'I want that donkey. Go buy that donkey.'

'What happens if it's dead?'

'Buy the corpse.'

The story had broken in the *Star* on 27 February 1987. It chronicled the cruel practices of a spring festival held in Villanueve de la Vera every year, wherein a fat man from the village rides a donkey until it collapses from exhaustion; then the children of the village hurl their bodies upon the animal until it is crushed to death. The story is headlined: 'DON'T SIT ON YOUR ASS, SENORS'.

MacKay loses not a moment; he is up and out of his chair, flying down the corridors of the *Star*, with Meagher, who once covered the Israeli Seven-Day war by taxi, close upon his heels. As they hightail it to Heathrow, the *Star* hastily assembles a front-page teaser: 'Hang on Blackie, we're on our way!' On Page Three, a lengthy story appears beneath the headline, 'WE'RE ON YOUR TAIL, SENORS'.

The Star was on its way yesterday to confront the sick senors of Spain.

For they have gone back on their promise to spare the life of Blackie the donkey.

And we don't intend to let them get away with it . . .

The mayor promised the *Star* he wouldn't kill Blackie, but now it appears that the mayor was only stalling.

But watch out, hombres of Villaneuva de la Vera. We're on our way with a posse.

You'd better watch your ass.

The story is run on 2 March. At the *Sun* offices, staffers, in the tradition of Villeneuva de la Vera, seem to have been sitting upon their asses. It isn't until 3 March that they wise up to the fact that Blackie the Donkey has emerged as the Number One tabloid story of the week. On 3 March, they run a catch-up story: 'FURY AT DONKEY'S SACRIFICE! Don't Kill Blackie! The *Sun* flies to the rescue.'

'Blackie' it turns out, is only the donkey's stage name; his real name is 'El Morinito', which translates too close to 'Little Darkie' for comfort. So the sub-editors have opted for the generic, at the same time sharpening up for the exchanges between *Star* and *Sun* that will, by the end of the week, dominate the week's news, with breakfast television picking up the story and the editors virtually, if not literally, at one another's throats.

MacKay and Meagher meantime have hired two regulars from the Madrid Press Service, one of whom actually knows the owner of the donkey who is doomed to death. They reach the village and within no time, MacKay has slapped down the cash to buy Blackie and stashed him away where he will be safe from the villagers – and the *Sun*.

MacKay's account of the events leading up to the sale appears on the front page, a photograph of him beside the rescued animal dominating. The headline, in memory of another of the *Sun*'s busts, is 'GOTCHA!' In the lower right-hand corner is a copy of the bill of sale. MacKay has fought his way through drunken, leering crowds, furious that their 'fiesta of fear' has been spoiled; he reaches, he buys, he saves the cowering animal. Writes MacKay,

This is the moment your caring *Star* saved Blackie the donkey.

I handed over 55,000 pesetas – about £280 – to Blackie's owner.

The donkey who had faced death in a barbaric fiesta ritual will end his days grazing peacefully in a Devon sanctuary.

On Page Three, in the space usually consigned to topless ladies, there appears a 'CARING STAR SPECIAL', and Blackie is 'OFF TO A NEW LIFE IN DEVON'. The same day, the *Sun* is making similar claims. 'WE SAVE BLACKIE!' they say, 'despite a lame rival newspaper's asinine attempts to mount their own rescue . . .'

By the next morning, obviously beaten, they have taken a new tack: 'LEAVE OUR BLACKIE ALONE'.

They start a 'Keep-Blackie-in-Spain' campaign. 'He'll just suffer in Britain', the story claims. In his move from 'sunny Spain' to 'dank Devon', Blackie will be unable to grow a coat thick enough to cope with the harsh winters, he will suffer psychological trauma, he may develop lung worm, he doesn't speak English; the list goes on. 'SEND FOR SUN BADGE! Just send a strong self-addressed envelope with an 18p stamp attached to 'Keep Blackie in Spain', The Sun, P.O. Box 450, London E1 9D4.'

The grapes of defeat are sour.

Walk along Fleet Street until you reach the old *Express* building. Cross over, and follow the narrow passageway to St Bride's Church. Go left along the alley. At the end is the City Golf Club.

Inside, old-time jazz is playing, and a few men, leftovers from the heydays of Fleet Street, stand at the wooden bar that curves into a horseshoe in the middle of the room. The carpet is green. Golf clubs hang upon the walls as decoration. This is the only connection between the club and the game of golf.

Don MacKay stands at the bar, drinking gin and ginger. He lifts his eyebrows, pins you with his eyes as he straightens his tie. In a Scottish brogue, he begins.

'I was sittin' in the office one day, feet up on the desk, twiddlin' away, you know, what time do the pubs open? Brian Hitchen comes in, "Are you doing anythin'?"

"Nothin' that can't wait."

"Find me Mrs Mengele."

'So I just looked at him and said, "Okay, Boss, sure." Thought about this for a short time. Made a couple of phone calls. Asked a few people, "Is there such a thing as a Mrs Mengele?"

'"Which one do you want, the first one or the second one?" I said, "Which one's still alive?" Answer, "The second one." I said, "That'll do." So I get the address. So the photographer and I go beltin' over to a little town in Northern Italy that used to be part of Austria. And we expect Alpine cottages and people with tin helmets and black boots and we go to the address. And there it is, "Mengele", right on the doorbell. Knocked on the door. She wasn't in. I thought, "Brian's gonna kill me." Been away on the story three weeks, phonin' and sayin', "Send more money, we need more money." Thought Hitchen was going to go through the roof.

'Anyway I was standin' lookin' into Mrs Mengele's

245

kitchen window, and thinkin', "What am I gonna write?" Turn my head to the side.

'And it was then that I realized God is actually a tabloid journalist, God is a hack. Because the street sign of the road behind Mrs Mengele's third floor flat is Anne Frank Strasse. It's true.'

He straightens his tie, rolls his eyes round, pins them on yours. Nods.

'So . . . I'm quite happily sitting drinking San Miguel. My competitors were runnin' around like mad, tryin' to find this donkey. And this is where I'd hidden the donkey. As you looked out of the verandah of this parador, over the rooftops of this village, there was an old church hall with a red roof, it was in there. Every morning they woke up they could see this church hall and they didn't know it was inside.

'Got sent on another story with Stan Meagher before he died. Brought back a British football fan who'd been lying in a Spanish hospital in a coma, near death, who hadn't woken up. Been in there for about six months. His family was out of money and couldn't bring him back, so we turned up like the saviours, waving the magic wand. Got a £25,000 air ambulance.

'Stan and I are in this hotel in Northern Spain, doing the coma-boy story, and I'm talking to the editor on Saturday morning. There's a bang on the door, and a voice says, "Room service, senor." Thought, "I didn't order room service." So . . . open the door and there's the competition saying, "Where the fuck's the donkey?"

'We get the donkey back to Britain. Everybody knew by this stage that we were bringing the donkey back. On the way back on the ferry to Portsmouth, and I hate boats – I get seasick on the Serpentine – I had to bodyguard this bloody donkey. Stan Meagher's on the ferry coming back. On an eighteen-hour ferry trip what does any tabloid journalist do? He sits at the bar. The odd dry sherry for the Queen Mother's birthday. Stan and I decide to go and visit Blackie in his horse box. I reckon it was the waves that were making us stagger like that.

'Stanley goes in the front end of this horse box and he's leanin' over and he's strokin' the snout of Blackie the donkey. I've gone in the back to get him some fresh water. The next minute he's standin' on my foot, and I canno' move the bloody donkey off my foot, and I say, "Stanley, help me," and he says, "Don't look at me, it's got me by the finger."

246

It was about half an hour before either of us got free of this fuckin' donkey.

'We come through the gates at Portsmouth and the whole of the British press contingent is there. So we stop before drivin' out the gates, and we casually look in the back, because this is the only time that any one else is going to get a picture of this donkey. So I slip in the back, and say, "OK, they're allowed ten minutes takin' pictures, that's it." And as I opened the back of the horse truck, I got covered with nothin' but unadulterated abuse because I'd thrown this very big red horse blanket over the back of this donkey, sayin', "*The Daily Star.*"'

Don MacKay pins you with his eye. An Ancient Mariner type. He straightens the tie again. He does a double take. He does another double take. 'There was *more money, more commitment, more editorial space* given to that one fuckin' story between the *Daily Star* and the *Sun* than there was about Ethiopia.'

247

13
20 THINGS YOU DIDN'T KNOW
ABOUT KELVIN MACKENZIE

1. Kelvin Calder MacKenzie succeeded Larry Lamb as editor of the *Sun* in June 1981, when he was thirty-five years old. The appointment was made on a Saturday, and MacKenzie spent the better part of that night on the telephone being instructed by Rupert Murdoch. At seven-thirty the next morning, he rang the home of his old friend and mentor, Vic Giles, asking if he could come by for breakfast. When he arrived, he was too jittery to eat. Instead, he spent the better part of the morning pacing up and down the corridor that stretches about fifty feet along Giles's Barbican flat, gobbling down an entire packet of Rennie's indigestion tablets. He kept asking Giles, 'Have I done the right thing? Have I done the right thing?'

2. MacKenzie is a public school boy who attended the same school as P. G. Wodehouse – Alleyns School, Dulwich. He tried for seven O levels at Dulwich, but passed only one – English literature; not art, woodworking or technical drawing as is sometimes reported. When he resat his exams a year later at Brixton College, he failed *all* of them. He seems slightly embarrassed he originally passed the literature, saying, 'I don't know how I got that . . . I never read the books.'

3. MacKenzie is reported to have vomited over the shoes of his first editor at an office party when he was a bit 'under the weather'. The story is probably apocryphal but tallies with office scuttlebutt that he is not a man who can hold his drink. Says one seasoned observer, 'He doesn't drink often, and when he does, he becomes very silly very quickly.'

4. A favourite MacKenzie maxim is, 'Am I or am I not a genius?'

5. Another of MacKenzie's *bons mots*, this one following the Elton

John fiasco, when perhaps as a result of self-censorship the paper went flat: 'We haven't had a libel writ in a week. And what we've got is a bloody awful paper.'

6. MacKenzie divides Britain's national press into two categories: 'the Popular Press' and 'the Unpopular Press'. The paper he appears to dislike most is the *Guardian*, which he says is 'indescribably boring.'

7. Known for his epic swearing, MacKenzie is perhaps most famous for the 'blue' exchange immortalized in Linda Melvern's *The End of the Street*. A features writer was told by MacKenzie her story wasn't good enough to go into the paper. 'How about "E" for Effort?' she asked. 'How about "F" for Fuck Off?' replied MacKenzie. In this regard MacKenzie is not unlike the legendary Joseph Pulitzer who sometimes halved his words in order to insert a curse. Pulitzer: 'Inde-goddamn-pendent'. MacKenzie: 'Soci-fucking-ology'.

8. MacKenzie is said to have an impregnable 'high-tech home', ostensibly to protect him and his family from the IRA, whom he has attacked many times over in the pages of the *Sun*. A salutary second benefit is no doubt the protection it affords him against invasions into his personal privacy.

9. MacKenzie's dislike of being interviewed or photographed by other journalists verges on the paranoic. He has broken his silence on only one occasion when he invited five reporters from the broadsheets to a quasi-news briefing in the wake of the £1 million Elton John libel settlement and his disastrous coverage of the Hillsborough football stadium disaster. One of the reporters later privately dismissed the luncheon as 'a performance'.

   During MacKenzie's 'anti-Frog' campaign – just after *Sun* reporters 'invaded France' on his orders – two photographers from *Paris Match* gained entrance into the *Sun*'s offices, chasing MacKenzie around the newsroom. They left without their photograph.

10. The few times MacKenzie has appeared on television, he has been less than successful. Asked if he thought a rival's newspaper had changed any, he answered on camera, 'It looks like the same crap to me.' 'Bloody television,' MacKenzie has been heard to say. 'They'll get you on and then say, "Why are you such a scumbag?"'

11. A source close to MacKenzie once said that his private philosophy can be summed up in a phrase, 'In the end, they'll let you down.' As is sometimes the case with a deeply held conviction, the maxim has become something of a self-fulfilling prophecy.

12. MacKenzie once told one of his star reporters that he had been hated all his life. 'I don't give a fuck,' he is reported to have said. But the reporter privately believes MacKenzie 'would desperately like to be loved.'

13. On the fiftieth birthday of the *Sun*'s news editor Tom Petrie, the office was brought to a standstill when, in the middle of the afternoon, the Coldstream Guards marched into the newsroom in full dress uniform playing 'Happy Birthday'. MacKenzie broke through their ranks, rushed up and gushed, 'Happy Birthday, Tom.' The military band then broke into a succession of songs which lasted about a half hour, going through their entire repertoire. Says one observer, 'Tom was delighted of course.'

14. At one time, the office possessed a megaphone, which either MacKenzie or Petrie would use to summon staff. One of the pair would suddenly jump up, put the megaphone to their lips and shout out across the newsroom: 'John Kay. John Kay. Come in John Kay. We've got a splash for you.'

15. The newsroom still has a musical triangle which hangs above the news desk. It is rung whenever there is 'a real story alert' (as opposed to 'a duff story alert').

16. It isn't unusual for MacKenzie to swing through the *Sun*'s doors singing old-fashioned songs. 'There will be blue birds over the white cliffs of Dover', can sometimes be heard as he saunters through the paper's newsroom. Another MacKenzie favourite: 'We'll meet again, don't know where, don't know when . . .' He never goes beyond the first few lines.

17. Subject to sudden mood changes, MacKenzie can be cheerfully singing one of his golden oldies when he will suddenly look up and say something to the effect of, 'Get the cunt that did this page down here. I want this fucking page done over.'

18. A rumour once went like wildfire through the *Sun* offices that MacKenzie didn't give a toss if you didn't know the name of the

Minister of Defence, but you had damn well better know the names of the entire cast of *Coronation Street* and be able to recite them on demand – or be prepared for a public dressing down.

19. Something of a fitness fanatic, MacKenzie often goes out of the offices at lunchtime to play a couple of games of squash, then comes back in to work the rest of the afternoon. Lately, at least one staffer has had the feeling MacKenzie is 'rather conscious of his middle-age paunch.' He also seems to be aware he is beginning to go bald, and like so many before him, combs his hair in such a way as to try to hide the bald spot.

20. There are various nicknames for MacKenzie. Says one reporter, 'What can I say? The guy really is "Mr *Sun*".' Others around the office sometimes refer to him as 'MacFrenzy'. *Time Out* magazine has called him 'MacNasty' while *Private Eye* refers to him as 'MacFilth'. Says one ex-staffer, 'I just think of him as "an evil shit". That sums up my feelings toward him.'

Now read on . . .

Ring, Ring.
The phone is ringing in the office of Paul Woolwich, editor of Channel 4's *Hard News*, the highly rated television series that takes newspapers to task over alleged improprieties. One of their most common targets – the tabloids. Woolwich picks up the phone.
'Paul Woolwich speaking.'
Says a voice on the other end of the line, 'Knowing the way you like *to be right up there* with journalist misdoings, I thought you'd like to know a guy is being suspended, a television researcher is being fired, for staging a fake interview . . . [specifies the case].
'It's an exclusive story. But I *thought*, knowing the way you like *to be right up there*, you know, in journalist [pause] misdoings . . . you might as well get *stuck into* the TV side as well as the newspaper side . . . I thought I would give you an early steer so you could *get up there* and get working on it.'
Woolwich agrees it's a good story, mentions the caller has missed his show's deadline and refers him to the *Media Show* or *Open Air* in Manchester.
'No, look, Mr Woolwich. We're giving *you* the early steer. We wouldn't want any other show to have it. Right! the others may lift it, but you must *get into it* with the same enjoyment you get into the newspapers. I'm relying on you guys *to really get stuck into these pricks* who do this sort of thing on TV.'

Woolwich agrees again that it's a good story, then asks the caller what he thought of the recent performance of the *Sun*'s deputy editor Martin Dunn on *Hard News*.

'I never saw it. I don't watch that kind of thing . . . The only thing I did see, which gave us a bit of fun, was a bloke writing in to us who said he's never been so disgusted in all his life and that as far as he was concerned Martin Dunn was a devious turd. We wrote back to that guy saying that "You saw him for only ten minutes, we've known him for ten years, and he's a slippery and devious turd."'

Woolwich again says he will call the story to the attention of the other television shows.

'No, No, No! We're relying on you, we're *depending* on you, Mr Woolwich. I'm gonna clean up TV if it kills me . . . We'll join forces together in this new campaign.'

The caller hangs up.

About the time Woolwich receives his telephone call, a writer for a popular London weekly magazine directs his readers' attention to the appearance of a new column in the *Sun*, called 'Hard Views'.

> I rang the hotline number which the *Sun* said would put me straight through to the special squad ['set up to deal with those TV fakers'] only to find the phone had been taken off the hook. It remained off the hook for three days on the trot. Finally I rang the news desk to find out what was happening. Never mind a special squad, there wasn't even a single reporter assigned to the column. The news desk suddenly got a bit nervous and I was referred to the managing editor whose record was stuck in a groove. I had barely told him that I was ringing about Hard Views before he said, 'We have no comment to make.' Why not? 'We have no comment to make.' When would he have a comment to make? 'We have no comment to make.' Sounded suspiciously as if the super, soaraway *Sun* was not being straightforward.

Welcome to the mind of Kelvin MacKenzie, the sometimes 'ogre', sometimes 'genius' of the tabloid press, whose stewardship of the *Sun* has, more than any other force, determined the direction of the popular press since he took over the newspaper in 1981.

MacKenzie has been credited with stopping the circulation slide after Larry Lamb carried the *Sun* through the dozen years that saw its successful launch, rollercoaster climb and unanticipated dip in readership which led, many believe, to his departure. Under MacKenzie, profits on the soaraway *Sun* have been variously reported as between £1 and £2 million weekly, with the sum £1.75 million a generally accepted middle-ground estimate. It has been said that the rich coffers of the *Sun* helped to finance Murdoch's purchase of other newspapers, among them *The Times* and *The Sunday Times*, as well as contributing heavily to Sky Television, the high-risk satellite venture that has recently accounted for Murdoch's selling off several of his more highly prized possessions in order to get the project off the ground. Some believe steady profits from the *Sun* were also of signal importance in helping Murdoch get his nascent 'fourth network', Fox Broadcasting, Inc., into operation in the United States.

On the debit side, MacKenzie's press ethics are by any accounting dreadful, and he has been sharply criticized for starting a dangerous trend in Britain that has drawn imitators into adopting his open-throttle style in their own national newspapers. These rough riders have together contributed greatly to threats of legislation in the forms of a Right of Reply bill and a threatened Law of Privacy, which most recently resurfaced in the proposals of the Calcutt Committee's Report to Parliament, which represent a bureaucratic and administrative nightmare to the press as a whole. The committee's recommendations have been endorsed by most of Britain's national newspaper editors as the unpleasant alternative to worse – new statutory limitations upon an already foundering freedom of expression.

MacKenzie's outrages have ranged from the merely mischievous to the wholly despicable. In some cases, the falsification was part of a 'stunt' designed to amuse readership; in others, an interview or story may have been falsified, to the extent that the *Sun* has gained a national reputation for unreliability. On the week of the *Sun*'s twentieth anniversary, in November 1989, the satirical magazine *Private Eye* ran a poem by its 'poet-in-residence' E. J. Thribb, which demonstrates the establishment's attitude toward the maverick newspaper:

Lines on the 20th Anniversary of the *Sun* Newspaper

So. Hats off
Then.
To the soaraway
Sun.

You are
Twenty.

'There's more
Fun in the *Sun*.'
That is
Your catch phrase.

Unfortunately,
Like everything
Else in the *Sun*,
This is
Not true.

E. J. Thribb (17½–34⅓–17½)

On a more serious note, MacKenzie has on occasion appeared to
show the characteristics of 'actual malice' as the term is defined
by the United States Supreme Court – 'prior knowledge of falsity,
reckless disregard of the truth, entertaining serious doubts, or
having a high degree of awareness of probable falsity.'* And it
should be remembered that this governmental body is considerably more liberal in its support of freedom of the press than
the British Houses of Parliament, who, unlike the American
Congress, not only can, but do suppress press freedom through
legislation.

In the early days of his editorship of the *Sun*, as the full range
of his power began to dawn, MacKenzie seemed to indulge in
character assassination. It was an inclination that met its natural
culmination in the Elton John case.

Arguably the most sordid single episode in the history of libel,
the case saw the singer issue seventeen writs before the *Sun* finally
capitulated, on the eve of what had promised to be a knock-down-
drag-out courtroom battle. They paid John a £1 million settlement,
publishing a full-page apology with the gigantic head 'SORRY
ELTON' dominating Page One.

What happened was, the *Sun* got it wrong.

On Wednesday, 25 February 1987, the *Sun* published a story
entitled, 'ELTON IN VICE BOYS SCANDAL', in which it was
alleged, on the basis of the 'confessions' of one so-called 'rent-boy'
turned pimp, that Elton John and pop manager Billy Gaff paid 'a

* The definition should not be confused with the common law concept of actual
malice, which implies hatred or ill will against the subject of a publication.

minimum of £100, plus all the cocaine they could stand' to some ten rent-boys, in exchange for their participation in practices most people would find deplorable. 'The singer', the Sun alleged, 'had snorted cocaine while begging tattooed skinheads to indulge in bondage.' Elton John issued his first writ.

As it turned out, John was in New York the night this exchange was to have taken place, and he had the limousine receipts to prove it. Moreover, a number of the singer's friends and acquaintances made statements to the effect that they had never seen Elton John at one of Billy Gaff's parties, or indeed even at his house. Nevertheless, the Sun continued to publish story after story, each of them in one way or another reflecting unpleasant, distasteful and, as it happened, false allegations. John issued writ after writ in retaliation.

There seemed inside the Sun to be the idea that John, who is openly bi-sexual, would finally lose his nerve if he had to face the prospect of actually testifying in open court about his sexual proclivities. But just in case he didn't, there was an effort to scour the globe for any instances of misconduct that could be pinned on him.

John's attitude, however, was demonstrated by a laid-back but gutsy statement that revealed what the Sun was up against: 'They can say I'm a fat old sod, they can say I'm an untalented bastard, they can call me a poof, but they mustn't lie about me.'

The Sun nevertheless pursued their original tack, certain it would pay off in the end. On 16 April 1987, they ran three compromising photographs of John, one of them a full-frontal nude, for which they had paid £10,000 according to rumours inside the industry. The photographs were pathetic, not for John, but for the Sun's editor. The internal pressure of the threatened court case, it seemed, had exploded onto the pages of the newspaper in the form of a reckless disregard for the reader.

There was puzzlement, confusion; Sun readers had no idea what was happening. They were certain of only one thing – they didn't like it.

Finally, the last of 'the anti-Elton' stories appeared: 'MYSTERY OF ELTON'S SILENT DOGS'. It alleged that Elton John had subjected his pet Rottweiler dogs to an operation which left them unable to bark. Elton John owns dogs, but they are Alsatians. And they bark. The publication of this final story boded ill for MacKenzie, since John's attorneys were able to bring this case to court first, meaning that the Sun would bear the burden of

255

proving this allegation before other, more embarrassing ones against the singer.

Facing this, the *Sun* quickly made for a magnanimous apology and unprecedented payoff, thus bringing to an end one of the most impressive journalistic kamikaze missions in the history of the press.

In its aftermath, it was said by an off-the-record source, libel seminars took place inside the Murdoch press, which included not only the *Sun* but also the *News of the World*. Most believe that these were originated by Rupert Murdoch, although at least one source close to Kelvin MacKenzie believes 'it's a cynical clean-up, all bullocks and bullshit.

'They are paying lip service,' he maintains. 'The *Sun* is on the downside, going through a healing period before show business people will talk to them again.'

Another veteran reporter from a Sunday tabloid shakes his head in disapproval at the mention of the Elton John case. 'Don't mention I said so,' he says in a lowered voice, 'but the story was offered to us first . . . and we turned it down.'

One senior sub-editor and a much respected member of the back bench, the late Graham Courtenay, referred before his death to the abrupt ending of the period when the *Sun* tended to dwell on character defects instead of news.

'We went through a period where we were delving into people's private lives too much, also too much into show business. If a *Neighbours*'s character sneezed, we reported it. It made hard news people on the staff uneasy. Stories about 'cricket captain takes chamber maid to bed, or *not*' – they were boring. I think the pendulum has swung back a bit. I have no concrete evidence, but I think Rupert has said, "Enough is enough."

'I know for a fact, Rupert is always asking, "Are we covering the heavy stories, the politics?" And this is where people tend to think of Rupert only as a yellow journalist and he's not.

'We have certainly tightened up on the veracity of stories in recent months, after the Elton John thing. At one period we were publishing stories about people from the soaps that turned out not to be true. The reporter would quote "insiders". You know, "insiders say this, insiders say that," and you suspected after a while that the "insider" was just a figment of this reporter's imagination. And certainly we paid out money to a lot of people [when] the story turned out not to be true. And this was one of our bad periods, where quite honestly, it was almost encouraged. Reporters were fearful of not turning in copy, not turning in stories, and it was almost as if – "Don't let the facts get in the way of a good story." And then people, like our night editor, would say, "How can this be right? This doesn't stand up." He would immediately be slapped down. By the editor.

'Then, of course, after we started having the libel actions and there were lots of them, suddenly it went the other way, and we would then be lectured on how important it was to be accurate. People on our side . . . that had been *our* feeling all along: we were now being instructed to do the very things we'd always been doing, as if we'd been neglecting those in the past. This was another instance where the editor lost a lot of respect from people.'

An area where MacKenzie rates particularly low is in his treatment of staff. Front-line reporter Harry Arnold speaks of waking up on a Monday morning dreading going to work. He refers to MacKenzie's sacking of a number of his friends, 'six or seven or eight people, they were good. He used to torment them by walking past, saying "Who's gonna be next?"'

Another ex-staffer equates MacKenzie with a public school bully.

'If he decides somebody has got to go, from that moment of decision, that person becomes a dead person. Kelvin will say, "I don't want that man in the office anymore." He takes a dislike to people, people who have done very good jobs. Suddenly, he walks up to Tom Petrie and says, "Get rid of so and so. Get rid of him." Often he doesn't do the firing himself; he gets Tom to do it, or one of his other underlings. Or on some occasions, Kelvin calls the person in, and they have a bloody row and that is it. Then, he's surprised that so many desert him.'

The MacKenzie Era has been a wild ride. From his early defiance of the unions, through the Falklands campaign, through the bumpy move to Wapping, there has been nothing like it in the history of the press.

All but forgotten is the 'scum of the earth' debate in which union workers tried to suppress a *Sun* story saying that striking miners, once 'the salt of the earth', could now rightly be reckoned as 'the scum of the earth'. That rift cost the paper four days. Another anecdote sees MacKenzie, confronted by union workers seeking an extra £25 per head for editorial changes, reaching into his own pocket, pulling out the cash and slapping it down on the desk in front of him.

The editor's heroic, almost single-handed defiance of the eleven-day strike by the National Union of Journalists that took place at the height of the Falklands campaign has become eclipsed by the series of jingoistic headlines that reflected the *Sun*'s coverage of the altercation. 'STICK IT UP YOUR JUNTA', 'THE SUN SAYS KNICKERS TO ARGENTINA' and the infamous 'GOTCHA!' published on 4 May 1982, after the sinking of the *Belgrano* – these are what stick. The *Sun*'s comic-book ZAP! and WALLOP! approach to the war, complete with a video game called 'Obliterate', wherein players had the chance to torpedo Argentine ships, climaxed with a leader in the *Sun* accusing commentators and newspapers who criticized the government's actions as 'traitors in our midst'. The paper was immediately branded 'the harlot of Fleet Street' by their rival, the *Daily Mirror*.

The best insight into the *Sun*'s coverage of the Falklands was captured by *Private Eye*'s incisive parody: 'Kill an Argie and Win a Metro!' It has been said, no doubt many times, that, had Kelvin MacKenzie thought of the idea, he probably would have used it.

Other sore spots have been charges of 'gay-bashing', sexism and racism in the pages of the *Sun*. In the case of the former, a typical *Sun* cartoon regarding homosexuals, this time dealing with the question whether gay judges should be permitted to sit in court, depicts a judge wearing silk stockings, high-heeled shoes and women's undies, who looks down at the proceedings. A convict is solemnly swearing, 'I Promise to Tell the Poof, the Whole Poof, and Nothing But the Poof!' It is accompanied by an article entitled, 'WHY WE SHOULD BAN GAY JUDGES'. To accompany a story hyping a new book on Elvis Presley that claimed the singer was homosexual, the *Sun* rewrites the names of ten of his top hits 'as he might have done them if he'd been feeling a little queer': '(Let Me Be Your) Teddy Bare', 'Return to Gender', 'All Poofed Up', and so on. Recently, in May 1990, under the headline, 'WE MUST DEFEAT MILITANT GAY CULT: THE GREAT HOMOSEXUAL DEBATE,' the *Sun* wrote, 'Today we publish part of a speech that SUN TV critic Garry Bushnell gave at the Oxford Union, the university debating society, opposing – with Judge Michael Argyle – demands for more rights for gays.' The anti-gay campaign continues unabated.

More embarrassing, perhaps, are accusations of sexism, many of which emanate from the continuing publication of photographs of topless Page Three Girls, recently relegated to Page Seven. The appearance of the relatively new women's pages, 'Sun Woman', and along with them, the Page Seven hunk, may be an attempt to dispel such charges.

With regard to the accusations of racism, recent clumsy attempts to show sympathy with minority groups have foundered from too little too late. On 14 June 1990, a Page One story proclaimed, 'RACISTS DAUB LENNY HENRY HOME', which detailed the National Front's 'sickening race hate attack on the home of comedian Lenny Henry.' By the next day, the *Sun*'s rival, the *Daily Mirror*, was proclaiming, in a story entitled 'THE LATE LATE NEWS':

> The sinking Sun was YEARS late yesterday with a story about top comic Lenny Henry and the National Front . . . Lenny Henry's PR girl, Samantha Royston, said, 'We were very surprised because Lenny says it was first revealed about four years ago and he has been making jokes about it in his stage show ever since.' In June 1986, the *People* carried a story headed 'NF Picks On Lenny'.

And yet, despite the unrelenting chauvinism of the *Sun* under MacKenzie's leadership, there *is* another side to his character that contributes to his undeniable charisma.

One of his senior staffers remembers an event that took place soon after the *Sun* had made the move down to Wapping, when inside the 'Wapping fortress' things were still disordered and hectic and outside angry pickets were clashing with police. In addition, there were, at the time, problems with distribution. 'In the midst of all this,' says the staffer, 'the phone rings on the back bench, Kelvin MacKenzie picks it up, and it was an old lady who hadn't got her paper for that day, and of course she hadn't got her bingo numbers. So, in the middle of this chaos, Kelvin got hold of the paper, and says, "Hang on a minute, Luv, have you got your card?" And he starts reading the bingo numbers off to her.'

MacKenzie rates high points for his '110 per cent commitment to the paper' as well. His capacity for work is legendary. A staffer once said MacKenzie could do twenty-seven times the work of anyone else in the office. He is in before anyone else, leaves after everyone else and truly loves his job, saying it is the best position in Fleet Street.

On a personal level, there is at least one instance of an attempt on his part to help out a socially deprived youngster, and on a long-term basis – even though this sort of thing tends to get buried under a blanket of silence. For some reason, he eschews public knowledge of private acts of kindness. One can speculate he fears these might be interpreted as signs of weakness. Says one relative, to whom he has extended a number of opportunities, 'He's been very good to me all my life. Kelvin is very sarcastic, and people can't handle him. Murdoch is probably the only man who can. But I get on with him.'

Then there is the speed-of-sound MacKenzie wit. Writes Linda Melvern,

> In September 1985 there was a feature series in the paper on Priscilla Presley's life with Elvis. The last day of the series carried a story headlined: 'How could Priscilla do this to our daughter Lisa?' It was Elvis's message to the *Sun* from beyond through the medium Doris Stokes. One joker picked up a phone and said to MacKenzie, 'Elvis for you.'
>
> Quick as a flash MacKenzie replies: 'Tell him his cheque's in the post.'

Another anecdote has Oliver Reed, whose bouts with the bottle are legendary, ringing the *Sun* to complain about a story. MacKenzie picks up the phone, saying matter of factly, 'Alcoholics Anonymous.'

In still another story, MacKenzie answers the phone, and according to a staffer, 'listened to a female reader who had rung in to complain. "Who's your newsagent?" he asked. When she told him, he said, "Right! You're barred from buying the *Sun* ever again!" There was a pause at the end of the line. Then the woman asked, "Does that mean my husband is barred from buying the *Sun* too?"'

Or, take a typical put-down from MacKenzie: 'You are what a hedgehog is to the M1 . . . fuckin' useless.'

Besides his audacious sense of humour, his great talent is his gift for using words to create a sense of excitement on the page, causing some to describe him as a 'genius'. Others believe MacKenzie's brilliance stems from his total understanding of the *Sun* reader, although one ex-staffer makes the distinction that he plays to 'the prejudices of the stereotypical reader, the ignorant lout who stands on the street corner with a fag hanging out of his mouth and a can of lager in his hand.' Says one editor of a national daily, 'Kelvin MacKenzie will stay editor of the *Sun* for a long time to come simply because he's still the best editor on Fleet Street.' The question is, how long can talent compensate for a series of publishing blunders that have lost the *Sun* prestige, respect and circulation.

In the same bleak period that witnessed the scandalous Elton John affair, the *Sun* faced MacKenzie's disastrous one-sided coverage of the Hillsborough stadium tragedy, the theft of a photograph from the Palace which eventually saw the *Sun* pay £100,000 to the Queen's favourite charities for breach of copyright, along with a front-page apology, and also, in the *Sun*'s Scottish edition, the exposure of a top Tory leader in Scotland for allegedly being involved in a 'spanking' episode with a prostitute.

Criticism for this sort of thing rolls, duck-like, off MacKenzie's back. When the *UK Press Gazette* criticized the *Sun*'s attack on the Scottish Tory Party leader, not least the methods used by *Sun* reporters in ferreting out the information used in the story, MacKenzie was offered a 'right of reply' – an entire page to answer the *Gazette*'s accusations. MacKenzie took full advantage of the opportunity, saying with customary sarcasm that the *Sun* was in the habit of publishing the news. The story was newsworthy, he implied, because of the possibility of blackmail against a rising Tory star. MacKenzie ended the piece totally in character: 'So you want to decide what appears in the *Sun* every day. What do you think would be the result? ANSWER: The sort of unsuccessful papers that you and your staff read.'

Although a public official should, more than any other individual in society, be prepared to answer publicly for private foibles, still, Murdoch, who was a personal friend of the then Prime Minister, Margaret Thatcher, couldn't have been exactly overjoyed by the exposé. And this raises the intriguing question of why, in the changing tenor of the times, when freedom of expression is under fire in Great Britain and questions of cross-ownership in the media are beginning to work their way to the top of the public agenda, Murdoch continues to retain MacKenzie as the *Sun*'s editor?

There is a general belief amongst *Sun*-watchers that MacKenzie, with all his faults, is kept on because Murdoch is grateful to him; grateful for the halt MacKenzie brought to the nosediving circulation of the paper when he took over, grateful for the way he handled the move to Wapping, grateful for the continuing profitability of the *Sun*. It's a sentimental, if not maudlin, interpretation of the motivations of the world's most powerful media baron. Far more likely is the possibility that Murdoch is not inclined to change the editor of his flagship publication until he has someone perfectly in tune to run it. Perhaps the man tagged to replace MacKenzie is editing a paper somewhere in Australia, just as MacKenzie once went to New York to hone down his journalistic skills.

Even if Murdoch is not so inclined, he is in no position to effect such a fundamental change in staff until his communications empire emerges from the shadow of debt that now threatens it.

By the summer of 1990, the real problem with MacKenzie's editorship had become – falling circulation. And a frequently cited explanation as to why it was happening could be found in the oft-repeated phrase, 'Kelvin's tired'.

Said MacKenzie's major competitor, *Daily Mirror* editor Roy Greenslade, once considered the biggest challenge to the Mac-Kensie steamroller, 'Kelvin's tired, and Rupert knows he's tired, but Rupert doesn't know what to do after him. At the apex of the *Sun* or *Mirror*, you've got to have somebody who is politically sensitive.' Greenslade, who took over the editorship of the *Mirror* on 1 February 1990, represented a serious threat to MacKenzie. He worked beside him as Assistant Editor for Features on the *Sun* for five and a half years, which means, as Greenslade put it, 'I know all the tricks.'

Greenslade *did* know all the tricks, and in addition, he had made a heavy commitment to hard news coverage on a day-to-day basis, which the *Sun*, under MacKenzie, has neglected. *Sun* staffers even refer to Page Two, where all the current news is carried, as 'the graveyard page.' In the area of flash news and disaster coverage, the *Sun* has, with the exception of Hillsborough, been of high quality, outpacing the broadsheets in most regards. But Greenslade supported an investigative unit, and in addition to the fluff, intended to keep the news – and politics – in his newspaper.

Politically, Greenslade falls to the left, which seemed for a time to fit neatly with the political persuasions of the paper's proprietor, Robert Maxwell. In his youth, Greenslade was, in his own words, 'a leading member of the local chapter of the Communist Party of Britain. That was a Maoist group.' University, however, 'de-politicized' him, and when he came out, his views had moderated sufficiently for him to work his way back into Fleet Street, and, after working as a sub on the *Sunday Mirror* and the *Daily Express*, to take over Features at the *Daily Star*. Eventually he was taken on to the *Sun* staff, despite his dismissal years earlier by Larry Lamb.

A couple of incidents serve to show Greenslade's thinking. While he was a sub on one of the Fleet Street papers, he became leader of the union. Says Greenslade, '1976 was a hot summer, and I used to get the lads to walk out until we got "a hot weather allowance."' In another episode, having worked late he was refused taxi money to get to Victoria on a Friday night, from whence he took the train to Brighton where his family was living. So, the following Friday, when it was time to catch the bus, 'I simply left my desk and got my bus. There was a horrendous ruckus. I said, "I can't pay for the cab, I work for a pittance, I simply got up when my shift finished." So they gave me the cab.

'Then one Friday, when my cab arrived, I took it and went to see a friend, who took me to Victoria later. I got an envelope from the managing editor of the paper with a note saying to send him a check for £3.14 for an illegal cab to Dalston. So I photocopied his letter and posted it, along with my check for £3.14 and my return letter to him, which said, "You have discovered that I have a homosexual male friend." He found it very funny, and we became friends because of it.'

Greenslade's maverick attitude, plus his experience working with MacKenzie, plus his serious commitment to news, made him an imposing threat to his old colleague. And in the spirit of a man who knows who his competition is, one of Greenslade's first moves was to hire the *Sun*'s chief sub-editor, Roger Wood, as well as three other sub-editors from the *Sun*. He also raided MacKenzie's reportorial staff, hiring Harry Arnold and Richard Wallace. Said Greenslade, 'They were lined up outside.'

Recognizing the threat, about six weeks after Greenslade came in, MacKenzie started a 'Spot the Ball' contest with a possible jackpot of £5 million. The *Mirror* immediately warned their readers that the odds of winning were 2,176,782,335 to 1; they then launched their own competition – this despite Greenslade's reluctance to get involved in a 'games' competition since he believed that 'games attract fickle readers who leave the paper when the game is over. Generally, they are older as well.'

But that was only the start of the competition between the two papers. When the *Daily Mirror* began incorporating the Scottish *Daily Record*'s circulation into their own, thus reaching the same circulation as the *Sun* practically overnight, MacKenzie retaliated by adding in the *Daily Record*'s circulation with *his* own – a classic MacKenzie tactic. Despite this show of spirit, though, the fact is that in 1990 the circulation of the *Sun* dropped precipitously low to just above the 3,800,000 mark; this from a high of upwards of 4.15 million.

Then, on 12 May 1990, MacKenzie went over the top. When truck driver Paul Ashwell, whose lorry was loaded with parts of the Iraqi supergun, was arrested and held for three weeks in a

Greek jail, the *Mirror*'s chief reporter Harry Arnold flew out, paid £19,000 bond to free him, and had a picture taken of him smiling with his family while wearing a *Mirror* T-shirt. MacKenzie stole the former *Sun*-reporter's by-line and air-brushed out the *Mirror* logo, replacing it with the *Sun*'s. He then ran the lot on Page One of the *Sun*. MacKenzie chalked it down to 'mischief', but the *Mirror* sued.

The stunt tended to show, once more, how easy it is to overstep the narrow line between entertainment and falsehood, and how simple a matter it is to misjudge the reactions of the reader.

Meanwhile, downmarket, MacKenzie faces Brian Hitchen's *Daily Star*, named Colour Newspaper of the Year for 1989–90. Although the *Star* hasn't the advertising revenues to make it a serious contender against the *Sun* or the *Mirror* – and its circulation remains under the 1 million mark – the general tenor under Hitchen's direction, as well as the paper's well-considered campaigns, have made it a distinctive new voice supporting the interests of the working class. Hitchen's campaigns have included drives for increased pensions for war widows, rises in pay for ambulance drivers, the distribution of blankets and food to refugees trapped in Jordan after the invasion of Kuwait by Saddam Hussein and a cessation to the dumping of toxic and nuclear waste in England and Wales. The paper has emphasized its stand against cruelty to animals, especially those nearing extinction. It also participated in a long-term fund-raising campaign for children with cancer. Another Hitchen touch is a kind of working-class consumerism, wherein front-page attention is brought to shops who penalize customers for suspected thefts amounting to a few pence, or bus drivers who expel young children, forcing them to walk home in the darkness for being short on the fare.

Hitchen is also a seasoned newsman who worked his way up from copy boy to being the *Mirror*'s foreign correspondent, a position he held for nine years before becoming an editor. He has covered war, riots, mayhem and political scandal. As he puts it, 'I've been maced in Memphis and gassed in Washington.' By the time he was sent to Vietnam, he had already covered two wars.

And there is no question his Tuesday editorials represent some of the best and most provocative tabloid writing in Fleet Street. Written on 14 November 1989, when the strike over the pay of ambulance workers was reaching its peak, this leader tells in plain talk exactly the effect the dispute could have on one individual's life.

It was twenty past eight on a Wednesday morning in June when an ambulance, its blue lights flashing and siren blaring, tore down the wrong side of the road along the Brighton seafront.

When oncoming morning rush-hour traffic didn't get out of the way in time, the wheelman expertly spun the ambulance on and off the pavement and around lamp posts in his race to save the life of a severely burned child.

In the back of the ambulance, cradled in the gentle arms of the driver's mate, a little three-year-old boy lay wide-eyed in deep shock.

Only moments before, the child's supposedly flameproof pyjamas had turned into a mass of glowing red coals.

He had set fire to himself with a table-lighter which had been thoughtlessly left within his reach.

The ambulance crew took only four minutes to reach his home.

Which is about the same time it took ambulance crews to reach the bomb-shattered wreckage of Brighton's Grand Hotel after terrorists tried to murder the Prime Minister and the entire British Cabinet at the Tory Party conference.

Some of those brave ambulance workers put their own lives on the line that night . . .

The whole building could have fallen in on them at any moment.

They knew the risks. But their skills were needed and they did their job.

Just as they wanted to do their job last week in London. But the Health Service wouldn't let them. They pulled the 999 plugs on the mercy men and stubbornly refused to even discuss increasing their miserable 6.8 per cent pay offer.

Authorities sent the Army on to the streets in military ambulances ill-equipped for civilian casualties. Their crews were armed with street directories . . .

How can those Top People have so soon forgotten the bravery and dedication the ambulance workers displayed on the night they needed them most?

Do they really expect these life savers to take home an average £130 a week as the lowest paid workers in the public sector?

That frightened little burned boy in the back of the speeding ambulance spent two months in the intensive care unit at Brighton Children's Hospital.

265

It was a long time ago. But had it not been for those ambulance workers he would have died. Next summer he takes his A-levels. That boy is my son.

Unlike some people, I have never forgotten those ambulancemen. And I never will.

The most generous predictions of how long MacKenzie could last against competition like Greenslade and Hitchen were, by autumn 1990, a bare six months. Then, back against the wall and sagging, MacKenzie got a respite in the form of the Gulf War. Forsaking 'bingoism for jingoism,' as one newspaper pundit put it, circulation began rising, no surprise during wartime.

Armed with new colour presses, MacKenzie nailed his colours to the mast, printing the Union Jack on the front page and literally identifying the *Sun* with the British flag.

Then he had an unexpected stroke of luck.

Roy Greenslade suddenly left the editorship of the *Daily Mirror* 'by mutual agreement' with proprietor Robert Maxwell after only fourteen months at the helm. Greenslade's farewell lunch was held on 14 March 1991, appropriately at the Bleeding Heart Restaurant. It is said that during the luncheon, MacKensie rang Greenslade's office and left a message assuring Greenslade he was 'always welcome whenever he wanted to come back to work for Murdoch' – this despite the two editors' heavily publicized broadsides against one another during their year of hot competition.

But regardless of his astounding good fortune and his undeniable talents, MacKenzie has been in the saddle nearly ten years; for a tabloid editor, it's the equivalent of a lifetime. And though few care to name him as the major cause of efforts to muzzle the press in Great Britain – perhaps from fear of retaliation, perhaps from respect for the Murdoch empire, perhaps from grudging admiration of his enormous talent – he is the man, more than any other, who has caused the national press to face the great legislative impasse that now threatens each and every newspaper publisher.

Flash back to a Sunday morning in June 1981, when a younger, less cynical, less jaded MacKenzie asks his friend, 'Have I done the right thing? Have I done the right thing?'

The answer is, probably not.

14
THE LITTLE KING

They are standing on the pavement outside Stringfellows, shivering in the first really cool evening of the hottest summer ever recorded in England: girls in leopard-spot dresses, elasticized see-through black lace hiphuggers, hot pink lipstick and push-up bras. One of them sports a raggedy haircut, deliberately stringy, bleached right up to inch-long black roots. Another has her hair clipped halfway round the back of her head, Delores-del-Rio style. They are rocking back and forth on four-inch stilettos, giggling like the teenagers of yesteryear, waiting for their boyfriends to arrive. Despite their whorish makeup, they appear young and vulnerable and sweet as they twist and turn in the shadows of St Martin's Lane, just in front of the white diagonal neon sign that designates one of the West End's most stylish nightclubs.

Next door to Stringfellows, seated at a pavement café, is the Manchester editor of the *Sport*, Peter Grimsditch – 'the man,' his ex-wife used to say, 'who put the tits in *Reveille*.' (Circulation went up for the first time in eleven years.)

Grimsditch, founder editor of the *Daily Star* in 1978, long-time Murdoch employee, and recently appointed editor of the Wednesday *Sport*, sits drinking and chain-smoking Marlboros as he argues with his girlfriend Janis, an attractive, level-headed woman in her mid-thirties. Grimsditch, who despite a lifetime in the news business remains something of a romantic, is espousing his theory that Page Three Girls are lonely. Janis disagrees. He thinks it's fine, he says, if a girl wants to display her breasts for profit. Janis isn't so sure.

A hundred yards away, youngish men arrive singly or in pairs. Their hair is slicked back into ponytails or greased into fashionable twenties cuts. They are dressed in wide-shouldered shiny suits, red silk handkerchiefs tucked into their breast pockets. They pick up their dates, swagger past the club's bouncers and into the invitation-only party.

Back at the table, the debate between Grimsditch and Janis is hotting up. 'Don't impress your views on others,' Grimsditch says. 'No, Peter,' Janis insists calmly (she is purposely non-aggressive), 'I am *stating* my views.'

Inside, a packed house. Hundreds of guests crowd the entrance, the bar, the dance floor downstairs. They are all in some way associated with pornography-entrepreneur-cum-newspaper-proprietor David Sullivan, forty, who is hosting the event. It is the first anniversary of the Wednesday *Sport*, the night of the newspaper's 'Glamour Girl Competition', and Sullivan's first public indication that he means to take his successful three-day-a-week national into daily production. Through the crowds, he can be spotted, wearing an expensive buff-coloured suit, his grey-brown frizzy hair coaxed carefully back, ducktailing slightly on his neck.

This is England's so-called 'King of Porn', whose kingdom is worth £100 million 'maybe more', according to him; £50 to £60 million according to *The Sunday Times*.

With him, his entourage – a remarkably beautiful girl with high cheekbones, wide green eyes and golden hair. In profile, she doesn't look like much, but catching a glimpse of her straight on, full in the face, quite takes one's breath away. She is wearing a plain dark suit. Beside her is a girl with red lips and black hair, which has been pulled severely back into a chignon. This girl stands quietly, moves very little; another class act.

It is all too much for the plump young Asian thing, who also tags along. She is wearing a long, Tahitian-looking skirt, a skimpy purple knit shirt that shows the tatoo on her shoulder. Her eyes look like big blue moons, the expression on her face one of pure rapture. There is a look of disbelief that the world can hold such things, and of rising determination. 'I must always have this,' her expression seems to say. At an appropriate moment, she pulls down her knit top, exposing creamy round breasts, and a photographer snaps in her direction.

Downstairs, Neil Fox of Capital Radio, has stepped out onto a dance floor made up of clear plastic blocks, with oddly shaped curls of bright neon pulsating randomly in each of them. He holds a microphone in his hand. A crowd gathers round the dance floor, most of them watching Fox, a few glancing covertly at their own images in the mirrors that line the walls. Stringfellows is a house of mirrors, an electronically and metaphorically closed system that feeds off its own images.

For this occasion, Fox is wearing a purple shirt, a black and white wide-shouldered sports coat, saddle oxfords and trendy specs. His lapel pin is shaped like a microphone. Not a handsome man, Fox has opted for the extreme; he looks like a cartoon parody of everyone else in the room. Loud music begins to pulsate; the crowd cheers.

Fox is here to host the Wednesday *Sport*'s Glamour Girl Competition, the theme of which appears to be Aliens from Outer Space. The music, however, is inner jungle.

MUSIC: UP FULL . . . FADE INTO AND UNDER ANNOUNCER . . . Fox begins his spiel. The winner, he says, will receive £1,000, plus modelling contracts; the runner-up, £300; the third-place contestant, £100. The crowd cheers. He introduces the judges, a platinum blonde scout from one of London's glamour agencies, editor Peter Grimsditch, David Sullivan himself, and the beautiful blond girl with the wide green eyes. She turns out to be Trine Michelson, a former Miss Denmark. Michelson sits solemnly, concentrating on Fox, as she slowly chews her gum.

In a few weeks, she will appear topless in the *Sport*, giving a first-hand account of what it was like to be gang-banged by fifteen hooligans at an acid-house-type party she attended in Italy. She tells of her ordeal, the *Sport* will explain, as a warning to what can happen to girls who don't watch out for themselves.

The girls begin their parade across the pulsating neon dance floor. They are wearing demure but garish swimsuits. As they walk past, music blaring, Fox yells out their specifications: 'Measures 34–24–34!' If the girl is busty, Fox has a standard joke: '59–24–36!' He ululates, slides into a wild animal cry that sounds like a high-pitched 'WOOOoooOOO.' Then he gargles. The crowd goes wild.

Backstage, the girls sit bunched along a bench, excited and trembling. Most have come down from the north, and it is easy to see this is their first London contest. They explain why they are here. Not for the money, 'No! *For the fame.*' One girl thinks it over before answering. 'For the recognition,' she offers.

A heavy-set woman in basic black stands waiting to hear who the winner will be. She is one of Sullivan's army of employees. She loves the lights, the music, the glamour. She turns away for a moment and says to a companion, 'I would be down there if I had the figure for it.' She is not complaining. It is a passing protest against the outrageous slings and arrows of fate and fortune.

'I *would*!' she says with sudden urgency. 'I *would*!'

In 1955, a small boy living in a council house in Wales prayed

269

every night to be granted three wishes. The first was to be captain of Wales and Cardiff at football. The second was to be a world champion boxer. The last was to be a millionaire.

Today, David Sullivan – the boy who made the wishes – admits he failed at the first two, but 'won on the last'. One of the things he continues to puzzle over as a grown man, is, *why at seven* did he set the goal that would determine the rest of his life?

Sullivan's childhood was uneven, at best. His mother stayed in Cardiff while his father, who was in the RAF, moved from base to base, coming home to see his family only at the weekend. 'Everyone was terribly poor,' Sullivan says, and he still remembers unpleasant arguments over money. Then, suddenly, when he was about ten, Sullivan, his brother Clive and his mother all packed up and went with his father to what is now South Yemen. For the next couple of years, Sullivan lived there in the luxury of a five-bedroom detached house, with a manservant to tend the family's needs. At twelve, he was sent away to boarding school, along with his brother. Clive flourished and stayed on for the next seven years, but the young David hated it and pestered his parents until they finally gave in and brought him home, enrolling him in the local state school.

'I was a shy little boy,' he recalls, 'and I felt it wasn't right of them not to have me at home. I missed my mum. I'm a mummy's boy and I felt a deep-down rejection.' Today, he speaks to his mother five nights a week. 'If she dies before I do, I will be very upset,' he says.

Clive was the bright one, and Sullivan's folks were always telling him, 'You'll never be as good as Clive, but do your best.' He did do his best. He took ten O levels, and three Grade-One A levels. 'I was little in size, but that made me more determined,' he says. In 1969, he was the Sir Edward Stern Scholar for London University, and his degree in Economics from Queen Mary's College was 'Second Class Honours (Upper Division).'

It was university, he says, that 'nearly knocked the ambition out of me. The lecturers used to say to me, "Oh, yeah, we know what you're like. But as you get older, you'll have to compromise like us."'

His first job as a Trainee Ad Account Executive, selling dogfood, earned him £1,500 per year, and for a time, he thought his lecturers were right. 'My boss took home four grand, he was twenty-four; his boss was twenty-six on six grand.' It all seemed pretty hopeless, and to make matters worse, Sullivan realized that, with his working-class accent and unimpressive appearance, he would never

270

be any good at 'chattin' up clients and takin' 'em out for lunches,' the main method for business getting in the company.

But by then, Sullivan had met a man who was working part-time selling girlie pictures. Sullivan threw in with him, and within six months, he was making £35 a week on his full-time job – £800 a week on his part-time job. Within the next few years, he would parlay this promising beginning into an empire with an estimated 170 sex shops, and he would become the publisher of a number of lucrative girlie magazines. The first one was called *Private*, but many others – with names like *Climax*, *Romp*, and *Whitehouse* – soon followed.

'I've made my money initially on . . . call it soft-core pornography. Or pornography. Call it anything you like . . . It's only a word . . . And I get castigated because of that,' he says, in an irritated tone of voice. What irks him is that he's a social outcast for selling girlie magazines while 'the tobacco people are knighted for sellin'' cigarettes.

'They're knockin' off tens of thousands of people every year, *and* they're causin' pain and aggravation to hundreds of thousands . . . in the interest of the profit motive. There is something,' he says emphatically, 'wrong with society's judgement. Cause, all I ever tried to do is to give people a bit of fun, a bit of happiness.

'I think I'm a nice guy. I'm not tough or anything. I'm not a sacker. I think a lot of the press people, if you look over their turnover of staff, it's phenomenal. I won't sack anybody, virtually. I think I did one of my editors because he used to spend all his time at the pub, but anyone who works hard and tries hard, I'll never get rid of.'

It's true, his employees respect him. Some even want to be like him. One of his staffers, a young one, says, 'I'll tell you what kind of guy *I* am. I am a David-Sullivan-type-of-guy.' A business associate confesses he was on the ropes when Sullivan took him aboard. 'I was having a crisis of confidence, and David Sullivan helped me out of it . . . And you can call him up,' he continues, 'I mean, he'll answer the phone himself, and you can ask him advice about *your* business, and he'll take time out, and he'll help you, like it was *his* business.' Others sing similar praise, volunteer it, uninvited. They would, they say in so many words, take a bullet for him.

They may get the chance. Sullivan's professional history is one of turbulence and unrest. Four of his sex shops were burned down, others vandalized, their locks filled with Superglue. The night after a London newspaper ran a centre spread on Sullivan,

271

naming him as Britain's biggest pornographer, his house was set on fire with a firebomb. He has been attacked by feminist groups from the earliest days of his career, and there were marches of protest against the *Sunday Sport*, when it was just starting out. Roundly condemned as 'a scurrilous rag,' its first issue featured no fewer than thirty-seven prominently displayed nipples, adding to the national nipple count that continues down to the present day by critics of the downmarket end of the tabloid press.

Sullivan remains angry about all this. 'I think they had some sort of fear about me, that I'm some sort of lunatic, you know? I've spoke to various editors of the newspapers, and I think the directive went out *to get me.*'

It's true the press, establishment or popular, hasn't much affection for the man they've dubbed, 'The King of Porn' – a label that continues to rankle Sullivan. And the photographs they chose to publish of him, especially those taken in the early days of his career, appear purposely selected to make him look bad. They are frequently high-angle shots that tend to emphasize his diminutive size. In a few, he looks shy, sweet but seedy; at best, a pudgy boy, perhaps even socially backwards. At worst, he looks unfocused and slightly stupid. In the later pictures, he is made to resemble a sleazy, overweight lout, the type who shows an overactive interest in the kinds of devices and reading matter he himself sells. His overlong hair, plastered against his forehead, didn't help that early image. Even today and in the best of conditions, Sullivan is still defeated by his own appearance. Like many really short men, he doesn't photograph well, even in custom-tailored suits. And his hair, now cut short and fashionably coiffed, tends to frizz without a fixer.

And then there is his self-confessed preoccupation with the models themselves. Eight years ago, a woman reporter went to his mansion in Chigwell, Essex, pretending to be a model seeking work. There had been charges he was pressuring women who sought work as glamour girls to have sex with him if they really wanted the job. In her story appearing in the *News of the World*, Tina Dalgleish wrote that she was taken to one of the bedrooms in Sullivan's mansion and told to strip to her undies, so he could take a look at her assets. Today Tina Dalgleish describes what Sullivan was like – 'a little dumpling, really. Kinda bland. That was his whole trouble, really.'

More recently, Sullivan has moved out of the newsprint pages of the more sensational tabloids and onto the slick ones of the Sunday magazines. But what the public still wants to know about is his sex life. And the ladies' methods of eliciting the information their readers want to know grow ever more sophisticated. Asked how many women he had had in his lifetime – he's had thousands, by the way – Sullivan said he would answer only if the reporter first told him how many lovers *she* had had. 'Hundreds,' she snapped back.

'It's really surprising,' he said later. 'A lady like that.'

Sullivan's all-time low came not from the press, but from the law. In 1982, he was found guilty of living off the immoral earnings of prostitutes, in a matter that evolved from his ownership of a massage parlour. To his own surprise, he ended up going to jail, first to Wormwood Scrubs and then to Ford Open Prison where he shared a hut.

'I spent seventy-one days in prison. Ten weeks and a day . . . yeah, with hardened criminals.' The experience turned out to be more boring than terrifying. The prisoners – most of them readers of his magazines – showed him 'massive respect'. They were convinced, he says now, he didn't belong there.

'The night before I'm comin' up for my appeal, there's all the guards readin' my books . . . And I thought, "This is a joke. They're all my customers."'

In a way, Sullivan seems actually to relish telling what he saw in prison, down to the smallest detail. 'Tell you what you lacked in prison,' he says authoritatively. 'You lacked meat. You used to get one slice of meat occasionally that was about a thousandth of an inch thick [he gestures], the thinnest slice of meat you can ever imagine . . . And once a week you got chips. And they used *to fight* over the chips. My first job, I used to dole out the food. And when you're dolin' out the chips, if you give one more than another, they sort of fight over them.

'In the cell there is no running water, there's no loos. There is a bucket. Literally, a bucket. And a bucket of cold water to wash your hands in, you know? I mean me, I understand biology a little bit. And when I was in a confined cell, I took no food and no water for five hours before I was locked in, so for about ten or twelve hours, I never had the disgrace of peein' in a bucket, you know what I mean?

'*I'm* not a criminal; I'm, if anything, a lawbreaker. I've offended perhaps a law on obscene publications, which I desperately disagree with. But basically, I'm a law abidin' citizen . . .' And he keeps a drawer full of cancelled cheques to prove it. Altogether, they

273

tally £30 million 'at least', paid to Inland Revenue since Sullivan started in business.

Released on appeal, Sullivan, who has always maintained his innocence, nevertheless continues to wish he had taken the easy way out and pleaded guilty. But 'believing in British justice, I pleaded "not guilty". And believe me, I *regret* doing it . . . I felt I let my family down. Nobody in my family at any time has ever been to prison. I felt I had let my mum down.'

Despite his bitterness, going to prison caused Sullivan to think about what he was doing for the first time, and afterwards, he went into semi-retirement to analyse his life, 'because I had spent thirteen years, and I'd had about five days holiday, and I thought, "What the hell am I doing with my life?" When you're locked up, you wonder, "What's it all about?"'

It was out of this crisis, this re-evaluation of his life and its purpose, that Sullivan's *Sunday Sport* was born.

The newspaper was to be a national weekly, aimed at young male readers aged between eighteen and twenty-five, and its main theme would be based upon the David Sullivan maxim, 'Sex Sells'. Its slogan, 'I get it every Sunday!' was, in Sullivan's words, 'pinched. All the best ideas are pinched. We pinched that from the *Sunday World* in Ireland. I think double innuendo humour appeals to people. It's sexy, but acceptable.'

So along with production of T-shirts with the now-familiar *Sport* slogan, Sullivan lined up forty-one television slots featuring comedian Jim Davidson for an eight-day run-up to launch. But it was here that he met with his first serious obstacle. The Independent Television Companies Authority, the IBA's television watchdog, refused to allow the newspaper television advertising on the grounds that the *Sport* wasn't the sort of thing families wanted to see promoted in their living rooms. Sullivan's request to buy commercial airtime was rejected 'on the general rules of taste and decency'.

Undeterred, Sullivan asked the High Court to rule that the IBA had 'broken guidelines which forbid discriminating between one advertiser and another.' And in September of 1986, the ruling came down. Mr Justice Taylor said the new tabloid was aiming at the 'sex, scandal and sports market,' and as such, it went 'one step too far' to permit advertising on the public airways.

'And that cost me £50,000,' says Sullivan. 'That was about £37,000 for their legal costs, about £14,000 for mine.'

In the days that followed, the *Sport* was picketed by the NUJ and became the object of public obloquy and angry demonstrations, as well as the target of a campaign led by labour MP Clare Short, whose objections to the new paper stemmed from her battle against the concept of Page Three Girls in general.

Fleet Street was also less than enthusiastic about the newspaper's survival. 'I mean, God forbid we succeed with a really raunchy newspaper,' says Sullivan. 'Where would it all stop? They were in [laughing] absolute terror.'

Inside the *Sport* offices, there was the general feeling of being besieged on all sides and serious doubt surfaced whether the paper would survive. 'There's two things that really boosted our circulation,' says Sullivan. 'Tina Small was the lady with the 84-inch boobs. And she saved *Sunday Sport*. We were very dicey, week to week. And it was very much "Shall-we-put-in-another-quarter-of-a-million-or-shall-we-call-it-a-day?" And Tina Small put thirty to fifty thousand on our sales and that was dramatic.' The second wave of success followed the newspaper's introduction of Jimmy Wrinkle to its pages. 'He's the guy, who used to weigh fifty-five stone, and dropped that to twelve stone, and he had all this [skin] hangin' [gestures]. And he sold papers like you wouldn't believe. And it was freaky. And all the fat people would think "I wouldn't like to look like that. Why should I lose all that weight?" So he made them feel good, Jimmy Wrinkle.'

It was 'like war,' one of Sullivan's editors said about the early days. 'If people are against you, it brings you closer together. The whole establishment was against us. It made us more determined that we'd stuff 'em in the end – and we have.'

Today, the Wednesday *Sport* and the paper's Scottish edition are produced from the company's editorial offices in Manchester, under the editorial direction of Peter Grimsditch. The *Sunday Sport*'s editorial department is housed in grubby offices on the third floor of an industrial building in north-east London.

Inside, there is the clutter of old-time newspaper offices, and the staff share an expression of old-time cynicism. At thirty, the London editor is Fleet Street's youngest – 'a dour grafter', Sullivan calls him – named Drew Robertson. Robertson, who doesn't eat lunch or supper until he gets home at night, sometimes not until 11.00, admits he drives his staff relentlessly. 'If you haven't got anything to do,' he yells at one staffer who has his feet up on a desk, 'I can give you something.'

Robertson is a solid man, with the rosy lips and cheeks of youth, and eyes like Rosemary's baby – red-rimmed and bloodshot from long nights of working late. Pugnaciously, he asks, 'If you can't work this hard when you're young, when *can* you do it?' If Robertson agrees with a point, he'll often say, 'yaah, yaah, yaah, yaah, yaah,' rapid-fire. If he disputes it, he leans forward and, without any hard feelings, says, 'nah, nah, nah, nah, nah,' making his disagreement seem a confidential admission rather than a negative opinion.

Robertson quit school in the middle of preparing for his A levels when his first job opportunity in journalism came up. 'I mean, I like newspapers. I can't imagine myself doin' anythin' else. As long as I can remember, I wanted to be a journalist.' By the time Robertson took over the *Sport*, he had already edited a group of newspapers in West London and worked as a reporter on the *Sun*. 'At the time, though, I knew in my heart of hearts, that being a reporter was not what I wanted.'

It was Robertson who gave the paper its 'Jimmy Wrinkle' look. 'We bought that picture off an agency. It cost us a total of £2,000 and we really used it. We really got our money's worth. That picture got turned down by the *News of the World* picture desk and by the *Sun* picture desk. But,' he shrugs philosophically, 'I could turn something down tomorrow, because I didn't have the perception to project it . . . the way it should be projected.'

The *Sport* was the first successful post-Wapping tabloid, and it is popular to say that David Sullivan was the first to benefit from what others accomplished. What this means is that Eddie Shah's early challenge to the unions and Rupert Murdoch's final, fatal blow at Wapping ushered in the new technology, the cold-type printing revolution that permits shoestring operations to proceed successfully within comfortable profit margins, even though they have relatively small circulations. The full-time staff of the London operation, for example, numbers only about twenty, with a draw from the pool of casual subs and reporters whenever they are needed.

The *Sport* has three production centres, one in the south, one in the midlands and one in the north, and from those centres the paper's four editions are produced. As far as the football is concerned, the backend of the paper changes according to location, the Scottish edition featuring Scottish sport.

The production centres are print centres as well, and the paper works from its base in Northampton where they have computer links with a centre in Burgess Hill and Blackburn. Basically, what happens is that they shoot data (stories) down the line on a high speed computer linkup to Blackburn and Burgess Hill, and then at those various centres, they paste the paper up, each edition essentially a separate pasteup operation. Apart from that, there are a certain number of early pages and colour pages, which are distributed on Saturday morning to the various print sites, and, in fact, there are four print sites on a Sunday. Thus, on a Saturday, they bike the colour prints to Kettering, the other centre, as well. 'It's not as complicated as it seems,' Robertson says, 'you just *do* it.'

To a large degree, the *Sport* is a 'bought-in' paper. It generates few news stories of its own, and a by-line usually means a simple rewrite. Nevertheless, readers take it seriously. Says Robertson, 'We've just received a letter praising the unbiased nature of our serious news stories. No one in the office thought we had *any* serious news stories, never mind unbiased ones.'

Under Robertson's leadership, the *Sport* evolved into what seasoned journalists were apt to call 'a hoot', and surprisingly, it developed a cultist Yuppie following. The secret of this, Robertson believes, is to gear the paper to a set market. 'You've gotta have a formula,' he says. 'You've gotta have a bizarre story. You've gotta have a sex-oriented story. You've gotta have a court case. You've gotta have a certain continuity of glamour pictures.'

But lately, the *Sport* has lost its spark, the touch of genius that gave it cultist standing. As it dwells more and more on the dark side of sexuality, it is losing more and more readers. By the summer of 1990, the newspaper's circulation had dropped dramatically.

The *Sport* is a sub's paper, and as such it gives the opportunity for subs to show what they can do. At its height, there was a jovial accentuation of the bizarre and the improbable, and these often turned out to be the readers' favourites. The paper staked its reputation on such stories as 'Statue of Elvis Found on Mars' and 'I Had Sex with an Alien'. These stories were, for the most part, purchased from downmarket American tabloids, which took them at straight-faced value. Robertson turned them upside down for the British market, and the result was a kind of working-man's satirical newspaper, a smutty and downmarket *Punch*.

Ask Drew Robertson about what's funny today, though, and you're likely to get a tired response. The mention of 'World War II Bomber Found on the Moon', and its followup 'World War II Bomber Found on the Moon Vanished', makes Robertson look slightly sick. 'I see it on a Sunday mornin'. I see it again, and I think, "Oh, my God, I didn't do this right, I didn't do that right." *The reader, he's* seein' it for the first time. Look at any comedian. He doesn't go around laughin' all the time. I do it because it's entertaining, because it's successful as journalism. Because you're

277

working with that type of story, that type of humour all the time, you think that it's just another story. OK, it makes you laugh, but not as much as it makes the reader laugh. *Ask a comedian* if his material is funny. Ask him.'

Robertson's brow wrinkles at the mention of the advertisements for 'X-rated' telephone chatlines which figure prominently in the pages of the *Sport*. He is convinced the paper would continue to prosper without the raunchy ads, whose titles – like 'No Knicker Naughties', 'Let Me Put My Panties on You', 'Pouting Pussy' – downgrade the tone of the paper's bizarre but humorous approach.

One call to the 'Kama Sutra Action Line', charged 'at 38p per minute, only 25p off peak', is enough to give the gist of the chatlines' services. Inexplicably, the first few seconds consist of peppy military marching music. Then a low and sexy female voice comes on the line. There is a hint of laughter in the way she speaks, a promise of wonderful things to come.

'Hi,' she says. 'Thank you for calling our extremely naughty number. I promise you a *very* naughty story . . . right after this recording' – which turns out to be . . . an advertisement for 'two other naughty numbers'. At last, the sexy, laughing lady continues: 'Now get ready for that really sexy story coming up now.

'Here comes the bride,' she sings, 'all dressed in white,' and the listener is given to understand that the story he's been waiting for has at last begun. 'It was only a few weeks ago,' our narrator begins, 'that tune was being played for *me* as I walked down the aisle to my Tom.' To be honest, she says confidentially, she didn't know Tom all that well when he '*popped*' the question, but . . . 'I know him now.' The narrative which follows falls in the tradition of naughty British seaside postcards or the 'Carry On' films of the 1960s. It ends with the revelation that our narrator didn't mind Tom dressing up in her wedding clothing on their wedding night, 'I just wish he wouldn't wear my best dress to the rugby club bashes every Saturday night!'

David Sullivan has his regrets about ads like these as well, but his differ from Robertson's. He is sorry he didn't buy into the telephone lines early. 'I thought,' says Sullivan, 'British Telecom will knock them over the head. And then I thought, well, anything that is a bit of fun, the government will stop them. They'll be an overnight wonder, because nobody is going to ring them. You'll ring up once, and realize it's only soft drivel. Might do it twice. But that's all. But I was wrong. And I *regret* it.'

278

Besides the *Sport*, which continues to circle downwards, Sullivan's other foray into the national newspaper market ended in disaster. On 4 September 1987, Express Newspapers, headed by Lord Stevens, bought a 24.9 per cent stake in Sullivan's Apollo Company with the understanding that Sullivan would take over production of the *Daily Star*, receiving a half penny for every extra copy sold. Sullivan sent in his then *Sport* editor Mike Gabbert, and for eight weeks, the pair sent shock-waves through Fleet Street. Gabbert became notorious for running teenage Page Three Girls with gigantic breasts, 'seventeen nipples in one issue,' according to one outraged commentator.

For his part, Gabbert blithely predicted he would put on at least a million in circulation and 'then the company will have to decide whether to compete with the *Sun* on advertising.' Instead, more than a dozen journalists on the *Daily Star* bailed out, and readership declined sharply. After only eight weeks, Lord Stevens himself was bailing out on the deal.

Sullivan's version of events goes like this: 'What really happened was, the other papers ganged up on the *Star* and on Lord Stevens and he just didn't anticipate the amount of adverse publicity that it would cause him and his company personally . . . and it wasn't a financial thing, it was purely the pressure, the social stigma of producing a product that he couldn't be associated with.

'So Mike Gabbert who went in as the editor – a brilliant man who has died of cancer, unfortunately . . . he was taken from achieving his life-long ambition, and in eight weeks he was right back to the floor again, being publicly sacked and humiliated.'

The establishment also delivered a blow to Sullivan when in May 1990 he tried to buy the Bristol Evening Post group of regional papers. His bid, referred to the Monopolies Commission, put Sullivan in front of a panel which included Sir Alastair Burnet. Sullivan was questioned for five or six hours, but knew in the first five minutes that it was a waste of time. 'To me, it's a joke that I could probably go to Hungary or Poland and produce a newspaper and I'd be welcomed with open arms; but I want to do it in Bristol and I'm like some pariah.'

Besides these setbacks, the new mellowed-out David Sullivan nurses few regrets. His image doesn't bother him anymore, personally, but he blames in part negative press reports for his failure to acquire the Bristol group. As a result, he no longer gives interviews to Fleet Street journalists. His hair, once dark and flat and greasy, has gone to grey, and cropped close to his face, makes him look more childlike than ever. When he sits on one of seven large zebra-patterned divans that fill the gigantic expanse of space where he greets visitors, a great hall that more nearly resembles an airport lounge than a living room, he is dwarfed even more. As he quietly talks, he chews his nails down to the quick, looks at them with interest, chews some more. Occasionally, he glances up to a portrait of his mother – a sweet-looking, grandmotherly matron – which stands in a prominent place on a shelf beside a bronze horse.

Sullivan is a good listener, and as he wraps his legs around one another in Yoga lotus position, there is a wide-eyed wonder about the way he approaches every topic of conversation, as though by talking about it, he'll learn something more about himself and what he might do next.

He makes no bones about his ambition to own a national daily, and he is determined to take the *Sport* into daily production or pick up another paper when the market is right. Maybe there was a time when he longed to be respectable, but that time is passed.

'I mean, respectability to me is the number of papers you sell, and if I was sellin' the most papers in the country, that would be the most respectability that I would want.'

15

PORK UP YA LOVE LIFE!

'It might start with the writer in consultation with the news editor,' says a former employee of the *Sun*. As an example, he uses a hypothetical about Princess Diana, who, let us say, decides to spend the day visiting a relative during a lengthy stay at Balmoral. Observed by the royal watchers who are permanently encamped just outside the castle, the Princess, accompanied by her two sons, sets off by car in the morning, returning home in the early evening.

The fact is reported back to the newspaper. Says the source, 'The news editor might say, "Put some spin on this." So the writer comes up with the idea Diana is bored rigid with Charles in this cold, drafty castle. Then the editor might say, "Let's splash it." And everyone else says, "And why not?"'

'You're not gonna get sued by the Royals,' says our ex-employee. 'They're the safest target in the world.' He is referring to the fact that, outside of Viscount Linley who sued *Today* for alleging he behaved badly in a local pub, no member of the Royal Family has ever brought suit against the press for defamation.

The second safest target in the world is the megastar. Since it is a hard-and-fast rule in Hollywood that celebrities speak to no one, many of the comments that appear in the newspapers as their words are either those of their publicist or of the reporter himself. If the statement isn't actionable, seems appropriate and doesn't show the celebrity in a bad light, it is unlikely to come back to haunt the writer.

The most obvious example of the non-event occurs when the old fan magazine formula of the past is resurrected in order to hype a new film. A story plugged on Page One of the paper as 'Danny Devito Divorce Shocker' turns out on the inner pages to be Devito's confession that he sometimes neglected his family when he was making *The War of the Roses*. If left unchecked, he says, this sort of thing can lead to a divorce, just like the one in the film.

'The modern editor of a paper,' William Randolph Hearst once said, 'does not care for facts. The editor wants novelty. The editor has no objection to facts if they are also novel. But he would prefer a novelty that is not a fact to a fact that is not a novelty.' The idea is not confined to America. Lord Northcliffe, proprietor of the *Daily Mail*, was the first to formalize the notion of a rewrite man who sensationalizes the news by making it more exciting and dramatic. In England, he has become known as the 'sub-editor', and such is the cult that has grown up around him that the mass-circulation dailies are said to be 'sub's papers', because the sub is the key to the whole operation. There are dozens of Fleet Street stories that purport to demonstrate the importance of the sub-editor, some accurate, some embellished through frequent retelling.

A young sub edits a story about a Second World War bomb found in a garden in South London which forces the evacuation of families living nearby. The chief sub calls him over. 'What does the word "evacuation" mean?'

'People had to leave their homes.'

'Then that's the way to write it.'

Says the sub, who went on to become a broadsheet reporter, 'I learned more about language from subbing in the tabloids than in my entire career.'

A similar story takes place when Belgian paratroopers are dropping into the Congo. According to the tale, *Daily Mirror* editor Dick Dinsdale yells out, 'What idiot is writing French in the *Daily Mirror*?'

'We all looked up at him blankly,' a sub-editor recalls.

Dinsdale clarified the question, 'Who subbed the Belgian Congo story on Page Two?' The sub-editor admits, 'I did.'

'Then maybe you can tell me what "élite" troops means.'

Sub-editor: 'It means "crack" troops.'

'Then use that. In the *Daily Mirror*, the readers can't fuckin' read English, let alone French.'

Dinsdale, now retired, can't remember the episode, 'But that doesn't mean it didn't happen,' he says. 'What I would never do is say anything that disparages the reader.' He pauses, gives it some thought. 'The swearing's all right, though. Just don't make it too bad, OK?'

Another story: A sub just starting out on the *Sunday Mirror* is given a really good story about a new type of aeroplane. He is told to condense it into three and a half column inches – about eighty or ninety words. The story has to answer *any* questions the reader might have, the chief sub explains. After a long struggle, the sub goes back to his boss, saying he can't tell it in three-and-a-half inches. 'Then spike it,' comes the answer. And that's what he did.

The tabloid is small and space is at a premium. Its format requires brevity, its readers clarity. Writing for a tabloid isn't as easy as it looks. Says Brian Hitchen, editor of London's *Daily Star*, 'Consider how difficult it would be to think of the words you use everyday, and then find smaller ones.'

Don MacKay, best known as a reporter but also trained as a sub, boasts that 'A tabloid journalist could write the Bible into a three-part series of salient points and still inform the readers of every single word, from page one to the last page. He can work on any broadsheet because he can say, "That's that point over, boom. Next point, boom." He'll understand the story a lot faster and a lot clearer and will translate it into whatever words are necessary for the readership. The tabloid journalist is often a far cleverer person than he is given credit for. If that isn't the case, why don't the broadsheets sell more than the tabloids?'

Peter Grimsditch, who is the weekday editor of the *Sport*, Britain's self-confessed, bottom-of-the-barrel tabloid, says of his staff, 'The guys that I've got producing the *Sport* up in Manchester could produce the *Daily Telegraph* tomorrow, without any culture shock. I could say, "We're not doin' that, we're doin' this." And there wouldn't be any problem. It's "rent-a-sub."'

In the autumn of 1989, *Sun* editor Kelvin MacKenzie made a public statement that his people could put out the *Guardian*, but the *Guardian* couldn't put out the *Sun* because, in MacKenzie's words, 'They haven't got the intellectual firepower.' According to MacKenzie, if a journalist on the *Guardian* had a popular idea, 'he would have to go into a dark room and lie down until it passed.'

Guardian editor Peter Preston immediately fired back a challenge to MacKenzie to exchange staffs for a day, offering a £10,000 charity wager that his side would win. MacKenzie refused, saying his circulation, which hovers just under 4,000,000, might plunge to the same level as the *Guardian*'s, which registers 400,000.

Several staffers on the *Guardian* nevertheless proceeded to publish their own version of the *Sun*, which they entitled the *Fun*. They splashed with 'Love Triangle That Ended in DJ's Death', subheaded, 'Club Bouncer Is Jailed Over Headless Body'. The lead: 'A nightclub bouncer at the centre of a love triangle row was jailed for 10 years yesterday for killing a disc jockey whose headless and handless body was found buried in a wood.' In the face of such an embarrassing attempt at tabloid style, *Time Out*

283

magazine commented, 'Looks like "the Dreadful Kelvin" might have a point.'

There is an old saying in the newspaper business: 'In the best of all possible worlds, you would have Australians to report the news, Americans to write it, and Brits to edit it.' Like most old sayings, this one holds a grain of truth. Within the industry, the Aussies are considered the most aggressive, the Brits the most canny; to the Americans go the honours of flat-out writing ability.

One of the best in the business is Jimmy Breslin, columnist in New York City for many years, Pulitzer Prize winner and prolific author. Says Breslin about the process, 'You come down to the key matter . . . sitting down and writing it accurately and entertainingly – so that someone can read it. That could take you six freaking hours at the machine. That's the part that nobody talks about because there's nothing to say. Either you do it or you don't. You must sit down and work and it takes hours and hours and hours.

'You don't do it in twenty minutes. Anything from a paragraph to a novel takes a long, long time. And I'm supposed to be supremo at making deadlines with short amounts of time. But I still want hours. I mean, I'll do what I gotta in eleven minutes if I have to, and it's worked wonderfully a lot of times. But when I start my column, I'm ready to go five or six hours. And that's the business – ARSE POWER.

'SIT. Don't walk around and talk about this story, don't swagger, don't tell me how much you had to drink, don't puff the cigarette and tell me how great you are or how tough it was. I don't want to hear anything. Just sit there and write, in silence please, preferably up against a blank wall. And have the names and addresses; don't give me a lot of blind quotes. I don't believe them. So don't waste my space and time by putting them in there.'

Breslin epitomizes the American ethos – the tough guy who thinks pure thoughts. He doesn't have much time for what he terms 'the post-Murdoch tradition.'

'Their papers are designed for people who are leading dreadfully dull lives, and they try to appeal to them with a great formula – animal stories, axe murderers and . . . bird of the day? It's not my style. New York City has a lot of news. You don't have to generate it. You don't have to come in with killer bees and things like that . . . You have so much news happening here in the course of a day that it's dizzying. You don't have to wake people up with a headline; the headline is there before you wake up in the morning.'

Most Americans in the business take a line similar to Breslin's, and nowhere do the Clark Kent values of the American press show up more prominently than in the offices of the New York *Daily News*. It was here, appropriately enough, the film *Superman* was filmed.

Says Chief Copy Editor Len Valenti, 'Plenty of times we blow up a story, a story that might not ordinarily be Page One that we put onto Page One in terms of significance. We had a badly burned kid brought to this city, he was an orphan. People were just pitching in, doctors volunteering to care for him. So we led the paper with this. But we just plain don't print stories that we know to be false. It would be abhorrent to us.' As copy chief, Valenti's job is to make sure everything the *Daily News* does is accurate and legal. 'We try to be fair.'

At the Philadelphia *Daily News*, the city tabloid that operates under a Joint Operating Agreement* with the more up-market Philadelphia *Inquirer*, veteran rewrite man Jack Morrison says that the British habit of putting a spin on a story just isn't acceptable. 'That would never be done over here . . . It's not only libel that would keep us from doing that. We don't report *what simply isn't true*! You have to know how far you can go. I mean, I like to set a scene too, and sometimes I'll exaggerate a little bit for the sake of drama, but to just invent something . . . If you want to write fiction, then write fiction. You won't find liberties taken like those in the British press in any paper in this country.' An afficionado of the tabloid format, however, Morrison remains open to possibilities. 'They're obviously in the entertainment business. *I think* we're in the entertainment business too, but nobody else does.

'People say, "How can I learn to write the way that you do?" And I say, "Well, you have to really want to do it, and then practice for forty years. It's experience." Where did that lead come from? It comes from forty years of experience, that's where it comes from. It really comes from your subconscious. You know, I'll be sitting

---

* A Joint Operating Agreement [JOA] is an arrangement whereby two competing newspapers share offices, presses and, in the case of the Philadelphia *Inquirer* and the Philadelphia *Daily News*, advertising contracts while maintaining separate editorial departments. The competition between the two newspapers is to some degree artificially maintained since the newspaper chain Knight-Ridder owns both. Joint Operating Agreements were created in order to prevent newspapers from going out of business. In terms of press freedom as defined by the First Amendment of the United States Constitution, the important factor is the preservation of two distinct editorial voices in what has been termed by the US Supreme Court as 'the marketplace of ideas'.

here, and I can't think of a lead. I'll get up, go get a soda or a drink of water from the fountain. By the time I come back, I've got it. And I don't even think about it. The unconscious is in there, thinking, "What in the heck can we do with this story?" I don't think I've been stuck for a lead or for a word in years. I enter a groove or a space . . . After two or three paragraphs, I'll be in that place. Kind of a flow.'

Morrison comes from the school of the anonymous rewrite man. 'Unless the story is exceptionally well written, the rewrite man is of no importance. Without the reporter there would be no story. The reporter got the story. The rewrite man is just taking the raw information and putting it together.'

In Philadelphia on 10 January 1990, it was business as usual. A double killing took place on the streets of the city. The *Inquirer*, a morning paper, led with a straight 'who-what-where-when-why-how' story, the bread and butter of the broadsheet format. 'Man Shoots Ex-girlfriend and Himself', says the headline. 'While startled students outside a North Philadelphia school looked on, a teacher's aide was shot in the head yesterday by an ex-boyfriend, who then turned the pistol on himself, police said.'

By late morning, Jack Morrison has found the real-life drama behind the shooting – in time for the first edition of the *Daily News*, an evening paper.

Double Shooting Erupts in Front of School Kids

Fear of her drunken, enraged ex-boyfriend had made Ana Ortiz a virtual recluse for the past several weeks, relatives say.

He stalked her in his car and on foot, threatening her repeatedly. She was desperate to flee to Puerto Rico but was worried about losing her job with the School District, her family said.

She never went out alone. She stopped going to her job as a teacher's aide at the William H. Hunter Elementary School in North Philadelphia. A protection order she had obtained against her ex-boyfriend apparently was useless.

At 8.30 a.m. yesterday, the crazed stalker caught up with his victim outside the school at Mascher and Dauphin Streets, police said, and heedless of the tender-aged children standing around waiting for school to open, shot her in the face with a .22-caliber pistol and then turned the gun on himself . . .

286

> Capt. Gerald Baker, of the 26th District, furious that the
> shooting had taken place in front of children, got two buck-
> ets of water from school maintenance men and personally
> washed the blood off the sidewalk.

The by-line goes to the reporter on the job, Joanne Sills, who left her notes for Morrison to work from. Morrison's assumption is that people reading the story already know what happened. They've heard about it on the radio, seen it on TV, maybe even read about it in the morning *Inquirer*. So Morrison tries to put a different lead on it. 'Traditional leads,' he says with certainty, 'are dull. And remember, our readers have taken the paper home after work, have done all their errands and are sitting down to read the news. They want the story *behind* the shooting.'

They open their paper to an entire page on the subject, entitled, 'Student Shock'. Besides Morrison's lead story, there is a sidebar on what the school district is doing to help the children who witnessed the killing, another on the neighbourhood – 'drug dealers on every corner' – yet another on a similar shooting in which the victim didn't die. There is even a map prepared by the *Daily News*'s graphics department showing exactly where the killing took place.

What attracted Morrison's attention when he first began writing the story was the police captain, 'who personally got two buckets of water from the maintenance man and washed off the sidewalk.'

Says Morrison, 'I thought that might make a good lead, so I pondered that. But I don't have anything from him. I need some quotes, you know, "This is terrible, these kids shouldn't have to see such a thing." *Something* to flesh that out.

'Now if I were in England, I would just make that up. Right?'

Well, maybe. It would depend upon the newspaper, the editor and the sub's relationship to God.

In the meantime, British sub-editors working in America have their gripes as well. Says Peter Grimsditch, who put in a tour of duty on the New York *Post*, 'Americans are much more precise on quotes, even if their readers are illiterate. Even at the *Post* level, the sub will put in any missing words in brackets.

'And they have an intensely annoying habit of saying that a robbery occurred six hundred feet south-east of the corner of Sixth and Fifth Streets. 99.95 per cent of readers *do not live six hundred feet south-east of Sixth and Fifth Streets*. It's precision gone mad.

'And the photographers are capable of taking only a few sorts of pictures. When I was on the *Post*, they loved taking pictures of firemen up ladders, surrounded by smoke. They loved taking pictures of "perps". "Perps",' Grimsditch explains, 'are perpetrators of crimes. All the "perps" that they took pictures of were black guys being led away in handcuffs. And the third type of picture they were extremely good at taking were of stiffs, bloody corpses all over the place, which are not really very difficult to get.

'The reporters and photographers all think they're bloody amateur policemen anyway, driving their cars up on the pavements. In fact, one of them on the *Post* even had a light to put on the top of his car so he could pretend to be bloody Kojak.

'There was an unwritten rule on the New York *Post*: If a black guy got murdered, it was certainly *inside* the paper and it was one or two "paras", perhaps. It may have made slightly more if there were certain circumstances about it that put it out of the ordinary. Somebody murdering a black guy would not on principle hit the front page. A black guy murdering a white guy would automatically hit the front page.'

Grimsditch believes that in America, people are 'convicted by newspapers.' He says that there is 'much greater frankness and publicity-seeking by the authorities, by assistant district attorneys, by coppers, by patrolmen, for God's sake. They all rush to get to a microphone, and they give all the bloody evidence about five minutes before they bang the guy in jail. That, of course, you would not be allowed to do in Britain anyway because of contempt.'

When Grimsditch managed to get his first copies of the New York *Post*, 'just about forty-eight hours before I left for the United States,' he had a shock. 'I couldn't understand any of the stories, but more than that, I couldn't understand the headlines.'

It's a common complaint, culture to culture. Headlines, like humour, rely on shared experience and the specialized vocabulary that goes with it. New York City heads, particularly, are an acquired taste.

The best-known headline ever written in America comes from the New York *Daily News*. Several years ago, when the city of New York was facing bankruptcy and basic services within the city were severely curtailed as a result, the mayor asked Washington for additional funding – a federal bail-out, as it is called. Gerald Ford was then President of the United States, and his answer to New York was that it should solve its own problems. The next morning, New Yorkers awoke to the headline, run in gigantic print across the top of the *Daily News*, 'FORD TO CITY: DROP DEAD'.

288

What the headline *really* said, employees of the *Daily News* will tell you, was 'FORD TO CITY: FUCK OFF.' The story is that a tough-talking metro editor named Richard Oliver got first news of Ford's rejection, wrote the profane version on a scrap of paper, wadded it up and threw it onto the desk of editor William Brink. Brink thought it was so good he modified it for publication for the next morning.

All well and good – except it never happened. Dick Oliver 'denies categorically' this version of events. 'Bill Brink just wrote the headline,' he says prosaically.

More recently, the New York *Daily News* has opted for a condensed style on Page One, which, as often as not, is printed in reverse – that is, white on black or white on tint, called WOBs or WOTs in England – against a full-page photograph. This is altogether fitting for the newspaper that bills itself 'New York's Picture Newspaper'. At the *Daily News*, the headlines appear in all-caps, thus eliminating ascenders and descenders. This cuts down on space by 25 per cent and allows for bigger headlines coming down the page. The overall effect is classic American macho.

Perhaps the outstanding example of just how short a *Daily News* head can run is the gigantic 'OURS!' printed in reverse over Manuel Noriega's forehead on Thursday, 4 January 1990, after the notorious general had surrendered to American troops in Panama. Or the head topping a story about City Hall voting itself additional perks when the city's policemen were getting nothing new: 'FAT CITY'. Or, imposed on the photograph of a man holding the body of a dead child, the headline, 'DROWNED'. Or, the man who held up his hand to stop the tanks rolling into Tiananmen Square, 'DEFIANCE'.

Or, the shocking photograph of a detective looking at a white cloth, spread *flat* against the pavement, underneath which is the body of an infant that had been tossed from a highrise window – 'IT WASN'T A DOLL'.

The most emotionally affecting sequence of headlines on a single event were those appearing day after day, in rapid succession, when New York City faced a new kind of crime. On 19 April 1989, a female stock broker out jogging in Central Park was attacked by a maruading gang of Harlem youths, who slashed and beat her, allegedly raped her repeatedly, then threw her body into a nearby ravine. She lost three-quarters of her blood and lay in a coma for weeks. Incredibly, she lived through the ordeal. 21 April 1989, the story breaks:

WOLF PACK'S PREY

RAPE SUSPECT'S JAILHOUSE BOAST: 'SHE WASN'T NOTHING'

ONLY ONE WAS SORRY

AMID TEARS AND ANGER

CALLS FOR CALM IN PARK ATTACK

'IT WAS FUN'

Park marauders call it 'WILDING'
and it's street slang for going berserk

And then on 4 May 1989, the miraculous 'SHE WAKES FROM COMA'. Nobody in New York City needed to be reminded who 'SHE' was.

Not to be outdone, *never* to be outdone, the New York *Post* – whose longtime flirtation with bad taste has often been consummated on Page One – is responsible for creating some of the most memorable headlines of all time. Many were written by British subs, imported to America by Rupert Murdoch when he took over the paper in 1976. In fact, the present editor of the *Sun*, Kelvin MacKenzie, wrote many of them. One of MacKenzie's most famous headlines was written when the Pope visited New York City. At that time, there were fourteen television stations in New York. Only two of them decided to cover the Pope's arrival. The others opted to stick with the previously scheduled football games. MacKenzie's front-page headline was 'POPE 2, FOOT-BALL 12'. It was said this so endeared MacKenzie to Murdoch that his position as editor of the *Sun* was insured at a stroke.

Another memorable *Post* headline – 'TERROR FROM THE SKIES' – was written after an air conditioner fell from a tall building, killing a passing pedestrian. Still another candidate for bad taste occurred when an escalator opened up, and a young mother fell into the machinery, dying a slow and agonizing death. The *Post* came up with 'STAIRWAY TO HELL'. Midway through the day, says Bill Hoffmann, who reports for the *Post*, a representative for the family rang the newspaper complaining that the dead woman was highly religious and would have deplored the implication she had gone to hell. 'So,' says Hoffman, 'they changed the head to "ESCALATOR SWALLOWS MOM".'

290

When New York police were given nets to deal with the criminally insane, the *Post* headed the story, 'COPS TO CATCH NUTS WITH NETS'. But perhaps the single most offensive *Post* headline, one destined to become immortalized on T-shirts as a cult item, was written by the late John Canning in connection with a teenager's suicide. Says Hoffmann, who covered the story, 'There had been a rash of teen suicides in New York, and I was assigned a story about a fifteen-year-old kid who went into his basement and drank gasoline. Just as his parents were coming home from a night out, he became very ill and began dying. He started throwing up, and he's next to the hot water burner, and the throw-up reaches to the flue of the hot water burner, and the flame follows it up to his body, and he bursts into flames. So the front-page headline the next day was "YOUTH GULPS GAS – EXPLODES".'

As cults go, the best-known headline ever to appear in the New York *Post* was the ever-classic 'HEADLESS BODY IN TOPLESS BAR'. Says Managing Editor Lou Colasuonno, 'Everybody on this newspaper wrote that head. Ask them. I'm the only one who'll tell you he didn't.' But the actual authorship is generally accorded to Drew MacKenzie, younger brother of Kelvin. 'It was staring everybody in the face,' says MacKenzie, 'I'm just the one who brought it in.'

America's preoccupation with the dark side of life might best be demonstrated by the number of newspaper stories connected with violence. The most graphic depiction is reflected in the heads. On the wall of the seventh floor of the building housing the Philadelphia *Daily News*, where copy-editors and headline writers daily ply their trade, over the years employees have cut and pasted up uneven rectangles of paper, each of differing age as shown by the yellowing. At some time or other, each of these rectangles has appeared as a headline in the pages of the paper. From the top downwards, they read, 'Mark of Death', 'Trail of Death', 'Highway of Death', 'Window of Death', 'House of Death', and 'City of Death'. Some anonymous joker has constructed a fake and pasted it up beneath all the others. It reads, 'Headline of Death'.

In the United States, there is probably only one true 'sub's paper', and that is the supermarket tabloid the *Sun*, part of Globe International's empire. According to *U.S.A. Today*, it takes only nine people, including reporters, editors and secretaries, to put out the paper, which has a circulation of 400,000. Says John Vader who edits the *Sun*, 'We're discovering that we're becoming a bit of a cult item with college kids. We think it's because of our headlines.'

Lining the walls of Vader's office are issues of the paper that prove his point. 'Drunk Swallows 8 Tennis Balls to Win a Bet', says one. 'Male Girl Makes Self Pregnant – Is Mom and Dad to Three Kids', says another. Then there is the thought-provoking, 'Circus Midget Shot from Cannon Flies thru Tent Roof and Disappears Forever.'

Vader is a headline addict. He doesn't seem to be able to get enough from his own publication, he collects and commits to memory personal favourites from other papers. He thinks the all-time greatest headline appeared in the New York *Post* when Generoso Pope died: 'Enquirer Editor Goes to Meet with Elvis'. Otherwise, he believes the best of the British heads was printed when Prince Charles announced his engagement to Lady Diana Spencer: 'My Shy Di'.

Every year, *New York Magazine* holds a headline-writing contest, inviting readers to write their own heads in the same spirit as the tabloids. Sitting atop a publication that often parodies itself, Vader still appreciates a parody of his parody. One of the funniest winners of the magazine's contest, Vader believes, is, 'Siamese Twin Kills Brother in Bungled Suicide Attempt'.

Other winners include, 'Boy, 8, Swallows Kitchen Magnet, Sticks to Refrigerator', 'Skydiving Mom Gives Birth During Free-Fall', and 'Doctor Leaves Own Finger in Patient'.

Compare these with actual headlines used in Vader's *Sun*: 'Missing Baby Found in Watermelon', 'Wife Mistakes Hair Restorer for Deoderant, Grows Hair on Chest', and 'Docs Remove 3-lb Frog from Boy's Stomach. He Swallowed Tadpole on a Dare'.

From time to time, a cover headline will attract high readership, but Vader can't figure out why. One such puzzler was 'Baby Born with Dead Dad's Tatoo. Docs Say It's Heredity; Psychics Say It's Reincarnation'. The headline was run beside a photograph of what appears to be an old man but who is really a young boy with a disease, which causes degeneration at an early age. The headline accompanying the photo said, 'Boy Fighting for Life'.

'That issue had a high sale,' says Vader, 'but I couldn't decide whether it was the head, or the picture of the boy, or the combination of the two. I've run headlines similar to 'Dead Dad's Tatoo' and not had good sales, pictures like the one of the boy and had average sales, and once, I actually repeated the same headline word for word. And again, it didn't sell as many copies.'

Although he never fathomed the mystery, Vader continues to create distinctive headlines like those of no other publication. How does he do it? 'You go into a kind of dream, almost like an Alpha state,' he explains. 'And sometimes a great story creates its own wild headline, like "Baby Born Holding Mom's IUD". Some are improved on after the story is written. And others just flash into your head.'

The 'flash-into-your-head' phenomenon is, at one time or another, experienced by every headline writer in the business. Said Graham Courtenay, senior sub-editor on the *Sun* in London, 'Some headlines come out of the blue. But more often, people spend a half hour or more thinking one up. If it's a story that lends itself to a daft headline, you just keep thinking of several puns. You look for word associations. You can get some really convoluted ones. The most convoluted one I ever wrote was about a soap star. The *Sun* discovered she had a Chinese lover. Our headline was, "Linda Has a Chink in her Armour". There were rumours that "an Australian" came onto the phone to Kelvin MacKenzie the next day and said, "Will you explain that headline to me?"'

At Murdoch's *Sun*, word association and punning, in conjunction with the natural British hostility toward the French, have given rise to some of the classics in the field.

'Eau No!' screams one head, 'Frog Food Has 50 on Hop at Big Bash':

> Top French chefs were flown in to cook a VIP banquet – and half the guests went down with FOOD POISONING.
>
> One hundred big wigs sat down to the £50-a-head civic feast of seafood and venison to celebrate Birmingham's centenary.
>
> But the fancy nosh served up by the three frogs was contaminated and diners came down with a dreadful dose of les Trots.

If a headline works once, it's bound to work twice: 'Eau No!' the *Sun* exclaimed, when traces of Benzene were found in bottles of Perrier. And just when you thought it was safe to go back into the water, the *Sun* tells us, 'N'eau Thanks: Restaurant Snub to Perrier Return'.

Joking aside, the headline is so important an element in the tabloid format that pages have actually been redesigned to accommodate a particularly successful one. It is said that several years ago, at an England–Scotland International, a picture on Page Five of traditional Scottish fans jumping in and out of fountains, run with the headline 'Scotland the Rave', so pleased Larry Lamb that he moved it to Page One.

Even today on Murdoch's *Sun*, the headline is decided first, and the page is then designed around it. As to the typefaces, the *Sun*

293

still uses fonts similar to the originals. When the paper was moved from Bouverie Street to Wapping, the goal was to preserve as far as was possible the paper's appearance, and computer programming created look-alike fonts that achieved this aim. When the new *Sun* hit the stands, readers couldn't actually see any difference from the old *Sun*. In fact, every aspect of production was mimicked with the new technology, so the transition from hot metal to cold type was practically painless.

In the old days, those working on the sub-editor's side wouldn't even speak directly to reporters. There was an air of formality, and sub-editors went through the news editor, whose main responsibility is gathering the news and directing reporters. Says one old-timer, 'The news editor could get very shirty if the sub-editor actually approached one of their reporters directly. It's a bit more relaxed now, but we've got to assume a story they give us is factual; we've got to accept things on trust. The sub-editors on the middle and backbench really do try to get the thing right, which is why it is so annoying when you keep getting settlements. Now, OK, we all make mistakes some of the time, especially in our case where virtually every story is rewritten . . . Usually, the sub-editor is actually rewriting the story from scratch, like the rewrite man in the United States.'

On the backbench at the *Sun*, four people sit facing one direction. They are, in order of seating, the assistant night editor, the night editor, the deputy night editor, and the late assistant night editor, who arrives around 4.30 p.m. In front of this table, there is another desk called the middle bench, and in the centre sits the chief sub-editor – the key man. To his right is his deputy and also the rough copy taster. He passes his copy back to the backbench copy taster, who has the power to consign a story to 'the hook', called 'the spike' on other newspapers. The editor, Kelvin MacKenzie, who as often as not sits beside the others at the backbench, is reputed to be able to see the potential of a story by skimming the first two or three paragraphs.

Surely, the most famous headline in Britain was the one MacKenzie wrote at the time of the sinking of the *Belgrano* during the Falklands campaign. Almost universally condemned as jingoistic pap, 'GOTCHA!' was written during a journalists' strike when MacKenzie was practically producing the paper by himself. Says one source, 'When he was persuaded that something like 2,000 people had drowned and maybe the headline wasn't in the best of taste, it was changed for the next edition.'

But overall, good taste is not the salient characteristic of the

MacKenzie touch. When in late February 1990, two babies died of overheating from an electric blanket, the *Sun* ran the headline: '158 Degrees: Four-week Twins Roasted to Death by Electric Blanket'.

So far as bad taste goes, however, MacKenzie's *Sun* doesn't hold the monopoly. 'Heart-Lung Swap Op Mum Dies' from the *News of the World* is surely a contender. In its defence, headline buffs will be quick to point out that, given the space constraints placed on headline writers for the tabloids, this one can be viewed as a thing of beauty. It conveys in only six words of one syllable each the story's basic thesis: 'The well-known mother who underwent a heart-lung transplant has died.'

Otherwise, the *Sunday Sport* must go down in newspaper history as the single most tasteless mass publication currently being published in the English language, beating out such serious contenders as Globe International's *Sun* and the *National Enquirer*'s sister publication *Weekly World News*.

'I Found Face of Jesus on My Fish Finger', says the *Sunday Sport* headline for 13 May 1990. It is written by 'Religious Affairs Correspondent Bertie Ollacks'.

> 'TREMBLING trucker Peter Edwards yesterday found the face of Christ . . . on a FISH FINGER!
>
> Poleaxed Peter, 28, was hungrily tucking into his supper when he had a bird's eye view of the Messiah's MUG gazing up at him . . .'

Then there is the 'Whoppas of Death' story, which appeared in the *Friday Sport* in late August 1989.

> TOP DOCS issued an urgent health warning last night, after our sister paper – *Sunday Sport* – vowed to publish pics of the KNOCKERS OF DEATH!
>
> Your caring, family newspaper originally kept Busty Heart's GIANT JUGS under wraps, after a fan who saw her bare boobs dropped dead!
>
> But floods of fan mail demanded an UNCENSORED eyeful of her dangerous curves.
>
> Now readers can judge the mammoth mega-melons for themselves in *Sunday Sport* . . .
>
> As a precaution, medics have recommended you:
>
> *DO NOT indulge in strenuous activity immediately before or after examining Busty's whoppas.

*DO take plenty of cold showers if you become giddy or over-heated.

*TRY to remain comfortably seated while making an assessment of Busty's mega-melons.

*DO NOT shout to friends: 'Cor, what a STUNNA!' across the room as hyperventilation can lead to a rush of blood to the head.

Much of the madness of the *Sport* can be credited, or discredited, as you please, to its young editor, Drew Robertson, who insists that none of the stories used in the paper are made up in the office. 'If it was that easy, life would be terribly boring, and we wouldn't have guidelines as to how far we could go. I can't have my staff making things up. We've got good journalists who are highly qualified and, though it may sound strange, we've got to set a certain standard. We've got pride in what we do. And we check the facts. If some guy claims he is a two-headed Santa who's just eaten his reindeer, who are we to argue?'

Since Robertson took over the helm, the *Sport* has run stories on people who eat worms, things that go 'bonk' in the night and a tragic thirteen-year-old boy who ate his mother ('Boy, 13, Eats Mum'). Other genre classics include 'Space Aliens Turned Our Son into an Olive', 'Marilyn Monroe is Alive and Working as a Nanny', 'Cheeseburger Kills Space Alien', 'Adolf Hitler Was a Woman', and the ever-popular, 'I Lived with Elvis Four Years After He Died'.

'My Cat's Come Home as Hitler, It's Puss in Jack Boots' is yet another Robertson creation. Under his editorial guidance, the *Sport* once ran an actual 'man-eats-dog' story.

During the hottest summer Britain has known for centuries, a wire-copy story worked its way into all the major tabloids to the effect that scientific studies showed human beings should cool themselves by rolling in mud, like pigs on a farm. A beneficial side effect to the activity was said to be an increase of the sexual drive of the male. The *Sport*'s subs beefed up Dominic Kennedy's original story and it appeared in late August 1989, under the title 'Pork Up Ya Love Life!'

How to Avoid Being a Boar in Bed

WILTING lovers have been told to spice up their sex lives – by rolling round in a PIG STY!

Experts say there's nothing like a cool MUD BATH to get in the mood for porking.

296

The advice was trotted out after the discovery of an amazing link between the sex lives of pigs and humans.

And since nothing perks up a porker more than a flop in the slop it could give MEN a bonking boost too!

Pig expert John Foster backed up the sow's-your-father claims.

He said: 'The most comfortable conditions for pigs are exactly the same as they are for humans.

'Prolonged hot weather can be dangerous when it comes to sexual performance.

'If a boar is subjected to heat stress he becomes less fertile.'

It can take boars six weeks to get in the mood for making bacon if they become overheated . . .

Vet John Seddon, of South London: 'What a load of HOGWASH!'

On occasion, the *Daily Mirror* will give a sub a free hand, more so since Roy Greenslade, who was once a key man on the *Sun*, took over as editor. In early March 1990, the *Mirror* ran the story of 'A Beastly Affair: It's One in the Eye for Toy Boy Basha!' by Kevin O'Lone.

Basha the randy rhino was feeling sore yesterday over an affair that messed up his image as a stud.

Toy boy Basha got bashed when he tried it on with a female twice his age, and he ended up swathed in bandages.

Basha, a 12-year-old likely lad, had wangled a date with June, 26, a mother of six.

Spring was in the air and the scene was set for a ton of love to make the earth move.

Unfortunately June was not in the mood.

But after a thundertiff, Basha was the one with the headache.

Angry June whacked him with her horn, just missing his eye, and sending him packing . . .

Say zookeepers: 'We'll try again – and hope they kiss and make up.'

Finally, in the unofficial sub's sweepstakes, the *Sun* has to remain world-class champion:

297

A Dead Cert! Punter Bill Tips a 4–1 Winner from Beyond the Grave

[by Tim Miles]

Racing fanatic Bill Brown left his friends with rich memories – by passing on a winning tip from beyond the grave.

Amazed mourners at the 60-year-old punter's funeral heard the vicar tell the congregation that Bill wanted them all to place a bet on Grey Generalin, the 2.30 at Wolverhampton.

And they were even more stunned when the horse stormed past the winning post at 4–1, an incredible TWENTY-FIVE lengths ahead of its nearest rival.

The Rev Bob White, who presides over the service in Southend, Essex, said yesterday: 'It was just the sort of thing Bill would do.

'He was a keen tipster and had a favourite expression: "One – and only one – for you boys."'

Friends and family who retired to the ex-hotel worker's local, the Southend Conservative Club, had a whipround and placed the bet.

And when the horse romped home, the club erupted with joy.

Close friend Graham Curnow, 39, said yesterday: 'It was as though Bill was looking down from the stars and saying "God bless you all."'

Bill's elder brother Jack choked back his tears and said: 'Bill placed a bet every day except Sundays.

'He just wanted to make all his friends happy for the last time.'

PART
Five

Ethics

16
THE TRUTH

Tabloid journalism is the direct application of capitalism to events and ideas. Profit, not ethics, is the prevailing motivation.

The other media buy and sell information, most notably magazines and network news – where impressive sums of money change hands routinely – but this is generally played down as much as possible. Practitioners of the tabloid press distinguish themselves by their total absence of hypocrisy about deal-making. They pay money, and they'll tell you they pay money.

Brian Hitchen, the editor of London's *Daily Star*, says, 'Information is only a commodity, like bread. It's the value of an individual's information to a commercial organization. We sell it, so why shouldn't they?'

A typical case occurred in late January 1990, when 'Baby Alexandra', who had been kidnapped soon after her birth from St Thomas's Hospital in London, was recovered by police and returned unharmed to her mother and father. The kidnapping became a *cause célèbre* in England when the baby's mother, Dawn Griffiths, went on national television to make an emotional appeal to the kidnapper. At the news conference where the press were allowed to take photographs of mother and child, all Griffiths would say was, 'I cannot describe it in words. Marvellous, marvellous.' That was because she and her boyfriend had reportedly sold exclusive rights to her story to the *News of the World* for a reputed £75,000.

Steve Dunleavy, former Metro Editor at the New York *Post*, paid cash for the letters of the so-called 'Son of Sam' serial slayer to his former teenage sweetheart, publishing them on Page One. 'You could actually see the letters changing,' says Dunleavy. 'They started off ordinary letters to a girlfriend. Then, you could see his deterioration.' With characteristic irony, Dunleavy reflects that at $500, 'they were cheap at half the price.'

Jeff Samuels recounts how he got the 'last night with Elvis' story for the *National Enquirer* in what he calls, 'a typical *Enquirer* deal.'

301

Samuels went to the house of the woman who was with Elvis Presley when he died. There he found the world press making bids in a kind of informal auction which was taking place on her front porch. 'They were all making offers,' says Samuels. '$30,000, $50,000, and I shouted out, "Samuels, *Enquirer*, $132,000." That stopped 'em all dead. And I got taken in there. I wrote her out a contract on a napkin, which, had she read it properly, she would have realized she was getting thirty-two grand for the story and the other hundred grand was optional for a four-part series, *if we'd wanted it*. So she could have got fifty from the real boys. I gave her thirty-two grand, then had to go through the rigmarole of doing a four-part interview knowing there was no intention ever of using it. And one of the things I had to ask her was the first time she fucked Elvis. And she said, "Why, Jeff, that's personal." I said, "For a hundred thousand dollars, you had better tell me." She told me all these details, dreadful stuff,' Samuels recalls. 'That was about it, really. When they're offering forty or fifty grand, you offer a hundred and thirty-two, but the contract says you only get thirty-two now, and down the line we have the option of either giving you the other hundred grand, or not. And of course, we didn't give it to her. Silly bitch. She should have read her napkin!'

In Los Angeles, New York, Aspen, or any Continental stop-off for world celebrities, there is a network of informants who are paid, each according to an established pecking order, based on a scale of whatever a star is currently thought to be worth. A Hollywood 'minder' explains how it works on the West Coast: 'You've got two-bit publicists, chauffeurs and secretaries all over Hollywood selling information to the junk press. Whenever you go to a restaurant frequented by celebrities, you can assume that the guy who parks your car is working with a paparazzo. He's got a slip of paper in his pocket with the name of a photographer on it, and he knows that if he calls with Madonna, he'll get $100, Brook Shields $50, George Michael . . . whoever. The junk press also monitors the airports.'

The source of such a network, the celebrity-based freelancer, is in a position to make big money, especially since freelancers began syndicating their own work globally.

When a client-star is fading, agents quickly sell whatever they can – information that their client has entered a drying-out clinic, is seeing a shrink, is fighting off bankruptcy, is involved in a particularly nasty divorce. This could very well be the last pay-off the star will see. Naïve readers sometimes blame the tabs for such

302

exposures when in fact, star and agent have cooked up the sale themselves.

More commonly, though, there is constant bombardment upon the friends, acquaintances and relatives of the celebrities to spill whatever they know. It is usually done for cash, but the ever-familiar motives of envy and revenge play their part as well. In matters of privacy, the stars are truly under siege. At the wedding of Michael J. Fox and Tracey Pollan, a bartender said she was offered $10,000 by a reporter from a supermarket tabloid to take a couple of surreptitious snaps with a concealed camera. She turned the offer down.

In England, a bodyguard who claimed to have been the ex-lover of Princess Anne was said by one editor of a national daily to have offered the story to him, along with circumstantial evidence, for a six-figure sum. The editor not surprisingly refused it. A deputy editor familiar with the case explained that even supposing such a story could be proved, the newspaper still would not have published it, because, in the long run, it wouldn't pay. There might be a temporary jump in circulation, but it would be followed by a backlash. People in the United Kingdom, he explains, have no desire to see the Royals' names dragged through the mire.

Meanwhile, an even more scurrilous version of the story appeared in the United States in the supermarket tabloid, the *Star*, then owned by Rupert Murdoch, under the stark title 'Princess Anne's Bodyguard Fathered Her Baby Girl'. In the US the Royal Family isn't held in such high esteem as in England, and libel laws require a higher standard of culpability in cases involving public figures. It is interesting to note, however, that standards have changed very little since Edward VIII was courting Mrs Simpson. Then as now, and despite their reputation for scandal-mongering, British tabloids do remain on the safe side of a line invisible to practically everyone except a handful of experienced editors.

For the year 1989, Rupert Murdoch's *Sun* in London paid freelancers something in the region of £6 million pounds for stories. The monthly rate was about £500,000, 'a figure which Murdoch himself keeps tabs on,' says a former employee of the *Sun*. However, in comparison with the total number of stories generated, these freelance sums are relatively small. Amounts between £30,000 and £50,000 or more are paid out only half a dozen times a year. In the *Sun* offices, it is said, you can sometimes hear editor Kelvin MacKenzie yelling, 'Start at £750 – no more than £2,000!'

Another former employee of the *Sun*, explains 'the reverse trick'. 'You can wind a guy up by starting at £750 and go down to £400. People fuck with you and you fuck them right back. It's a deceitful business, dog eat dog. If you hear it, you bank it in the paper before anybody else. People's lives *do* get ruined.'

The other standard operating procedure, and the *Sun* here seems to lead the pack, is to promise money and then renege on the deal. 'There are a lot of times,' says a former freelancer, 'when I told people that the *Sun* would pay them X amount. You only do that on instruction from your editor. Then, when you've got the interview, the editor, on numerous occasions will say, "No, fuck 'em." Or "tell them to fuck off." He'll either offer a lesser amount or he'll say none at all. Unless they have the gumption or resources to see a lawyer, then they are left high and dry.'

In one case, a woman said she had slept with one of the stars of the American television series *Miami Vice*. A *Sun* reporter interviewed her, with the promise to pay her $5,000 – $10,000, depending on the value of her disclosures. Although the story ran, there was no real proof whether the woman had really slept with the star, as she claimed. On balance, the evidence seemed fairly circumstantial. She could describe the home of the star and other details, but, as the reporter puts it, 'How do you prove a thing like that? We ran the story, though. Kelvin then turned around and said, "No, give her a thousand dollars, that's all it's fucking worth."'

Says the reporter, 'It's fine for Kelvin to do that, sitting in an office in London, not having to deal with these people. And he seems unfazed we have given someone our word. But then *you* have to face them and explain, "We're not paying. They've decided it's not worth that." This woman said to me, "But you agreed." I said, "I'm sorry, I know we did, I'm sorry." Nothing you are saying on behalf of your newspaper might actually be true. You don't know where you stand.

'I don't think if Kelvin was faced with the circumstance of doing it himself, he would actually do it. I don't think he is such an ogre behind closed doors as he acts like he is in the office, his public persona.'

Another former employee of the *Sun*, however, says the freelancers themselves are often the ones to blame. 'They promise a source a percentage of their story, or a flat fee, and then, after the story is published, they refuse to pay,' he says. 'They won't take any calls from the informant, won't answer any letters. The only thing they will answer is a writ.' He remembers an occasion when he confronted a freelancer with not paying his source. The freelancer's answer: 'Oh, that. That was just a come-on.'

How far will a freelancer go? A vicar in the south of England, who prefers his name be kept off the record, found out the hard way when he had to face a series of upsetting events involving his daughter. In the spring of 1990, the vicar was first beset by a Sunday broadsheet reporter, who said he was investigating a report that the vicar's seventeen-year-old daughter had become pregnant, that the vicar had attacked the parishioner responsible in a local pub, 'smashing his face in', and that he had to be hauled off the man by locals in the bar. Neither report was true.

The broadsheet reporter nevertheless came to the village, investigated the matter, then left, saying 'there was no story for him there.' Soon after, reporters from the Sunday tabloids showed up in the village. Again, they went to local pubs, speaking with locals in the village and generally giving the vicar the feeling of being personally harassed.

At last, the boyfriend of the girl was approached by a reporter who identified himself as being from a Sunday tabloid, offering the young man £12,000 for the story and £5,000 for any photograph of the girl herself that might be 'interesting'. The boyfriend refused the offer.

Says one veteran reporter, 'With sums like these, you can be sure the reporter never intended actually paying the money promised. The young man would never have seen a penny of the money.'

Says the vicar, 'My daughter was devastated by the affair. She was in the middle of A levels at school, and she was unable to complete them. Her whole confidence was undermined, and she became depressed. So it did have a traumatic effect on her.'

Otherwise, the vicar has no idea who planted the story with the press; someone among his parishioners must have made the telephone call that set the series of events into motion. The press unwittingly became the vehicle for someone who wished the vicar ill. Meanwhile, the vicar is unable to confront his accuser.

And for the freelancer who went after the story, how much could he have expected to make? Well, something in the neighbourhood of £750 for a Sunday tabloid, if the story led the page. So for a potential profit of £750, a young girl misses out on her A levels and a village vicar faces his parishioners with unpleasant suspicions in his mind, perhaps undermining his work in the community.

Occasionally, it's not the freelancer who is to blame, it's a *member of staff* who won't put down the credits for a story. 'It's not that they are trying to keep the money. They just want credit for the story; they don't want to admit they have been given the story by a contact. Later on, when the source calls and says they were promised money, they will begrudgingly say, "Oh, yeah, go ahead and pay them." My advice to anyone doing business with a tabloid,' says our former employee, 'is, "Get it in writing".'

Indeed, the entire industry is riddled with minor rip-offs that can take in not only an unsuspecting informant but on occasion the editors themselves. According to one foreign correspondent, many of the by-lines in newspapers and magazines are actually pseudonyms because reporters working for one newspaper are actually writing undercover for feature magazines. Says the correspondent, 'You can't let your editor find out. He'll say, "That was a good story. Why didn't you send it to us?" The reason of course is, "If I'd brought it to you, I wouldn't have got diddly squat." You can get at least £250–£300 for a page lead in Britain, more for a Sunday. And you can do that in a couple of hours. But on the magazine pieces, you can get anywhere between £750 to £1,200. You do a clip job, and it can take you three or four hours to put them together.'

It's not a bad rate of pay, especially considering that the reporter is already drawing his regular salary, plus his expenses.

Together, salary and expenses make up a tidy sum. A novice *Sun* reporter can expect to make somewhere in the region of £25,000 plus about £100 per week expenses. A sub-editor starts at £28,000 plus expenses. A big-name reporter pulls in £45,000 or more and can expect to pick up £10,000 or so on expenses – extra. Inside the industry, one of the gripes of reporters is that they actually have to pay out for legitimate expenses, and sub-editors, who rarely leave the office, do not.

These 'expenses' are, as one veteran reporter puts it, 'part of the system'. He views them as a form of bonus for working unsociable hours, and 'you would be very silly not to accept them.' Each week, reporters and subs file weekly claims, many of which are totally fictitious. The form has blanks for stories and for the amount of cash expended, and in some cases, the reporter simply makes up a headline for a story that never happened. These make fascinating reading, since they detail mileage to and from locations never visited, hospitality never paid, dinners never eaten and so on down the line. The headlines are often wonderfully imaginative, 'Secretaries Rebel Against Sexist Managers', says one; 'Yuppies Arrested on Drugs Charges', reads another. Telephone calls from the reporter's home as well as phone rental are usually paid by house agreement, in addition to the Value Added Tax. And

306

although the forms instruct the claimant to attach receipts, 'nobody really has to bother', says one former employee. There is an idea among newsmen that 'the fewer receipts, the better, because the Internal Revenue Service just argues with them anyway.'

Another school of thought holds it's best to get whatever receipts you can and attach them. Says one reporter, 'I was at a political conference at Blackpool in a restaurant, and I went to the toilet, which happened to be up a flight of stairs. As I was going up, I saw a bunch of blank receipts, so I picked them up automatically and stuffed them into my pocket. I got back to my table, and we all sat there for quite a long while. The food just wasn't arriving. Nobody was getting any meals. And the whole restaurant went slowly into chaos. Finally we called over a waiter, an Italian, and asked him what was the matter. He said, "There's been a punch-up in the kitchen. The chef claims there have been no orders, and the waiters claim there have. We put them on the stairs by the restaurant upstairs." So what I had picked up was all the orders for the cook at the restaurant.'

The way in which money is handled, or mishandled, within the tabloid industry gives a good measure of the ethical conduct of reporters and editors. But there are other criteria just as revealing.

One freelancer, who got out of the business, said he simply became worn out by what he called 'doing dirty deals'.

'It's intensely competitive if you are a freelancer, and you *have got to make it work*, and some people will go to all sorts of lengths to do that. Stories become almost legendary about how people cheat and lie to get interviews. There are the common ones. Certain newspapers develop certain reputations, so if you said "I'm from the *Sun* or *Star*," you wouldn't get in. So you don't say where you're from. Here is the White Lie: "I'm from News International." Then there is the next one up: "I'm from *The Times*." The rationale here is that we are all owned by the same person. But people do get a bit upset when they find what they thought was an interview with an organization with a reputation for being trustworthy turns out to be the *Sun*.'

Then, there is the quote that was never quoted. Reporters will and do make up quotes. 'There is pressure to get stories, pressure to be seen to be good, pressure to make things fit. The old ploy, and perhaps it is excusable, is the one where you say, "You must have felt terrible," and they say, "yes," and that translates, "I felt terrible." But it goes a stage further in lots of cases, where reporters will change the quotes, so it comes out, "This was the most terrible

307

day of my life. I thought I was going to die." It gets embellished. It's 10 per cent there, and they make it 110 per cent. And that it inexcusable. But the pressure is *intense*. There are two ways to justify it: a) In the case of ordinary people, it's what he *meant* to say, it's what he would have said if he could. b) Then there is the thing with Hollywood stars.

'Hollywood, showbiz, if you like, is built on the PR system. They will feed stories, embellish stories for publicity, so the reporter thinks, "Why can't *we* do it? It's a game." So show-biz reporters will actively inspire PR agents to make up stories about their clients so their clients will get good press, and the reporter will get good stories. The showbiz reporter might say, "Oh, what's the difference?" And you might say, "But none of it ever happened." "That doesn't matter," he says. "No one will ever know." And it goes down in history. When someone comes back to write a profile of this star, there is the story to be repeated. History is altered, and the star begins to believe his own publicity. And it never happened!'

The classic quote that never happened? Says Jeff Samuels, 'Well, one time, I quoted Elvis from the grave.'

One newswoman who didn't object to rearranging reality a bit was the redoubtable Wendy Henry, who holds the distinction of being the first woman to hold the position of editor of two national newspapers and leave both under less than sanguine circumstances. Described by colleagues as 'a unique talent', Henry first gained notoriety when she 'lifted' an interview with Simon Weston, the Falklands hero who suffered extensive burns, from another publication, for which she received a month's suspension from the *Sun*. Later, it was said she left her position as editor of the *News of the World* because Rupert Murdoch did not like the general 'tone' the paper had taken.

After moving to the editorship of Robert Maxwell's Sunday *People*, she made waves when she ran photographs of the victims of the DC-10 crash in Sioux City, Iowa, along with the headline, 'Horror of Flight 232: the pictures television couldn't use.' A second caption read, 'Mangled: a corpse sprawls grotesquely in death'.

But Henry's real gift lay in her special, perhaps intuitive under-standing of the prurient directions curiosity can take. In her short story 'Petrified Man' Eudora Welty penned the lines that come nearest to explaining the universal appeal of freaks of nature. Referring to a local fair, a beauty parlour operator named Leota says to her client, 'Aw. Well, honey, talkin' about bein' pregnant an' all, you ought to see those twins in a bottle, you really owe it to yourself . . . Born joined plum together – dead a course.'

Not unlike Leota, Wendy Henry frequently dwelled on the bizarre, featuring a kind of 'weekly freak' neatly packaged as a humanitarian service. She followed naturally in the tradition of William Randolph Hearst, whose New York *Journal* was filled with stories 'about 2-headed virgins, jugular veins of patients, and Siamese twin marriages.' A certain type of feature typified the *People* when Henry edited it: There was the story plus photographs of a baby girl who lost half her face from a rare virus. *People* raised a special fund of £14,000 and a US plastic surgeon agreed to treat the baby free of charge, the paper claimed. Another story showed a close-up of a baby with a rare skin disease which caused her skin to encrust with thick, crater-like flakes. Another week: A young girl cut in half who walked on her hands. And most amazingly, Siamese-twins Masha and Dasha Krivoshlyapova, who for twenty years had been kept in an institution on the outskirts of Moscow, where finally, 'with the advent of glasnost, [they have] been allowed to tell of their life of appalling hardship – and miraculous courage.'

What brought Henry down was a front-page photograph of Prince William, headlined, 'The Royal Wee', with the caption, 'Willie's Sly Pee in Park', which Henry ran on the front page of the paper on 19 November 1989. When the photograph of the future King of England urinating met with unqualified criticism, Henry defended herself by saying, 'It is a charming picture taken in a public place.' In the meantime, a statement was issued on behalf of the Prince and Princess of Wales complaining that the photo was 'intrusive and irresponsible'.

By 7.00 p.m. the next day, the announcement was being broadcast on the evening news that Wendy Henry had been sacked. In issuing the announcement, proprietor Robert Maxwell said, referring to the photo, 'the intrusion into privacy is not acceptable to me.'

Since that fateful day, little has been seen of Henry on the London newspaper scene. Rumours that she was soon to re-surface in Florida were substantiated when Globe International announced in November 1990, that Henry would become the editor of its flagship publication the *Globe*, replacing Paul Levy, who moved to the editorship of the *National Examiner*.

As a kind of farewell statement to Fleet Street, Henry said, 'I can, and have been accused of many things, but don't let anyone say I didn't know how to flog a few papers.'

Inside the same issue that featured 'The Royal Wee' on Page One, there appeared on Page Three a colour photograph of Sammy Davis Jr. just after he had undergone a throat operation for cancer. The dark pink of the open wound on his neck looked like raw meat, and many believed part of the reason Henry had been dismissed was this photograph. The same photograph appeared in another tabloid without causing public furore because it was printed in black and white.

Earlier in the year, on 25 August, the *Daily Star* ran a full-page colour photograph of the pram of a baby who had been crushed to death when a brick wall fell on it. In the photo, blood seeped through the pram's cover, changing in colour from red to an almost black hue and giving the impression of matter actually sticking to the fabric.

Says editor Brian Hitchen, 'I couldn't see any matter at all [in the original], and I wouldn't have used it if matter had been in there . . . I cropped the photo very tightly so you wouldn't get the blood because I don't want to upset people like that. I had to show the terrible tragedy of the thing but at the same time, I didn't want the gore in, and there certainly wasn't any flesh.' What Hitchen cropped out was 'a yard of blood to the left of the picture.' Despite this, the effect of the photograph was deeply upsetting.

This photograph and the one of the dying Sammy Davis Jr. raise the question of how the relatively new colour technology can affect a reader's reaction to a picture. Discussions within the industry about 'getting the colour mix right' don't seem to be taking into account the shock effect colour photography can have.

Of course, photographs in black and white can raise serious ethical questions. A photograph of Mandy Smith, nineteen-year-old wife of Rolling Stone Bill Wyman, presumably taken by telephoto lens in the clinic where she was staying, shows a stick-like creature weighing only five-and-a-half stone. It was run on the front page of the *Sun* on 4 July 1990, the day the Stones opened their British tour at Wembley Stadium in London.

Perhaps more alarming was the picture of David Blundy, the well-known and popular British journalist who was shot dead in San Salvador in late November 1989. The *Sun* ran a photograph of his body on the mortuary slab which outraged the whole of Fleet Street. The Press Council, reflecting the mood of editor Kelvin MacKenzie's peers, was quick to criticize the *Sun* for printing the picture. Although the tabloid business is often referred to as 'cut-throat' and 'dog eat dog', there is a tacit rule that in reality 'dog *don't* eat dog', meaning journalists don't prey upon one another.

MacKenzie's decision to publish the Blundy photograph showed an unwillingness to pander to this double standard. He is as likely to make a meal of his own kind as anything else that comes across his desk.

A former *Sun* employee, at one time within a heartbeat of MacKenzie, refers off the record to 'a huge siege mentality' that exists inside the offices of the *Sun*, perhaps as a result of the thirteen-month strike that marked the tumultuous birth of Wapping. At one time, the kinds of comments issuing forth out of the *Sun* offices, says the source, were things like, 'When this comes out, this guy is going belly-up', or 'Amazing story: we print this, the guy can kiss his ass goodbye.'

If it is true that ultimate power is ultimately corrupting, says the source, who knows from first-hand, 'apply the same thing to journalists as well.'

But *National Enquirer* editor Iain Calder disagrees. 'I don't think this kind of comment is so much corruption as desensitization . . . To some extent, it's black humour, and some of it is defensive black humour. If you don't laugh, you'll cry. As you know, at funerals, sometimes you find people after the funeral go back to a person's home, and it's like an Irish wake. They are devastated by the death, but it's a way of keeping mentally sane, because if you don't do this, it could get to you. It's not an exact parallel, but people who make jokes like these, it doesn't necessarily mean what you think it means.'

In MacKenzie's case, it might. There is the well-documented case of the falsification of an interview with Mrs Marica McKay, widow of Sergeant Ian McKay, one of two women whose husbands were posthumously awarded the Victoria Cross for exceptional acts of heroism during the Falklands campaign. When the *Daily Mirror* got the exclusive interview with McKay, the *Sun* simply falsified their interview, calling it 'a World Exclusive'.

The *Sun*'s version:

> Victoria Cross's widow Marica McKay fought back her tears last night and said: 'I'm so proud of Ian, his name will remain a legend in the history books forever . . .
>
> Hugging her children at their home in Rotherham, Yorkshire, she said: 'I'm proud of Ian's Victoria Cross

. . . but I'd exchange all the medals in the world to have him back.'

In its comment column, the *Mirror* accused writer John Kay of asking secretaries at the *Sun* how they would feel if it were them and then assigning versions of their quotes to McKay in his story. Whatever the case, the *Sun*'s interview with McKay could not have taken place because she was being interviewed by the *Mirror* at the time the *Sun* claimed to be seeing her.

More recently, on 16 August 1990, John Kay's name appeared above a story accompanying a page-one photograph of Prince Charles. It captured, as the newspaper put it, a 'royal snuggle', the Prince wearing bathing trunks as he 'holds old flame Lady Penny Romsey in a lingering, warm embrace at a hideaway villa in Majorca . . .

'The gorgeous blonde', the story went on to explain, 'once tipped as his future bride, nuzzled his neck and put her right hand on his left shoulder.' What the story failed to point out was that Lady Romsey's husband had been only yards away at the moment of the embrace. It also neglected to give the circumstances behind it.

This task was left to Lord Romsey who issued a public statement the day the photograph appeared:

> The picture published in this morning's *Sun* is the picture of a caring human being comforting my wife.
>
> The photograph was taken at the moment we told Prince Charles our four-year-old daughter Leonora had been diagnosed with a serious cancer.
>
> Prince Charles was obviously as upset as we were and immediately consoled Penny who was in tears.

It was said that Prince Charles himself called the *Sun*'s treatment of the event 'appallingly cruel'. Two days later, besieged by the *Mirror* and the *Mail*, the *Sun* at last apologized for the story, which, it explained, 'contained innuendos which were false.'

There is a strange corollary to all this.

John Kay, the writer of these two stories, both of which grossly misrepresent actual events, killed his first wife. The circumstances are buried in the past, but he and his wife were in the bathtub where he drowned her. Obviously in a state of great distress, he then tried to commit suicide, but failed. Kay pleaded guilty to manslaughter on the ground of diminished responsibility and was ordered to enter Friern Hospital, Barnet, for treatment. His plea of not guilty to murder was accepted at St Alban's Crown Court. All Fleet Street knows the story, but it is generally considered to be in bad taste to mention it. The tacit rule, 'dog don't eat dog', comes into full play with John Kay, who is unusually well liked and indeed respected by his colleagues. That MacKenzie keeps Kay on the payroll has been cited as evidence of a kind and humane side to MacKenzie's personality.

Irony: it is *not* considered reprehensible to falsify an interview; it *is* considered reprehensible to mention John Kay's past.

Aside from that puzzling ethical paradox, the real measure of MacKenzie's editorial abilities occurred during the week following Britain's worst football crowd disaster when ninety-five people were crushed to death at Hillsborough Stadium, Sheffield, at the FA Cup semi-final between Liverpool and Nottingham Forest. A late surge of 3,000 fans at the turnstiles to the stadium was allowed to enter through a tunnel, pushing those already inside against wire fences, where many died. In the wake of the disaster, an acrimonious debate took shape over who held the responsibility, some blaming police for allowing the crowd to enter the stadium, some blaming fans for coming to the game drunk and unruly.

Four days after the tragedy, on 19 April 1989, the *Sun* ran an article in gigantic letters, labelled 'THE TRUTH'. At the top of the page was that week's logo, 'Gates of Hell', which showed in reverse a thumbnail photograph of the fans being squeezed behind the wire fence. The article featured large underlined heads that read:

*Some fans picked pockets of victims
*Some fans urinated on the brave cops
*Some fans beat up PC giving kiss of life

The article was met with fury, especially in Merseyside, where a students' organization gathered 7,000 names on a petition protesting against the manner in which the piece presented its information. In its investigation of coverage of the disaster, the Press Council singled out 'THE TRUTH', saying that the policeman named in the article had stressed that only a small minority of Liverpool fans behaved 'so badly'. It went on to criticize the article for being 'generally one-sided, offering no other counter to the allegations it included.'

> Whether or not any of these allegations can be sustained, the article was unbalanced and its general effect misleading. The headline THE TRUTH was insensitive, provocative and

313

unwarranted. The *Sun*'s own ombudsman declared that the article should not have been published in the form in which it appeared. The Press Council condemns its publication.

Perhaps more punishing to the *Sun* was the boycott by readers in Liverpool and elsewhere, which, according to some reports, cost the newspaper upwards of 300,000 in circulation. (Inside the *Sun*, private audits of the numbers of readers lost were said to be much lower.) Whatever the actual number, it was enough. MacKenzie ended up making an unprecedented public apology for the article on Radio 4's *The World This Weekend*. In it, he drew attention to the fact that the allegations in the article had not been made by the *Sun* but by sources cited in the story. 'What we simply did,' said MacKenzie, 'was to report them, as did other newspapers, including the *Daily Telegraph*. I must say that it was my decision – and my decision alone – to do that Page One in that way, and I made a rather serious error. We have taken on board not only what has been said in this report by the Press Council but far more importantly, the beliefs of the Liverpool people who were, prior to the way we covered Hillsborough, one of our most important areas of readership.'

It was said that MacKenzie's apology was 'personally approved by Mr Rupert Murdoch,' but the deputy editor of the *Sun* denied this, saying 'it was the newspaper's own decision.'

The result of 'THE TRUTH' had a rather startling effect in the pages of the *Sun*, especially in relation to the Hillsborough disaster. On 30 November 1989, some eight months after 'THE TRUTH' appeared, a report ran on Page Two of the *Sun* detailing an article published in a police magazine 'which claimed reports of drinking Liverpool soccer fans were "whitewashed" by the official inquiry.' Examples from the article were given, as well as reactions to the article by relatives of fans who had died in the disaster. A boxed graphic juxtaposed the two opposing views of the disaster, with a policeman quoted as saying, 'They were acting like animals and worse'; a father of girls who died there saying the claims were 'scandalous, offensive and insensitive.' All in all, the article, written by Simon Hughes, could have served as a textbook example of journalistic fairness and objectivity.

The Hillsborough tragedy was a lesson in objective reporting for MacKenzie, and one well-learned if the follow-up article was any measure. And it underlines a fact most press pundits forget. In the marketplace of ideas, there exists a self-righting mechanism – the public.

There is that moment when the public step back, take a long look and reject the product. It happened with the *Daily Star*, when editor Mike Gabbert took it too far down-market; it happened with Elton John, when the *Sun*'s attacks on his personal life offended readers; it happened with Wendy Henry, when she crossed the bad-taste barrier with the Royals.

Most importantly, it happened with the Hillsborough tragedy when the public signalled the demarcation line of a dangerous no-go area. Editors who enter this zone do so at their own peril.

There is a rule of thumb regarding press freedom that is well worth remembering. A press remains free only so long as it maintains an acceptable level of responsibility. To some degree this is true of any press, even that of the United States, where the First Amendment to the Constitution guarantees that 'Congress shall make no law . . . abridging freedom of speech, or of the press . . .'

This correlation between responsibility and freedom exists because, in actual fact, hardly anyone really believes the press should be free.

From time to time, some group of researchers in the United States takes it upon themselves to prove this by rewording the Bill of Rights so it cannot be easily recognized, then carrying out a statistically correct random survey of the population to determine how many today would actually support the ten amendments to the US Constitution that guarantee each citizen's rights. Inevitably, the large majority would be willing to give away their personal freedoms without a backward glance, most especially their freedom of expression.

In England where there is no First Amendment to protect it, the press is in constant danger of legal constraints that come about by government fiat or by carelessly crafted laws that limit what can be printed. Ironically, in the country which gave birth to freedom of expression after the Dark Ages, there is no Freedom of Information Act, no 'Sunshine Laws', no distinction made between public figures and private individuals for purposes of adjudicating defamation cases. There *is* an Official Secrets Act analogous to America's long discarded Espionage Act of 1917, a piece of war-time legislation intended to prevent insubordination in the armed forces and to protect vital information about troop movement; there are injunctions against publication, that is, prior restraint, the absence of which has long been considered by American legal scholars as the very *least* protection freedom of the press must have in order to flourish. There are moreover the most repressive libel laws of any self-styled democratic country; the dreaded 'D-notice'; the Criminal Rehabilitation Act of 1974; contempt of court; the list goes on – in short, a chamber of horrors.

Now editors must face the possibility of privacy legislation as well. And they have been offered, as a 'bite-the-bullet' alternative, the opportunity 'to put their own house in order' or face an extra-judicial, governmentally appointed committee with powers to order newspapers to publish precisely-worded apologies, their size and location, with the extra added constraint of a possible 'hotline' to warn editors against publishing an impending 'intrusion upon privacy' – in other words, a hotline to prior restraint. If publications do not voluntarily adhere to the findings of the panel, they then face the establishment of a statutory tribunal with the legal power to restrain the press according to a code of fair practice.

These are the findings of the Report of the Committee on Privacy and Related Matters, chaired by David Calcutt QC, which was set up to prevent excessive intrusion upon the privacy of public and private individuals. Julian Critchley MP, who is both a journalist and a Parliamentarian, sees a division between the tabloid press and 'the responsible press'. The former, he believes, is entertainment; the latter, a legitimate information-disseminating institution. Says Critchley, 'From the tabloid point of view, it doesn't matter whether you are a celebrity. You can be humble and still have your life ruined by intrusion. People have an insatiable appetite for a parade of other people's misfortunes.

'The kind of person who becomes a foot-in-the-door journalist is extremely streetwise and by definition pretty unscrupulous. If that were not the case, they would be working for *The Times*, the *Independent*, the *Guardian* or the *Telegraph*.'

What Critchley is forgetting, however, is that, in a good many cases, *they are*. The cross-over from tabloid to establishment press is a well-known fact inside the industry, although few outside the business are informed of it. *Mirror* editor Roy Greenslade – to name but one of many – took his turn on the *Sun* and the *Express* before joining *The Sunday Times* staff and finally taking over at the *Mirror*. Says Greenslade, 'Three of the best people on *The Sunday Times* when I was there were from the tabloids. And that showed what I've long suspected, that there is a large number of tabloid journalists who could do the job.'

It has also happened that journalists who report for the tabloids during the week become subs for the establishment press on the weekend. It's not that certain journalists successfully crossed over

316

from tabloid to broadsheet: in some cases, they are the very same people.

In 1979, at about the time Members of Parliament were scheduled to vote whether to bring back legalized execution to Britain, the sister of Ruth Ellis, who in 1955 was the last woman to be executed in England, voiced a strange request to reporter George Lynn. She wanted to meet the man who hanged her sister.

Arthur Pierrepoint, who had during his career as Britain's official hangman put to death over 400 people, was then about seventy, and he was running a small pub in the English countryside. An agreement was struck in which there would be a story for the *Sun*, and in return, Ellis's sister would be given the opportunity to speak privately with the hangman. They would then go together to the cemetery where Ruth Ellis was buried under her maiden name, Ruth Hornby. Says Lynn, 'The arrangement was that we should not take any pictures of Albert Pierrepoint and Ruth Ellis's sister *in* the graveyard. That would be too bizarre. So I gave my word.'

Lynn accordingly set up the meeting, a lunch at a hotel, and then, after introducing the pair, left the table for an hour as agreed. Then Lynn, the sister, Pierrepoint and a photographer drove to the graveside, where both the sister and Pierrepoint visited the grave – 'they both of them stood there, silently, and then we all drove back and that was it. That was all.

'But then, I discovered, to my horror, that the photographer had taken a picture at the graveside. Of course, a photo like this would have been worth a fortune! So I went into Ken Donlan, my news editor at the time. I said, "Ken, I've done the story," and I said, "But I gave my word we would *not* take the pictures." And he said, "You did?"

'And he took the photos and negatives, and he said, "Go through them and see if you can find any taken at the graveside." And I went through them, and I found this bloody picture, and you could see the pair quite clearly. And I gave it and the negative to Ken, and he said, "Give me a pair of scissors." And he took them, and he cut them up in pieces. And that's what you call ethics.

'I mean, can you imagine? The hangman of the last woman to be executed in England and her sister at the grave.'

Later, it would be Ken Donlan who, as official ombudsman of the *Sun*, publicly deplored the form in which the story 'THE TRUTH' appeared on the newspaper's front page.

In the spring of 1990, Paul Woolwich, producer of the highly rated television show *Hard News*, received an atypical letter from a viewer. Woolwich, it should be remembered, and his moderator, Raymond Snoddy, media correspondent of the *Financial Times*, declared war on the excessive practices of the tabloid press, devoting much air time to exposing their scams and scandals. But this letter gave Woolwich pause.

It came from an observer at the Royal Marsden Hospital, calling attention to efforts by the *Daily Star* to raise £1,000,000 of the £25,000,000 needed for a new unit for children suffering from leukaemia. The writer of the letter said he had viewed *Hard News* many times and couldn't help wondering why Woolwich didn't do a show on the *Star*'s long-term fundraising campaign for the hospital. The writer mentioned that *Star* editor Brian Hitchen had come around to the hospital to visit the children and was 'a really nice man'. Why didn't Woolwich mention this on the show?

The answer is unclear. The fact remains, however, that when the tabloids act scandalously and unscrupulously, the establishment press is hard on their heels. When they act humanely, rendering undeniable services to the community at large, they are either viewed cynically – or ignored altogether.

In late August 1988, Ariel Glaser seven-year-old daughter of Elizabeth and Paul Michael Glaser, former star of television's *Starsky and Hutch*, died after an extended illness. Predictably, the family was grief-stricken.

The young girl had a vulnerable, waif-like appearance, penetrating dark eyes and a direct stare that could be disarming. It seemed that life could hold no greater cruelty than the death of this promising child. But there was more.

Ariel Glaser died of AIDS, and the day the family discovered she had the disease, they also learned that both Elizabeth Glaser, infected from transfusions of unscreened blood when Ariel was born, and her four-year-old son, infected in the womb, carried the HIV-virus. In Elizabeth Glaser's words, 'We discovered that an entire family was going to be lost.' Only Paul Michael Glaser was untouched by the disease.

The effect upon Elizabeth Glaser was extreme. She withdrew from society, frightened that if someone gave her a glass of water in their home, they might not wash it properly afterwards. She no longer watched television or read newspapers because reports about the advance of the disease frightened her. 'I felt like a leper,' she later said. Then, about six to eight weeks before the anniversary of Ariel's death, a series of strange events came about.

There were 'unexplained calls' to Glaser's insurance company, leaving a number. When Glaser or some other member of his family returned the call, they found no such person existed. A stranger approached the Glaser home, asking whether they knew where 'a good pool man' could be found.

Family and friends began to be bombarded by telephone calls, all in some way related to Ariel's illness. When they changed their telephone numbers, the calls resumed almost immediately, despite the fact the numbers were unlisted. One of the calls was to Paul Michael Glaser's sister from someone pretending to be an old chum of his from college: 'Oh, I heard about the AIDS from the family . . .'

In another episode, individuals called the Crossroads School, where Ariel had studied until her illness forced her to withdraw. They identified themselves as parents of a child with AIDS, saying that 'Elizabeth Glaser had recommended the school to them.'

'On all these calls,' says Josh Baran, who represents the family to the public, 'the homework had been done. The caller knew where the family lived, when they were in school, all the details that made the callers seem authentic. They showed exceptionally good detective work.

'In one extremely upsetting episode,' says Baran, 'a man went to the hospital ward where Ariel had died, trying to talk to the five or six private nurses who had helped her when she was sick and dying. These nurses were also called at home.

'But perhaps the most upsetting single incident involved a man who called on close friends of the Glasers saying he was the son of a rabbi for the memorial service on the yearly anniversary of her death. No service had been planned.'

Then, a call came from the *National Enquirer*. They advised Baran that they were planning to publish an article on the Glasers, identifying the disease, because Paul Michael Glaser was a world-wide celebrity, and as such, the illness of his family was newsworthy.

In addition to the loss of their daughter then, the impending deaths of mother and son and the bizarre series of inquiries about their personal life that had been taking place for nearly two months, the family now had to face publication of their plight. 'For Paul and me,' Elizabeth Glaser later told a reporter, 'this is very frightening to imagine that people we don't know will find out the most private parts of our lives. But our fear is the greatest for our son. He doesn't know that he isn't a normal, healthy little boy, and he doesn't know that his mother isn't a normal, healthy mom. It's our right to tell him when he is strong enough and old enough to handle the information. Now we may not have that choice.'

What Baran characterized as 'difficult negotiations' between himself, the Glaser's family attorney and the *National Enquirer* now began taking place. When, after a period of four to six weeks, it became apparent that the supermarket tabloid would publish, despite the family's wishes to the contrary, the decision was made to pre-empt them. The family went to the Los Angeles *Times* with their story, which was immediately flashed on to front pages across the world, a few days ahead of the *National Enquirer*'s publication date.

Quite literally, the Glasers scooped the *National Enquirer*.

The *Enquirer*, it turns out, wasn't the first media outlet to pick up the story. *Entertainment Tonight* had called before the *Enquirer*, asking the family's permission to broadcast the story. Informed of the family's wishes to the contrary, they complied. Not so the *Enquirer*. Baran characterizes the *Enquirer*'s actions as 'a complete and total invasion of the family's privacy.'

Says Iain Calder, editor of the *National Enquirer*, 'What *we* do is to find out . . . or someone else finds out . . . who forces the celebrities into the situation where they actually become role models for society. With *Starsky and Hutch*, we found out his wife had the virus. "We'll do a compromise," we say, "we won't say she or her surviving child has the virus out of respect for their privacy." We didn't say how their daughter got AIDS, only that she died from it, and this was the tragedy of their lives.'

The Glaser family then went public with the full story that went far beyond what the *Enquirer* published. 'We *didn't* publish it. We went to the stands with a story that absolutely didn't say that. Now his publicity made our circulation go up. He didn't intend it. But we had a very good sale. And what has happened since? The family has got more love and affection. They've been able to raise money for AIDS, and the community has come around them. They no longer have this terrible dark secret to come out. The actual disease is still there for them. But the dark secret isn't there. And they've helped other people. It's a situation, if more people come out, the social stigma will fall away from it, like happened with cancer. For these people, who through no fault of their own have got this terrible disease, why treat it as if there is something to be ashamed of? We were absolutely willing and able not to say the wife and child had AIDS.

320

'What the *Enquirer* did turned out to be a good thing for the family and AIDS sufferers in general.'

Paul Levy, editor of the *Globe*, agrees with Calder, but he doesn't expound the view that the purpose of publication of the story would be to create role models for society. His is the clear, cold rationalization of the hardened newsman. '*When I worked for the Philadelphia* Bulletin, *if the mayor was sick, I was gonna find out what was wrong with him*. There isn't a paper in the country that would not run on the front page, if they found out, that their mayor had AIDS, including the New York *Times*. I would have run it – the Starsky and Hutch AIDS story – and my answer, had I made that decision, *which I did not*, would be that if Mayor Koch had children, and they had AIDS, the New York *Times* would have run it, or Mayor Bradley in LA, the Los Angeles *Times* would have run it. And they would have made some excuse, "Well, he's a public official." But the fact that he's a public official doesn't change the fact they would be running it because it is news and it is interesting.'

Elizabeth Glaser, after Ariel's death and before the publication of the story of the family's tragedy, had made the decision to lobby Congress privately about appropriations for the paediatric AIDS budget. She visited President Ronald Reagan, the Surgeon General, Barbara Bush, congressmen, senators and Admiral James D. Watkins, who then headed Reagan's AIDS task force. She is credited personally for getting the budget raised from 3.3 to 8.8 million dollars to fund thirteen paediatric clinical treatment units instead of the previously planned four. She then co-founded a charity named the Pediatric AIDS Foundation, which has raised 4 million dollars through charity benefits and contributions.

Since publication of her story, despite the knowledge that she will die from the disease – as will her remaining child – she has become the international spokeswoman for children infected with the disease AIDS, and she campaigns indefatigably on their behalf. The face of her dead daughter appears on her foundation's poster urging against discrimination towards children with AIDS. The same woman who feared to take a drink of water at the home of a friend has accepted the role that was thrust upon her. And the remaining years of her life are dedicated to alleviating the pain of others similarly situated as herself, but who are without her voice in the international marketplace of ideas.

Not long after the Glasers were forced to publish these intimate facts of their family's personal tragedy, the *National Enquirer* rang

Josh Baran back. They told him they were planning to run a follow-up story on the Glasers. Did the family wish them to run the name of Elizabeth Glaser's charity and its address alongside the story, for readers' contributions?

The Glaser family, Baran informed the tabloid, wanted nothing from the *National Enquirer*.

Josh Baran will now hang up the phone, turn back to his desk and begin working on one project or another. For all practical purposes, he has finished dealing with the *National Enquirer*.

Somewhere within the inner sanctum of the *Enquirer* offices, the decision is taken to go ahead and run the name and address of the Pediatric AIDS Foundation. It will appear in bold letters, boxed in, at the end of a heart-warming story telling how the entire nation has responded with sympathy to the Glaser family's tragedy.

And so it goes.

PART SIX

Appendices

CHANGES

Since the writing of *Shock! Horror!*, a number of the key characters have changed positions. John Mahoney no longer reports for the London *Daily Star* from Los Angeles, but has been promoted to news editor of the paper's Manchester office. His colleague Chris Anderson has left tabloids in order to write a book.

Wendy Henry, publicly sacked by Robert Maxwell from her position as editor of the *People*, now edits the *Globe* for Globe International, Inc. in Boca Raton, Florida. Paul Levy, who did hold that position, has moved laterally to the editorship of the *National Examiner*, also a Globe publication. Phil Bunton, formerly executive editor of the *Star*, left when MacFadden Enterprises bought the supermarket tabloid from Rupert Murdoch; he now holds the same position at *Globe International*. Roger Wood stayed with the *Star*, retaining his position as editorial director.

Drew Robertson, the youngest editor of a London national, was, in his own words, given the opportunity to resign as editor of the *Sunday Sport* in November 1990, but chose to be sacked instead. 'When you're sacked, you're sacked,' says Robertson. He is now working in the field of graphics.

Joyce Hopkirk, who was editor of *She* magazine, has gone to 'TVPlus'. Paul Woolwich, formerly editor of Channel 4's *Hard News*, is now editor of *This Week* at Thames Televison.

In the Honours List that followed the resignation of Mrs Thatcher as Prime Minister, Nick Lloyd, editor of the *Daily Express*, was knighted. Brian Hitchen, editor of the *Daily Star*, was made a Commander of the British Empire.

GLOSSARY OF TERMS USED IN BRITISH TABLOIDS

assets *n*. Ladies' breasts. *See* boobs, knockers, melons, stunnas, whoppas, wobblers
attractive *adj*. Unattractive
bang *excl*. Exclamatory remark as in Bang!
bang *v*. To have sex with. *See* bonk, pork
bash *v*. To wallop, in the best English tradition
bash *n*. *Wild* party, in the best English tradition
barmy *adj*. *Wild* and crazy! *Fun*-lovin'. *See* madcap
bawdy *adj*. ¹. Wildly sexy, in the best English tradition. ². What sexual activity should be
boffin *n*. Expert, authority
bonk *v*. To have sex with. Nicely combined with 'barmy' as in 'bonk-barmy'. *See* bang, pork
bonked *adj*. To have been subjected to sexual intercourse by a partner, in the best English tradition. *See* zonked
boobs *n*. Ladies' breasts. *See* assets, knockers, melons, stunnas, whoppas, wobblers
bot *n*. In the human anatomy, the bottom. *See* bum. *Var*. botty
bottle *n*. ¹. Nerve. ². Guts. ³. Balls. What male readers of the popular press should have alotta
bum *n*. In the human anatomy, the rear end. *See* bot
cheek *n*. Nerve, in the worst British tradition
chinks *n*. Respected citizens of China, Korea, Thailand, Vietnam, etc. *See* Frogs, Japs, Krauts, Nips, Yanks
cor blimey! *excl*. Goodness gracious me. *Var*. Goo blimey!
crash! horror! *adj*. Mildly unpleasant. *See* shock! horror!
dishy *adj*. Sexy and attractive. Derives from 'nice little dish'
dosh *n*. Cash money
eiffel *n*. French for eyeful
frogs *n*. Garlic-swilling, wife-swapping, stinking Frenchmen. The women are a bit of *OK*! *See* Chinks, Krauts, Japs, Nips, Yanks
fuels *n*. Pun for fools

327

gobsmacked *adj.* [1]. Covered in slime, as in wet kiss. [2]. Covered in slime, as in ectoplasm. [3]. Struck dumb with wonder

gutbucket *n.* Fat person

horny *adj.* Alert to sexual possibilities. *See* randy

hubby *n.* Husband. *See* missus

hunk *n.* Male counterpart to Page Three Girl

japs *n.* Respected citizens of Japan (slanty-eyed, though). *See* Nips

kinky *adj.* What all sex is, if done right

knickers *n.* Undergarments, usually women's

knockers *n.* Ladies' breasts. *See* assets, boobs, melons, stunnas, whoppas, wobblers

krauts *n.* Respected citizens of Germany. *See* Chinks, Frogs, Japs, Nips, Yanks

loadsa *idiom.* Loads of. *Var.* loadsacash, loadsa money, loadsa trouble, loadsafun, etc.

lotta *idiom.* A lot of. *See* loadsa

lout *n.* Yob

loveplums *n.* Male genitalia. *See* wedding tackle

madcap *adj.* *Wild* and crazy! *Fun*-lovin'. *See* barmy

megabucks *n.* Many dollars

melons *n.* Ladies' breasts. *See* assets, boobs, knockers, stunnas, whoppers, wobblers

milko *n.* Milkman. *See* postie

missus *n.* Wife. *See* hubby

nips *n.* Respected citizens of Japan; clever devils. *See* Japs

nookie *n.* Sexual intercourse, in the best English tradition

nosh *n.* Snack

outta *dble prep.* Out of

pork *v.* To subject to sexual intercourse, in the best English tradition. *See* bang, bonk

postie *n.* Postman. *See* milko

randy *adj.* Alert to sexual possibilities. *See* horny

raunchy *adj.* Sexually disgusting, in the best English tradition. *See* rude

romeo *n.* Lover boy. *Ex.* pint-sized romeo – short lover boy

rude *adj.* Dirty, but pleasing nevertheless. *See* raunchy

rumpy-pumpy *n.* Sexual intercourse, in the best English tradition. Russian *var.* rumpski pumpski

saucy *adj.* Cute and sassy. *See* rude

shock! horror! *adj.* Fairly shocking. [Currently, out of use.] *See* crash! horror!

sizzlin' [1]. Hot off the griddle. [2]. Hot off the mark. [3]. Ready to go, in the best sense of the word

skimpy *adj.* ¹. Little of it. ². What women's underwear, swimming costumes, sports garments should be, whenever possible
smasher *n.* Sexually attractive woman; often used in conjunction with 'Cor blimey!' and 'Wotta . . .'
steamy *adj.* ¹. Hot. ². What many sex sessions tend to be
stunnas *n.* ¹. Ladies' breasts. ². The ladies themselves. *See* assets, boobs, knockers, melons, whoppas, wobblers
swap *n.* Transplant, as in body part, i.e., liver, heart, lungs, etc. *adj.* of or pertaining to a transplant, as in body part, ex. 'Heart-lung-swap-op girl'
36DD *adj.* Ideal size, as in cup
topless *adj.* Preferred state of womankind
tot *n.* Substitute for 'child'; (it fits a narrow head count)
wacko *adj.* *Wild* and crazy! *Fun*-lovin' in the best English tradition. *See* barmy. *See* madcap
wedding tackle *n.* Male genitalia. *See* loveplums
whoppas *n.* Ladies' breasts. *See* assets, boobs, knockers, melons, stunnas, wobblers
wobblers *n.* Ladies' breasts. *See* assets, boobs, knockers, melons, stunnas, whoppas. *See* topless. *See* 36DD
worra *n.* Worry
yanks *n.* Oversexed, overpaid, and *still* over here. *See* Chinks, Frogs, Krauts, Japs, Nips
yob *n.* Lout
zonked *adj.* Located in outer space, as this directly pertains to drug usage, alcohol usage, or elaborate sexual activity; conveniently, rhymes with 'bonked'

SOURCES

Chapter 1: The Education of Sir Larry Lamb

1. Interview with Vic Giles, Retired Design Director, the *Sun*, 12 April 1990, London.
2. Interview with Joyce Hopkirk, Former Editor *She*, 6 September 1989, London.
3. Larry Lamb, *Sunrise* (London: PaperMac, 1989).
4. Interview with Marian Davison, Former Secretary to Larry Lamb, 10 April 1990, London.
5. Charles Wintour, *The Rise and Fall of Fleet Street* (London: Hutchinson, 1989).
6. Henry Porter, *Lies, Damned Lies and Some Exclusives* (London: Chatto & Windus, 1984).
7. Interview with George Lynn, Retired Editorial Executive, the *Sun*, 26 June 1989, London.
8. Interview with Mike Nevard, Director of Special Projects, *National Enquirer*, 22 January 1990, West Palm Beach, Florida.
9. Interview with Nick Lloyd, Editor of the *Daily Express*, 2 April 1990, London.
10. Interview with Sue Snell, Film Fashion Designer, 15 September 1989, London.
11. Interview with Roy Greenslade, Editor of the *Daily Mirror*, 15 March 1990, London.
12. James Curran and Jean Seaton, *Power without Responsibility: The Press and Broadcasting in Britain*, 2nd edition (London: Methuen, 1985).
13. Simon Jenkins, *Newspapers: The Power and the Money* (London: Faber & Faber, 1979).
14. Yvonne Paul with Madeleine Pallas, *The Glamour Game* (London: Nexus, 1989).

15. Patrick Pilton, *Page Three Girls* (London: Sun Books, n.d.).
16. Roslyn Grose, *The Sun-Sation: Behind the Scenes of Britain's Bestselling Daily Newspaper* (London: Angus & Robertson, 1989).

Chapter 2: Page Three Phenomena

1. Yvonne Paul with Madeleine Pallas, *The Glamour Game* (London: Nexus, 1989).
2. Patrick Pilton, *The Page Three Girls* (London: Sun Books, n.d.).
3. Roslyn Grose, *The Sun-Sation: Behind the Scenes of Britain's Bestselling Daily Newspaper* (London: Angus & Robertson, 1989).
4. Larry Lamb, *Sunrise* (London: PaperMac, 1989).
5. Interview with George Lynn, Former Executive Editor, the *Sun*, 26 June 1989.
6. Interview with Joyce Hopkirk, Former Editor *She*, 6 September 1989, London.
7. Interview with Sue Snell, Film Fashion Designer, 15 September 1989, London.
8. Hansard Reports on the House of Commons, 'Indecent Displays (Newspapers)'; initiated by Clare Short, MP for Birmingham Ladywood, 12 March 1986; 13 April 1988.
9. Interview with Len Valenti, Chief Copy Editor, New York *Daily News*, 17 January 1990, New York.
10. Interview with Christina Kirk, Associate Editor, the *Star*, 17 January 1990, New York.
11. Interview with John Vader, Editor, the *Sun*, Globe International, Inc., 22 January 1990, Boca Raton, Florida.
12. Interview with Marcelle, Agent for Page Three Girls, 22 August 1989, London.
13. Interview with Shelley Lawrence, Photographer's Agent, 11 August 1989, London.
14. Interview with Daniel Mayor, Glamour Photographer, 11 August 1989, London.
15. Interview with 'Tracie', Page Three and Glamour Model, 11 August 1989, London.

Chapter 3: I Cut Out Her Heart and Stomped On It

1. 'The Murder of John Ostrom', *National Enquirer*, 8 January

1967; from the Archives of the *National Enquirer*, Lantana, Florida.

2. Interview with Iain Calder, Editor and President of the *National Enquirer*, 24 January 1990, Lantana, Florida.

3. Interview with Mike Walker, Gossip Editor and Columnist, *National Enquirer*, 25 January 1990, West Palm Beach, Florida.

4. Beth Ann Krier, 'When the National Enquirer Pounces, Sales Jump – And So Do Its Critics', Los Angeles *Times*, 11 June 1987.

5. Iain Calder, 'Elegy for Gene Pope', 5 October 1988; from the Archives of the *National Enquirer*.

6. Interview with Brian Hitchen, Editor of London's *Daily Star*, 13 September 1989, London.

7. Interview with Paul Levy, former Senior Editor at the *National Enquirer*, now Editor of the *Globe*, 23 and 26 January 1990, Boca Raton, Florida.

8. Interview with David Duffy, Gossip Columnist, *National Enquirer*, 25 January 1990, Lantana, Florida.

9. Interview with Tony Brenna, Senior West Coast Correspondent, *National Enquirer*, 2 January 1990, London.

10. Interview with James Sutherland, Managing Editor of London's *Daily Star*, 29 November 1989, London.

11. Interview with Jeff Samuels, Chief Writer for 'Lifestyles of the Rich and Famous', 7 February 1990, New York.

12. Interview with Tony Miles, Publisher of Globe International Inc., 22 January 1990, Boca Raton, Florida.

13. Interview with Vic Giles, Retired Design Director, the *Sun*, 12 April 1990, London.

14. Interview with Mike Nevard, Director of Special Projects, *National Enquirer*, 22 January 1990, West Palm Beach, Florida.

15. Interview with Christina Kirk, Associate Editor, the *Star*, 17 January 1990, New York.

16. Interview with Phil Bunton, Executive Editor, the *Star*, 1 February 1990, Tarrytown, New York.

An artist and a businesswoman

1. Interview with Laurie Brady, Astrologer for the *Star*, 29 January 1990, Chicago.

Chapter 4: The First Casualty

1. Interview with Rafe Klinger, Former Columnist and Reporter for the *Weekly World News*, 24 January 1990, Boynton Beach, Florida.
2. Interview with Phil Bunton, Executive Editor, the *Star*, 1 February 1990, Tarrytown, New York.
3. Interview with John Vader, Editor of the *Sun*, Globe International Inc., 22 January 1990, Boca Raton, Florida.
4. Interview with Mike Walker, Gossip Columnist and Editor, *National Enquirer*, 25 January 1990, West Palm Beach, Florida.
5. Interview with Christina Kirk, Associate Editor, the *Star*, 17 January 1990, New York.
6. Interview with Tony Miles, Publisher, Globe International Inc., 22 January 1990, Boca Raton, Florida.
7. P. J. Corkery, 'Inside the *National Enquirer*: An Eyewitness Account', *Rolling Stone Magazine*, 11 June 1981, pp.19–21.
8. Interview with Paul Levy, Editor of the *Globe*, Globe International Inc., 23 January 1990, Boca Raton, Florida.
9. Interview with Iain Calder, Editor of the *National Enquirer*, 24 January 1990, Lantana, Florida.
10. Interview with Jeff Samuels, Chief Writer for 'Lifestyles of the Rich and Famous', 7 February 1990, New York.
11. Interview with Tony Brenna, Senior West Coast Correspondent, *National Enquirer*, 2 January 1990, London.

That popcorn diet in full

1. Interview with Richard Ellis, European Correspondent, the *Sunday Times*, 20 March 1990, London.
2. Cuttings from the *Sun*, *Interview Magazine*.

Chapter 5: Fifteen Minutes

1. Interview with Christina Kirk, Associate Editor, the *Star*, 17 January 1990, New York.
2. Daniel J. Boorstin, *The Image, or What Happened to the American Dream* (London: Penguin, 1963).
3. Alastair Hetherington, *News, Newspapers and Television* (London: Macmillan, 1985), p.13.

4. Interview with Andrew Cowan-Martin, Rock Group Manager, 9 April 1990, London.
5. Interview with Iain Calder, Editor and President of the *National Enquirer*, 24 January 1990, Lantana, Florida.
6. Interview with James Sutherland, Deputy Editor, the *Daily Star*, 29 November 1989, London.
7. Adam Raphael, *My Learned Friends* (London: W. H. Allen, 1989).
8. Interview with Bill Burt, Former Editor of the *National Examiner*, 23 January 1990, Boca Raton, Florida.
9. Interview with Mike Walker, Gossip Editor and Columnist, *National Enquirer*, 25 January 1990, Lantana, Florida.
10. Interview with Brian Williams, Reporter for the *National Enquirer*, 25 January 1990, Lantana, Florida.
11. Interview with David Duffy, Gossip Columnist, *National Enquirer*, 25 January 1990, Lantana, Florida.
12. Interview with Phil Bunton, Executive Editor, the *Star*, 1 February 1990, Tarrytown, New York.
13. Interview with Paul Levy, Editor of the *Globe*, Globe International Inc., 23 January 1990, Boca Raton, Florida.
14. Interview with John Vader, Editor of the *Sun*, Globe International Inc., 22 January 1990, Boca Raton, Florida.
15. Interview with Roger Wood, Editorial Director, the *Star*, 6 February 1990, New York.
16. Joint interview with Vince Eckersley, Lee Harrison and Roy Foster at 'Tycoon', Boca Raton, Florida.
17. Interview with Harry Arnold, Chief Reporter, the *Daily Mirror*, 8 May 1990, London.
18. Harry Arnold, *Charles and Diana* (London: New English Library/Times Mirror, 1981), p.41.
19. Interview with James Whitaker, Royal Reporter, the *Daily Mirror*, 1 December 1990, London.
20. Interview with Joyce Hopkirk, Former Editor *She*, 6 September 1989, London.

Chapter 6: Hollywood

1. Interview with Tony Brenna, Senior West Coast Correspondent, *National Enquirer*, 2 January 1990, London.
2. Interview with Phil Ramey, Freelance Photographer, 19 October 1989, Los Angeles.

3. Interview with John Mahoney, Foreign Correspondent, the *Daily Star*, 17 October 1989, Los Angeles.
4. Interview with Chris Anderson, Foreign Correspondent, the *Daily Star*, 17 October 1989, Los Angeles.

Ageing actress turns back on fans

1. Cuttings from the *Sun* and the *Star*.

Chapter 7: Let Fucking Dogs Lie

1. Interview with Laurent Sola, Photographer for *Paris Match*, 1 December 1989, London.
2. Interview with Tony Brenna, Senior West Coast Correspondent, *National Enquirer*, 2 January 1990, London.
3. Interview with Brian Hitchen, Editor of the *Daily Star*, 13 September 1989, London.
4. Interview with Kurt Heine, Crime Reporter for the Philadelphia *Daily News*, 11 January 1990, Philadelphia.
5. Interview with Jack Morrison, 14 January 1990, Rewrite Man for the Philadelphia *Daily News*, 14 January 1990, Philadelphia.
6. Tom Wolfe, *The Bonfire of the Vanities* (New York: Farrar Straus Giroux, 1987), p.201.
7. Interview with Peter Fearon, Producer on 'Inside Edition', 7 February 1990, New York.
8. Interview with George Lynn, former Editorial Executive on the *Sun*, 26 June 1989, London.
9. Interview with Stuart Winter, Deputy News Editor, the *Daily Star*, 20 September 1990, London.
10. Interview with Chris Anderson, US Foreign Correspondent, *Daily Star*, 17 October 1989, Los Angeles.
11. Interview with Bill Boyle, Deputy City Editor, New York *Daily News*, 17 January 1990, New York.
12. Interview with Rafe Klinger, former columnist and reporter, *Weekly World News*, 24 January 1990, Boynton Beach, Florida.
13. Interview with Lee Harrison, Executive Editor, the *Globe*, 23 January 1990, Boca Raton, Florida.
14. Interview with Richard Ellis, European Correspondent, *Sunday Times*, 20 March 1990, London.

15. Interview with Sue Snell, Film Fashion Designer, 15 September 1989, London.
16. Alastair Hetherington, *News, Newspapers and Television* (London: Macmillan, 1985).
17. Interview with Trevor Kempson, Chief Investigative Reporter, *News of the World*, 21 November 1989, London.
18. Interview with John Mahoney, US Foreign Correspondent, *Daily Star*, 17 October 1989, Los Angeles.
19. Pamella Bordes, Guest Appearance on 'An Hour with Jonathan Ross', Channel 4, 12 November 1989.
20. Tape recording of Jimmy Tayoun, provided by Anonymous Source, 16 November 1988, Philadelphia.
21. Interview with James Sutherland, Deputy Editor, the *Daily Star*, 29 November 1989, London.
22. Interview with Vince Eckersley, Freelance Photographer, 23 January 1990, Boca Raton, Florida.
23. Piers Brendon, *The Life and Death of the Press Barons* (London: Secker & Warburg, 1982).
24. Interview with Mike Nevard, Director of Special Projects, the *National Enquirer*, 22 January 1990, Palm Beach, Florida.
25. Interview with Derek Jameson, Radio Host, BBC2, 22 November 1989, London.
26. Interview with Peter Grimsditch, Manchester Editor, the *Sport*, 17 August 1989, London.

Chapter 8: War

1. Interview with Bill Hoffmann, Reporter, the New York *Post*, 18 January 1990, New York.
2. Interview with Mike Walker, Gossip Columnist and Editor, *National Enquirer*, 25 January 1990, West Palm Beach, Florida.
3. Marc Fisher, 'The King of Sleaze', *Gentleman's Quarterly*, 1990, pp.185–198.
4. Interview with Richard Ellis, European Correspondent, the *Sunday Times*, 20 March 1990, London.
5. Interview with Brian Hitchen, Editor, the *Daily Star*, 13 September 1989, London.
6. Interview with Lou Colasuonno, Managing Editor, the New York *Post*, 16 January 1990, New York.
7. Interview with John Cotter, Metro Editor, the New York *Post*, 1 February 1990, New York.

8. Interview with Peter Fearon, Producer, 'Inside Edition', 7 February 1990, New York.
9. Interview with Roger Wood, Editorial Director, the *Star*, 6 February 1990, New York.
10. Interview with Steve Dunleavy, Senior Reporter, 'Current Affairs', 7 February 1990, New York.
11. Interview with Mike Nevard, Director of Special Projects, the *National Enquirer*, 22 January 1990, West Palm Beach, Florida.
12. Terri Schultz-Brooks, '*Daily News*: Can News Team Rout Rupe?' *Columbia Journalism Review*, May/June, 1985, pp.55–60.
13. Mitchell Stephens, 'Clout: Murdoch's Political Past', *Columbia Journalism Review*, July/August 1982, pp.44–46.
14. Interview with Peter Grimsditch, Manchester Editor, the *Sport*, 17 August 1990, London.
15. Interview with Jim Hoge, Publisher, New York *Daily News*, 8 February 1990, New York.
16. Interview with Phil Bunton, Executive Editor, the *Star*, 1 February 1990, Tarrytown, New York.
17. Interview with F. Gilman Spencer, former Editor, New York *Daily News*, currently Editor, Denver *Post*, 5 February 1990, by telephone.
18. Interview with Jimmy Breslin, Columnist, New York *Newsday*, 16 January 1990, New York.

Chapter 9: Subterranean Cellar Dwellers

1. Interview with Bill Boyle, Deputy City Editor, New York *Daily News*, 17 January 1990, New York.
2. Interview with Bill Hoffmann, Reporter, the New York *Post*, 18 January 1990, New York.
3. Interview with Jimmy Breslin, columnist for New York *Newsday*, 16 January 1990, New York.
4. Interview with Len Valenti, Chief Copy Editor, 17 January 1990, New York.
5. Interview with Jim Hoge, Publisher, New York *Daily News*, 8 February 1990, New York.
6. Interview with Jack Morrison, Rewrite Man, Philadelphia *Daily News*, 14 January 1990, Philadelphia.
7. Interview with Kurt Heine, Reporter, Philadelphia *Daily News*, 11 January 1990, Philadelphia.

8. Jeffrey K. Taylor, Unpublished MS, Reporter, *Wall Street Journal*.

Chapter 10: Personal Services

1. Interview with Peter Fearon, Producer, 'Inside Edition', 7 February, New York; 6 May 1990, by telephone.
2. Interview with Keith Deves, former 'Dirty Affairs Correspondent', the *Sun*, 23 March 1990, by telephone.
3. Interview with Trevor Kempson, Chief Investigative Reporter, the *News of the World*, 21 and 27 November 1989, London.
4. Interview with Lindi St Clair, Summer 1990.
5. Interview with George Lynn, Former Editorial Executive, the *Sun*, 26 June 1989, London.
6. Interview with Tina Dalgleish, Former Investigative Reporter, the *News of the World*, 14 December 1989, London.

Chapter 11: Trevor and Tina

1. Trevor Kempson, Chief Investigative Reporter, the *News of the World*, 29 November 1989, London.
2. Tina Dalgleish, Former Investigative Reporter, the *News of the World*, 14 December 1989, London.

Dear Marje

1. Interview with Marjorie Proops, Personal Advice Columnist and Associate Editor, the *Daily Mirror*, 15 March 1990, London.

Chapter 12: News Junkies

1. Interview with Richard Ellis, European Correspondent, the *Sunday Times*, 20 March 1990, London.
2. Interview with Martine Dennis, News Reader, Sky Television, 3 April 1990, London.
3. Interview with Don MacKay, Reporter, the *Daily Mirror*, 4 January 1990, London.

4. Interview with George Lynn, Former Editorial Executive, Reporter, the *Sun*, 26 June 1989, London.
5. Interview with Gladys Lynn, Housewife, 4 April 1990, by telephone.
6. Interview with Nick Lloyd, Editor of the *Daily Express*, 2 April 1990.
7. Interview with Eve Pollard, Editor of the *Sunday Mirror*, 16 March 1990, London.
8. Interview with Marjorie Proops, Personal Advice Columnist, Associate Editor, the *Daily Mirror*, 15 March 1990, London.
9. Interview with Brian Hitchen, Editor, the *Daily Star*, 13 September 1989, London.
10. Interview with Derek Jameson, Radio Host, BBC2, 22 November 1989, London.

God is a hack

1. Interview with Don MacKay, Reporter, the *Daily Mirror*, 4 January 1990, London.
2. Cuttings from the *Daily Star* and the *Sun*.

Chapter 13: 20 Things You Didn't Know about Kelvin MacKenzie

1. Interview with Vic Giles, Retired Design Director, the *Sun*, 12 April 1990, London.
2. Roslyn Grose, *The Sun-Sation: Behind the Scenes of Britain's Bestselling Daily Newspaper* (London: Angus & Robertson, 1989).
3. John Sweeney, 'Gotcha! The FIRST Profile of Kelvin MacKenzie, the Elusive editor of the Oafish *Sun*', *Tatler*, October 1986.
4. Interview with the late Graham Courtenay, Senior Subeditor, the *Sun*, 11 September 1989, London.
5. Interview with George Lynn, Former Editorial Executive, the *Sun*, 26 June 1989, London.
6. Linda Melvern, *The End of the Street* (London: Methuen, 1986).
7. Interview with Lou Colasuonno, Managing Editor, the New York *Post*, 16 January 1990, New York.

8. 'The Media Show', Channel 4, 19 March 1990.
9. Interview with Harry Arnold, Chief Reporter, the *Daily Mirror*, 8 May 1990, London.
10. Telephone tape of Kelvin MacKenzie calling Paul Woolwich, Editor 'Hard News'.
11. Alkarim Jivani, 'Sun Sets: Time In & Broadcast Guide', *Time Out*, 16 November. 1989.
12. John Sweeney, 'The Sun and the Star', the *Independent Magazine*, 11 February 1989.
13. Robert Harris, *Gotcha!: The Media, the Government and the Falklands Crisis* (London: Faber and Faber, 1983).
14. Kelvin MacKenzie, 'Public Mask Can't Hide Private Shame', *UK Press Gazette*, 25 September 1989.
15. Interview with Roy Greenslade, Editor, the *Daily Mirror*, 15 March 1990, London.
16. Interview with Brian Hitchen, Editor, the *Daily Star*, 13 September 1989, London.
17. Cuttings from *Private Eye*.

Chapter 14: The Little King

1. Interview with Peter Grimsditch, Manchester Editor of *Sport*, 17 August 1989, London.
2. Interview with David Sullivan, Proprietor of the *Sport*, 8 August 1989, London.
3. Queen Mary and Westfield College, 'Certificate of Confirmation of Degree Studies, Undergraduate Courses' for David Sullivan, graduated 1 July 1970.
4. Interview with Tina Dalgleish, former Investigative Reporter, the *News of the World*, 14 December 1989, London.
5. Interview with Drew Robertson, Editor, the *Sunday Sport*, 16 August 1989, London.

Chapter 15: Pork Up Ya Love Life!

1. Fritz Spiegl, *Keep Taking the Tabloids: What the Papers Say and How They Say It* (London: Pan, 1983).
2. Interview with Dick Dinsdale, former Managing Editor, the *Daily Mirror*, 1 August 1989, by telephone.
3. Interview with Don MacKay, Reporter, the *Daily Mirror*, 4 January 1990, London.

4. Interview with Peter Grimsditch, Manchester Editor of the *Sport*, 17 August 1989, London.
5. *Time Out*, November 22–29, 1989.
6. Interview with John Leese, Editor, the *Evening Standard*, 4 December 1989, London.
7. Interview with Jimmy Breslin, Columnist, New York *Newsday*, 16 January 1990, New York.
8. Interview with Len Valenti, Chief Copy Editor, New York *Daily News*, 17 January 1990, New York.
9. Interview with Jack Morrison, Rewrite Man, the Philadelphia *Daily News*, 14 January 1990, Philadelphia.
10. Conversation with Richard Oliver, former Producer for 'The Reporters', 7 February 1990, New York.
11. Interview with Vic Giles, Retired Design Director, the *Sun*, 12 April 1990, London.
12. Interview with Bill Hoffmann, Reporter, the New York *Post*, 18 January 1990, New York.
13. Interview with Lou Colasuonno, Managing Editor, the New York *Post*, 16 January 1990, New York.
14. Interview with Drew MacKenzie, Sub-editor, the New York *Post*, and Freelancer, 2 February, 1990.
15. Interview with John Vader, Editor, the *Sun* for Globe International Inc., 22 January 1990, Boca Raton, Florida.
16. Interview with Drew Robertson, Editor, *Sunday Sport*, 16 August 1989, London.
17. 'The Third Degree: Drew Robertson on the *Sunday Sport*', *Company Magazine*, September 1989.
18. Interview with the late Graham Courtenay, Senior Sub-Editor, the *Sun*, 11 September 1989, London.

Chapter 16: The Truth

1. Interview with Brian Hitchen, Editor, the *Daily Star*, 13 September 1989, London.
2. Interview with Steve Dunleavy, Senior Reporter for 'Current Affair', 7 February 1990, New York.
3. Interview with Jeff Samuels, Chief Writer for 'Lifestyles of the Rich and Famous', 7 February 1990, New York.
4. Michael J. Fox and Michael Pollan, 'Michael J. Fox's Nuptials in Hell!' *Esquire*, June 1989, pp.137–52.
5. Interview with Iain Calder, Editor, the *National Enquirer*, 24 January 1990, Lantana, Florida.

6. 'The Press and the People', 29th/30th Annual Report of The Press Council, 1982/1983.
7. 'The Hillsborough Inquiry: Press Coverage of the Disaster at Hillsborough Stadium, Sheffield on 15 April 1989', published by the Press Council, 1989.
8. Interview with Julian Critchley, MP, 7 March 1990, by telephone.
9. Interview with George Lynn, Former Editorial Executive, the *Sun*, 26 June 1989, London.
10. Interview with Paul Woolwich, Producer, 'Hard News', 6 March 1990, London.
11. Interview with the late Graham Courtenay, Senior Sub-Editor, the *Sun*, 11 September 1989, London.
12. Interview with Josh Baran, Publicist for the Glaser Family, 22 October 1989, Los Angeles.
13. Interview with Paul Levy, Editor, the *Globe*, 23 January 1990, Boca Raton, Florida.
14. Henry Porter, *Lies, Damned Lies and Some Exclusives* (London: Chatto & Windus, Hogarth Press, 1984), p.9.

*In writing this book, the author relied on a large number of newspaper cuttings too numerous to list here.

**In addition to the interviews listed above, the author accumulated a number of off-the-record remarks which appear as such in the text of the book. Altogether, the number of interviews conducted exceeded 120.

BIBLIOGRAPHY
AND RELATED READINGS

Arnold, Harry. *Charles and Diana*. London: New English Library/ Times Mirror, 1981.

Black, Jeremy. *The English Press in the Eighteenth Century*. London: Croom Helm, 1987.

Bleyer, William Grosvenor. *Main Currents in the History of American Journalism*. Boston: Houghton Mifflin Co., 1927.

Boorstin, Daniel J. *The Image, or What Happened to the American Dream*. London: Penguin, 1963.

Boot, William. 'Capital Letter: The Chuck and Di Show', *Columbia Journalism Review*, Jan/Feb, 1986, pp.38–41.

Bower, Tom. *Maxwell, the Outsider*. London: Arum Press, 1988.

Brendon, Piers. *The Life and Death of the Press Barons*. London: Secker & Warburg, 1982.

Brenton, Howard and David Have. *Pravda*. London: Methuen, 1985.

Chippendale, Peter and Chris Horrie. *Stick It Up Your Punter! The Rise and Fall of the Sun*. London: Heinemann, 1990.

Churchill, Allen. *Park Row*. New York: Rinehart & Co., Inc., Toronto, 1958.

Clarkson, Wensley. *Dog Eat Dog: Confessions of a Tabloid Journalist*. London: Fourth Estate, 1990.

Cook, Roger and Tim Tate. *What's Wrong with Your Rights?* London: Methuen, 1988.

Corkery, P.J. 'Inside the *National Enquirer*: An Eyewitness Account', *Rolling Stone Magazine*, 11 June 1981, pp.19–21.

Cranfield, G.A. *The Press and Society: From Caxton to Northcliffe*. London: Longman, 1978.

Cudlipp, Hugh. *At Your Peril*. London: Weidenfeld & Nicholson, 1961.

Curran, James and Jean Seaton. *Power Without Responsibility: The Press and Broadcasting in Britain*, 2nd ed. London: Methuen, 1985.

Elkins, Charles. 'The Voice of the Poor: The Broadside as a Medium of Popular Culture and Dissent in Victorian England', *Journalism of Popular Culture*, 14:2, Autumn, 1980, pp.262–74.

Emery, Edwin and Michael Emery. *The Press and America: An Interpretive History of the Mass Media*, 5th ed. Englewood Cliffs, N.J.:Prentice-Hall Inc., 1984.

Evans, Harry. *Good Times, Bad Times*. London: Weidenfeld & Nicholson, 1983.

Fisher, Marc. 'The King of Sleaze', *Gentleman's Quarterly*, April 1990, pp.185–86+.

Fox, Michael J. and Michael Pollan, 'Michael J. Fox's Nuptials in Hell!' *Esquire*, June 1989, pp.137–52.

Gifford, C.A. 'Ancient Rome's Daily Gazette', *Journalism History* 2, Winter 1975–6, pp.106–07+.

Grose, Roslyn. *The Sun-Sation: Behind the Scenes of Britain's Bestselling Daily Newspaper*. London: Angus & Robertson, 1989.

Haines, Joe. *Maxwell*. London: Macdonald, 1988.

Harris, Michael. *London Newspapers in the Age of Walpole*. London: Associated University Presses, 1987.

Harris, Robert. *Gotcha! The Media, the Government and the Falklands Crisis*. London: Faber and Faber, 1983.

Heren, Louis. *The Power of the Press?* London: Orbis, 1985.

Hetherington, Alastair. *News, Newspapers and Television*. London: Macmillan, 1985.

Hodgson, Godfrey. 'Dateline Britain: The Revolt of the Press Barons', *Columbia Journalism Review*, Sept/Oct, 1986, pp.53–55.

Holden, Anthony. *Charles*. London: Fontana/Collins, 1988.

Jameson, Derek. *Touched by Angels*. London: Ebury Press, 1988.

Jenkins, Simon. *Newspaper: The Power and the Money*. London: Faber and Faber, 1979.

Jivani, Alkarim. 'Sun Sets: Time In & Broadcast Guide', *Time Out*, 16 November 1989.

Keay, Douglas. *Royal Pursuit: The Palace, the Press and the People*. London: Severn House, 1983.

Kersh, Cyril. *A Few Gross Words: The Street of Shame, and My Part In It*. New York: Simon & Schuster, 1990.

Lamb, Larry. *Sunrise*. London: PaperMac, 1989.

Leapman, Michael. *Barefaced Cheek: The Apotheosis of Rupert Murdoch*. London: Hodder & Stoughton, 1983.

MacArthur, Brian. *Eddy Shah: Today and the Newspaper Revolution*. London: David & Charles, 1988.

MacKenzie, Kelvin. 'Public Mask Can't Hide Private Shame', *UK Press Gazette*, 25 September 1989.

Melvern, Linda. *The End of the Street*. London: Methuen, 1986.

Mott, Frank Luther. *American Journalism: A History of the Newspapers in the United States through 250 Years, 1690–1940*. New York: Macmillan Co., 1941.

Munster, George. *Rupert Murdoch: A Paper Prince*. New York: Viking, 1985.

Northmore, David. *Freedom of Information Handbook*. London: Bloomsbury, 1990.

Paul, Yvonne with Madeleine Pallas. *The Glamour Game*. London: Nexus, 1989.

Pilton, Patrick. *Page Three Girls*. London: Sun Books, n.d.

Pinkus, Philip. *Grub Street Stripped Bare*. London: Constable, 1968.

Porter, Henry. *Lies, Damned Lies and Some Exclusives*. London: Chatto & Windus 1984.

The Press Council. 'The Hillsborough Inquiry: Press Coverage of the Disaster at Hillsborough Stadium, Sheffield on 15 April 1989.'

The Press Council. *The Press and the People*. Annual Reports of the Press Council. London, in series 1970–88.

Raphael, Adam. *My Learned Friends*. London: W.H. Allen, 1989.

Shaw, Donald L. and John W. Slater. 'In the Eye of the Beholder? Sensationalism in American Press News, 1820–1860,' *Journalism History* 12:3–4, Winter/Autumn 1985, pp.86–91.

Shultz-Brooks, Terri. '*Daily News*: Can News Team Rout Rupe?' *Columbia Journalism Review*. May/June, 1985, pp.55–60.

Somerfield, Stafford. *Banner Headlines*. Shoreham, Scan Books, 1979.

Spiegl, Fritz. *Keep Taking the Tabloids: What the Papers Say and How They Say it*. London: Pan, 1983.

Stephens, Mitchell. 'Clout: Murdoch's Political Past', *Columbia Journalism Review*. July/August, 1982, pp.44–46.

Stephens, Mitchell. 'Sensationalism and Moralizing in 16th and 17th Century Newsbooks and News Ballads', *Journalism History*, 12:3–4 Winter/Autumn 1985, pp.92–95.

Stevens, John D. 'Sensationalism in Perspective', *Journalism History*. 12:3–4, Winter/Autumn, 1985, pp.78–79.

Sweeney, John. 'Gotcha! The FIRST Profile of Kelvin MacKenzie, the Elusive Editor of the Oafish Sun', *Tatler*, October, 1986.

Sweeney, John. 'The Sun and the Star', the *Independent Magazine*, 11 February 1989.

Tannenbaum, Percy H. and Mervin D. Lynch. 'Sensationalism: The Concept and Its Measurement', *Journalism Quarterly* 37, Summer, 1960, pp.381–92.

Tannenbaum, Percy H. and Mervin D. Lynch. 'Sensationalism: Some Objective Message Correlates', *Journalism Quarterly* 39, Summer, 1962, pp.317–23.

Taylor, Jeffrey. Unpublished MS, *Corrupt & Content: Philadelphia City Politics*, 1988.

'The Third Degree: Drew Robertson on the *Sunday Sport*,' *Company Magazine*, September, 1989.

Warren, Francke. 'An Argument in Defense of Sensationalism: Probing the Popular and Historiographical Concept', *Journalism History* 5: Fall, 1978, pp.70–73.

Waterhouse, Keith. *Daily Mirror Style*. London: Mirror Books, 1981.

Westmancoat, John. *Newspapers*. London: The British Library, 1985.

Wintour, Charles. *The Rise and Fall of Fleet Street*. London: Hutchinson, 1989.

Wolfe, Tom. *The Bonfire of the Vanities*. New York: Farrar Straus Giroux, 1987.

INDEX

351

352